A Modern History of German Criminal Law

Thomas Vormbaum
Michael Bohlander
Editor

A Modern History of German Criminal Law

Translated by Margaret Hiley

Springer
VolkswagenStiftung

Thomas Vormbaum
FB Rechtswissenschaften
FernUniversität Hagen
Hagen
Germany

Editor
Michael Bohlander
Durham Law School
Durham University
Durham
United Kingdom

ISBN 978-3-642-37272-8 ISBN 978-3-642-37273-5 (eBook)
DOI 10.1007/978-3-642-37273-5
Springer Heidelberg New York Dordrecht London

Library of Congress Control Number: 2001012345

Printed on acid-free paper

Springer is part of Springer Science+Business Media (www.springer.com)

Foreword

The Federal Republic of Germany has built a democratic society on the foundations of the Basic Law. Its legislative bodies, judicial system, academic community, and media have all played a crucial role in enabling Germany to join the group of rule-of-law nations respected on the global stage. In a globalised world, where domestic legal systems compete, German law has become the subject of growing interest. In response to this greater interest, the leading institutions of German legal life have joined forces with the Federal Ministry of Justice to form the *Alliance for German Law*.

The Federal Ministry of Justice publishes English-language translations of key German legislation. While the latter can offer a basic insight into German law, legal provisions alone do not suffice to impart a clear understanding of our country's legal structures, systems, and dynamics. This is where Germany's legal academics must take up the gauntlet.

It is therefore highly commendable that Professor Vormbaum's book, *A Modern History of German Criminal Law*, has been published in English. I would like to thank the editor, Professor Bohlander, and the Volkswagen Foundation, which has supported this project. I agree entirely with the author that, in order to understand the law as it stands, knowledge is required of its origins, as well as its development from the age of enlightenment to the present day. The aim of this book is to make such knowledge widely accessible to an audience outside of the German-speaking world.

I therefore hope that the English-language version of this book will enjoy the broad readership it deserves.

Sabine Leutheusser-Schnarrenberger

Preface to the Second edition

The favourable reception of the first edition has made it possible for a second to follow after a comparatively brief space of time. The aims of the study remain the same. For those student readers whose interest in matters of legal history already shows their desire to gain not only an understanding of the (naturally indispensable) technical requirements of their subject but of its structural problems also, it aims to provide a way of acquiring a basic overview of the history of modern criminal law that will enable them to engage critically with those technical requirements. It also aims to give "late starters", such as lawyers and others interested in legal matters who have already entered working life, an opportunity to catch up on this knowledge. The fact that the editorial team of the journal *Juristische Schulung* (JuS) selected this book as one of its "legal educational books of the year" (cf. JuS 2009, 1160) would seem to confirm that these aims have been recognised.

Besides correcting a few technical and editorial errors, this new edition diversifies and goes deeper into some points, which means the book has become slightly longer. Important new publications—particularly essays—have been taken into account, and here and there older literature has also been considered afresh. Due to its scope, which remains limited, this work cannot of course be comprehensive in this regard.

Many thanks to all whose suggestions and comments on the previous edition helped me to see some points more clearly. Particular thanks are due to the Berlin teachers of criminal law who gave me the opportunity to present and discuss my ideas and concepts in their seminar.[1]

Once again, I was able to rely on the support of *Zekai Dagasan* and *Anne Gipperich* for the new edition.

Hagen, Germany
Summer 2010

Thomas Vormbaum

[1] A shorter version of the discussion of methods presented under § 1 was included in the internet portal *Docupedia Zeitgeschichte* run by the Zentrum für zeitgeschichtliche Forschung Potsdam (Centre for contemporary historical research Potsdam) under the title "Juristische Zeitgeschichte" (Legal contemporary history): http://docupedia.de/docupedia/index.php?title=Juristische_Zeitgeschichte&oldid =71531, where it is also possible to comment on this discussion.

Acknowledgements

Literature in English about German criminal law is still relatively thin on the ground. This is especially true when we look at works on German legal history, and here again the area of criminal justice seems particularly underrepresented. It is therefore with great pleasure that I present this volume, which is a translation of the 2nd edition (2011) of the *Einführung in die moderne Strafrechtsgeschichte* by Thomas Vormbaum, one of Germany's foremost scholars in legal history.

The book provides an insight into the development of German criminal law, both substantive and procedural, in the modern period from the late 18th century onwards. Its aim is to show the broad lines along which the modern law was shaped rather than merely to string major dates and events together. Together with my own two books on German criminal law and procedure with Hart Publishing, the reader should now have a reliable foundation to obtain a thorough first impression of the roots and the current state of affairs of modern German criminal law.

This book would not have been possible without the generous funding provided by the German Volkswagen Foundation (Grant No. 85 679), which covered the entire cost of the translation. I would especially like to thank Dr Thomas Brunotte for the smooth and efficient cooperation during the production of the book. I am also grateful to Springer Publishers for accepting the volume into their programme.

However, even abundant funding and a publishing contract are not enough unless one has a translator who is up to the task of tackling such a major project. I was very fortunate to be able to work together, through the good offices of Ms Anja Löbert from Textwork Translations, with Dr Margaret Hiley, who with a high degree of professionalism mastered the often difficult terminology superbly and produced a translation that I am sure will engender a wider interest and understanding of the topic in the Anglophone readership and beyond. I will always remember our linguistic conversations during the work phase when we tried to find the best English equivalent to some arcane German concept or other. One will always be able to find alternatives to the translations chosen, but we hope that our efforts remain as faithful to the original as possible.

I am deeply grateful to Sabine Leutheusser-Schnarrenberger, Minister of Justice of the Federal Republic of Germany, for gracing the volume with a foreword.

Last, but by no means least, thanks are due to Professor Thomas Vormbaum of the Fernuniversität Hagen, Germany, for agreeing to the translation of his work and for the occasional clarifications.

Durham, UK
February 2013

Michael Bohlander

List of Abbreviations

ALR	*Allgemeines Landrecht für die preußischen Staaten* = Prussian General Code
ArchCrR	*Archiv für Criminalrecht*
ARSP	*Archiv für Rechts- und Sozialphilosophie*
Art.	Article
bayStGB	*Bayrisches Strafgesetzbuch* = Bavarian Penal Code
BGB	*Bürgerliches Gesetzbuch* = Civil Code
BGBl.	*Bundesgesetzblatt* = Federal Law Gazette
BGH	*Bundesgerichtshof* = Federal Court of Justice
BGHSt	*Amtliche Sammlung der Entscheidungen des Bundesgerichtshofs in Strafsachen* = Official Gazette of the Decisions of the Federal Court of Justice in Criminal Matters
BMJ	*Bundesministerium/Bundesminister der Justiz* = Federal Ministry of Justice/Federal Minister of Justice
BT	*Bundestag* = National Parliament of the Federal Republic of Germany
BVerfG	*Bundesverfassungsgericht* = Federal Constitutional Court
BVerfGE	*Amtliche Sammlung der Entscheidungen des Bundesverfassungsgerichts* = Official Gazette of the Decisions of the Federal Constitutional Court
CCC	First general German penal code, issued under Charles V (Latin: Constitutio Criminalis Carolina)
CD	Commission Draft
CDU	*Christlich Demokratische Union* = Christian Democratic Union
cit.	Cited
Col.	Column
CrimO	*Preußische (C) Kriminalordnung* = Prussian Criminal Ordinance
CSU	*Christlich-Soziale Union* = Christian Social Union
D(t)StrRZ	*Deutsche Strafrechtszeitung*
DDP	*Deutsche Demokratische Partei* = German Democratic Party

Dept.	Department
DJV	*Deutsche Zentralverwaltung für Justiz* = German Central Administration of Justice
DJZ	*Deutsche Juristenzeitung*
DNVP	*Deutschnationale Volkspartei* = German National People's Party
DP	*Deutsche Partei* = German Party
DVP	*Deutsche Volkspartei* = German People's Party
E	Entwurf (Draft)
e.g.	For example (Latin: exempli gratia)
ECHR	European Convention on Human Rights
Ed.	Edition(s)
Ed./ed.	Editor/edited
EGOWiG	*Einführungsgesetz zum Ordnungswidrigkeitengesetz* = Regulatory Offences (Introduction) Act
EU	European Union
FDP	Free Democratic Party
Fn.	Footnote(s)
Frhr.	*Freiherr* = Baron
Fschr.	*Festschrift*
GA	*Goltdammers Archiv für Strafrecht*
GB/BHE	*Gesamtdeutscher Block / Bund der Heimatvertriebenen und Entrechteten* = All-German Bloc/League of Expellees and Deprived of Rights
GDR	German Democratic Republic
Gestapo	*Geheime Staatspolizei* = Secret State Police
GG	*Grundgesetz* = Basic Law
GmbH	*Gemeinschaft mit beschränkter Haftung* = Limited Company
GVG	*Gerichtsverfassungsgesetz* = Constitution of Courts Act
GWU	*Geschichte in Wissenschaft und Unterricht*
HGB	*Handelsgesetzbuch* = German Commercial Code
Intro.	Introduction
IVR	*Internationale Vereinigung für Rechtsphilosophie* = International Association for Philosophy of Law and Social Philosophy
JJZG	*Jahrbuch der Juristischen Zeitgeschichte*
JoJZG	*Journal der Juristischen Zeitgeschichte*
JuS	*Juristische Schulung*
JW	*Juristische Wochenschrift*
JZ	*Juristenzeitung*
KJ	*Kritische Justiz*
KPD	*Kommunistische Partei Deutschlands* = German Communist Party
KritV	*Kritische Vierteljahresschrift für Gesetzgebung und Rechtswissenschaft*
KZ	*Konzentrationslager* = concentration camp

MdtStrD	*Moderne deutsche Strafrechtsdenker*
MfS	*Ministerium für Staatssicherheit* = Ministry for State Security
MschrKrim.	*Monatsschrift für Kriminalpsychologie und Strafrechtsreform*
n.d.	No date
n.v.	New version
NArchCrimR	*Neues Archiv des Criminalrechts*
NATO	North Atlantic Treaty Organization
NJW	*Neue Juristische Wochenschrift*
No.	Number(s)
NRW	North Rhine-Westphalia
NS	Nazi-/National Socialist
NSDAP	*Nationalsozialistische Deutsche Arbeiterpartei* = National Socialist German Workers' Party
ÖKV	*Österreichische kriminalistische Vereinigung* = Austrian Criminalistic Association
OLG	*Oberlandesgericht* = State Supreme Court
Orig.	Original
o.v.	Old version
PD	Preliminary draft
PDS	*Partei des Demokratischen Sozialismus* = Party of Democratic Socialism
Pr(euß)StGB	*Preußisches Strafgesetzbuch* = Prussian Criminal Code
Pr.	Prussian
Pr.GS	*Preußische Gesetzsammlung* = Prussian Statute Book
RepSchG	*Republikschutzgesetz* = Law for the Protection of the Republic
RGBl.	*Reichsgesetzblatt* = Reich Law Gazette
RGSt	*Amtliche Sammlung der Entscheidungen des Reichsgerichts in Strafsachen* = Official Gazette of the Decisions of the Supreme Court of the Reich in Criminal Matters
RGVG	*Reichsgerichtsverfassungsgesetz* = Code of the Reich on the Constitution of Courts
RJM	*Reichsministerium der Justiz (Reichsjustizministerium)* = Reich Ministry of Justice
RStGB	*Reichsstrafgesetzbuch* = Reich Criminal Code
RStPO	*Reichsstrafprozessordnung* = Reich Code of Criminal Procedure
s.l.	Sine loco (Latin: no place of publication)
SA	*Sturmabteilung* = Stormtroopers
SBZ	*Sowjetische Besatzungszone* = Soviet Occupation Zone
sc.	"Science" (Latin: scientia/scientiae)
SchwZStrR	*Schweizerische Zeitschrift für Strafrecht*
SD	*Sicherheitsdienst* = Security Service
SED	*Sozialistische Einheitspartei Deutschlands* = Socialist Unity Party of Germany

SMAD	*Sowjetische Militäradministration in Deutschland* = Soviet Military Administration in Germany
SPD	*Sozialdemokratische Partei Deutschlands* (SoPaDe) = Social Democratic Party of Germany
SS	*Schutzstaffel* = Protection Squadron
StA	*Staatsanwaltschaft* = Prosecution (Service)
StÄG	*Gesetz zur Änderung des Strafrechts (Strafrechtsänderungsgesetz)* = Law to Change the Criminal Code
Stasi	*Staatssicherheit* = State Security
StGB	*Strafgesetzbuch* = Criminal Code
StPÄG	*Gesetz zur Änderung der Strafprozessordnung und des Gerichtsverfassungsgesetzes (Strafprozessänderungsgesetz)* = Criminal Procedure Amendment Act
StPO	*Strafprozessordnung* = Code of Criminal Procedure
StrD	*Strafrechtsdenker*
StrRG	*Gesetz zur Reform des Strafrechts (Strafrechtsreformgesetz)* = Criminal Law Reform Act
StVollzG	*Strafvollzugsgesetz* = Execution of Prison Sentences Act
StVRG	*Gesetz zur Reform des Strafverfahrensrechts (Strafverfahrensreformgesetz)* = Act to Reform Criminal Procedure
Subpara.	Subparagraph
Suppl.	Supplement
SZ	*Süddeutsche Zeitung*
UIDP	International Union of Penal Law
USSR	Union of Soviet Socialist Republics (Soviet Union)
VfZ	*Vierteljahreshefte für Zeitgeschichte*
VO	*Verordnung* = Decree
Vol./Vols.	Volume/volumes
VolksGH	*Volksgerichtshof* = People's Court
vs.	Versus
VStGB	*Völkerstrafgesetzbuch* = Code of International Criminal Law
WRV	*Weimarer Reichsverfassung* = Weimar Constitution
ZNR	*Zeitschrift für neuere Rechtsgeschichte*
ZPO	*Zivilprozessordnung* = Code of Civil Procedure
ZRG	*Zeitschrift der Savigny-Stiftung für Rechtsgeschichte*
ZRP	*Zeitschrift für Rechtspolitik*
ZStW	*Zeitschrift für die gesamte Strafrechtswissenschaft*

Contents

List of Figures

Introduction

This textbook follows two objectives. Firstly, it aims to give a reliable overview of the development of criminal law from the end of the Enlightenment to the present day. Secondly, its goal is to facilitate a methodological understanding enabling a critical historical approach to contemporary criminal law. The basic idea informing this book, discussed at greater length in the first chapter, is that the time period presented here constitutes a single *legal-historical epoch* that is characterised by fundamental traits and that the strengthening or weakening of these traits allows conclusions to be drawn regarding the position of law and criminal law during specific periods within this epoch.

The textbook forms an *introduction* in both regards. Its scope is limited to the content necessary to convey a basic knowledge of the history of criminal law in the 19th and 20th centuries to both law students, as well as those who have come to the conclusion at a later point in their lives that historical knowledge helps them to better understand the current legislation. Furthermore, it hopes to give an idea of how this newly acquired knowledge might be used in a critical historical evaluation of the current law.[1]

The history of criminal law, of which this book provides an account, did not take place in a political or social vacuum. Thus, political and social history is included in the account where it is deemed necessary for an understanding of legal history.

The history of criminal law as a subject of research, as is the case with every historical account, is *also* an interpretation, and particularly so in the case of a book such as the present one, which besides presenting *facts* also has a methodological aim. Of course, this does not mean that facts are chosen and weighted at random. Our journey through the legal-historical epoch should be imagined as traversing the

[1] The bibliographical information contains suggestions for further reading for those wishing to gain deeper knowledge and understanding. A more detailed exploration will soon be available in the multi-volume *Handbuch der Strafrechtsgeschichte* (Handbook of the History of Criminal Law) published by Springer, in which the author is writing about the 20th century. A final suggestion is the collection of texts "Strafrechtsdenker der Neuzeit" (Early Modern Theorists of Penal Law) edited by the author (referenced in the Bibliography).

entire length of a long island covered in jungle (perhaps similar in shape to Cuba). Someone undertaking this journey can use a machete to cut his or her own way through the forest, but the path is not solely a matter of personal choice, for the terrain's topographical features will have to be taken into account: mountains to be circumvented, dried-up river beds used, those carrying water crossed at the right places, and natural paths and clearings sought out and used to ease the way. Anyone starting out on this journey must therefore consider to which extent he or she wants to use those tracks already made by others—at the risk of detours or being led astray. The author hopes and is confident that he will guide readers successfully through the jungle to their goal (i.e. learning target)[2] while making them aware of the topographical features so that they will be able to undertake the journey again, maybe this time on paths they themselves have cut.

On the whole, the subject of this account is the history of *German* criminal law. Additions result from the fact that German criminal law was closely linked to criminal law in other European countries and pan-European developments both at the beginning and the end of the epoch under discussion. Not only are there many shared features in "common" criminal law during pre-revolutionary and pre-Napoleonic times, but the internationally debated concept of reform also emerged at this point in time. Present times reveal the first outlines of a European criminal law, the—sometimes quite problematic—features of which will be investigated briefly towards the end of the account.[3] But even in the time of national criminal codes, there was an international debate on criminal law in which German theory of criminal law played an important part. Lastly, the author admits to a personal interest in the development of criminal law in Italy, which is thus occasionally referred to, and as he is of the opinion that German criminal law theory and research about the history of criminal law, regardless of its undisputed quality, could benefit from its Italian counterpart, these references are considered relevant to the subject.[4]

The idea that the history of law is merely a superfluous addendum to legal training and has no relevance to the practice of law is both common and wrong—even if one is of the opinion that "education" must be measured against its "practical" applicability: a lack of knowledge of the history that conditions current

[2] It was only noticed later that the island example selected here, Cuba, lies close to Guantanamo Bay. It cannot be denied, however, that the characteristics of modern criminal law allow for the possibility of "Guantanamo".

[3] In a 2006 contribution on the development of criminal law in the EU published in German, the Italian scholar of criminal law *Massimo Donini* identifies the beginnings of a "new Middle Ages of criminal law", referring to "a new network of territorialism and universalism reminiscent in some regards of [the coexistence of *ius commune* and statutory law] of the Middle Ages": *Massimo Donini*, Ein neues strafrechtliches Mittelalter? Altes und Neues in der Expansion des Wirtschaftstrafrechts, in: ibid., Strafrechtstheorie und Strafrechtsreform. Beiträge zum Strafrecht und zur Strafrechtspolitik in Italien und Europa. Berlin 2006, p. 203 ff., 217.

[4] *Manfred Maiwald* gives an excellent introduction in his Einführung in das italienische Strafrecht und Strafprozessrecht. Frankfurt am Main 2009.

law means one is not only helpless when it comes to solving many technical questions of *current law* but also helpless in the face of *power*. That punishment by the state is an expression of power is of course obvious. But power needs to be the subject of constant critical scrutiny—regardless of whether and how well that power is legitimised.[5] For those who share the author's opinion that *criminal law and theory* should be tools used to scrutinise power and to rein in and control state punishment, the history of criminal law will form an indispensable part of criminal law research and teaching, for vigilance vis-à-vis power grows above all out of a knowledge of its abuses, and where these abuses are found, it is usually easy to find criminal laws that legitimise them too.

This textbook is informed by parts of my course of the same name written for the consecutive degree "Master of Laws" at the FernUniversität in Hagen. Thus, it has benefited from suggestions, contributions, and proofreading for that course by my colleagues *Dr. Martin Asholt*, stud. iur. *Katharina Kühne*, *Dr. Kathrin Rentrop*, stud. iur. *Dana Theil*, and Dipl. iur. (Münster) *Nadeschda Wilkitzki*. *Anne Gipperich* and stud. iur. *Zekai Dagasan* were indispensible in creating the master copy for printing. My warmest thanks are due to all of them.

[5] A recent publication on this subject is *Mario Cattaneo*, Recht und Gewalt. Ein problematisches Verhältnis. Münster 2008.

§ 1 Delimiting the Time Period and Methodology[1]

The "modern history of criminal law", the subject-matter this book is intended to provide an introduction to, could also be termed "contemporary history of criminal law" or "contemporary criminal history". Thus three thematic areas are alluded to, forming concentric circles and progressing from the largest to the smallest as follows:

- "Contemporary history";
- "Contemporary legal history"[2];
- "Contemporary criminal legal history";

As there is no general agreement on what these basic terms denote, they first must be defined or at least rendered plausible.

[1] General secondary literature on this topic: *Justizministerium Nordrhein-Westfalen* (Ed.), Perspektiven und Projekte (Juristische Zeitgeschichte NRW. 2). Düsseldorf 1994 (with contributions by Klaus Bästlein, Norbert Haase, Birte E. Keppler, Helmut Kramer, Klaus Marxen, Dieter Strempel, Hans-Ulrich Thamer, Thomas Vormbaum); *Wolfgang Naucke*, Über protokollierende und summierende (neuere) Strafrechtsgeschichte, in: Der praktische Nutzen der Rechtsgeschichte. Hans Hattenhauer zum 8. September 2001. Heidelberg 2003, p. 353 ff.

[2] The German term "juristische Zeitgeschichte" (English: contemporary legal history) was apparently coined by Klippel; see *Diethelm Klippel*, Juristische Zeitgeschichte. Die Bedeutung der Rechtsgeschichte für die Zivilrechtswissenschaft (Gießener rechtswissenschaftliche Abhandlungen. 4). Gießen 1985; its common usage in legal and legal-historical discourse can be attributed to the essay collection *Michael Stolleis* (Ed.), Juristische Zeitgeschichte—ein neues Fach? Baden-Baden 1993 (with contributions by Diemut Majer, Joachim Rückert, Jan Schröder, Rainer Schröder, Reiner Schulze, Thomas Vormbaum, Gerhard Werle); the series *Juristische Zeitgeschichte*, edited by the author, is expressly concerned with contemporary legal history, as are the periodicals *Jahrbuch der juristischen Zeitgeschichte* (edited by the author since 1999/2000) and *Journal der juristischen Zeitgeschichte* (edited by the author since 2007) and the series edited by the NRW ministry of justice, *Juristische Zeitgeschichte NRW*.

T. Vormbaum and M. Bohlander, *A Modern History of German Criminal Law*,
DOI 10.1007/978-3-642-37273-5_1,

I. Contemporary History

Everyone has heard the words "contemporary history", and everyone has their own associations with the term that probably correspond as far as their basic facts are concerned. Nonetheless, a precise definition is anything but easy. Certainly no one will doubt that contemporary history deals with matters particularly close to the observer.[3] However, is the observer already (or still) part of it? Does something from yesterday's paper already count as "contemporary history"? Then again, do the Reformation, the Thirty Years' War, the Napoleonic conquests or the foundation of the German Reich in 1871 still form part of contemporary history?

1. Subjective Approach: "Living History"

When students are confronted with questions such as these, their overwhelming response is that contemporary history is the history of the time that "one" has experienced oneself, or—as the respondents are all young—that it is the history of the time that people alive today have experienced. This response actually makes more assumptions than it would seem at first glance. The first tacit assumption is that "contemporary history" is primarily defined by a (recent) historical period, but not by a particular methodology. This assumption is already controversial—at least as far as contemporary *legal* history is concerned; objections to it will be dealt with at a later point.

The second tacit assumption is an understanding that can be referred to—using terminology common among lawyers—as "subjective theory"; non-lawyers would probably prefer to speak of a "subjective understanding" or "subjective approach". Terminology regardless, what is meant is that the definition's starting point is formed not by objective historical events or situations but by personally belonging to the contemporary period, regardless of the characteristics and particular traits of those events and situations. The death of the last person who experienced the time of World War I would thus mean that time would no longer fall under the category of "contemporary history", and the same would soon go for the National Socialist period—even though these two periods are among the most studied and debated in German history, and the former has been the focus of increased attention particularly in recent times. Contemporary history would thus—at least as far as its chronological subject area is concerned—be a yardstick measuring 70–80 years

[3] I am purposely avoiding the wording "particularly close *in time* to the observer", for there is no unanimous answer to the question of whether contemporary history—or at least contemporary *legal* history—should restrict itself to a chronologically delimited period. This already refers to *Senn* and *Gschwend's* view; on this, cf. this chapter, Section III. On the following, see also *Reinhart Koselleck*, Stetigkeit und Wandel aller Zeitgeschichten. Begriffsgeschichtliche Anmerkungen, in: Ibid., Zeitschichten. Studien zur Historik. Frankfurt am Main. 2000, p. 246 ff.; also p. 250 ff. on the history of the word and term "Zeitgeschichte" (contemporary history).

(its length corresponding with human life expectancy), moved along the timeline of world history day by day. For the study of contemporary history this means that new research topics are added on "in front", while topics drop away at the opposite end. The consequences of this understanding for research practice are both realistic and useful, for it is largely compatible with the approach described above: many historians concerned with the First World War may not regard themselves as "contemporary historians"; and whether the National Socialist period will still be regarded as "contemporary history" by those living 20 years from now, when the generation who actually experienced that period will have died out, is unclear (whatever one's opinion one of such a prospect might be). However, there seems to be little doubt that the cultural shift marked by the year 1968, the history of the GDR, German reunification and the radical changes in world politics after 1989 are now topics of contemporary history.

Methodologically, too, the subjective approach has certain advantages: certain research options are *per definitionem* available to it. Interviews with contemporary witnesses banally require that they are still alive. Refining empirical social research methods fits in with the trend in modern historiography to research everyday life, in particular the life of the lower social classes, of those social groups with less access to education and culture who therefore leave no or fewer *active* historical traces. To give these people a voice is one of the tasks that "oral history" has set itself; interviews with contemporary witnesses are not used primarily to explore individual lives, rather larger numbers of autobiographical individual comments can be used to make general statements.[4]

2. Objective Approach: "History of the Contemporary Epoch"

The approach presented above is "subjective" because *people* living in present times form its point of reference to the present. This contrasts with an objective approach that is based upon *structures* and thus upon objective facts. One structure used to demarcate historical topics chronologically is the *epoch*. An epoch can be understood as a period of time that forms a unity due to dominant (subjective and objective) traits that its political, cultural, social and economic lives have in common.

---

[4] On this, cf. *Werner Fuchs*, Biographische Forschung. Eine Einführung in Praxis und Methoden. Opladen 1984; *Wolfgang Vogel* (Ed.), Methoden der Biographie und Lebenslaufforschung. Opladen 1987; *Peter Alheit/Erika M. Hoernig*, Biographisches Wissen. Beiträge zu einer Theorie lebensgeschichtlicher Erfahrung. Frankfurt, New York 1989; *Matthias Peter/Hans-Jürgen Schröder*, Einführung in das Studium der Zeitgeschichte (UTB. 1742). Paderborn, Munich, Vienna, Zurich 1994, p. 55 ff. Further methodological issues are discussed in *Gabriele Metzler*, Einführung in das Studium der Zeitgeschichte (UTB. 2433). Paderborn, Munich, Vienna, Zurich 2004.—Apart from its "emancipatory" aspect, this approach is also coloured by a particular understanding of the value of historical sources; Koselleck notes that attempts to write "contemporary history" in all their variety from Herodotus to Churchill still share the same assumption that "[t]he incorrect testimony of a contemporary witness is still a more immediate source [than later compilations], even if it is exposed later".

According to this approach, contemporary history is the history of the *contemporary epoch*. In practice, this is the approach commonly followed at present; however, research subjects are usually tailored in such a way that any debate on the basic understanding of "contemporary history" becomes redundant as both approaches overlap. If one follows the objective approach, the boundary, in this case the *beginning* of the contemporary epoch, must be defined. Naturally, the method formerly used in school history lessons—using the dates of the lives or reigns of potentates or other events in national politics or war, and seeing them as indicative of epochal shifts—should be avoided. Of course there are "epochal" happenings such as the French Revolution; but even it had its prehistory, if the social-historical aspect is included, and the storming of the Bastille was certainly not its most incisive event.[5] Usually, epochs are not strictly demarcated by clear turning points. Instead, so-called *saddle periods* lie in between, during which processes leading to a new historical "situation" grow increasingly frequent—in more theoretical terms, during which an accelerated change of quantity into a new quality occurs. Of course, this change can manifest itself particularly strongly in spectacular events.

For example, simply stating that the *Early Modern Period*[6] begins with the Reformation or the discovery of America is insufficient explanation in itself. However, when searching for accumulations of important processes, changes and events, it becomes clear that both of these events do indeed fall into a saddle period: the Great Plague of 1348, which wiped out a third of the population of Europe, occurred during a period of climate change described in historiography as the beginning of a "Little Ice Age". Social unrest, caused not least by the worsening of the climate, occurred in several parts of Europe (the revolt of the "Ciompi" in Florence, the Jacquerie—a peasant uprising—in France, and, following close on the heels of the Reformation, the great Peasant War in Germany).[7] Around 1450, Gutenberg invented the art of printing books using movable type, without which the later spread of the Reformation is unthinkable; in 1492, Columbus discovered

[5] On the history of the word and term "epoch", cf. *Hans Blumenberg*, Die Epochen des Epochenbegriffs, in: Id., Aspekte der Epochenschwelle. Frankfurt a.M. 1976, p. 7 ff.—On the symbolic, rather than practical, importance of the storming of the Bastille on 14 July 1789, cf. *Hans Jürgen Lüsebrink/Rolf Reichart*, Die "Bastille". Zur Symbolgeschichte von Herrschaft und Freiheit. Frankfurt am Main 1990, p. 49 ff. Following *Rudolf Vierhaus*, Aufklärung und Reformzeit. Kontinuitäten und Neuansätze der deutschen Politik des späten 18. und beginnenden 19. Jahrhunderts; in: Reformen im rheinbündischen Deutschland. Ed. Eberhard Weis, assisted by Elisabeth Müller-Luckner. Munich 1984, pp. 267–301, here p. 289, "the effects produced by the French Revolution are usually exaggerated. Colossal change also took place in Germany around 1800".

[6] On the following, cf. *Reinhart Koselleck*, Wie neu ist die Neuzeit? in: *Ibid.*, Zeitschichten (above Fn. 3), p. 225 ff.

[7] On this, see *Ruggiero Romano/Alberto Tenenti*, Die Grundlegung der modernen Welt. Spätmittelalter, Renaissance, Reformation. (Fischer-Weltgeschichte. 12). Frankfurt am Main. 1967 (incl. many new editions), p. 25 f. (Jacquerie), 26, 61 (Florentine Ciompi), 295 ff. (German Peasant War).

America[8]; around 1515, Copernicus developed his eponymous heliocentric worldview, and in 1517, Luther took the decisive steps towards the Reformation, which in terms of intellectual history was itself dependent on the Renaissance and Humanist worldview (even where it defines itself in opposition to it). Even before Luther, Girolamo Savonarola in Florence, John Wycliffe in England, Johann Zwingli in Switzerland and Jan Hus in Bohemia had all put forward reformatory theses. This concentration of fundamental events and processes—of "unheard-of novelties" (Koselleck)—within a relatively short space of time and the resulting impact on the following time period mean this space of time can be called a "saddle period".[9]

So when does the contemporary epoch begin? There is no prevalent opinion on this. The title of the *Weltgeschichte des 20. Jahrhunderts* published by the Institute of Contemporary History in Munich reveals a (presumably pragmatic) understanding of the area of contemporary history. A chronologically more limited understanding can be seen in the apostrophisation, common in recent years, of the First World War as an "ur-catastrophe".[10]

Hans Rothfels sets 1917 as the chronological boundary: only when America joined the war did it really become a "world war"; in the same year, the October Revolution paved the way for Russia and the Soviet Union's rise to global power. Both processes lay the foundation for political "globalisation".[11]

In *research practice*, "contemporary history" seldom goes further back than the National Socialist period or the Weimar Republic. Of course, this also has to do with the particular academic remit of departments and chairs as well as personal research interests.

We need not provide an answer to the question of period boundaries in regard to general contemporary history, as we are dealing with contemporary *legal* history. Even if the objective understanding of contemporary history is given preference over the subjective, this in itself does not determine whether the period boundary assumed by the former also goes for contemporary *legal* history, as there may be differences specific to the field. For example, social historiography might see contemporary history beginning with the development of the "Fourth Estate" (the working class or proletariat) in the middle of the nineteenth century; legal history

---

[8] In the same year, an edict was pronounced in Aragon and Castile offering all Jews the choice between emigrating within 4 months or being baptised; on this, cf. *Bernd Rother*, Die iberische Halbinsel, in: Kotowski/Schoeps/Wallenborn (Eds.), Handbuch zur Geschichte der Juden in Europa. Darmstadt 2001. Vol. I, p. 325 ff., here p. 344 f.; the "modern" aspect of this event is that, following the edict, those "Conversos" whose conversion was thought to be insincere were persecuted. Their descendants were barred from many offices and professions on grounds of "purity of blood" (op. cit., p. 348).

[9] Of course, the term "Early Modern Period" only appeared in the nineteenth century; on this, cf. *Koselleck*, Neuzeit (Fn. 6), p. 227.

[10] Thus for example the title of the 17th volume of the 10th edition of *Gebhard's* Handbuch der Deutschen Geschichte: *Wolfgang J. Mommsen*, Die Urkatastrophe Deutschlands. Der Erste Weltkrieg 1914–1918. Stuttgart 2002. This designation appears to derive from G.F. Kennan, without being restricted to Germany; cf. *Mommsen*, op. cit., p. 14, incl. further references.

[11] *Hans Rothfels*, Zeitgeschichte als Aufgabe, in: Vierteljahrshefte für Zeitgeschichte (VfZ) 1 (1953), p. 1 ff.

has to go back even further, as will be seen shortly. However, it will soon become evident that any search for the beginnings of the *legal-historical* period must also take account of processes and structures that form part of general history but nevertheless impact particularly upon the development of law.

3. Emphasis and Implications

The methodological advantages of the subjective approach have already been outlined above. It has its disadvantages also. Without wishing to detract from the value of research methods, it is nonetheless difficult to use them to establish the boundary of an epoch. But as far as this boundary is concerned, it seems arbitrary to use the lifespan of those currently living as its criterion, i.e. to assume a time span that moves through history, parts of which continuously break away behind and grow in front, with no other criterion of content other than the biological one of the human lifespan. It does not seem appropriate to the subject of contemporary history that ultimately the advance of medical research should determine its area and scope.

Then again, the objective approach certainly has its difficulties in ascertaining criteria for defining the period boundary; it fact, it will almost certainly lead to a failure of general consensus. However, this drawback must simply be accepted, for debating these different understandings when defining epoch boundaries will reinvigorate considerations of the characteristics of one's own epoch and thus prove fruitful for both the study and the politics of history. Conversely, this approach allows for questions that are not possible when adopting a subjective approach—as will be discussed in connection with contemporary *legal* history.

Even if the objective approach is adopted for the reasons given here, the advantages of the subjective approach—whether tacit or openly acknowledged—and their respective value nonetheless remain available, for in practice the described possible methods of a "history of contemporaries" will lead to research activity concentrating on precisely these contemporaries. For example, the German version of the internet encyclopaedia *Wikipedia* first describes Rothfels's (objective) understanding before stating that "since the end of the twentieth century, contemporary history has been understood as the period following the end of World War II, for living contemporary witnesses of the time before the Second World War have died or are dying out". Thus it implicitly refers to the subjective approach—if only as a supplement, for it subsequently goes on to state: "The period following 1945 is a time of peace for most Europeans, Asians and Americans and is not characterised by a large-scale war", thus again using an objective criterion as its basis.[12] Then again, *Rothfels* takes as his starting point the definition that contemporary history is "the period of living fellow humans and its scholarly discussion";

[12] http://de.wikipedia.org/wiki/Zeitgeschichte, last accessed 17 January 2012—Translator's note: The previous version read "with the beginning of the 21st century" and was used in that form in the German original.

the year 1953, when *Rothfels* wrote his essay, was only 36 years after 1917, so that setting this year as the boundary meant that the subjectively defined time period was actually *narrowed*.

In the following, the objective approach is adopted due to the advantages presented above. Accordingly, contemporary history is seen as **the history of the contemporary epoch.**

II. Contemporary Legal History

If contemporary history is the history of the contemporary epoch, then contemporary legal history is the **history of the contemporary legal epoch**. This calls for an outline of the present legal-historical period, i.e. an investigation of its chronological boundaries (see 2. below). But prior to this, a few brief queries related to the methodology and subject of enquiry require discussion, as these are important for further understanding.

1. Methodology and Subject of Enquiry

Up until the second half of the twentieth century, traditional legal history consisted largely, though not exclusively, of the history of doctrine and theory. If these subject boundaries were crossed, then usually in the direction of cultural history and—mainly in the area of constitutional history—political history. These restrictions have been increasingly criticised since the 1970s.

It should be added, of course, that general history itself up until the mid-twentieth century was limited to political history in the narrower sense of the word, or to the history of a particular state. As has already been mentioned, history lessons in school consisted for the most part of the dates of the reigns of emperors and kings and of events in state politics, diplomacy or war. Much has changed in this regard over the last three decades. The history of political events has been both enriched and partly driven back by structural-historical elements. Large parts of social history, that is the history of social groups and classes which is not characterised by spectacular events but precisely by structures and structural shifts, have been included in political history; as is evident in *Hans Ulrich Wehler's* standard work, recently increased to five large volumes to include an introduction to the present-day period.[13]

But traditional legal history can be criticised not only from a general historical point of view, but also from the points of view of the philosophy of law and legal theory, in brief: from the point of view of legal studies (on this, see b).

[13] *Hans Ulrich Wehler*, Deutsche Gesellschaftsgeschichte. 5 volumes (cf. references).

Before these demands are addressed and their justification examined (and agreed with), it should be made clear that *doctrinal legal history* was and is valid and important, and will in all likelihood remain so. As the history of the construction and gradual shifts and changes of doctrinal theory, it is able to make valuable contributions to an understanding of present-day doctrinal concepts—as well as put them in perspective. The doctrine of current law tends to present its results as necessary and imperative, but doctrinal history is able to prove that legal problems have been solved in different ways (in terms of both law and doctrine), and that the solution favoured at present is not the only one possible.

For example, if the current theory of attempts invokes[14] the current legal framework (§ 22 (1) StGB)—though it is not imperative to do so—and sees the cause for punishing the attempt in an intent which is manifestly hostile to the law, not in creating an objectively dangerous situation or at least ex ante and evidently endangering a legally protected interest, it thus concludes that any mitigation for the attempted offence can only be *optional* in nature (see § 23 (2) StGB), for the offender's criminal intent is (usually) just as great in an attempted as in a completed offence. Taking our thoughts back yet another step, we can deduce from the legal decision in § 23 (2) StGB that the task of rules is to *guide and control* human behaviour; in an attempted crime, this control has failed just as much as if a crime had been committed.—However, if we know that, prior to a change of law in 1943, the criminal code made mitigation *compulsory* for attempts and that the current rule was only introduced by National Socialist legislature,[15] and that many democracies committed to the Rule of Law in fact do not cover this aspect in their criminal codes,[16] then this puts the "necessity" of these constructions in perspective and reveals an alternative model (one that used to be prevalent), where prosecuting authorities only see grounds to become active where someone's rights or legally protected interests have been infringed or at least endangered. But as endangering objectively constitutes a lesser wrong than infringement, from this point of view mitigation is seen as necessary. In this alternative model, the task of rules to guide and control is merely a desirable side effect; the main focus is to detect and sanction wrongdoing.[17]

---

[14] On this, see *H.J. Hirsch*, Versuchstheorie, op. cit., p. 89 (text of Fn. 75).

[15] For further discussion of the extreme subjective theory of attempts and its connection with National Socialist doctrine of criminal law, see *Hirsch*, op. cit.

[16] Supporting evidence in *H.J. Hirsch*, Versuchstheorie, op. cit., p. 65 f., 89; for *Italy* see for example Art. 56 (2) of the Codice penale (the so-called Codice Rocco—which dates from the Fascist period!).

[17] The subjective theory of attempts is sometimes depicted as a consequence of the theory of personal unlawfulness. As *Hirsch*, himself one of the proponents of this theory of unlawfulness whilst an outspoken critic of the subjective theory of attempts, details in his contribution noted in Fn. 14, in terms of doctrine this statement is based on a misunderstanding that equates personal theory of unlawfulnesss with subjectivisation (op. cit., p. 497). Two levels become apparent here: while Hirsch's elaborations are certainly correct as far as *doctrine of criminal law* and *doctrinal history* are concerned, seen from the broader perspective of the history of criminal law the question arises of how this misunderstanding—which, as *Hirsch* demonstrates, even some of the "greats" of

a) Inclusion of History

Criticism of a history of (pure) doctrine demands that legal-historical research include or at least consider general history. Taken on its own, doctrinal history gives only an abridged version of legal developments. As part of political, cultural, social and economic developments, law and its development can only be understood adequately as part of this overall development. Legal history should therefore open itself up to the social and political implications of law and embed itself into its social and general historical context. Accepting this demand of course does not mean that legal history should simply dissolve into general history; rather, in the same way as social history or cultural history, it should be understood as the *history of a particular aspect*, i.e. a view of history from the particular perspective of law. Such a widening of perspective can result in a broadened insight into legal developments also—as can be seen in the following example.

In Germany in January 1924, the so-called Emminger Decree abolished jury trials. (Following the Anglo-American pattern, jury trials had existed in Germany since 1877 on the level of the Reich, if only with limited jurisdiction and *without* jurisdiction over precisely those crimes they had originally been created for by the nineteenth century bourgeois revolutionary movement: political offences and press offences.) A doctrinal history of criminal procedure would include this process in a representation of the discussion, with its many arguments both for and against, at the time hotly debated in criminal law theory.[18] However, a fully rounded representation can only be achieved by considering the further changes in court organisation and criminal procedure resulting from the Emminger Decree and—crucially, in our context—by taking account of the political and social "side effects". (This term is put in inverted commas as it would be more correct to say that the rules of the Emminger Decree were a result of these political developments.) The most important changes besides the abolition of jury trials were: a huge shift of first-instance responsibility to the criminal judge as a single judge, and first inroads into the principle of mandatory prosecution in criminal proceedings (the obligation to prosecute in a prima facie case, § 152 StPO) that up until then had been universally valid—at least on paper. Concurrent political circumstances become clear if we bear in mind that 1923 was probably one of the most spectacular and crisis-ridden years in German political history.[19] The Reichstag was on holiday, having delegated powers almost completely to the government of the Reich through an enabling law, and much evidence suggests that this situation was being exploited by conservative forces.[20] Giving the *political*

criminal doctrine have fallen prey to (op. cit., p. 495 on *Bockelmann*, p. 496 on *Eb.* Schmidt)—fits into a historical line of development. This results in challenging and intriguing methodological consequential problems for the relationship between criminal doctrine and modern history of criminal law that unfortunately cannot be examined further here.

[18] On this, see *Vormbaum*, Lex Emminger, p. 134 ff.

[19] Cf. *Vormbaum*, Lex Emminger, p. 21 ff.

[20] Though tolerated by social democratic forces, e.g. Gustav Radbruch; cf. *Vormbaum*, op. cit.

excuse of combating inflation and the *legal* excuse of legal concerns, they used an emergency decree to abolish an institution they saw (not without reason) as a consequence of the 1848 Revolution and which had always been a political thorn in their side.

b) Inclusion of Law

The call to include general history in contemporary legal history reveals an emphasis on the element of *contemporary history*. The discipline of law further demands a *legal* element. What does this mean in our case?

If the inclusion of general history means broadening our perspective in *factual* terms, i.e. extending the subject-matter and objects of enquiry, then an inclusion of legal-theoretical aspects means a *normative* extension. Limiting contemporary legal history to a *legal-historical period*, i.e. one particular period of time characterised by shared fundamental traits, necessarily means that certain legal principles are declared valid during this legal-historical period.

This opens up the possibility of tracing how these principles are realised (or not realised) during the process of their development (or regression). Thus both the demands of law itself and the demands made of it in terms of legal theory can be used to measure law and its development. If this is approached from a historical angle, an epoch's particular lines or curves of development can be revealed and it becomes possible to evaluate developments as positive or disastrous (measured against legal demands), and perhaps to use this to make suggestions for present-day actions—something subject historians usually regard sceptically but in actual fact frequently practice themselves.[21]

The main objection raised is that it is naïve to believe that a simple development can be seen in or indeed a "lesson" learnt from historical events and processes. Any unconditional understanding or even evaluation of past times and their (legal) historical texts is impossible, as any such process requires the "lens" of the interpreter and is thus seen through it. Whether consciously or unconsciously so, the interpreter's prior understanding forms part of their interpretation, so that even the question formulated conditions the (inevitable) selectivity of the subject-matter (the so-called *hermeneutic circle*).

That this is a valid objection cannot be denied. The sciences particularly affected by the problem of the hermeneutic circle are those concerned with interpreting and explaining texts and other carriers of meaning (scholars of law, theology, literature, and history; also, for example, geographers when interpreting maps). Those who undertake interpretation uncritically (particularly towards themselves) fall victim to

---

[21] On this, see *Hans-Ulrich Wehler*, Aus der Geschichte lernen? in: Id., Aus der Geschichte lernen? Munich 1988, p. 11 ff.

the ironic suggestion made by Goethe in his satirical *Zahme Xenien*: "Be brisk and lively in your interpretation,/If you find no meaning in it, at least put something under it".

Self-criticism and self-monitoring require above all an awareness of one's own prior conceptions and understanding, followed by the application of the basic tenets of critical source analysis, in particular the tenet that historical sources are *polyvalent* on principle. Their classification is a matter of interpretation, which again leads us to the problem of the hermeneutic circle. This phenomenon thus cannot be excluded. As already mentioned, prior knowledge and assumptions determine what subject-matter is selected. Selectivity cannot be avoided when choosing the subject-matter, as only selectivity makes it possible to write historiography, the art and science of which consists precisely in selecting "essential" facts from the infinite range of daily events and occurrences. Here, too, the arbitrariness of selection can be minimised by weaving as detailed a "tapestry" of facts as possible. However, this process will have to be broken off at a more or less arbitrary point, as there is no defined limit to the ideal level of detail; furthermore, the more one goes into the details of events, the more their connection with other events is lost.[22] This creates another insurmountable obstacle, as historiography is concerned precisely with making "connections". All in all, the attempt to eliminate prior understanding through density of facts will not be able to cross a certain threshold of concretisation.

As demonstrated by the so-called sociology of knowledge, there is however such a thing as a *collective* prior understanding that a society can "come to an understanding" on. This is particularly important as it is this collective understanding and agreement that plays a role in the development of epochs and legal-historical epochs.[23]

Of course, this understanding is only valid *within* the "collective". The related danger of a "politics of history" directed against those outside the collective should not be overlooked. In methodological terms, it can be observed that the existence of collective prior understanding reduces communicative difficulties *within* a culture or an epoch, facilitating the development of accepted interpretations.

In a contribution to a discussion (that unfortunately remains unpublished), *Klaus Marxen* suggested differentiating between "contemporary legal history" and a

[22] It is well known that only astronauts' photographs, taken from vast distance, were able to show us the earth in its "connected" entirety.

[23] The standard work of the sociology of knowledge is: *Peter L. Berger/Thomas Luckmann*, The Social Construction of Reality. A Treatise in the Sociology of Knowledge (1966). Paperback English edition, London 1980; see also the anthology of important contributions to the sociology of knowledge: *Volker Meja/Nico Stehr* (Eds.), Der Streit um die Wissenssoziologie. Vol. 1: Die Entwicklung der deutschen Wissenssoziologie. Vol. 2: Rezeption und Kritik der Wissenssoziologie. (Suhrkamp TB. 361). Frankfurt am Main 1982.

"contemporary history of law". The contemporary history of law becomes "contemporary legal history" only when the interpretational element discussed here is included.[24]

2. *The Legal-Historical Period*

a) Searching for Its Beginnings

Although ultimately it was possible to leave the general question of when the *historical period* begins open, this is not an option when it comes to the *legal-historical period*, for despite all the particularities of the history of criminal law it cannot be separated from general developments in law and thus from a definition of the legal-historical period. Thus the question of when our legal-historical period begins must first be answered in order to address the question of the time period covered in the history of modern criminal law. This result can be achieved by going back as far as it takes to reach that point in time or comparatively short time period—a "saddle period"—during which the conditions and elements that shape the law today developed.

It should be noted here that the year **1989**, often referred to as an "epochal year", cannot (or not yet) be properly called the threshold of an epoch, despite its spectacular events and the changes wrought by them—all the more as these events primarily did not affect the area of law, and even where this was the case they were really only formal legal sanctions of political and social occurrences. As far as German legal history and history of criminal law are concerned, there is also the additional fact that any change in legal developments only affected the GDR; but even there, it simply meant reconnecting to developments that had continued in Germany's larger half after 1945 and were now (again) expanded to include the GDR. Whether the development of law and criminal law in the GDR really constitutes a "break" of course requires further discussion.[25]

Whether the next threshold in question—going backwards—should be the year 1945 or maybe the year **1968** is open to debate. After all, the changes in everyday and social life following the year 1968 are quite profound: they start with clothing, continue with notions of family, authority, sexuality, the role of women and culminate in unmarried and (legally sanctioned) same-sex civil partnerships. Nonetheless, 1968 cannot be called the threshold to a *legal* epoch, for neither in legislation and jurisdiction nor in legal theory were there any significant new principles or contours added to the current law.

[24] However, cf. *Klaus Marxen*, Strafrecht nach der Überwindung zweier Unrechtsregime in Deutschland. Ein Plädoyer für eine zeithistorische Rechtsschule im Strafrecht, in: Festschrift 200 Jahre Juristische Fakultät der Humboldt-Universität Berlin. Berlin 2010; in fine. An attempt to gain further insight from this differentiation can be found in: *Vormbaum*, Judeneid.

[25] See in the first instance the reference in *Vormbaum*, GA 1994, p. 94.

1945, above all 8 May, was felt by many Germans to be the "Stunde Null", "zero hour". But even disregarding the fact that this is not the case for many other nations, for whom this year meant—and importantly so—the return of peace and freedom from German occupation and oppression and not a break in their political and cultural development, in *legal* terms we cannot speak of a new epoch even if we assume a discontinuity between the National Socialist period and the following period,[26] for legal developments after 1945 do not signify a new beginning in the sense that hitherto unknown elements were added to existing law. Rather, links were re-established to the legal state of affairs *prior to 1933*, as far as attempts at disassociation from National Socialist law were made.

For this reason, **1933** and the transfer of power to the National Socialists cannot be regarded as the threshold of an epoch, either—simply because most of the ensuing radical political changes were reversed 12 years later. The question of continuity will be addressed in later sections.

Going back, the transition from the Kaiserreich to the Weimar Republic in **1918** presents itself as the next possible threshold. In actual fact, apart from the change in the form of government, this transition did not even constitute a significant break with respect to the political institutions. On the one hand, the Prussian three-class voting system had been abolished and a parliamentary form of government introduced throughout the Reich during the final phases of imperial rule.[27] On the other hand, the revolution only meant that one political elite was replaced by another, broader one (and this only partially). The bureaucracy and justice system remained more or less unchanged; there were no significant alterations in civil and criminal law.

The **First World War** certainly produced some innovations, not least in criminal law, that will be discussed later; but they consisted more of changes in the style of legislative technique than long-term changes of normative content.

Going further back, we reach the time period between **1870 and the change from the nineteenth to the twentieth century**. This would seem to present itself as the threshold to a new legal epoch for the simple reason that a host of codifications were introduced at this time.[28] Meanwhile, a closer look reveals that the innovative range of this wave of codifications was only limited (for example introducing freedom of advocacy), while a large part of territorial law had already been anticipated. The innovative aspect thus lay in *unification* and *standardisation*. However, this in itself does not warrant defining this time as an epochal threshold.

---

[26] This controversial question, responses to which nowadays usually focus on *continuity*, will be discussed during the relevant part of this study.

[27] For detailed information on this subject, see: *E.R. Huber*, Deutsche Verfassungsgeschichte seit 1789. Vol. V: Weltkrieg, Revolution und Reichserneuerung. Stuttgart et al. 1978, p. 388 ff.

[28] 1870: Reich Criminal Code—1877/1879: the so-called Reichsjustizgesetze (Code of Civil Procedure, Code of Criminal Procedure, Court Organisation Act, Insolvency Act, Legal Profession Act)—1896/1900: German Civil Code—1897: revision of the General German Commercial Code (created by the German Confederation and adopted as Reich law in 1871), now the "Commercial Code", as well as the Public Limited Companies Act in 1884 and the Limited Liability Companies Act in 1892.

I remain convinced of this opinion even following a heated discussion with Berlin teachers of criminal law in April 2009, during which the codifications mentioned in Fn. 28 were held up as counter-examples. I agree that the last three decades of the nineteenth century constitute the only alternative to the beginning of the legal-historical (at least as far as criminal law is concerned) contemporary epoch suggested in the present study. It is undeniable that a change in political and legal conditions took place during that time, which can be seen as—using a term taken from analytical geometry—a *point of inflection*, a turning point, but not as *the threshold of a new epoch*. Specific characteristics of this turning point will be discussed in § 4.

Going back further in time through the nineteenth century, there are decades where no clues justifying the assumption of an epochal threshold appear. The failed revolution of 1848 set no new direction *effective in practical terms*, apart from the (limited) parliamentarisation of Prussia and a few other German states already anticipated by the southern German states, and the introduction of jury courts in several German states.[29]

b) Defining Its Beginnings

Thus we reach the shift from the eighteenth to the nineteenth century. And here we do actually find accumulated signs of an epochal threshold in the development of law. External signs of change are—moving backwards—the end of the old German Reich in 1806 (Francis II. gives up the German Imperial Crown), and 3 years earlier the German Mediatisation that resulted in the end of prince-bishoprics and the mediatisation of most smaller principalities, radically restructuring the political map of Germany. Of course, this was simply the institutional consequence of changes at the European level for Germany; for the second half of the eighteenth century was a time of revolutionary change in which the end of the old German Reich only constitutes the final point. In general, these changes are concerned with elements that are (also) revolutionary in general historical terms; however, they also have revolutionary consequences for the development of *law*, indeed some affect partly or mainly only legal developments.

The **political revolutions** that come to an end with the end of the old Reich or, ultimately, with the Congress of Vienna (1815) and its long-term restructuring of Europe begin with the French Revolution (1789), pre-empted by the American Revolution of 1776, and continue with Napoleon's conquering of most of Europe, because he propagated the ideas of the Revolution throughout his territory—if only in a watered-down form distorted by authoritarianism.

[29] The effects of this revolution on *France* were similar to the effects of the 1918 revolution in Germany.

At the same time, **social revolutions** take place. The age of feudalism and nobility comes to an end, the peasants are set free and the political rise of the bourgeoisie begins.

The **Industrial Revolution**, which started earlier in England, spreads throughout the continent at the end of the eighteenth century.

It is combined with **economic revolutions**. Building railways demands greater amounts of capital than a wealthy individual can raise. This is the dawn of the age of large banks and stock companies (the latter initially hampered in France by a distrust—sown by Rousseau—of powerful organisations on a level between the individual and the state, and in Germany by precisely the opposite, the ruling elite's distrust of a non-governmental concentration of power). The demand for iron and steel (railways, rails!) leads to an expansion of mining and metallurgy and thus to a corresponding growth of the working class.

Of particular importance for law are the **revolutions in culture and the history of ideas**. One of Enlightenment philosophy's main areas of application is law and particularly criminal law. Eberhard Schmidt[30] summarised its demands for this area with the following key words: *secularisation, individualisation, rationalisation* and *humanisation*. **Immanuel Kant**, who both perfected and went beyond Enlightenment philosophy, places the human being at the centre of his theories as a free and autonomous individual; it is fair to say that his work creates significant impulses for ensuing legal developments. It was Kant who, at the time the Enlightenment was already in its final stages, created the definition still famous today:

> Enlightenment is man's emergence from his self-imposed immaturity. Immaturity is the inability to use one's understanding without guidance from another. This immaturity is self-imposed when its cause lies not in lack of understanding, but in lack of resolve and courage to use it without guidance from another. Sapere Aude! Have courage to use your own understanding!—that is the motto of enlightenment.

This requires further discussion. The first definition of **human rights** in the *Déclaration des droits de l'homme et du citoyen* declared by the French National Assembly on 26 August 1789, based on the American model, also belongs to this context

To summarise, these revolutions cover all material, cultural, economic and legal areas.[31] As these factors are interconnected and because people experienced this time as a break with the past, we are fully justified in speaking of a "saddle period"

---

[30] *Eb. Schmidt*, SchwZStrR 1958, 341 ff.

[31] In passing, one should also mention that significant changes took place in the fields of literature and music: German *literature* at least undergoes a significant shift in terms of its quality and modernity in the middle of the eighteenth century; indeed, Schlaffer only begins his "short history of German literature" with this time (*Heinz Schlaffer*, Die kurze Geschichte der deutschen Literatur. Munich, Vienna 2002); at the same time, *music* shifts from the baroque era and its use of figured bass to the Viennese classical school. In the latter, aural perception is dominated by melody, resulting in a significant shift in ways of listening (see e.g. *Herbert Rosendorfer*, Don Ottavio erinnert sich. Unterhaltungen über die richtige Musik. Kassel 1989, p. 205 f.).

in the sense initially referred to. In history and philosophy, this time is referred to as the beginning of "modernity".[32]

Of course, the same goes for this periodisation as for all other periodisations: they are "rationalisations made in hindsight that structure the course of the historical process and attempt to comprehend conceptually the mass of events and connections".[33] However, the objective factors that form the basis of this interpretation are, after all, of great import.

The results of our considerations so far can be summarised as follows:

1) Contemporary legal history is the legal history of the contemporary epoch.
2) The current legal-historical period begins with the saddle period towards the end of the eighteenth century and thus (so far) includes the nineteenth and twentieth centuries.
3) Contemporary legal history includes general, cultural and social history in its consideration. Thus it can be seen as a "history of aspects".
4) Contemporary legal history interprets and evaluates the development of law (also) according to legal criteria.

III. The Approach of Senn/Gschwend

The understanding of contemporary legal history adopted here lies halfway between the widely spread (if not expressly acknowledged) approach that—insofar as it is objective—reduces the scope of general contemporary history and contemporary legal history to the twentieth (and, in the near future, the twenty-first) century or even only part of it, and the approach advocated by the legal historians *Marcel Senn* and *Lukas Gschwend*. Their approach does not see contemporary legal history in terms of epochs at all; instead, the entire inventory of problems solved throughout world history is used to find answers to current legal issues. According to this understanding, the specific characteristics of contemporary legal history lie in the investigator's perspective and the contemporary reference of the *question*, instead of a reference to any particular epoch. (Senn quotes Hölderlin: "It is, however, not the time..."). Contemporary legal history is not—in the pointed words of Marcel Senn—legal history where "smoke is still rising from the ashes".[34] Accordingly, *Senn* and *Gschwend's* textbook on "contemporary legal

---

[32] This definition on the whole corresponds to what is also called history of "recent times"; on this, see *Koselleck*, Neuzeit (Fn. 6), p. 228; in addition to the characteristics listed in the text, he includes "exponential time graphs", that "confirm accelerated change": world population, speed of travel, communication technology, artistic epochs, scientific and technical innovations are updated and modernised at increasingly closer intervals.

[33] Thus *Rudolf Vierhaus*, Aufklärung und Reformzeit (as in Fn. 5), p. 288.

[34] *Marcel Senn*, JJZG 6 (2004/2005), p. 224.

history"[35] examines questions such as "violence, power and law", "law and the elite", "race and law", "gender and law", "anthropology and law" and "economics and law", using source texts to trace them back over the years and centuries they have been discussed, in some cases back to ancient times.

As has already been demonstrated, I agree with *Senn* and *Gschwend* insofar as I consider the practice of questioning legal history in order to gain insights or even instructions for the present both acceptable and desirable. However, I do think it an over-extension of the term "contemporary history" to use it in a sense where any grounding in and reference to the present is abandoned. Of course there is a canon of problems and suggested solutions that covers timeless human issues; but precisely because they are timeless they cannot be historical. I would class them as philosophical or legal-philosophical problems. Critical questions of a science that calls itself "contemporary legal *history*" must refer to a historical period; and as the term "contemporary history" in its (more or less) general usage refers to a recent, if not the present, period, thus contemporary *legal* history must refer to the contemporary *legal-historical* period.[36]

IV. Current Legal Issues

Until when does an event form part of (legal) contemporary history? This is a problem that only really affects contemporary history, for all other historical periods with their fixed beginnings and endings are behind us—or indeed before our eyes as the object of our enquiry. The historian Johann Gustav Droysen states in his *Historik* (1882), one of the most important works on the theory of history (not only) of the nineteenth century:

> The restlessly moving present of the civilised world is a never-ending chaos of activities, conditions, interests, conflicts, passions [. . .]. No person of sense enacts or intends whatever occurs in it on a daily basis to be history. Only a particular way of viewing what has occurred retrospectively turns activities into history (§ 45).

However, if—in line with the approach adopted here—contemporary legal history is to include criticism of legal developments (see above: the demands of

[35] *Marcel Senn/Lukas Gschwend*: Rechtsgeschichte II—Juristische Zeitgeschichte. 2nd edition. Zurich 2004.

[36] Further discussion of the approach of Senn/Gschwend: *Marcel Senn/Thomas Vormbaum*, Dialog über juristische Zeitgeschichte, in: JJZG 6 (2004/2005), p. 219 ff.—That the approach of *Senn/ Gschwend* can also be helpful in furthering the approach adopted in the present study is shown in a quote by Koselleck (who himself develops a definition of contemporary history similar to that of the two authors mentioned here): "Contemporary history, properly defined, is more than the history of our time. Only when we know what parts of history can repeat themselves (even if not all at once) will we be able to measure what really is new about our time. Perhaps less than we imagine. But it is this little that counts"; *Reinhart Koselleck*, Stetigkeit und Wandel aller Zeitgeschichte (as in Fn. 3), p. 246 ff., 263.

theory of law), then contemporary processes can also be factors or symptoms that confirm or refute the processes analysed, and this speaks for including present-day developments. Of course, this not only poses the question of where the line between current legal issues and contemporary legal history should be drawn, but also raises the well-known problem that it is usually difficult to judge whether a present event will turn out to be of historical "importance". The "blurred" boundaries between current legal issues and contemporary legal history are a necessary consequence of the concept presented above and must simply be accepted. The difficulty of evaluating the importance of current issues cannot be eliminated entirely. At least an attempt can be made to bring out their particularity on the level of language by calling this border area "current legal *issues*".[37]

V. Modern History of Criminal Law

Everything discussed in regard to contemporary legal history in general also applies to the modern history of criminal law or the contemporary history of criminal law (or, to be precise, according to *Marxen's* classification: the contemporary legal history of criminal law). That is: the modern history of criminal law also focuses on the contemporary legal-historical period, the beginning of which can be dated to the end of the eighteenth century.

[37] The attempt to examine current issues in terms of their importance for posterity goes back to the beginnings of historiography (the most famous example being the Annals of Tacitus).—An attempt to document current legal issues over a 5-year period using the reports of a daily newspaper was undertaken in: *Heribert Prantl/Thomas Vormbaum* (Eds.), Juristisches Zeitgeschehen in der Süddeutschen Zeitung. 5 vols. (for the years 2000–2004 of the SZ). Berlin 2001–2005 (Juristische Zeitgeschichte. Section 5, vols. 9, 11, 13, 15, 17). In the present book "current legal issues" is used pragmatically to refer to developments since 1989. Later editions would, of course, have to query this categorisation, for even in 2010 over 20 years have passed since the political turning point of 1989 (a much longer period than the entire National Socialist era).

§ 2 Criminal Law at the Beginning of the Legal-Historical Period

If the decisive characteristics of the current legal period were formed towards the end of the eighteenth century, then it should be possible to identify key shifts in law and legal theory away from that of the previous period of legal history. An analysis of the criminal law and legislation of the time serves to confirm this.

I. Criminal Law of the Enlightenment

1. Forerunners of Modern Criminal Law

With **Benedict Carpzov** (1595–1666; major work: *Practica Nova Imperialis Saxonica Rerum Criminalium*, 1635),[1] German criminal law began to shake off the overriding influence of Italian, French and Spanish models, themselves significant agents in the modernisation of legislation, a development facilitated by the rising importance of the universities and the increasingly scholarly nature of judicial decision-making. *Carpzov* himself was of course still heavily influenced by the theocratic concept of law, which saw maintaining the dignity and authority of the divinely ordained state as the main purpose of punishment; connected to this theocratic understanding of law is the idea of the "necessity" of punishment as a retribution understood to be the "mirror of divine justice in this world" (Robert von Hippel), as the criminal's act of reconciliation with God and the people's act of atonement. Punishment as a "cautionary example" does appear in Carpzov, but only constitutes a side aspect of his thought.

Alongside the discipline of general criminal law founded by Carpzov which dominated both universities and courts well into the eighteenth century, modern

[1] Excerpt in Vormbaum, StrD, p. 26 (references in appendix).

T. Vormbaum and M. Bohlander, *A Modern History of German Criminal Law*,

DOI 10.1007/978-3-642-37273-5_2, © Springer-Verlag Berlin Heidelberg 2014

natural law developed. Beginning with Hugo Grotius (1583–1645),[2] it substituted the man of reason for the medieval man of faith.[3] Law's true foundations were no longer sought in God, but instead—in spite of verbal concessions—in the nature of man himself: law was gradually breaking away from the influence of theology.

In a time still informed by close ties between state and religion, this approach also placed proponents of natural law at personal risk. The church, where orthodox views prevailed, launched attacks on *Grotius*, *Pufendorf*, and *Thomasius*; Grotius's work *De iure belli ac pacis* was listed on the Catholic Church's *Index librorum prohibitorum* into the twentieth century; other books on natural law, such as Montesquieu's *Esprit des Lois*, suffered the same fate when first published.

Should one wish to determine a starting point for the *secularisation*, *rationalisation* and *individualisation* of law and criminal law, Hugo Grotius's formula *etiamsi daremus* constitutes an apt beginning. In his major work (*De iure belli ac pacis*, 1525) he explains that his theories must be valid *etiamsi daremus – quod sine summo scelere dari nequit – non esse Deum, aut non curari ab eo negotia humana* ("though we should even grant, what without the greatest Wickedness cannot be granted, that there is no God, or that he takes no Care of human Affairs"). By using this caveat, Grotius opened up scope for the foundation of a purely secular legal system, which (at least in theory) did not clash with faith in God. (His task was of course made easier by theological developments such as late scholastic natural law and Luther's "two kingdoms" theory.) The secularisation of law and criminal law is also evident in individual points of Grotius's work, which are sometimes oblique or subtly nuanced, and sometimes quite open in their secularism.

Samuel Pufendorf (1632–1694), **Christian Thomasius** (1655–1728) and **Christian Wolff** (1679–1754) updated Grotius's ideas, systematising and developing them into the *law of reason*.[4]

2. *Theory of Punishment in Natural Law and Enlightenment Thought*

While a religiously influenced doctrine of retribution and atonement had still been foremost in Carpzov's thought, the secularisation of legal theory increasingly led natural law philosophers to the conclusion that the main purpose of criminal law was to deter from future crime, and that this was why punishment should be meted

[2] On Grotius in general, see *Senn/Gschwend*, p. 246 ff.; excerpt from his work "De iure belli ac pacis" in *Vormbaum*, StrD, p. 13 (references in appendix).

[3] *Eb. Schmidt*, Introduction, § 144. Of course, these two characterisations only touch on the central interpretative strategies of the approaches they represent.

[4] Excerpts from their works "De jure naturae et gentium" (1672), "Institutiones Jurisprudentiae Divinae" (1688) and "Grundsätze des Natur- und Völckerrechts" (1754) in *Vormbaum*, StrD, p. 50 ff., p. 67 ff., p. 104 ff. (references in appendix); see also *Rüping/Jerouschek*, p. 78 ff.; for detailed information on Pufendorf, see *Senn/Gschwend*, p. 257 ff., on Thomasius ibid. p. 266 ff.

out. They made use of both general and specific grounds of deterrence, primarily referring to the former in its guise as *deterrence by punishment*. For example, Cesare Beccaria writes:

> the purpose of punishment is not that of tormenting or afflicting any sentient being, nor of undoing a crime already committed. [. . .] The purpose [. . .] is nothing other than to prevent the offender from doing fresh harm to his fellows and to deter others from doing likewise. Therefore, punishments and the means adopted for inflicting them should, consistent with proportionality, be so selected as to make the most efficacious and lasting impression on the minds of men with the least torment to the body of the condemned.[5]

Towards the end of the eighteenth century, German enlightened absolutism in particular produced theorists of criminal law whose main focus lay on individual/special prevention. These were, first and foremost, **Ernst Ferdinand Klein** (1743–1810), **Gallus Aloys Kleinschrod** (1762–1824) und **Christoph Carl Stübel** (1764–1828),[6] and later also included **Karl Grolman** (1775–1829),[7] a friend and opponent of Feuerbach—although he adopted this stance for different reasons. However, their approach was overshadowed by the influence of Kant's retributive theory of punishment and Feuerbach's theory of general deterrence. *Stübel* failed to complete his textbook oriented on special prevention; in 1800 (despite one last attempt at resistance), *Grolman* admitted defeat in the controversy in the title of an essay on the theory of criminal law.[8]

3. *The Demands of Criminal Law Enlightenment*

Thomasius's later years already fall into the Enlightenment period, which reached its high point in the eighteenth century. Major impulses also came from France—**Charles-Louis de Montesquieu**[9] (1689–1755), **Voltaire** (1694–1778), **Jean**

---

[5] *Cesare Beccaria*, Beccaria: 'On Crimes and Punishments' and Other Writings. Ed. Richard Bellamy, transl. Richard Davies. Cambridge 1995, p. 31. Excerpt included in: Vormbaum, StrD, p. 119 ff. (references in appendix).

[6] Excerpts of all these in *Vormbaum*, StrD, p. 267, 223, 205 (references in appendix); for excerpts of Ernst Ferdinand Klein, see also: *Vormbaum*, MdtStrD, p. 69 ff. (references in appendix).

[7] On Grolman cf. *Mario A. Cattaneo*, Karl Grolmans strafrechtlicher Humanismus. Baden-Baden 1998; see also *Ibid.* Die Bedeutung der Strafgesetzgebung in der deutschen Aufklärungsphilosophie, in: Ibid., Aufklärung und Strafrecht, p. 225 ff., particularly p. 285 ff.

[8] *Karl Grolman*, Sollte es denn wirklich kein Zwangsrecht zur Prävention geben? In: Magazin für die Philosophie und Geschichte des Rechts und der Gesetzgebung 1 (1800), p. 241 ff. Excerpt in *Vormbaum*, MdtStrD, p. 61 ff. [In the language usage of that time, "prevention" meant "special or individual prevention", not deterrence]; on this cf. *Radbruch*, Feuerbach, p. 44 ff.

[9] On his theory of criminal law, cf. *Eb. Schmidt*, Montesqieus "Esprit des lois" und die Problematik der Gegenwart von Recht und Justiz, in: Festschrift Kiesselbach. Hamburg 1947, p. 177 ff.; Heike Jung, Montesquieu und die Kriminalpolitik, in: JuS 1999, 216 ff.; Mario A. Cattaneo, Montesquieus Strafrechtsliberalismus. Berlin 2002.

Jacques Rousseau (1712–1778)[10]—and from Italy—**Gaetano Filangieri**[11] (1753–1788), **Mario Pagano** (1748–1799)[12] and **Cesare Beccaria** (1738–1794)[13]; **Joseph von Sonnenfels** (1732–1817)[14] should also be mentioned as an Austrian exponent (Figs. 1, 2, 3, and 4). In the meantime, the theory of natural law had developed the principles noted above further, and thus it entered a phase where it was able to move from diagnosing and systematising a rational right to therapy to demanding a change in the existing state of legal affairs.[15] In addition to the demand for *secularisation*, *rationalisation* and *individualisation* of all spheres, and criminal law in particular, the demand for *humanisation* arose.

In this respect, demands were directed at ending *witch trials* (the last witch was burned in Germany in Regensburg as late as 1775[16]), abolishing *torture* (the first, initially only partial abolition occurred in Prussia when Frederick II. succeeded to the throne in 1740), *mitigation of punishment* (*Beccaria*: "dolcezza delle pene"; *Montesquieu*: proportion between punishment and crime), above all abolishing cruel forms of *corporal* and *capital punishment* (so-called "*geschärfte Todesstrafen*"), and in some individual cases (e.g. *Beccaria*, if with exceptions) the abolition of capital punishment. *Thomasius* voiced doubts in relation to the justification of threats of punishment for bigamy (*De crimine bigamiae*, 1685) and heresy (*An haeresis sit crimen,* 1697).

Doubts were also cast upon the justification of punishment for (attempted) *suicide*.

---

[10] Excerpts of all these in *Vormbaum*, StrD, p. 90, 136, 114 (references in appendix).

[11] Excerpt of his main work *Scienza della legislazione* in *Vormbaum*, StrD, p.179 ff. (references in appendix); for more general information cf. *Paolo Becchi/Kurt Seelmann*, G. F. und die europäische Aufklärung. Frankfurt am Main 2000; particularly p. 45 ff.: Filangieri und die Proportionalität von Straftat und Strafe.

[12] *Sergio Moccia*, Die italienische Reformbewegung des 18. Jahrhunderts und das Problem des Strafrechts im Denken von Gaetano Filangieri und Mario Pagano, in: GA 1979, p. 201 ff.

[13] On all of these *Otto Fischl*, Der Einfluß der Aufklärungsphilosophie auf die Entwicklung des Strafrechts in Doktrin, Politik und Gesetzgebung. Breslau 1913 (2nd reprint Aalen 1981); on **Beccaria** see *Wolfgang Naucke*, Die Modernisierung des Strafrechts durch *Beccaria*, in: Id., Zerbrechlichkeit, p. 13 ff.; *Id.*, Introduction: Beccaria. Strafrechtskritiker und Strafrechtsverstärker, in: Beccaria, Verbrechen, p. IX ff.; *W. Küper*, Cesare Beccaria und die kriminalpolitische Aufklärung des 18. Jahrhunderts, in: JuS 1968, 547 ff.; *Herbert Deimling* (Ed.), C. B. Die Anfänge moderner Strafrechtspflege in Europa. Heidelberg 1989.

[14] On Sonnenfels: *Mario A. Cattaneo*, Beccaria und Sonnenfels: Die Abschaffung der Folter im theresianischen Zeitalter, in: Id., Aufklärung und Strafrecht, p. 49 ff.; on Sonnenfels's role in the abolition of torture in Habsburg territories see also *E. Dezza*, Der Feind der Wahrheit. Das Verteidigungsverbot und der Richter als "Faktotum" in der habsburgischen Strafrechtskodifikation (1768–1873), in JJZG 9 (2007/2008), Footnote 11; *Ezequiel Malarino*, Kommentar I, in: Th. Vormbaum (Ed.), Pest, Folter und Schandsäule. Der Mailänder Schandsäulen-Prozeß in Rechtskritik und Literatur. Berlin 2008, esp. footnote 84.

[15] *Eb. Schmidt*, Introduction, § 203; many other exponents of the criminal law of the Enlightenment are discussed in *Fischl*, p. 25 ff.

[16] On this cf. Wolf Wimmer, Anna Maria Schwägelin († 1775). Die letzte Hexenexekution in Deutschland, in: JZ 1975, 631 ff.

Fig. 1 Christian Thomasius (1655–1728)

Fig. 2 Charles-Louis de Montesquieu (1689–1755)

The crime of infanticide, which until the early modern period had been punished as an unmitigated form of homicide, had become a central topic of discussion during the Enlightenment (e.g. the "Gretchen tragedy" in *Goethe's* "Faust"). As a

Fig. 3 Cesare Beccaria (1738–1794)

Fig. 4 Ernst Ferdinand Klein (1743–1810)

result of this debate, it was gradually downgraded to a less serious form of homicide with an accordingly mitigated punishment (which of course initially meant only that no particularly cruel forms of capital punishment were used).[17]

[17] *Wächtershäuser*, Kindesmord; *Andrea Czelk*, Frauenbewegung.

The philosophy of law and criminal law of the Enlightenment gained influence due to its *understanding of laws*.[18] Natural law and early Enlightenment thought, reacting to the threat of brutal corporal punishment and severe forms of capital punishment (e.g. in Charles V.'s "Peinliche Gerichtsordnung" or *Carolina* of 1532), demanded that the judge hold a free and sovereign position in the interest of humanising criminal law (*Thomasius*, *Hommel*, *Gmelin* and others). However, in the course of the eighteenth century a countermovement developed, supported by an emphatic understanding of laws that placed positive law close to natural law and was influenced by *Montesquieu's* theory of the separation of powers. Accordingly, legislators acting according to rational principles were viewed as the guarantors of civil liberties, while judges with their civil-servant-like status came to be seen as a threat in need of containment through strict observation of the binding nature of law.[19] Montesquieu had already called judicial power "en quelque façon nulle", basically nonexistent or without any substance of its own. *Beccaria* expresses this as follows:

> Nor can the authority to interpret the law devolve upon the criminal judges, for the same reason that they are not legislators. [...] The judge should construct a perfect syllogism about every criminal case: the major premise should be the general law; the minor, the conformity or otherwise of the action with the law; and the conclusion, freedom or punishment. Whenever the judge is forced, or takes it upon himself, to construct even as few as two syllogisms, then the door is opened to uncertainty (*Beccaria*, On Crimes, Chap. IV).

Enlightenment thinkers could not fail to notice that this idealisation of the legislator meant that criminal law was placed at the mercy of those in political power. There appear to have been several reasons why they clung to their demand nonetheless. On the one hand, they trusted that reason would assert itself and, in the long run, control the legislator; this hope would have been strengthened by the emergence of enlightened absolutist princes (Frederick II. of Prussia; Emperor Joseph II.; Archduke Leopold, Prince of Tuscany). Given that the humanitarian line of argument regularly pointed out the status quo's lack of practicability and the greater practicability of the reforms demanded, this hope was not unfounded. On the other hand, the threat posed by judges' arbitrariness, which directly affected the individual accused, seemed greater than that posed by a legislator restricted to passing general, abstract laws. Even in the case of a harsh criminal law, the latter at least guaranteed equal treatment—and in this regard, the call for judges to be bound more strictly to the law also expresses the aspiring bourgeoisie's desire for legal certainty.

---

[18] On the following, see *Küper*, Richteridee, p. 39 ff.; *Ogorek*, Richterkönig, p. 37 ff.; *Massimo Nobili*, Die freie richterliche Überzeugungsbildung. Baden-Baden 2001; *Ettore Dezza*, Strafprozeß.

[19] For detailed information on this subject, see *Schreiber*, Gesetz und Richter, p. 46 ff.; an examination of the partially different developments resulting from the four principles deduced from this binding nature of law (prohibition of customary law, prohibition of retrospective legislation, prohibition of analogy, prohibition against lack of specificity) in *Krey*, Keine Strafe ohne Gesetz, p. 1 f.

In demanding the abolition of *torture* in criminal proceedings, an enlightened theory of criminal law challenged a central aspect of inquisitorial trials under the *ius commune*, whose procedural model assigned the power both to prosecute and make decisions to the court. A formal defence only took place at a very late stage in the proceedings. In order to compensate for this strong position of the court, its decisions were tied to rules of evidence. According to the *ius commune* based on Art. 22 of the *Lex Carolina* of Emperor Charles V., a sentence could only be passed if the crime was proven by either two eye-witnesses or the confession of the accused.[20] As on the one hand reliable eye-witnesses are rather the exception, particularly in the case of serious crimes, and on the other there was usually no great willingness to confess (particularly seeing the punishments threatened at the time), torture was used to "encourage" confession in cases where solid evidence, particularly the incriminating testimony of *one* eye-witness, existed.[21] Removing torture from this system would impede justice as long as the judge was not allowed to base his judgement on his own (well-founded) conviction, regardless of rules of evidence.

Enlightenment philosophers mainly based their arguments on the inexpediency of torture, which gave resilient guilty parties a chance of acquittal, but placed weaker innocent parties at risk of making a false confession.[22]

4. Enlightenment and Humanisation

It is doubtful whether the theory of criminal law—or rather: the criminal policies—of Enlightenment philosophy can really be credited with a tendency towards "humanisation", and with good reason.[23] *Eb. Schmidt* (§ 208) has pointed out that

---

[20] *Mumme*, E.F. Klein, p. 28; *Thäle*, Verdachtsstrafe, p. 24 ff.; *Ignor*, Geschichte, p. 62 ff. with detailed references in footnote 112; for detailed information on the abolition of torture, see *Mathias Schmöckel*, Humanität und Staatsräson. Die Abschaffung der Folter in Europa und die Entwicklung des gemeinen Strafprozess- und Beweisrechts seit dem hohen Mittelalter. Cologne 2000; *Evans*, Rituale, p. 147 ff.

[21] In cases where factual evidence would seem to any reasonable observer to prove the guilt of the accused, torture might appear at least understandable as means to an end, if not humane. But in practice, torture was often used beyond these obvious cases, particularly in witch trials; *Jerouschek*, Die Carolina—Antwort auf ein "Feindstrafrecht"? In: Hilgendorf/Weitzel, p. 79 ff., 90; *Ignor*, Geschichte, p. 101 ff. Of course, the question remains whether this insistence in the practice of the *ius commune* on obtaining a confession was (also) due to Christian ideas of confession and repentance, beyond procedural issues; for more detail on this, see *Ignor*, Geschichte, pp. 62–73.

[22] *Pietro Verri*, Betrachtungen über die Folter (1777), in: Thomas Vormbaum (Ed.), Folter und Schandsäule (as in footnote 11). p. 49 ff.; *Beccaria*, Crimes op. cit. (footnote 4), p. 33; cf. also the reference in *Mumme*, Klein, p. 29.

[23] In greater detail: *Naucke*, Einführung; *Id.*, Modernisierung op. cit.; *Vormbaum*, Judeneid, p. 266 ff.

Voltaire condemns the death penalty as "anti-economic", as it prevents the state from exploiting the labour of the offender *(un homme pendu n'est bon à rien)*. In their award-winning *Abhandlung von der Criminalgesetzgebung* (1783), *v. Globig* and *Huster* object to mutilation as corporal punishment on the grounds that "the state will be forced to maintain the infirm and mutilated culprit",[24] and *Pietro Verri* introduces his discussion of the question whether torture is a means of ascertaining the truth (the answer he arrives at is no) with the words[25]:

> If the search for the truth using torture is in itself an atrocity [...], nonetheless an enlightened citizen will suppress and smother this isolated surge of emotion, and will set the pain caused to a person suspected of a crime against the good that comes of discovering the truth about crimes; he will calmly weigh the pain of one against the peace of thousands.

Beccaria's line of argument against capital punishment is exemplary in this regard. He starts with two contractarian (that is, derived from social contract theory) arguments: the social contract decrees that each party entering the contract give up part of his freedom—but only as much as absolutely necessary, the smallest possible part—for the shared greater good. However, this smallest possible sacrifice cannot include the sacrifice of the greatest of all possessions, life.[26] At first, this line of argument is astonishing; indeed, there is something rabulistic about it, for theoretically in *borderline cases* the smallest possible part can also be the whole, unless it could be proved empirically that such cases do not exist. Thus Beccaria already points towards utilitarian arguments.

The second contractarian argument is as follows: as man is not in command of his own life, he cannot have had it at his disposal in the social contract either (p. 48 f.). This argument is only intrinsically logical, for Beccaria himself elsewhere declares himself to be against sanctioning suicide.

Beccaria's transition from these two contractarian arguments to the following ones (again, there are two) is as follows:

> Thus, the death penalty is not a matter of *right*, as I have just shown, but is an act of war on the part of society against the citizen that comes about when it is deemed necessary or useful to destroy his existence. But if I can go on to prove that such a death is neither necessary nor useful, I shall have won the cause of humanity (p. 66).

The contractarian argument against capital punishment—which (in the English edition used here) only takes up about half a page—is followed by seven pages concerned with the *inexpediency* of the death penalty. Beccaria declares himself willing to accept two reasons for putting a citizen to death, if they are proven. The first:

> when it is evident that even if deprived of his freedom, he retains such connections and such power as to endanger the security of the nation, when, that is, his existence may threaten a dangerous revolution in the established form of government (p. 66).

---

[24] *Rüping/Jerouschek*, 4th ed., p. 61; see also 5th ed., p. 82.

[25] *Pietro Verri*, Betrachtungen über die Folter (as in footnote 22), p. 49.

[26] *Beccaria*, p. 48. The following remarks summarise *Vormbaum*, Beccaria.

In other words: in times of political turmoil, a dangerous citizen may indeed be killed. But this deduction also only takes up half a page. All of the rest is concerned with the second argument (the fourth altogether): "if [. . .] his death is the true and only brake to prevent others from committing crimes" (p. 67)—or, using legal phrasing: if necessary on grounds of general deterrence. As there are no crime statistics yet in his day, Beccaria is unable to bring numerical proof that these grounds do not exist; instead, he provides another reason: he invokes the nature—meaning: the empirical nature—of man (p. 67). The human mind is impressed not so much by the intensity of a punishment as by its extent. Seen from this point of view, the death penalty is inexpedient, for its enactment is a "terrible, but fleeting" spectacle (p. 67). Thus it is not ideally suited to deter men from crime, and is *therefore* unjust. More effective and thus more just is lifelong, publicly enforced servitude (as a "beast of burden"), as this confronts onlookers with the consequences of crime over and over again.

Modern criminology and sociology confirm some, but not all, of the empirical arguments used by Beccaria. The sentence "[i]f a punishment is to be just, it *may* be pitched *only* at that level of intensity which suffices to deter men from crime" is certainly ambiguous. Reformulating the sentence to "if a punishment is to be just, it *must* be pitched at that level of intensity which suffices to deter men from crime" is not simply a matter of wordplay, but reveals a very real danger: whoever wants to deter also wants to make doubly sure, and this limitation can quickly turn to legitimation.[27]

It remains unclear what is to happen in individual cases if these empirical assumptions do not apply. Beccaria treats both of the—fairly weak—contractarian arguments rather superficially. There is no clear conclusion indicating that the extended empirical discussion really only consists of supporting arguments. All in all, Beccaria's writing reveals "again and again [. . .] that the effectiveness of punishment is the argument that solves everything".[28]

From the point of view of *legal history* and *legal theory*, criticism of Enlightenment philosophy's utilitarian line of argument thus seems justified. However, a *historical* consideration needs to interpret and understand people's actions within the context of their time. Beccaria and his fellow Enlightenment theorists of criminal law along with their policy arguments were in a "comfortable" position due to the dire state of criminal law at the time. In France, whoever failed to remove their hat in front of the monstrance during a Corpus Christi procession could receive the death penalty,[29] and in most states torture was used, presenting a veritable arsenal of a whole range of critical arguments—focusing on both justice and utility. But this is where history's cunning—or rather, deceitfulness—lies hidden: because

[27] Translator's footnote: the standard translation in the List of Translated Texts has been adapted here slightly, as it does not contain the crucial distinction between "may" and "must".

[28] *Naucke*, Beccaria, p. 25.

[29] For a detailed discussion of the trial and execution of the Chevalier de La Barre in Abbeville (1766), made famous throughout Europe by Voltaire's "An Account of the Death of the Chevalier de la Barre", see *Max Gallo*, Im Namen des Königs! Justizskandal am Vorabend der Französischen Revolution. Frankfurt am Main, Berlin 1989.

politicians, i.e. those in power, are most easily convinced by utilitarian arguments, using these seemed the most likely way to make oneself heard. And those fighting subjectively for the humanisation of criminal law—which Beccaria and the other Enlightenment thinkers admittedly were doing—are also prepared to argue against the death penalty for infanticide on grounds of its inexpediency, as it would deprive the state of those children that the woman thus punished would have borne.[30]

How delicate this argument was (and is) can be seen in the fact that Enlightenment thinkers included theorists of criminal law who *advocated* capital punishment on utilitarian grounds.[31]

II. Influence of the Enlightenment on Penal Legislation

The *Lex Carolina* of 1532, a code of procedure also containing some substantive law aspects, was a remarkable body of laws at its time of composition,[32] but was unable to withstand the criticism directed at it by the theory of natural law and the demands of Enlightenment philosophy. Court practice (which had, at first, frequently chosen to ignore the protective regulations the *Carolina* did in fact contain) increasingly revised it, becoming more and more lenient.[33]

After laws such as the Bavarian *Codex Juris Bavarici Criminalis* of 1751[34] and the Austrian *Constitutio Criminalis Theresiana* of 1768 had succeeded in compiling the legal status quo but had made only insignificant changes in terms of content, the demands of Enlightenment philosophy found expression in the criminal code of

---

[30] Thus *Voltaire* in his Commentaire sur le livre des délits et des peines (1766), in Vormbaum, StrD, p. 136 f.

[31] *Sellert/Rüping* I, p. 372: capital punishment is more economical than building penitentiaries (*Michaelis*); it is a more effective deterrent (*Frederick II. of Prussia*, similarly *Ernst Ferdinand Klein:* "assassins are among those people that the state can only protect itself against by sentencing them to death", see *Mumme*, Klein, p. 18 f.).

[32] On the Carolina, see most recently *G. Jerouschek*, Carolina (as in footnote 17); earlier: *Gustav Radbruch*, Zur Einführung in die Carolina, in: Die peinliche Halsgerichtsordnung Karls V. von 1532 (Carolina) (Reclam 2990/a). Stuttgart 1967. p. 3 ff.; *Peter Landau/Friedrich-Christian Schroeder* (Eds.), Strafrecht, Strafprozess und Rezeption. Grundlagen, Entwicklung und Wirkung der Constitutio Criminalis Carolina. Frankfurt am Main. 1984; *Friedrich-Christian Schroeder* (Ed.), Wege der Forschung. Die Carolina. Darmstadt 1986; on territorial criminal codes of the eighteenth century see *Ignor*, Geschichte, p. 129 ff.

[33] Supported, in part, by theory; for more detailed information, see *Küper*, Richteridee, p. 39 ff. (on Carl Ferdinand **Hommel**, Christian **Thomasius**, Christian Gottfried **Gmelin**).

[34] On its creator W.X.A. Frhr. v. **Kreittmayr** see *Richard Bauer/Hans Schlosser* (Eds.). W.X.A. v. K. Ein Leben für Recht, Staat und Politik. Festschrift z. 200. Todestag. Munich 1991; part. *K. Schlosser*, Der Gesetzgeber K. und die Aufklärung in Kurbayern (p. 3 ff.); *R. Heydenreuter*, K. und die Strafrechtsreform unter Kurfürst Max III. Joseph (p. 37 ff.). In 1768, K. wrote a commentary on the civil, procedural and criminal codes he had shaped: *W.X.A. Kreittmayr*, Compendium Codicis Bavarici. Reprint of the 1768 edition. Ed. and with an introduction by Richard Bauer and Hans Schlosser. Munich 1990 (on the Codex Criminalis pp. 519–572).

Archduke Leopold of *Tuscany* of 1786 (the so-called *Leopoldina*)[35] and in the General Code on Crimes and their Punishments of Emperor Joseph II. of 1787 (the so-called *Josephina*) in *Austria*.[36] The Prussian *Allgemeines Landrecht (ALR)*, the General Code of 1794, summarised the criminal law in the extensive 20th title of its Part II (containing over 1,500 sections). All of these shared an emphasis on the role of the *law* and endeavoured to restrict judges' freedom in making decisions.

> Part the First § 13 of the Emperor's new code of criminal laws: 'The criminal judge is bound down to the sense and letter of the law, according as the law established, concerning such or such offence, the magnitude and kind of punishment are exactly and expressly set forth. He is not at liberty, under pain of being rigorously responsible, to lessen or increase the punishments prescribed by law [. . .]'.

The sheer scope of the ALR's part concerned with criminal law points to an extensive number of case histories that limited judges' discretionary powers to a large extent.[37]

The **death penalty** was abolished in the Tuscan *Leopoldina*, as it was in the Austrian *Josephina*, with the exception in the latter of courts-martial (Part the First § 20). By contrast, the Prussian Civil Code even contained "geschärfte Todesstrafen" (punishment of treason in the first degree according to § 102 ALR II 20: "[He] is to be dragged to the place of execution, killed by rolling the wheel over him from the bottom upwards, and the body bound to the wheel"). Capital punishment was reintroduced in Tuscany in 1790, and in Austria in 1803 by the *Gesetz über Verbrechen und schwere Polizeiübertretungen (Act on Felonies and other Serious Offences)*.

Even where capital punishment was abolished, the punishments that remained were still very harsh; the *Josephina* still contains punishments such as chaining (Part the First § 25),

> The criminal suffers severe imprisonment, and is so closely chained, that he has no more liberty than serves for the indispensable motion of his body. The criminal condemned to the chain, suffers corporal punishment every year, for an example to the public,

most rigorous imprisonment (§ 27),

---

[35] The text of the *Leopoldina* is now available in a German translation for the first time since it was written: *Hans Schlosser*, Die "Leopoldina". Toskanisches Strafgesetzbuch vom 30. November 1786. Original text, German translation and commentary. Berlin 2010. On the importance of the *Leopoldina* see *Hinrich Rüping*, Das Leopoldinische Strafgesetzbuch und die strafrechtliche Aufklärung in Deutschland, in: L. Berlinguer/F. Colao (Eds.), La "Leopoldina" nel diritto e nella giustizia in Toscana. Milan 1989, vol. 5, p. 140 ff.; see also the introduction to *Schlosser*, op. cit., which also includes further references.

[36] On how Habsburg criminal legislation of the pre- and post-Napoleonic period was transposed to Italian territories, see the contributions in: *Ettore Dezza/Loredana Garlati*, Beiträge zur habsburgischen Strafgesetzgebung in Italien. Münster, Berlin 2010.

[37] *Küper*, Richteridee, p. 64 ff.; see also *W. Naucke*, Hauptdaten der preußischen Strafrechtsgeschichte 1786–1806, in: Id., Zerbrechlichkeit, p. 49 ff.—A further reason for the number of laws included in this title is the inclusion of many prophylactic police regulations.

> In cases of the most rigorous imprisonment, the criminal is confined day and night to the spot assigned him, with a ring of iron fastened about his middle; and he may be loaded with additional irons, if the kind of work imposed on him permit, or the danger of his escape render it necessary,

severe imprisonment (§ 28), milder imprisonment (§ 30), hard labour on public works (§ 31), "corporal punishment, with whip, rod, or stick" (§ 32) and exposure in the pillory (§ 33). These could all be rendered more severe by public notification of the criminal, the confiscation of their property and the loss of nobility (§ 34).

As far as **criminal procedure** is concerned, *torture* was abolished in the *Leopoldina* (which also contained regulations on procedural law), the Austrian *Gesetzbuch über Verbrechen und schwere Polizeiübertretungen* of 1803 (the substantive part of which replaced the *Josephina*) and the *Preußische Criminalordnung* of 1805. This raised the question of how to proceed in cases where substantial evidence pointed against the accused, but did not meet evidence requirements according to general criminal law.

In these cases, the *Leopoldina* permitted punishment on suspicion,[38] while Austrian law of 1803 provided for the option of the "Lossprechung von der Instanz" (*absolutio ab instantia*) instead of entering an acquittal (and thus not triggering *res judicata*).[39] In the Prussian Criminal Code of 1805 the gap was filled by punishments for lying ("strokes with the whip or the rod" for the "stubborn and devious criminal, who through bold lies and fabrication or through obdurate denial or complete silence" attempts to "elude just punishment").[40] Related structural questions will be addressed in the following chapter.

It is possible to see the **harsh or even brutal** aspects of these codifications of natural or Enlightenment law as sorts of "skid marks", as a defeat of Enlightenment thought or "failed Enlightenment", and for a long time they were interpreted as such. However, taking into consideration the humanisation discussed above, there is more that speaks for seeing them as *one* side of the criminal law of the Enlightenment[41]:

---

[38] Art. CX; on this, see *Rüping*, Leopoldina, op. cit.

[39] On this, see *Dezza*, Versöhnung, op. cit.

[40] On this, see *Vormbaum*, Strafrecht und Strafprozeß, op. cit. incl. reference. Structurally, punishment on suspicion and punishment of lying evolved out of the general *poena extraordinaria*, of which they can be seen as representing special cases; on both this and views on punishment on suspicion in legal theory see *Thäle*, Verdachtsstrafe; *Mumme*, E.F. Klein, p. 32 ff.; *Elemér Balogh*, Die Verdachtsstrafe in Deutschland im 19. Jahrhundert. Münster, Berlin 2009. There was a close connection between the *poena extraordinaria* and the *punishment by hard labour* ("opus publicum") that (re-)emerged in the seventeenth century and became dominant in the eighteenth and early nineteenth century; for detailed information on this subject, see: *Hans Schlosser*, Motive des Wandels in den Erscheinungsformen und Strafzwecken bei der Arbeitsstrafe, in: Schulze/Vormbaum et al. (Eds.), Strafzweck und Strafform, p. 145 ff.

[41] This insight should not lead to a rejection of Enlightenment ideals; rather, any criticism of the faults of Enlightenment philosophy must itself be informed by Enlightenment thought. I have attempted to demonstrate this generically in *Vormbaum*, Judeneid, p. 266 ff.; *Vormbaum*, Kant e la critica illuministica del illuminismo, in: Mario A. Cattaneo (Ed.), Kant e la filosofia del diritto. Naples 2005, p. 37 ff.

> The Enlightenment's liberation of criminal law from entrenched irrationality linked criminal law to the demands of public security. Every move in domestic politics was translated into criminal law.[42]

The retention of publicly executed harsh punishments can be explained as a calculated utilitarian strategy of prevention; the torture substitutes mentioned above (punishment on suspicion, *absolutio ab instantia*, punishment of lying) can be explained by the fact that the abolition of torture had removed a central element of the inquisitorial system, which as long as no new system was in place appeared to require replacing; the fear of unjustified acquittals was prevalent.

The influence of Enlightenment thought was *clearly mitigating* particularly where criminal offences were identified as contrary to rational and secular thought (witchcraft, blasphemy, violation of morals, bigamy). These offences were either abolished or received milder punishments, and/or (in the Austrian law of 1803) were moved from criminal law to police law.

III. Criminal Law at the End of the Eighteenth Century

Two thinkers shaped the discipline of criminal law in Germany at the turn of the century: **Immanuel Kant** and **Paul Johann Anselm (von) Feuerbach** (Figs. 5, 6, 7, and 8). It is not intended (or even possible) to give an in-depth philosophical analysis of their theories here, for we are concerned only with their *historical* importance.[43] Sketching the key aspects of their theories of criminal law must suffice.

1. Immanuel Kant (1724–1804)

The following assumptions are central to Kant's theory of criminal law.[44]

Distinction between legality and morality: Kant differentiates between "juridical" and ethical legislation. The difference between the two consists not in that they apply to different fields of action or norms, but rather that the driving force

---

[42] *Naucke*, Hauptdaten op. cit., p 52; on *Michel Foucault's* similar insights, see in the following § 3 IV.

[43] Excerpts from the texts of both of these thinkers can be found in *Vormbaum*, MdtStrD, p. 36 ff. and 82 ff. (references in appendix).

[44] Among the vast literature on Kant: *Wolfgang Naucke*, Kant und die psychologische Zwangstheorie Feuerbachs. Hamburg 1962; *Daniela Tafani*, Kant und das Strafrecht, in: JJZG 6 (2004/2005), 261 ff.; reprinted in: JoJZG 1 (2007), 16 ff.; *Byrd/Hruschka* JZ 2007, 957 ff.; *Georg Steinberg*, Sittliche Strafwürdigkeit als Rechtfertigung staatlichen Strafens nach Kant, in: Schulze/Vormbaum et al., Strafzweck und Strafform, p. 175 ff.

Fig. 5 Immanuel Kant (1724–1804)

Fig. 6 Paul Johann Anselm Ritter von Feuerbach (1775–1833)

(= motive) behind ethical legislation is duty, while juridical legislation can have any kind of driving force. An action that conforms to law (regardless of its motive) is **legal**, an action that conforms to law and that beyond this is motivated by duty is **moral**.

Fig. 7 Karl Ludwig Wilhelm von Grolman (1775–1829)

Fig. 8 Wilhelm von Humboldt (1767–1835)

Somebody who does not steal because he fears to be discovered and punished acts legally, but not morally. If he refuses to steal out of respect for the property of others, he acts (legally and) morally.

The **principle of law** thus is: "You should act in such a way that your will can coexist with the freedom of everyone, according to general law". This principle is the application of the *general* categorical imperative of morality

– "Act only according to that maxim [i.e. according to that guideline] whereby you can, at the same time, will that it should become a universal law" –

to practical relationships between people. Thus, like this imperative, it is an unconditionally valid (social) law that derives from practical reason (that is, reason related to practical action as opposed to the pure reason of natural law). It follows that the creation of the juridical condition, i.e. the state, is commanded by reason.

While for philosophers of the Enlightenment, the state's purpose lies in assuring the security of its citizens (i.e. in an empirical objective), for Kant the state is the juridical condition and thus the guarantee for justice.[45] It is with some justification, then, that Kant is widely seen as the originator of the concept of the rule of law. *What* the juridical condition actually is can be surmised from his definition of justice:

Justice is "the aggregate of those conditions under which the will of one person can be conjoined with the will of another in accordance with a universal law of freedom".[46]

This definition of justice and this justification of the state have consequences for **criminal law**. If the principle of criminal law—as an application of the principle of law—is a categorical imperative, then it cannot be subject to negotiation for empirical purposes. Therefore, punishment *must be independent of any further purpose* (Naucke). The state should not use the criminal as a means to an end or include him "among objects of the Law of things [*Sachenrecht*]"; neither should the state be able to revise justice, for then it would be contradicting itself. According to Kant, the only way to ensure this is the **law of retribution** (*ius talionis*), from which the punishment for the respective crime arises as of its own accord.

Although Kant does not really follow in the tradition of Montesquieu, this line of thought is evidently influenced by Montesquieu's idea that it constitutes a triumph of freedom if every punishment is derived from the particular nature of the crime. Nothing arbitrary remains. The punishment depends only on the nature of the crime in question.[47]

---

[45] *Naucke*, Kant und Feuerbach, p. 28.

[46] *Immanuel Kant*, Metaphysical Elements of Justice, transl. John Ladd. Indianapolis 1999, p. 30; see also *Mario A. Cattaneo*, Menschenwürde und ewiger Friede. Kants Kritik der Politik. Berlin 2004, p. 32 ff., 37.

[47] *Montesquieu*, De l'esprit des Lois/The Spirit of the Laws. Book 12, Chapter 4, printed in *Vormbaum*, StrD, p. 100 f.; however, M. elsewhere associates *ius talionis* with despotic states (op. cit., Book 6, Chapter 19, p. 99); furthermore, the sentence quoted refers more to the *kind* of punishment than to its *extent*.

At the same time, the result is a rejection of all relative theories. *Naucke* (p. 37 f.) rightly emphasises that even though Kant's theory of criminal law sometimes appears to derive from his dissociation from relative theories and thus seems negative in origin, it actually is derived positively from his philosophy.

Of course, Kant knew as well as any other that both the threat of punishment and punishment itself could have a preventative effect. However, in his theory this can only ever be a side effect, if not an undesirable one. It cannot in itself constitute a legitimation of punishment.[48]

Kant's endorsement of **capital punishment**, which he derives from the law of retribution, is particularly controversial. From a contemporary (European) point of view, this must indeed appear as a major flaw in his theory. However, in his examination of Beccaria's criticism of capital punishment, Kant identifies its argumentative weak points:

> For Kant, [...] Beccaria's position constitutes a 'tort', as he makes the creation of a law which holds the same status as moral law a mere matter of agreement between contracting partners and an evaluation of their respective interests. He calls it 'sophistry' as it conceives of criminal law as deriving from an act of will instead of a rational decision, which leads to the nonsensical outcome that punishment is reduced to an evil the criminal himself desires.[49]

Kant does not utterly refute this reference to the will of the murderer. However, he focuses not on the murderer's empirical judgement, but on the rational judgement the culprit possesses as much as any other. According to Kant, this rational judgement informs the criminal that he is being punished not because he desired to be, but because the punishment is just (*Naucke*, p. 35).

A current interpretation of Kant might take this as its starting point: the law of reason certainly dictates that the heaviest crime should receive the heaviest punishment. But whether this is the death penalty, and whether—as Kant believes—the murderer himself would see this punishment as appropriate seems doubtful. Furthermore, one gains the impression from reading Kant's reflexions that his opposition to arguments against the death penalty[50] carry a particular emotional emphasis. This can be seen above all in his example of the island, where even for example, if the people inhabiting an island decided to separate and disperse themselves around the world [...], the last murderer remaining in prison [would] first [have to] be executed, so that everyone will duly receive what his actions are worth and so that the bloodguilt thereof will not be fixed on the people because they failed to insist on carrying out the punishment; for if they fail to do so, they may be regarded as accomplices in this public violation of legal justice.[51]

---

[48] This has recently been disputed by *Daniela Tafani*, JJZG 6 (2004/2005) 261 ff. and JoJZG 1 (2007), 16 ff., who claims that the so-called absolute theory in Kant only refers to the extent of punishment, but not to the reason behind it; on this discussion see contributions by *Pawlik* (JoJZG 2007, 26), *Rother* (JoJZG 2007, 27 f.), *Cattaneo* (JoJZG 2007, 59 f.); explicitly contradicting Tafani also *Byrd/Hruschka*, JZ 2007, 957 ff.

[49] *Daniela Tafani* (as in footnote 42) JoJZG 1 (2007), 16 ff., 25; see also *Naucke*, p. 34 f.

[50] Translator's note: The English translation of the text here amends an error in the second German edition.

[51] *Kant*, Metaphysical Elements, p. 140; on this, see also *Senn/Gschwend*, p. 277 f.: "Kant's reaction model is convincing because it appears logically compelling. However, in its categorical

From a *historical* point of view, we can grant Kant that general sensitivity towards the legitimacy of capital punishment is a very recent phenomenon. The same goes for thoughts on castrating sexual offenders, which can also be found in Kant; even current law still allows for this—however, crucially, on a voluntary basis. One should take into account that opera audiences in Kant's time took delight in the singing of castrati mutilated in childhood.

2. *Paul Johann Anselm Feuerbach (1775–1833)*

a) Life and Works[52]

Paul Johann Anselm (von) Feuerbach—father of the materialist philosopher Ludwig Feuerbach and grandfather of the painter Anselm von Feuerbach (the philosopher's nephew)—can perhaps be called the most important German theorist of criminal law (if such categorisations are considered useful). Unlike Kant, his life was very eventful; it has been described in Gustav Radbruch's informative and sensitive biography. Born before his parents' marriage, he first took a doctorate at the University of Jena with the Kantian Reinhold, which at that time was a stronghold of Kantian philosophy, but then economic pressure—the birth of his first child was imminent—caused him to take up the study of law so as to be able to earn a living. He took a second doctorate in this subject. After teaching in Jena and Kiel,

---

consequence and its express rejection of any consideration of the social conditions and the criminal's point of view, it quickly reaches its limits. Kant's statements in connection with the argument of 'bloodguilt', as used in seventeenth century theocratic theory of criminal law, are highly problematic. Thus his reasoning becomes irrational". I doubt whether—as *Senn/Gschwend*, p. 278 believe—Kant misunderstood the Old Testament *lex talionis*, which meant a "limitation" and not a categorical insistence on punishment; in the case of the death penalty as the heaviest punishment its effects can only go in one direction; with all other punishments, in both directions; precisely therein lies its purpose within the rule of law. Kant derives the *duty* to punish not from *lex talionis* but from the nature of criminal law as a categorical imperative.

[52] *Eberhard Kipper*, Paul Johann Anselm Feuerbach. Sein Leben als Denker, Gesetzgeber und Richter. Cologne, Berlin, Bonn, Munich 1969; *Gustav Radbruch*, Paul Johann Anselm Feuerbach. Ein Juristenleben. 3rd edition. Göttingen 1956; on individual aspects of Feuerbach's theory of criminal law, see also *Max Grünhut*, P.J.A. Feuerbach und das Problem der strafrechtlichen Zurechnung. Hamburg 1922. Reprint Aalen 1978; important contributions to more recent research and theory of criminal law are included in the conference proceedings edited by *Gröschner/Haney*; *Wolfgang Naucke*, Feuerbachs Lehre von der Funktionstüchtigkeit des gesetzlichen Strafens, in: Hilgendorf/Weitzel, Strafgedanke, p. 101 ff., that sees as the main flaw in Feuerbach's theory of criminal law "the unsuccessful dovetailing of effective utilitarianism, which tends to move beyond the boundaries of criminal law, and Kantian absolute justice"; even more decidedly, *Id.*, Die zweckmäßige und die kritische Strafgesetzlichkeit, dargestellt an den Lehren P.J.A. Feuerbachs (1775–1832), in: Quaderni Fiorentini 36 (2007), 323 ff.; an extensive reconstruction of Feuerbach's theory of criminal law in *Greco*, Lebendiges und Totes; further references to his life and works in *Vormbaum*, MdtStrD, p. 362.

he was offered a chair at the Bavarian university of Landshut, as his criticism of Gallus Aloys Kleinschrod's draft of a criminal code[53] (the focus of which was on special prevention) had caught the Bavarian government's attention and they wished to consult him on their planned legal reforms. After a disagreement with the Landshut faculty, Feuerbach moved to Munich, where he worked in the Ministry of Justice and where was responsible for the abolition of torture.[54] There, too, the Bavarian Criminal Code of 1813 was developed, which was based on his ideas and largely drafted by himself. Despite its flaws, which can be attributed to the period in which it was written, it remains one of the most important bodies of legislation in German history. In Munich, Feuerbach was again involved in many personal disputes, partly due to intrigues against him as a "foreigner" and partly due to his own character. After completing his statutory drafting he had worked on many other issues, including pardons, and now he moved into the justice system, becoming the second president of the Court of Appeal in Bamberg and finally president of the Court of Appeal in Ansbach. During his time in Ansbach he became involved in the famous Caspar Hauser affair and in his work *Kaspar Hauser. Beispiel eines Verbrechens am Seelenleben des Menschen* (1832, last reprinted 1983) first put forward the theory that Hauser was a suppressed child of the princely family of Baden, turning Hauser into a "European celebrity".[55] In 1833, shortly after Caspar Hauser's murder, Feuerbach himself died while visiting his sister in his home city of Frankfurt.

While Feuerbach's work also includes contributions on philosophy, civil law and comparative law as well as the *Aktenmäßige Darstellung merkwürdiger Verbrechen* (*Narratives of Remarkable Criminal Trials*) still in print today, his main focus lies on criminal and criminal procedural law. Three particular works are of importance: his two-volume monograph *Revision der Grundlagen und Grundbegriffe des positiven peinlichen Rechts* (1799/1800), wherein he develops his system of criminal law based on general deterrence; his *Lehrbuch des in Deutschland gültigen peinlichen Rechts* (1801), reprinted in many new editions even after his death (the last and 14th edition in 1847)[56] and remaining the predominant textbook during the first half of the nineteenth century; and the *Bayerisches Strafgesetzbuch von 1813*, valid in Bavaria until 1862, which influenced many criminal codes in other German territories. Feuerbach's splendid style, completely unlike what might be expected of a lawyer or a professor,

[53] *Paul Johann Anselm Feuerbach*, Kritik des Kleinschrodischen Entwurfs zu einem peinlichen Gesetzbuche für die Chur-Pfalz-Bayrischen Staaten. Gießen 1804.

[54] As had already been the case in 1740, King Frederick II. of Prussia instructed the Bavarian King Maximilian Joseph not to make the decree on the abolition of torture public. According to one account, he is said to have stated: "May Feuerbach answer for it if criminals now escape punishment", Feuerbach, p. 75.

[55] *Kipper*, p. 170.

[56] *Paul Johann Anselm Feuerbach*, Revision der Grundsätze und Grundbegriffe des positiven peinlichen Rechts. 2 vols. Erfurt 1799/Chemnitz 1800 (Reprint Aalen 1966); *Id.*, Lehrbuch des gemeinen in Deutschland gültigen peinlichen Rechts (first published 1801).

contributed to the success of his writings. Hans Magnus Enzensberger recently compared the language of Feuerbach with that of the poet lawyer Heinrich von Kleist.

Feuerbach propounded his theory of criminal law repeatedly in other texts besides the "Revision", sometimes emphasising particular points. Of note are: "Anti-Hobbes oder: Über die Grenzen der höchsten Gewalt und das Zwangsrecht der Bürger gegen den Oberherrn". Gießen 1797 (Reprint Darmstadt 1967), and "Über die Strafe als Sicherungsmittel vor künftigen Beleidigungen des Verbrechers". Chemnitz 1800 (Reprint Darmstadt 1970). – Feuerbach's character is described in detail in *Jakob Wassermann's* novel "Caspar Hauser oder die Trägheit des Herzens".

b) Criminal Law

Feuerbach's theory of criminal law takes Kant's legal theory as its starting point; however, unlike Kant, Feuerbach arrives at a theory of general deterrence. Like Kant, he sees the state's main function in its "establishment of the juridical condition".[57] As this is an external condition, the state is prohibited from imposing moral punishments. However, it must take precautions so as to avoid any violation of *law* (§ 9). These precautions are of necessity "compulsory precautions". As *physical* coercion (both antecedent and subsequent) is an insufficient means of reaching the goal desired (§ 11), the possibility of an antecedent "psychological" coercion must be explored.[58]

At this point, Feuerbach departs from Kant, for he ignores the question of "whether [...] there can be an absolute juridical external punishment of the kind based by Kant on the categorical imperative". He has thus tacitly turned state, law and freedom—transcendental terms in Kant—into empirical terms.[59]

This coercion cannot be carried out by *imposing* punishment (neither as a specific nor as a general deterrent), for this would mean using a person as a means to the ends of others—here Feuerbach follows Kant. Feuerbach therefore focuses on the *threat* of punishment; this threat is directed not at a specific person, but at a number of people whose individual identities are not yet known. The *mechanism* that comes into effect here he describes as follows:

All violations have their psychological origin in sensuality, to the extent that the human capacity for desire is fuelled by lust or actions taken to satisfy that lust. This sensual incitement is overridden by the fact that everyone knows his deeds will inevitably be followed by an evil greater than the displeasure resulting from the frustrated urge to act. In order to support the general realisation that such evils and their indignities are necessary, I) a law must define these as the necessary consequence of the action (legal threat). And so that the reality of that legally defined ideal connection is imprinted in the minds of all, II)

---

[57] Lehrbuch § 8; Excerpt in *Vormbaum*, MdtStrD, p. 82 ff.

[58] Correct in linguistic terms would be "mental" coercion. However, Feuerbach speaks of psychological coercion, therefore this term is retained here. Then again, the designation of his theory as "a theory of psychological coercion" is correct.

[59] Cf. *Naucke*, p. 44 ff.

that causal link must appear in reality; therefore, as soon as the violation has occurred, the evil connected with it by law must be applied (enforcement, execution). The effectiveness of executive and legislative powers in agreement for the purpose of deterrence constitutes psychological coercion.

The purpose of the legal *threat* of punishment thus is—in modern terms—to balance the gain in pleasure (in the widest sense) anticipated through carrying out an action with an increase of displeasure (through punishment) and thus exercise *psychological coercion* on those inclined to act so they refrain from doing so. The "enforcement, execution" of the punishment is only intended to prove that the threat of punishment is genuine.[60]

Feuerbach has an easy time *legitimising* this psychological coercion *by threat of punishment*. He explains that in exerting this coercion, the state is only doing what everyone is allowed to, namely to threaten coercion if an infringement of one's rights occurs. The demand not to commit the legally defined crime connected to the threat of punishment requires that those inclined to crime do nothing other than that which they are obliged to anyway, namely observe the positive law.

The *purpose* of *imposing* and *executing* punishment, as already mentioned, lies *not* in the immediate attainment of a criminological goal, but solely in proving the genuine nature of the threat of punishment. However, Feuerbach expressly admits that an antecedent threat does not *legitimise* imposition and execution; rather, he refers here to the culprit's *consent*. Empirically, this is of course unlikely; indeed, the culprit could—as Feuerbach himself recognises—topple this assumption by stating expressly that he does *not* consent to the punishment. But Feuerbach—on second attempt—does not remain focused on empirical consent of this kind; he explains that the right to administer the punishment threatened is based "not on the criminal's actual consent to the punishment, but on the legal necessity on the part of the criminal (legal obligation) to submit to punishment"[61]—a line of argument reminiscent of Kant's analysis of Beccaria.

All in all, despite its many "Kantianisms", Feuerbach's theory is once again closer to Enlightenment criminal law theory. However, he does differ markedly from it in using not the imposition and execution of punishment but the *threat* of punishment as a means of general deterrence. The idea that a human being may not be "instrumentalised" has taken root in his thought to this extent.

More recently, various attempts have been made to contrast Feuerbach's abstract "ivory tower" views with those of Karl Grolman, which seem to do more justice to actual human beings.[62] To me, such a contrast seems rather dubious. *Grolman* takes as his starting point

[60] There is certainly no great difference between this statement and the one that punishment should strengthen the authority of the law; whether punishment is thus identical with the law (thus *Naucke*, Quaderni Fiorentini 2007, 331, 337 (as in footnote 50)) I am not so sure.

[61] *Feuerbach*, Über die Strafe als Sicherungsmittel vor künftigen Beleidigungen des Verbrechers (1800), extract in *Vormbaum*, MdtStrD, p. 82 ff.

[62] *M.A. Cattaneo*, Strafgesetzgebung (as in footnote 7), p. 305 ff.; *Id.*, Grolman (as in footnote 7), passim; *Günther Kräupl*, Die strikte Tatstrafe, der Täter und das Opfer in der Werkbiographie P.J. A. Feuerbachs, in: Gröschner/Haney, p. 78 ff.

the idea that the criminal has shown, through his crime, that he does not accept positive law as his guideline. Therefore he cannot regain freedom before he has given an appropriate guarantee of a change of heart. From today's point of view, this may be interpreted in the sense of a "humanism of criminal law" (*Cattaneo*), drawing the conclusion that no imprisonment may last longer than required for the social rehabilitation of each individual convict. This however fails to take account of both the historical context and the significance of Grolman's theory for legal history and criminal theory: a *historical* account has to consider the context of the time; at this time of—at best!—a "caring" police state, any individual consideration of and influence on the accused or convict contradicted the emerging ideal of liberalism and the interests of the bourgeoisie that supported it in their desire for emancipation[63]; their prime interest lay in keeping the power of the state within legally defined boundaries, and this desire contradicted Grolman's approach. From the point of view of the *theory of criminal law*, Feuerbach pointed out the decisive flaw in this approach: any examination of whether the convicted criminal took the rule of law as his guideline would lead to a criminal law based on convictions and to a mixing of morality and legality.[64] Grolman has actually been invoked even in recent times as a crucial witness for the debate about whether the distinction between these spheres is to be abolished or lessened.[65]

Objections to Feuerbach's theory saw it as condoning possibly severe threats of punishment in order to ensure that its compensatory effect was successfully reached, or in other words, saw his theory as supporting "terrorism at the cost of humanity and other functions of the state".[66] Feuerbach countered these objections in various ways. While his *Lehrbuch* states that the severity of the punishment threatened is up to the "discretion of the legislative state (criminal policy)",[67] his essay "Strafe als Sicherungsmittel" develops a theoretical line of argument: "In my theory, the coercion cannot be greater than is necessary to remove the obstacle of freedom". Of course, this argument once again has to rely on empirical evidence and policy, for the question of how great the "necessary coercion" is cannot be answered theoretically. This becomes clear when juxtaposed with one of Beccaria's key statements: "[i]f a punishment is to be just, it may be pitched only at that level of intensity which suffices to deter men from crime"[68]; the difference is simply one of terminology, not an essential one. By contrast, Kant's introduction of the *lex talionis* had aimed at excluding precisely this empirical connection.

The **conclusion** that Feuerbach draws from the mechanism of psychological coercion is important for the further development of criminal law: if this coercion is to have any success, the person inclined to a crime must know exactly what to

[63] The bourgeoisie of course also wanted the state to protect its property interests against the lower classes; this is one of the factors that explain why the criminal law of the liberal period was by no means always lenient.

[64] *P.J.A. Feuerbach*, Über die Strafe als Sicherungsmittel (as in footnote 51), in: *Vormbaum*, MdtStrD, p. 82 ff.

[65] See e.g. *Welzel*, Über den substantiellen Begriff des Strafrechts (1944); excerpt in: *Vormbaum*, MdtStrD, p. 291 ff.

[66] *Feuerbach*, Lehrbuch, § 18, Note.

[67] Ibid.

[68] *Beccaria*, p. 68.

expect if he commits it, so he can develop counterarguments. This assumes that crime and threat of punishment are defined by the *law*, that they are *not* implemented *ex post*, that they are worded *definitively* and are not interpreted in a sense that goes beyond their literal meaning, i.e. *not through analogy*. These four consequences (the prohibition of customary law, prohibition of retrospective legislation, prohibition of indeterminate criminal laws and prohibition of analogy) are summarised nowadays in Feuerbach's statement: *nulla poena sine lege* (from his "Lehrbuch"; today often appearing with the contemporary addition of *nullum crimen sine lege*). Feuerbach himself only formulated the first of these four consequences; however, the other three can be inferred from his theory. Here, Feuerbach is once again continuing an Enlightenment tradition that can also be found in Beccaria, for example, but he provides a new theoretical foundation for it.

3. Shared Traits

The question of the extent to which Feuerbach can be called "Kantian" will not be pursued further here.[69] Despite all the differences that certainly exist between Kant, Feuerbach and the other theorists of criminal law of the late eighteenth century,[70] from a historical perspective the following shared fundamental ideas can be identified in or deduced from their theories:

1. The notion of autonomy leads to the idea that it is not the state's business to investigate human beings' (including criminals') personal convictions, and that the state should not try to take an educative influence on its citizens. Punishment as a means of prevention would—in modern terms—"instrumentalise" a person (in Kant's words: "include [him] among objects of the Law of things"). As has already been discussed, this is why Feuerbach focuses not on *punishment* but on the *threat* of punishment as a means of prevention.
2. The definition of justice leads to the idea that the canon of what can be punishable, i.e. that which the state legitimately can issue punishment for, must be limited to violations of *law*. Anything beyond this falls outside the state's responsibility, which lies in creating the juridical condition (or better: that itself should be the juridical condition). The criminal's convictions are of no concern to the state. Morality and criminal law are separate.
3. Taken together, the first and second points result in a (sometimes unspoken) demand that criminal law be independent of politics. Because of this independence Kant is prepared to defend capital punishment, as he sees the law of retribution as a rule of law free of arbitrariness and derived from reason. With the central position it gives to positive law, Feuerbach's theory does contain the

[69] In detail, providing a negative answer to this question: *Naucke*, p. 52 ff.

[70] On these, see *Cattaneo*, p. 262 ff.

danger of availability to politics and a consequent expansion of criminal law. At least he himself was aware of this danger and emphasised the necessity of a congruency between positive criminal law and violations of law.

4. The principle *nullum crimen, nulla poena sine lege* applies, from which the principle of specificity of prescription which applies in criminal law is derived. As a consequence of the first point, *the crime* is the main focus of criminal law, not the criminal.
5. The demand to abolish torture marked a first step towards reforming the general inquisitorial criminal procedure. This reform's theoretical armoury includes the application of the separation of powers to the court procedure, which thus is conceived as a counter model to the concentration of powers held in the hand of the court.[71] However, it was to take some time before the demands that went beyond abolishing torture could be at least partially enacted.

All in all, these points reveal the broad outline of the **programme of liberal criminal law**, based upon a combination of Kant's theory of criminal law and Enlightenment theories reshaped by Kantian terminology.

Wilhelm von Humboldt's essay "Ideas for an endeavour to define the limits of state action" of 1792 can be seen as the classic manifesto of this liberal view of the state.[72] It was only published in full in 1851, probably due to fears of problems with censure, and thus had only a limited effect on legal policy. Humboldt's theses are however representative:

> 1. [. . .] The State must inflict punishment on every action which infringes on the rights [!—T.V.] of the citizens, and (in so far as its legislation is guided by this principle alone) every action in which the transgression of one of its laws is implied.[73]
> 2. The most severe punishment must be only that which is the mildest possible, according to particular circumstances of time and place. [. . .]
> 3. Criminal laws are to be applied only to one who has transgressed them intentionally or culpably [= negligence—T.V.], and only to the extent to which the criminal thereby showed a disregard for the rights of others.
> 4. In the inquiry into crimes committed, the State may indeed employ every means consistent with the end, but none which would treat the citizen who is only suspected as already a criminal, nor any which would violate the rights of man and citizen (which the State must respect even in the criminal), or which would render the State guilty of an immoral action.
> 5. The State must only adopt special arrangements for preventing crimes not yet committed, in so far as they avert their immediate perpetration. [. . .].[74]

---

[71] On Montesquieu's influence on Italian criminal law of the eighteenth century (*Cremani, Renazzi* et al.), see *E. Dezza*, Anklageprozeß und Inquisitionsprozeß in der Rechtslehre des 18. Jahrhunderts; in: Id., Strafrecht, p. 7 ff.

[72] Extract including Humboldt's recommendations regarding criminal law in *Vormbaum*, MdtStrD, p. 5 ff. and references p. 356.

[73] Strictly speaking, this also marks a limitation of police law.

[74] *Wilhelm v. Humboldt*, The Limits of State Action. Ed. J.W. Burrow, transl. Joseph Coulthard. Cambridge 1969, p. 120 f. On Humboldt's text see also *Friedrich Schaffstein*, Das Strafrecht in Wilhelm von Humboldts Schrift über die Grenzen der Staatswirksamkeit (first published 1973), in:

Kantian theory of criminal law and those theories it influences are characterised by their *idealistic nature* (philosophically speaking), which has had a strong and lasting influence on German theory of criminal law to this day, regardless of its respective content. Both German theory and doctrine of criminal law are characterised by a "spiritualisation of the social".[75] In contrast to France and English-speaking countries, the insights of social science only enter into German thought in highly sublimated forms.

This development was not independent of the **political situation**. Unlike in Germany's Western neighbours, German attempts at "explaining the world" for a long time did not only have no *chance* to measure themselves against political reality—they had no *responsibility* to do so either. German thinkers were both denied and spared this "testing out" of their theories against reality. Thus, Germany relied on—as Heinrich Heine put it—"the high horse of the idea".[76] And thus German philosophy, again in the words of Heine, massacred the idea of God as the French Revolution had its real monarchy:

> This book [sc. "Criticism of Pure Reason"] is the sword with which deism [i.e. belief in God] has been put to death in Germany. Honestly, you French, in contrast to us Germans you are tame and moderate. You were only able to kill a king. [. . .] *We* had emeutes in the world of ideas, just as *you* had in the material world, and we were just as passionate in destroying old dogmatisms as you were in storming the Bastille.

German theory of criminal law partakes of this idiosyncrasy. As German idealist philosophy triumphed outside Germany, particularly in Southern European countries, German theory of criminal law also gained worldwide influence. The secret of its success to this day lies in its general nature and level of abstraction, which enables its "ruthless" methodical and conceptual consistency.[77] One result of this influence is a certain "dematerialisation", which one the one hand makes it possible to remain committed to ideals regardless of the (political) reality opposing them.[78] On the other hand, this also meant that in Germany, unlike in English-speaking countries for

---

Id., Abhandlungen zur Strafrechtsgeschichte. Aalen 1986, p. 247 ff. *Felix Herzog*, Über die Grenzen der Wirksamkeit des Strafrechts. Eine Hommage an Wilhelm von Humboldt. (Humboldt-Universität Berlin. Public lectures. Booklet 11). 1993.

[75] *Amelung*, Rechtsgüterschutz, p. 32.

[76] *Heinrich Heine*, Gefängnisreform und Strafgesetzgebung, in: Thomas Vormbaum (Ed.), Recht, Rechtswissenschaft und Juristen im Werk Heinrich Heines. Berlin 2006, p. 136.

[77] There is no space here to pursue *general* questions that arise at this point. Suffice it to suggest that national characteristics—a term that can, of course, only be used with great caution—usually derive their greatest strength as well as their more problematic aspects from the same source: *here* we have the intellectual discipline of German idealist philosophy, methodologically and conceptually consistent down to the smallest level of detail, *there* the logic and consistency of racial theory, giving madness a method, and the resulting systematic, methodical mass murder of the holocaust. Naturally, these considerations need to be looked at in greater depth and differentiation.

[78] Many references to Kant's defence of a metaphysics of justice against a theory of law based purely on empirical evidence can be found in *Mario A. Cattaneo*, Menschenwürde und ewiger Friede. Kants Kritik der Politik. Berlin 2004, p. 32 ff.; *Naucke/Harzer*, Rechtsphilosophie, p. 77: "Kant's metaphysics of justice is an attempt to control a system of law based merely on metaphysics".

example, it was not possible to ground certain minimum standards of the rule of law in everyday legal culture as an unquestioned part of social heritage, requiring no further explanation.[79] Of course, this result was more a precondition than a consequence of the idealistic focus of German theory of criminal law,[80] in other words it was a result of the *political development*.

If idealist philosophy is approached from the angle of *epistemology*, then its political extension is the *formal rule of law*. From a political point of view this rule of law is ambiguous, for—as shown by the Bismarck-Reich—any kind of content can be used to fill its form.[81] However, if idealist theory of criminal law is imagined combined with the realisation of the points listed above, then the principle of the rule of law, and its particular aspect of criminal law, emerges, limiting state power (also in terms of content). Therefore, if any accusation is to be levelled at the discipline of criminal law, this would be less a matter of lacking social theory[82]—which could take different forms in reality (including authoritarian), but rather that many believed they had to accommodate "practice". After 1815 this "practice" was first that of the Restoration, then of the *Vormärz*, then of the Reaction and finally of the authoritarian Bismarckian state. This will be shown in the following chapter. And at the end of the nineteenth century it would be seen exactly how problematic this "opening up" of the theory of criminal law to empirical science could be.

[79] The debate still ongoing today about the legality and legitimacy of the Enabling Act of 1933 can be seen as symptomatic in this regard. Art. 79(3) of German Basic Law attempts to define and ensure such a minimum level.

[80] It might be interesting to explore whether the aversity to theory of German legal practitioners that every junior lawyer encounters during his or her practical training is a phenomenon complementary to the development described in the present text.

[81] *Müller*, Generalprävention, p. 30.

[82] Although this accusation can be found in *Amelung*, Rechtsgüterschutz, p. 33.

§ 3 Nineteenth Century Developments

I. Criminal Law Theory

As set out in § 1, this chapter intends to trace how the principles put forward at the beginning of the legal-historical period were put into practice and developed further.

1. Definition of Crime

First we must return to the subject discussed at the end of the previous paragraph, namely that criminal law is limited to reacting to *infringements of rights*. This affects the question of the legitimate *extent* of criminal law, which must precede any questions on so-called purposes of punishment. *What* is the state allowed to render punishable and sanction if necessary?

This can also be viewed as a question of the **material definition of crime.**[1] *Formally*, a crime is simply what legislators positively define as a crime. A *material crime* is what can be punished following a consideration of its *substance*. If the actual legislator is not to issue penal laws at whim, then this material, pre-positive definition of crime is an essential "yardstick" for the (formal, positive) legislator,[2] and any formal, positive or statutory criminal law that exceeds the area of material crimes constitutes illegitimate abuse on part of the legislator.

But what then is the yardstick for this legitimate criminal law, based on a material definition of crime? The earlier religious foundations of criminal law

[1] *Naucke,* Materieller Verbrechensbegriff, p. 269 ff.

[2] Whether the material definition of crime only defines the *outer* limits of state punitive force, or whether it also establishes a *duty* to punish, is another question. Kant's understanding of criminal law as a categorical imperative can only be understood as the latter. On the attempt to establish a different understanding, see below § 7, at the end of the afterword.

T. Vormbaum and M. Bohlander, *A Modern History of German Criminal Law*,
DOI 10.1007/978-3-642-37273-5_3, © Springer-Verlag Berlin Heidelberg 2014

(e.g. in *Carpzov*) had regarded every crime as a violation of divine commandments with punishment as the criminal's act of atonement and the people's way of achieving redemption from the blood guilt that lay upon them. However, for theorists of criminal law during the **Enlightenment** period, concerned with providing a secular foundation for criminal law and the individual punishments threatened, this no longer sufficed. Literature on criminal law raised the theory of the *social contract.* One of the central concerns of contractarian theories was how the legitimate extent of state punishment could be defined and delimited. Following the transition from a state of nature to a state of society, human beings' peaceful coexistence was to be achieved by a guarantee of each individual's rights. Any encroachments upon individual freedom (particularly criminal laws) that did not serve this purpose were not covered by the social contract.

However, it was already perceived during the Enlightenment that, besides the punishments of criminal law that serve the immediate preservation of peace, a law of sanctions exists that ensures the *practical realisation and preservation* of this peaceful condition of "good policy". Thus for a long time this law of sanctions was called police law, later also administrative criminal law, and corresponds to today's law governing administrative offences. This opens up the possibility of ("partial") decriminalisation, transforming those offences of criminal law that do not (or no longer) measure up to its material criteria, into offences under the remit of this legal category, rather than causing in a complete lack of sanctions. The delimitation of these two areas is a theme that runs throughout 19th and 20th century discussions of criminal law. However, in the absolutist state, where police powers are not restricted to maintaining security but aim to secure public prosperity, there is no criterion that sets any limits to police powers themselves.[3]

Immanuel Kant shifted the central focus of the theory of criminal law to *infringements of rights.* We have already traced how this approach is derived from his definition of justice. As state punishment can only be applied to infringements of freedom, but freedom itself finds its concrete expression in *subjective rights*, legitimate state punitive violence is restricted to the punishment of *infringements of rights.* Kant thus provided a new foundation for a doctrine already espoused by critical philosophers of the Enlightenment.

This meant that a clarity still unmatched today (at least in theoretical terms) was gained regarding the legitimate extent of the criminal law. Around 1800, various teachers of criminal law influenced by Kant attempted to construct a system of those rights worthy of protection by criminal law, based on the theory of infringement of rights that Kant had provided the philosophical foundation for.

It is noteworthy that the two most famous of these teachers—*Paul Johann Anselm Feuerbach* und *Carl Grolman*—do not follow Kant's absolute theory of punishment. As already outlined, Feuerbach advocates a theory of punishment of general deterrence by threatening punishment, Grolman a theory of special prevention. One could say that Kant limits the purpose of criminal law to *requiting* infringements of *rights*, and Feuerbach and Grolman to *preventing* these from occurring.

[3] *Amelung*, Rechtsgüterschutz, p. 22 ff.

In Kant, the limitation of the scope of criminal law to the infringement of subjective rights is a postulate philosophically derived from his definition of (objective) justice. However, as a practising criminal legislator in Bavaria, **Feuerbach** was made to feel the political and social resistance to this restriction of criminal law. The concessions made to convention by the Bavarian Criminal Code of 1813 that he helped to shape (cf. II. 2. a) are in fact a kind of compromise.

The way Feuerbach developed *police law* further represents a political compromise with state criminal policy. It includes acts that do not violate any inherent rights, but indirectly harm the purpose of the state:

> Inasmuch as the state is legitimately allowed to work towards its purposes *indirectly* through *police laws* and use these to forbid acts not unlawful in themselves, there exist *special rights of the state to demand that its subjects refrain from these specially forbidden acts*, even though they were originally legally entitled to them. If the *right of the state to obedience towards a certain police law is rendered punishable*, the concept of *misdemeanour, infringement of police law* arises.[4]

On the one hand, this theoretical construct limits the capacity of criminal policy to define criminal offences against police law to cases where the state's purpose is indirectly harmed. On the other hand, it also accommodates criminal policy—for there can be little doubt that "indirect harm to the purpose of the state" is something easily conceptualised. Feuerbach himself was aware of the dangers of police law:

> Police law can easily be misused to place all human freedom in chains, and to make of the citizen a living Chinese doll, unable to take even the most innocent step without incurring punishment.[5]

At least the doctrine of infringement of rights theoretically placed criminal law beyond legislative whim; basically, it represented a codification of natural law, and to this extent the act of legislation remained *declaratory*. The demand that punishment be issued only for violations of subjective rights thus remained a challenge and an argumentative problem for criminal law politicians (to the extent that they could be swayed by the theoretical arguments of criminal law at all). However, they were soon to receive support.

According to current popular opinion, this support first came from the teacher of criminal law **Johann Michael Franz Birnbaum**. In 1834 he introduced the term "***Gut***" (possession or interest) to the theory of criminal law, from which the term "***Rechtsgut***" or **protected legal interest** later developed. Today, Birnbaum is remembered basically only for his 1834 essay *Ueber das Erforderniß einer Rechtsverletzung zum Begriffe des Verbrechens.*[6] His starting point in this essay was the—certainly terminologically valid—assumption that rights as such could not be infringed, but only the *legal interests* that are the object of rights.

---

[4] *Feuerbach*, Lehrbuch, § 22, (p. 46) (emphases in the original); cf. also *Amelung*, Rechtsgüterschutz, p. 34.

[5] *Feuerbach*, Lehrbuch, § 22 footnote 2 (p. 48). Feuerbach singles out the draft of a Bavarian Criminal Code created during the Restoration period (1822) as a "shocking example" of such legislation; however, it did not become law.

[6] Excerpt in *Vormbaum*, MdtStrD, p. 148 ff.

A thief who steals an object from someone effects no change in ownership, for the property *right* of the victim of theft still exists. A victim of bodily harm as defined in § 223 StGB does not lose his or her *right* to physical well-being and physical integrity; an imprisoned individual does not lose his or her *right* to freedom of movement and so on. Only the substrata of these rights can be violated by hindering the beneficiaries from exercising them.

In fact, Birnbaum's insight was a trivial one, pointing out that the legislator and legal theory use imprecise terminology when speaking of the "infringement" of a right. In any case, this change in terminology produced no change in the *extent* of criminal law. Nowadays, replacing the word *Recht* in § 823 (1) BGB with the word *Rechtsgut*, or reformulating its phrasing as "A person who, intentionally or negligently, unlawfully injures the right to life, health, freedom, property or the exercise of another (absolute) right of another person", does not redefine the area this law or other comparable laws apply to.[7] As far as the *extent* of what was punishable was concerned, *Birnbaum* himself thus remained restricted to individual rights. However, the necessity of justifying the definition of a criminal offence by citing the right it protected became redundant. Thus Birnbaum's approach objectively opened up the possibility for criminal law also to be applied to those *Güter* or protected legal interests that are not the object of *rights*. In actual fact, Birnbaum's teacher **Carl Joseph Anton Mittermaier** (1787–1867)[8] had already crossed this threshold with regard to this matter, without using the term *Gut*.[9] The shift away from this paradigm of an infringement of *rights* legitimated threats of punishments for acts that did not violate the rights of a natural person or legal entity, particularly those acts that only went against principles of morality and decency.

Birnbaum no longer provided any theoretical foundation for the idea of the protection of "*Güter*", believing it to be plausible without. Thus he created a path which his successors followed to arrive at theories of crime in which this missing theory of the prerequisites of human coexistence is actually replaced by the political whim of the subject pronouncing judgment. [. . .] The idea of the protection of legal interests transforms the doctrine of social harm into purely a matter of judgment and thus returns it—which *Birnbaum* of course fails to see—to the only reliable authority of judgment, the legislator.[10]

Amelung's observation is quite remarkable, for today the idea of the protection of legal interests is used primarily as a method for *limiting* criminal law. However, it should be noted that the idea of protected legal interests in fact came about due to a desire to **expand the scope of criminal law.**[11]

---

[7] Thus also *Knut Amelung*, J.M.F. Birnbaums Lehre vom strafrechtlichen "Güter"-Schutz als Übergang vom naturrechtlichen zum positivistischen Rechtsdenken, in: Diethelm Klippel (Ed.), Naturrecht im 19. Jahrhundert. Goldbach 1997, p. 349 ff., 354.

[8] *Frommel,* Präventionsmodelle, p. 155.

[9] *Naucke*, Verbrechensbegriff, p. 280 f.

[10] *Amelung*, Rechtsgüterschutz, p. 49, 50.

[11] Thus also *Silva Sanchez,* Expansion, p. 62 ff.; in 1972, Amelung already pointed out the arbitrariness of the doctrine of protected legal interests: "It is doubtful whether those who have recently placed the reform of criminal law relating to sexual offences under the aegis of protected interests are in fact aware that the theory of an infringement of legal interests was introduced to serve a restorative purpose, particularly in this precise area. The term 'interest' is so broad that it covers everything Birnbaum would like to see protected by the state: human beings and morals, objects and fear of God"; *Amelung*, Rechtsgüterschutz, p. 47.

The transition from a doctrine of infringement of rights to a doctrine of infringement of protected legal interests can be classed as the fallout of general developments in criminal law:

Politically, this transition takes place during the period of the **Restoration** and the Vormärz; the constitutional situation of the pre-Napoleonic period had been "restored"—except in some South German states.[12] The governments of the **German Confederation** founded in 1815 attempted to suppress social developments towards an increased participation (primarily) of the middle classes, not least by using criminal law (on this, see II. below). An understanding of philosophy of law and criminal policy that aimed to limit the state's punitive power to infringements of rights did not fit well into this political context.

In terms of the *history of ideas and culture*, the "dilution" of the theory of infringement of rights by the theory of the infringement of protected legal interests falls into the final years of the **Romantic period**, which contrasted the techno-rationality of Enlightenment thought with the idea of the organic, an emphasis on the subjective, and on individuality (of people, states and nations). The theory of the infringement of rights, felt to be mechanistic and doctrinaire, was unable to stand up to Romanticism's organic concept of the state and the way it lovingly immersed itself in national history, lore and idiosyncrasies—even less so as Romanticism, which originally had been a movement with considerable emancipatory potential, had become entangled with conservative ideas in the wake of the so-called wars of liberation against French foreign rule.[13]

From the point of view of *legal history*, this shift away from the theory of an infringement of rights must be seen in relation to the **German Historical School**, whose most important exponent was *Friedrich Carl von Savigny*. Savigny's theoretical and doctrinal work was focused primarily on private law,[14] but also influenced other areas of law. Like Romanticism, of which it can be seen to be an offshoot, the Historical School replaced the generalising tendencies of the Enlightenment with the individual, its rationalising tendencies with the irrational, its terminology aimed at timelessness with one that had evolved historically, and its passion for codification with the "silently working forces" of a law originating

[12] On Southern German so-called early constitutionalism (Bavaria, Baden, Württemberg, Hesse) see *Huber*, Verfassungsgeschichte I, p. 314 ff.; also for an overview of the constitutions pertaining to the estates of the realm in the states of the German Confederation.

[13] Recently discussed in *Rüdiger Safranski,* Romantik. Eine deutsche Affäre, Munich 2007, particularly p. 172 ff.; the *emancipation of the Jews*, which had made significant progress at the turn of the nineteenth to the twentieth century, suffered setbacks in consequence of the changes made during the period after 1815; see *Vormbaum*, Judeneid, p. 214 ff. incl. references.

[14] On **Friedrich Carl von Savigny** *Stintzing/Landsberg*, III, 2 (text volume), particularlyp. 185–253; *Franz Wieacker,* Privatrechtsgeschichte der Neuzeit. 2nd edition. Göttingen 1967, particularly p. 381 ff.; *Senn*, Rechtsgeschichte, p. 331 ff.; *Wolf,* Rechtsdenker, p. 467 ff.; *Iris Denneler*, Karl Friedrich von Savigny (Preußische Köpfe 17). Berlin 1985.

in the *Volksgeist*, the national spirit[15]. As far as the material definition of crime is concerned, it follows that the values and opinions held by the people are the yardstick by which the limits of state punishment are to be measured. A correspondence can be noted to the extent that Birnbaum's concept of "Gut" easily covers a definition of these opinions as "Güter".[16]

Naturally, this should not be taken to mean that the theorists of criminal law of the early nineteenth century consciously saw themselves as "representatives" of one of the three tendencies mentioned here. The intellectual influence of politics, the *Zeitgeist* and prevalent scholarly opinion is never one-dimensional (at least not in the case of serious scholars); however, some connections only become obvious to later generations with the passing of time.[17] In addition, the parameters and tendencies mentioned did not completely supplant earlier streams of thought. The concepts of natural law, Enlightenment and Kantian thought remained—sometimes in a fragmented state—as undercurrents, and could still be discerned more or less clearly. Both rationality as well as a consideration of emotion seeped into the attitudes of everyday culture as a result of the eras of Enlightenment and Romanticism; the intertwining of these popular currents of rationalism[18] and romanticism, with phases when alternatively one or the other component gained the upper hand, characterises the course of the modern period.

The liberalism emerging at this time thus developed within many different force fields. For this reason, it is sometimes difficult to determine the political orientation of theorists of criminal law. For example, **Carl Joseph Anton Mittermaier**, who railed against the "doctrinarism" and "generalising tendency" of Feuerbach,[19] was an exponent of moderate liberalism and for many years a member and, at times, the president of the legislature in Baden; he was the president of the Frankfurt

[15] *Friedrich Carl von Savigny*, Vom Beruf unserer Zeit zur Gesetzgebung und Rechtswissenschaft, in: *Jacques Stern* (Ed.), Thibaut und Savigny (1914). Newly edited by Hans Hattenhauer. Munich 1973, p. 79.

[16] Worthy of singling out from the extensive literature on **Carl Joseph Anton Mittermaier's** biography and a general appraisal of his work are: *Landwehr,* Mittermaier, op. cit., as well as the 200th anniversary conference proceedings edited by *Wilfried Küper* with contributions among others by: *Frommel, Küper, Maiwald, Müller-Dietz, Naucke, Schlosser, Schulz.* Heidelberg 1987; further, *Götz Landwehr*, Karl Joseph Anton Mittermaier (1787–1867). Ein Professorenleben in Heidelberg, in: Wilfried Küper (Ed.) Heidelberger Strafrechtslehrer im 19. und 20. Jahrhundert. Heidelberg 1986, p. 69 ff.; *Klaus Lüderssen*, Karl Joseph Anton Mittermaier und der Empirismus in der Strafrechtswissenschaft, ibid., p. 101 ff.

[17] Of course this greater clarity, to put it in modern terms, is the result of a reduction in complexity, and is furthermore subject to the conditions of the "hermeneutic circle" (cf. § 1 II. 1. b).

[18] On this cf. *Hans Rosenberg*, Theologischer Rationalismus und vormärzlicher Vulgärliberalismus, in: Id., Politische Denkströmungen im deutschen Vormärz. Göttingen 1972, p. 18 ff.

[19] Excerpt of his text directed primarily against Feuerbach "Über die Grundfehler der Behandlung des Kriminalrechts" of 1819 in *Vormbaum*, MdtStrD, p. 122 ff.

Pre-Parliament, a member of the Frankfurt Assembly and a member of its constitutional committee.[20] He came to reject capital punishment, although his deliberations on this had several stages.[21] Methodologically, his rejection of theoretical constructs was, of course, in line with the spirit of the Restoration period and the Vormärz.

The positive aspects of romantic and historicist (i.e. going back to the German Historical School) influence should not be overlooked. Romanticism was as important in initiating the exploration of the criminal mind as historicism was in the development of historical and comparative legal research[22] – both of these are of course elements that are just as ambiguous as the rationalism of the Enlightenment. A historic point of view can prove how relative and conditional currently valid law is, and thus show its by no means "timeless" character, its need of reform (already discussed towards the end of § 1 II. 1. a); however, it can also lead to the demand – as Karl Marx accused the German Historical School – that the ship should "ignore the river and row only on its source-head",[23] or the assertion "sterling today, for yesterday 'twas sterling".[24] The exploration of the criminal mind can be seen as complementing the objective side of the offence and result in a limitation of punishment; however, it can also promote a criminal law based on the criminal and the danger he or she poses. Only the criminal law of the twentieth century has fully acknowledged this ambivalence and made it clear.

At any rate, we can note that the anti-theoretical or sceptical attitude of Mittermaier and other teachers of substantive criminal law led to the material definition of crime becoming less focused, and thus was a considerable factor in the arbitrariness of the legitimation of criminal laws.[25]

Mittermaier's polemics against Feuerbach's theory of punishment gained a particular – problematic – emphasis, as it was he of all people who continued to edit Feuerbach's textbook for several editions following its author's death (last edition 1847).[26] That such an outspoken critic of the textbook author's position[27] took on this position is less surprising

[20] References in the works listed under footnote 16.

[21] *Martin Fleckenstein*, Die Todesstrafe im Werk Carl Joseph Anton Mittermaiers (1787–1867). Zur Entwicklungsgeschichte eines Werkbereichs und seiner Bedeutung für Theorie- und Methodenbildung. Frankfurt am Main 1991.

[22] Mittermaier is seen as one of the "fathers" of comparative law, cf. *Konrad Zweigert/Hein Kötz*, Einführung in die Rechtsvergleichung. 3rd edition. Tübingen 1996, p. 54 ff.; *Landwehr*, Mittermaier (as in footnote 16), p. 97 f.—However, Feuerbach had already undertaken in-depth study of comparative law as part of a planned "universal history of law"; on this, cf. *Radbruch*, Feuerbach, p. 190 ff.

[23] *Karl Marx*, The Philosophical Manifesto of the Historical School of Law (1842), in: Marx/ Engels Collected Works. Vol. 2. Moscow 1975, p. 203.

[24] *Schiller*, Wallenstein's Death, Act 1, Scene 4. The time frame of course has been shifted (the original has "Sterling tomorrow, for today 'twas sterling!").

[25] *Frommel*, Präventionsmodelle, p. 153 ff., pleads for greater understanding for Mittermaier's position, as she sees its results as not far removed from those of Feuerbach.

[26] For an extensive and differentiated discussion of this, see *Neh*, Posthume Auflagen.

[27] Cf. the contribution published in 1819, during Feuerbach's lifetime (above footnote 19). Mittermaier's preface to the first edition he revised (the 12th) is one long criticism of Feuerbach's textbook and of its author's position: "[...] His textbook is no less flawed, in that his theory of

when considering that Mittermaier on several occasions worked as Feuerbach's secretary. Feuerbach valued Mittermaier's proficiency in languages (particularly Italian) and used it for his comparative studies of law.[28] Mittermaier had also contributed to new editions of the textbooks in Feuerbach's lifetime, though mainly in an editorial capacity.[29] Therefore he was an obvious choice to continue the textbook as one of Feuerbach's "disciples". There were probably also publishing reasons for continuing the textbook after the death of its founder. Feuerbach's textbook had become a standard work and was used by many of his colleagues as the basis of lectures on criminal law, as was usual at the time. The advertising effect of the original author's name was to be preserved as a "brand" – as is still common today.[30] But how could a continuation of the textbook actually be possible on the basis of Mittermaier's utterly different position? The solution was to preserve Feuerbach's text (including the notes) unchanged, but to supplement it with many extensive "Notes by the Editor", additional paragraphs and even a "comparative account of further developments in criminal law due to recent legislation". In the end, these additions took up almost as much space as Feuerbach's text. They contain supplementary, but primarily historic discussions of the topics covered on the one hand, and on the other critical comments on Feuerbach's opinions. However, Mittermaier's line of argument did not produce what amounts to a second textbook; rather, his comments often make a rather pedantic, carping impression. Even though Mittermaier was one of the most productive writers of the 19th century on criminal law in terms of quantity,[31] and although he listed his criteria for a desirable textbook on criminal law in the preface to the 12th edition of the Feuerbach textbook, he never wrote such a textbook himself.[32]

In any case, the overall result is that the shift away from the doctrine of infringement of rights produced a first weakening of the reform programme that had marked the beginning of the legal-historical period. The discrepancy between the persisting reality of criminal legislation and the theory of criminal law, which remained liberal and strictly focused on the rule of law, was not resolved by the theoreticians' patient insistence on theory in the face of actual practice. Rather, theory grew ever closer to practice.

criminal law, which cannot be justified, affected every single theory; that the aspect of the infringement of rights, which he made the basis of every crime, led him to an unsuitable systematic order of crimes and to erroneous points of what was punishable for individual crimes" (p. III f.). In the preface to the 14th edition, Mittermaier writes: "[...] The editor, who fully acknowledges of the difficulty of adapting the notes on the work of an author, with whose basic principles the editor disagrees [...]" (p. XIV f.).

[28] *Neh*, Posthume Auflagen, p. 38 ff.; on Feuerbach's comparative work, see footnote 21 above.

[29] *Neh*, Posthume Auflagen, p. 60 ff.

[30] In the preface to the first edition he revised (the 12th), Mittermaier himself writes: "After Feuerbach's death, when the publisher requested that I edit this work, it was my intention to completely revise it". But even collecting the materials for such a textbook would have gone far beyond its scope, for "it was desirable to reprint Feuerbach's book, which is so widespread among practitioners" (p. V f.).

[31] On this, cf. *Landwehr*, Mittermaier (as in footnote 16), p. 99: "31 independent works, many containing several volumes, and more than 600 essays".

[32] Even in the last (14th) edition of Feuerbach's textbook, Mittermaier states that he, the editor, had hoped to "present the readers with a textbook of his own instead of the revision of the 14th edition of Feuerbach. Many distractions" however "prevented him from undertaking this project". In the nearly 20 further years of his life, Mittermaier failed to produce a textbook on criminal law; *Landwehr*, op. cit., p. 93.

This does not mean that no practical progress was made during the nineteenth century in the liberalisation of criminal law. But the doctrine of infringement of rights plays only a marginal role in it. In the main, we are dealing with the successes of political liberalism—most of these achieved by way of compromise. To the extent that political liberalism developed a theoretical understanding of criminal law, this understanding was a product of **legal positivism**—the line of thought that considered the positive legislator and its dictates the ultimate legitimising authority. The doctrine of the infringement of protected legal interests resonated much better with this line of thought than the doctrine of infringement of rights. The "pragmatic" nature of the doctrine of the infringement of protected legal interests accommodated both conservative and liberal politicians, whom the increase in their parliamentary activity from the mid-century onwards—earlier in southern Germany—had made dependent on compromises that naturally did not always measure up to the standards of theory. For the individual trying to negotiate a compromise, demands of theory that limit his room for manoeuvre (in advance) and show the compromise reached in an unsatisfactory light (in retrospect) are irritating in the long run; the temptation to denounce them as unrealistic was as great then as it is now.

Thus the idea of the protection of legal interests established itself in the course of the nineteenth century. Not in the formal sense that it became established in theory—this would have contradicted its anti-theoretical tendency. Birnbaum's essay might have been forgotten, had it not been rediscovered later by Karl Binding.[33] But the idea of protected legal interests was *put into practice*.

In 1855, *Köstlin* was able to state that it was "generally accepted that a 'natural' criminal law which held importance for practice did not exist". While Feuerbach's efforts as a theoretician and legislator had aimed at constructing the offences of positive (criminal) law so as to conform as closely as possible to infringements of rights (defined by natural law), the Hegelian *Köstlin* sees "the idea of law [...] as subject to the imperatives of the developments of world history and the gradual progress towards perfection, encompassing multiple imperfect phenomena conditioned by place and time, of its finite life".[34] Thus the material definition of crime is, to a large extent, at the mercy of politics. Objectively, Hegelian philosophy of criminal law converges with criminal legal positivism.

Towards the end of the nineteenth century, the idea of protected legal interests also established itself in formal terms. **Karl Binding**, who rediscovered Birnbaum's essay, replaced the term "*Gut*" with that of "*Rechtsgut*" and tried to define it more closely, draws the ultimate conclusion that the question of *which* protected legal interests or *Rechtsgüter* were to be recognised and guaranteed by a definition of their infringement as a criminal offence would have to be determined by the legislator itself, as there was no other authority that legitimates positive law.

[33] *Frommel,* Präventionsmodelle, p. 155, points out that Birnbaum's essay was basically not quoted for decades, not even by his teacher Mittermaier.

[34] *Köstlin*, System, § 13, reproduced in *Vormbaum*, MdtStrD, p. 169.

Binding criticises an "understanding of crime in which the offence is supposed to correspond to the culpable infringement of subjective rights" as "narrow and restricted". The task of the criminal legislator possesses "universal character". Not subjective rights are to be protected, but the "actual conditions for a healthy life of the community", i.e. the *Rechtsgüter*.[35]

As Binding's theoretical opponent **Franz von Liszt** also discussed the term of the protected legal interest, it became one of the central terms within twentieth century debates surrounding theory of criminal law.[36] To this day, practical effects—in the sense of the legislator dispensing with a new criminal offence or a constitutional court verdict based on the absence of a respective protected legal interest—have of course remained rare. This is not surprising, for Binding's reasoning means that the idea of protected legal interests is no longer an external pre-existing measure applied to criminal law in order to limit the reach of the legislator, but at most a means of self-regulation for the legislator. If the legislator itself defines the legal interest protected by a criminal offence, it can only do so in practical terms by formulating precisely this offence. Thus the offence itself becomes the measure by which it is later to be interpreted. As the legal definitions of offences rarely make express reference to the protected legal interest, its definition regularly falls to legal academia and to the courts; thus the point made in the previous sentence can actually be logically reduced to: whoever interprets a criminal offence at the same time determines the measure used to interpret the criminal offence—circular reasoning. Accordingly, there is a tendency for the determining of a protected legal interest as a *measure of limitation* and its use as a *guide for interpretation* to converge.[37]

2. Theories of Punishment[38]

a) Fichte

Johann Gottlieb Fichte (1762–1814) is perhaps the greatest idealist philosopher after Kant to concern himself with theories of the purpose of punishment around the turn of the eighteenth to the nineteenth century. Like Kant and also Feuerbach and

---

[35] *Karl Binding*, Die Normen und ihre Übertretung. Eine Untersuchung über die rechtmäßigen Handlungen und die Arten des Delikts. Vol. I. 2nd edition. Leipzig 1890, p. 339 ff.; on this, cf. *Felix Herzog*, Gesellschaftliche Unsicherheit und strafrechtliche Daseinsvorsorge. Studien zur Vorverlegung des Strafrechtsschutzes in den Gefährdungsbereich. Heidelberg 1990, p. 10 ff.

[36] See also *Amelung*, Rechtsgüterschutz, p. 52.

[37] Amelung, who has examined and analysed the history of the idea of protected legal interests as no other, draws the conclusion to use it only in this second sense; see most recently *Amelung*, Der Begriff des Rechtsguts in der Lehre vom strafrechtlichen Rechtsgüterschutz, in: Roland Hefendehl/ Andrew von Hirsch/Wolfgang Wohlers (Eds.), Die Rechtsgutstheorie. Legitimationsbasis des Strafrechts oder dogmatisches Glasperlenspiel? Baden-Baden 2003, p. 155 ff., 159 ff.

[38] On the legal-philosophical points of departure see *Müller*, Generalprävention, p. 57 ff.

Grolman soon after, in his *Grundlagen des Naturrechts nach Principien der Wissenschaftslehre* of 1796/97[39] Fichte assumes a strict distinction between law and morality: "Each has a claim only to the other's *legality*, but by no means to his *morality*." However, everyone has a claim that others undertake only those actions they would carry out *if they had* a thoroughly good will (p. 125). Fichte now asks which arrangements can be made to "keep people from engaging in wrongful actions". Similarly to Feuerbach, he reaches the conclusion that these arrangements must be directed at the *will*; the will must be "necessitate[d to] will only what is rightful". When honesty and trust have been lost, security can thus be re-established, "and it would render the good will superfluous for the realization of external right, since a bad will that desires other people's things would be led—by its own unrightful desire—to the same end as a good will" (p. 127). Fichte calls this kind of arrangement a *law of coercion*.

Like Feuerbach shortly after, Fichte claims that this does not result in a restriction of freedom, for "[n]o external law is given to someone who is righteous; he is completely liberated from such a law, and liberated by his own good will" (p. 249). A human being should "exercise precisely as much care not to violate the rights of others as he does to prevent his own rights from being violated". However, if the law of coercion turns any violation of the rights of others into a violation of one's own rights, he must take care not to violate the rights of others for the sake of his own security. Of course, Fichte adds that this law of coercion does not represent a categorical right, but is only problematically rightful (in simplified terms: only permissible in situations of self-defence or emergency). Thus "it is always unjust actually to apply coercion, as if one had a categorical right to it" (p. 132). This justification of coercion appears both more prosaic and more differentiated than the thesis of an agreement either feigned or commanded by reason, a Kantian feature which Feuerbach transplants into the context of his theory of prevention.

In *practice*, Fichte assumes that every violation of the civil contract leads to the violator losing "all his rights as a citizen and as a human being", becoming "an outlaw with no rights at all" (p. 226)—a thought already encountered in Rousseau.[40] As the state's "interest [is] to preserve its citizens", this conclusion should not be acted upon where "there is no risk to public security [...] to impose alternative punishments for offenses that, strictly speaking, merit exclusion" (p. 227). Here, Fichte imagines a contract of all with all "not to exclude [the other] from the state for their offences (provided that this is consistent with public security". Fichte calls this contract **expiation contract** (***Abbüßungsvertrag***).

---

[39] Excerpt in *Vormbaum*, MdtStrD, p. 19 ff.; then the following page references in the text. For an extensive discussion of Fichte's theory of criminal law, see *Rainer Zaczyk*, Das Strafrecht in der Rechtslehre J.G. Fichtes. Berlin 1981; see also *Daniela Tafani,* Recht, Zwang und Strafe bei Fichte, in: JJZG 9 (2007/2008), p. 267 ff.

[40] *J.J. Rousseau,* Du contrat social, Chapter 5; excerpt in Vormbaum, StrD, p. 116 ff.

The sentence "Punishment is not an absolute end" distances Fichte from Kant.[41] According to Fichte, punishment is a means for achieving the state's end, which he defines as public security. The purpose of criminal law is to never actually be put into practice—a statement clearly indebted to the idea of deterrence by threat of punishment.

Fichte infers that the consequence of the expiation contract he constructs is a (political, not moral) *reform* of the convicted criminal; the institutions for reform should however also be *deterrent* at the same time. Those who are reformed within a certain time period should be able to return to society with all of their rights restored, but the others are to be "excluded from the state as unreformable" (p. 240). However, the death penalty is only compulsory for *intentional, premeditated* murder (p. 241).

Consequently, based on the above, Fichte "has transformed Kant's theory of retribution into a utilitarian theory of general and special prevention".[42]

b) Hegel

The main line of development in nineteenth century theories of punishment was given a significant boost by the theory of criminal law advocated by probably the most influential philosopher of the nineteenth century, **Georg Wilhelm Friedrich Hegel** (1770–1831), in his *Elements of the Philosophy of Law*.[43,44] It forms an integral part of the view of the progress of world history Hegel develops in *The Phenomenology of Spirit*. During this progress, the *Weltgeist* or world spirit as (merely) "objective spirit" thinks itself, i.e. makes itself the object of its thought. In order to do so it divests itself of itself, in order to then return to itself as "absolute spirit" and thus be "with itself". The structure of this progress is the dialectic three-part step "*thesis* (or position)—*antithesis* (or negation)—*synthesis* (or negation of the negation)". All that is limited, all that is "posited" (position), precisely because of its limitations necessarily generates its opposite (or its challenge) out of itself

---

[41] This becomes clear in the following passage, where he writes: "The claim that it is (whether stated explicitly or through propositions that implicitly presuppose such a premise, e.g. the unmodified, categorical proposition that 'he who killed, must die') makes no sense" (p. 228).

[42] *Müller*, Generalprävention, p. 63.—The similarities between Fichte's remarks on how punishments might be executed and the Prussian "General Plan" for the execution of punishments presented only a few years later (on this, see § 3 IV. 2. below) are striking.

[43] Translator's note: standard editions translate the German "Recht" in the title of this work as "right", but in this context "law" seems more appropriate. References are nonetheless made to translations using 'Right'.

[44] On Hegel's theory of criminal law, see *Ossip K. Flechtheim*, Hegels Strafrechtstheorie. Brno 1936 (Reprint Berlin 1975); *Kurt Seelmann*, Hegels Strafrechtslehre in seinen "Gundlinien der Philosophie des Rechts", JuS 1979, 687 ff.; *Naucke/Harzer,* Rechtsphilosophische Grundbegriffe, p. 79 ff.; *Daniela Tafani,* Pena e libertà in Hegel, in: Carla De Pascale (Ed.), La civetta di Minerva. Studi di filosofia politica tra Kant e Hegel. Pisa (Edizione ETS) 2007, p. 197 ff.; on individual aspects of his theory of criminal law, see *Klesczewski*, Hegels Straftheorie; further references in *Vormbaum*, MdtStrD, p. 365.

(negation), and in disputing and grappling with it returns to itself (negation of the negation), but not in the sense of restoring its original state, but rather on a qualitatively new level, for it has "proved" itself in the preceding dispute; both the original state as well as its opposite are thus sublated.[45] This three-part step not only characterises the general structure of world progress, but is reproduced in its individual aspects. Thus dialectics shape every sphere of life. Everything that is limited has an opposite that challenges it and that it must grapple with. This also goes for law and right. Where there is right, there is also wrong.[46] In grappling with wrong, right must "prove" itself, in order to subsequently return to itself on a new qualitative level, as "proven", strengthened and established right.[47]

An obvious (and historically likely realistic) objection would be: why is wrong not that which is posited, i.e. the thesis, and right its antithesis? Hegel answers this question by denying crime any (rational) existence of its own; it is exhausted in the negation of right. In criminal law in particular, it becomes obvious that crime in the end is simply a function of law: the offences of criminal law define *wrong*, i.e. that which negates right. Thus wrong's illusory existence only derives from right. The will of the criminal directed at wrong is thus an "individual will which has being only for itself".[48]

Punishment thus is the negation of the negation of right which is constituted by crime. Right proving itself against wrong however assumes that the criminal him- or herself is recognised as a rational being, for right can only prove itself as an expression of rationality by grappling with wrong: "For it is implicit in his action, as that of a *rational* being, that it is universal in character, and that, by performing it, he has set up a law which he has recognized for himself in his action, and under which he may therefore be subsumed as under *his* right." Similarly to Kant, Hegel claims that punishment for the sake of right must be derived from the crime itself, with no consideration of its purpose or usefulness: "In so far as the punishment which this [i.e., the criminal's actions] entails is seen as embodying *the criminal's own right*, the criminal is *honoured* as a rational being. He is denied this honour if the concept and criterion of his punishment are not derived from his own act".

Feuerbach's theory of general deterrence by threatening punishment is thus rejected. According to Hegel, it "presupposes that human beings are not free, and seeks to coerce them through the representation [*Vorstellung*] of an evil. But right and justice must have their seat in freedom and the will, and not in that lack of freedom at which the threat is directed. To justify punishment in this way is like

---

[45] Translator's note: Hegel uses the German word *aufgehoben*, which combines the meanings of "eliminated" and "lifted up".

[46] It can even be said—with what only appears to be a paradox: Justice produces injustice; *Flechtheim*, p. 93.

[47] Of course, this brief sketch represents a gross simplification of Hegel's thought. A more precise account of Hegel's differentiated thoughts on levels of injustice can be found in *Vormbaum*, MdtStrD, p. 137 ff.: unprejudiced injustice, deception, crime—this three-part division has not been able to establish itself; particularly the term "deception", which differs completely from usual terminology, has suffered general rejection; on this, see *Flechtheim*, p. 78 f.

[48] *Hegel*, Philosophy of Right, § 104, p. 131; see also *Flechtheim*, p. 84 f.

raising one's stick at a dog; it means treating a human being like a dog instead of respecting his honour and freedom".[49]

Hegel differs from Kant in regard to the practical consequences of criminal law primarily in that he understands retribution not in terms of an "equality in the specific character" of the punishment (like several philosophers of the Enlightenment before him, he points out the consequences of the "an eye for an eye, a tooth for a tooth" principle for one-eyed and toothless individuals), but of "equality [. . .] in its character in itself", of its value. On the level of value, theft and robbery on the one hand, and fines and imprisonment on the other are "comparable". However, he makes an exception for murder, "which necessarily incurs the death penalty. For since life is the entire compass of existence [*Dasein*], the punishment [for murder] cannot consist [*bestehen*] in a value—since none is equivalent to life—but only in the taking of another life".[50]

In *basic* terms, the difference between Kant and Hegel lies in the way they view the position of the state. Both agree that the state should ensure the individual citizen's freedom. In Hegel, however, the state is not only the means of securing justice (and thus freedom), but "the means by which freedom actually becomes freedom in the first place. Freedom guaranteed by law is part of the state. [. . .] The opinion that freedom is only arbitrary will or whim is on the rise once more".[51] Over the next one hundred years, this idealisation of the role of the state led to the frequent use of Hegel's theory in support of authoritarian concepts of state and society.

c) General Tendencies

The aspects in which the theories of Kant and Feuerbach, and later Hegel, overlap (see the conclusion of § 2) dominated the theory and practice of criminal law for much of the nineteenth century. These aspects consist of a combination between the theory of retribution and general deterrence. Phrases that imply an absolute theory of punishment according to Kant are usually employed to bolster ideas of general deterrence.[52] This proclamation of theories of general deterrence using Kantian terminology is usually successful because—similarly to Feuerbach—terms understood as transcendental concepts, such as state, right and freedom, are transformed into empirical terms. For the theorists of law that use these Kantian phrases, the guarantee of external freedom—which for Kant is the precondition of being able to act morally—becomes the precondition of a quiet and secure life, i.e. of securing peace. Kant's philosophy is thus turned into a vehicle presenting utilitarian punishments as just punishments.[53]

---

[49] *Hegel*, Philosophy of Right, § 99, addition.

[50] Op. cit., § 101, p. 129 f.

[51] *Naucke/Harzer*, Rechtsphilosophische Grundbegriffe, p. 88 f.

[52] *Naucke*, Einfluss Kants, esp. p. 144 ff.

[53] Ibid., p. 149.

Fig. 9 Carl Joseph Anton Mittermaier (1787–1867)

Hegelian theory of criminal law develops in a similar way. This theory gains many followers among legal theorists, who—after some initial hesitation[54]—work their way through its doctrinal details. The most important among them are **Julius Friedrich Heinrich Abegg** (1796–1868),[55] **Albert Friedrich Berner** (1818–1907),[56] **Christian Reinhold Köstlin** (1813–1856)[57] and **Hugo Hälschner** (1817–1889).[58] The Hegelians' characteristic style, which tends to dress up simple statements in elaborate language, at first glance may appear to encourage the continuation of the Hegelian theory of "retribution negating injustice".[59] However, a closer examination reveals that ideas of deterrence, particularly general deterrence, into which theories of punishment are "smuggled", are sometimes prevalent even among the Hegelians (Figs. 9, 10, 11, and 12).[60]

[54] On this, see *Loenig*, ZStW 3 (1883), p. 219 ff., p. 349.

[55] On Abegg, see *Eb. Schmidt*, Einführung, § 269 (p. 297 ff.); *Müller*, Generalprävention, p. 224 ff.; in general, *Stintzing/Landsberg*, Geschichte III, 2, p. 669 ff.

[56] On Berner, see *Eb. Schmidt*, Einführung, § 270 (p. 299 ff.); *Stintzing/Landsberg*, Geschichte III, 2, p. 680 ff.; on his textbook of criminal law see *Radbruch*, Drei Strafrechtslehrbücher, op. cit., p. 13 ff.

[57] On Köstlin, see *Eb. Schmidt*, Einführung, § 268 (p. 295 ff.); *Stintzing/Landsberg*, Geschichte III, 2, p. 672 ff.; *Müller*, Generalprävention, p. 229 ff.; see also the excerpt in *Vormbaum*, MdtStrD, p. 165 ff.

[58] On Hälschner, see *Eb. Schmidt*, Einführung, § 271 (p. 301 ff.); *Stintzing/Landsberg*, Geschichte, III, 2, p. 669 ff.

[59] *Müller*, Generalprävention, p. 138.

[60] On this, see the references in the preceding footnotes.

Fig. 10 Johann Michael Franz Birnbaum (1792–1877)

Fig. 11 Johann Gottlieb Fichte (1762–1814)

Fig. 12 Georg Wilhelm Friedrich Hegel (1770–1831)

3. *Doctrinal Issues*

a) Understanding of Law

In the nineteenth century, the influence of Feuerbach and of the philosophy of the Enlightenment dominated the understanding of law. However, the principle *nullum crimen, nulla poena sine lege* was only gradually recognised in writings of the time. During the first decades of the century, voices were still found in literature demanding that unwritten criminal law—whether as a revival of the idea of a "natural" crime, or under the influence of the German Historical School—be taken into account.[61] Over the course of the century, the principle was established. One of its most vehement opponents towards the end of the nineteenth century was *Karl Binding*. As has already been described, Binding criticised the doctrine of infringement of rights as an "expression of narrowness and restriction", and in this point, too, he fails to live up to the reputation as a liberal which he still enjoys to the present day. He spoke of the "tyranny" exercised by the *nullum crimen, nulla poena sine lege* principle. He was able to base this position on his theory of law, according to which *penal laws* are not directed at the (potential) offender, but at those in charge of the application of law. Only (frequently unwritten) prohibitions are

[61] *Schreiber*, Gesetz und Richter, p. 121 ff., 124 ff.

directed at the offender, and according to Binding it is only these prohibitions that he should have been aware of. For these reasons Binding considered the regulation made in § 2 RStGB a mistake.[62]

The increasingly positivistic nature of criminal law derived not least from the tradition of legal certainty and specificity established by Feuerbach. Two opposing interests appear to have come together in the tendency to restrict judicial discretionary powers. On the one hand, the Enlightenment and its philosophy of law had regarded professional judges with suspicion—a suspicion that remained even after the Enlightenment period. On the other hand, those in power during the nineteenth century were wary of judges who, on account of their recognised independence, were not under their control. The liberals who in the course of the nineteenth century, particularly its second half, had fought to have a say in legislation, also had an interest in ensuring the judges appointed by the ruler were bound by the laws that the parliamentary representatives of liberalism had helped to shape.

After the end of his legislative activity, the father of the theoretical principle *nullum crimen sine lege*, Feuerbach, was confronted with the practical ramifications of his law, first as an advisor in clemency matters in the Bavarian Ministry of Justice, then as a judge in Bamberg and Ansbach. He later distanced himself from the rigour of his code and granted judicial discretionary powers a greater role in his draft reform of 1824.[63]

b) Individual Issues

In line with positivist and historical thinkers, the main emphasis of the nineteenth century debate on criminal theory shifted from the theory of crime and criminal policy to the doctrine of criminal law. Partly building on the dogmatic lines to be found in the *ius commune* and the Enlightenment,[64] but above all on French criminal law, and developing new patterns of argumentation, the criminal theory of the nineteenth century coined **definitions of offences** still valid today in many areas of the General Part[65] and the Special Part[66] of the core criminal law. The

[62] *Schreiber*, Gesetz und Richter, p. 169 ff., Binding's followers and opponents are also presented here (p. 174 ff.).

[63] For more detail, see *Gernot Schubert*, Feuerbachs Entwurf zu einem Strafgesetzbuch für das Königreich Bayern aus dem Jahre 1824. Berlin 1978.

[64] On this, see the collected contributions of *Friedrich Schaffstein*, Abhandlungen zur Strafrechtsgeschichte. Aalen 1986 (including on homicide, lèse majesté, robbery and blackmail, coercion, fraud and the development of a system of offences).

[65] See e.g. on the **doctrine of attempt** *Sergio Seminara*, Versuchsproblematik, op. cit., with many quotes from contemporary literature; on the **doctrine of secondary participation**, where under the influence of French law the doctrine of intellectual authorship was gradually replaced by the three-part division of principal offender, abetting and aiding still valid today, see *Raimund Hergt*, Die Lehre von der Teilnahme am Verbrechen. Heidelberg 1909; an overview is provided in *Dennis Miller*, Die Beteiligung am Verbrechen nach italienischem Recht. Frankfurt am Main 2006, p. 64 ff.; on **derivative omission offences** see *Manfred Seebode*, Zur gesetzlichen Bestimmtheit des unechten Unterlassungsdelikts, in: Festschrift für Günter Spendel (1992), p. 317 ff.

[66] On this in reference to territorial legislation, see II. below.

theory of criminal law and the attempts to codify criminal law that set in throughout all states of the German Confederation during the first third of the nineteenth century (on this, see II. below) benefited from mutual exchange. The gradual recognition of the principle of *nullum crimen sine lege* strengthened attempts to define criminal offences as closely as possible.

This was evident in the doctrine of **political criminal law** among other things. The term of *crimen laesae majestatis*, which during the eighteenth century was still used to cover all crimes against the state, was broken down and structured from the beginning of the nineteenth century onwards. A distinction between the two forms of treason *Hochverrat* (high treason against a person) and *Landesverrat* (treason against a nation) is first found in the Prussian Civil Code of 1794[67] and is defined even more precisely in the theory of Kleinschrod and Feuerbach; the definition of *Majestätsbeleidigung*, lèse majesté, was narrowed as part of this development.[68] This new structure entered the literature under the influence of Feuerbach's textbook, it entered the Bavarian Criminal Code of 1813 under the influence of his legislative activity, and from thence it entered territorial legislation.

II. Penal Legislation

1. The Influence of French Legislation

Penal legislation in Germany in the nineteenth century is strongly influenced by French legislation of the late eighteenth and early nineteenth centuries. In 1789, the Revolutionary National Constituent Assembly's legislation[69], inspired by Voltaire, Beccaria, Rousseau and other thinkers of the Enlightenment, produces the Declaration of the Rights of Man and of the Citizen, which is subsequently integrated into the constitution, realising the key demands of Enlightenment philosophy in criminal and criminal procedural law[70] and abolishing estates-based privileges among other things. After a brief period during which the death penalty was abolished, the guillotine—the "great leveller"—becomes the icon of egalitarian revolutionary

[67] Arguing against the opinion that this innovation is due to the influence of the famous 1782 essay by Hanns Ernst v. Globig and Johann Georg Huster, Abhandlung von der Criminal-Gesetzgebung, *Schroeder*, Schutz von Staat und Verfassung, p. 39 f.; on the essay by Globig/Huster *Stefani Schmidt,* Die Abhandlung von der Criminal-Gesetzgebung von Hanns Ernst von Globig und Johann Georg Huster. Berlin 1990.

[68] More detail in *Schroeder*, Schutz von Staat und Verfassung, p. 48 ff.; *A. Hartmann,* Majestätsbeleidigung, p. 11 ff. A collection of pertinent texts, including by Globig/Huster, Kleinschrod, Feuerbach, can be found in *Friedrich-Christian Schroeder* (Hrsg.), Texte zur Theorie des politischen Strafrechts Ende des 18. Jh./Mitte des 19. Jh. Darmstadt 1974.

[69] *Wolfgang Naucke,* Zur Entwicklung des Strafrechts in der französischen Revolution, in: Id., Zerbrechlichkeit, p. 29 ff.

[70] For a discussion of the concept of the public and of public prosecutors up to the French Revolution, see *Haber*, ZStW 91 (1979), 189 ff.

criminal law.[71] It was not only with the Revolution's sudden descent into terror, carried out in the name of (alleged) good[72], which set it in action. Political revolutionary protective legislation openly uses the threat of capital punishment. The two aims of making humanity happy and utility entwine in political practice. Laws contain preambles whose undertones threaten the enemies of the Revolution. The Rousseau-esque aversion to corporations, *corps intermediaires* standing between the individual and the state,[73] thus takes on legal form in anti-corporation legislation enforced by punishment. Evidence would appear to support the claim that the totalitarian traits appearing openly during the Reign of Terror from 1791 onwards were already present (if latently so) beforehand.[74] After Napoleon's gradual accession to power, the five Napoleonic codes (Code civile, Code de procédure civile, Code de commerce, Code pénal, Code d'instruction criminelle) created a technically exemplary legislation that put a clear authoritarian spin on the humanitarian and utilitarian principles it proclaimed.

In the form of Napoleonic law, French criminal and criminal procedural legislation (Code d'instruction criminelle of 1808; Code pénal of 1810), together with other social and legal achievements following the Corsican's wars of expansion and conquest, became the model for the reform of states with late feudal and/or absolutist constitutions. Of course, these reforms—particularly in criminal procedural law—partly only set in with considerable delay in the context of the 1848/49 revolution. French law influenced the founding of many Napoleonic states, particularly in Germany, Italy and Poland (Grand Duchy of Warsaw). In Germany, these were the Grand Duchy of Berg and the Kingdom of Westphalia.

With the *Kingdom of Westphalia*[75] and the *Grand Duchy of Warsaw*, Napoleon had placed two states with which he wanted to make "moral conquests" on Prussia's flanks. The 1807 constitution of the **Kingdom of Westphalia** declared open justice of judicial proceedings and jury courts—two procedural institutions that only became generally widespread across Germany 40 years later. The new institutions

---

[71] On this, see *Daniel Arasse*, Die Guillotine. Die Macht der Maschine und das Schauspiel der Gerechtigkeit. Reinbek bei Hamburg 1988.

[72] In German literature, this is depicted most famously in *Georg Büchner's* drama "Dantons Tod" (Danton's Death); text with a critical literary commentary by Sven Kramer and a critical legal commentary by Bodo Pieroth: in Section "Role of the accused; defence" (Recht in der Kunst—Kunst im Recht) of the series "Juristische Zeitgeschichte". Berlin 2007.

[73] On this, see *Thomas Vormbaum*, Die Rechtsfähigkeit der Vereine im 19. Jahrhundert. Berlin 1976, p. 29 ff.

[74] On all this, see *Naucke,* Revolution, p. 44 f.

[75] *Helmut Berding*, Napoleonische Herrschafts- und Gesellschaftspolitik im Königreich Westfalen 1807–1813. Göttingen 1973; *Heiner Lück/Mathias Tullner* (Eds.), Königreich Westphalen (1807–1813). Eine Spurensuche. (Sachsen-Anhalt. Geschichte und Geschichten. 2007/5). s.l. 2007; *Elisabeth Fehrenbach*, Traditionelle Gesellschaft und revolutionäres Recht. Die Einführung des Code Napoléon in den Rheinbundstaaten. 2nd edition Göttingen 1978; *Heinz-Otto Sieburg*, Die Auswirkungen des napoleonischen Herrschaftssystems auf die Verfassungsentwicklung in Deutschland, in: Id. (Ed.), Napoleon und Europa. Cologne 1971, p. 201 ff.—On developments in Italy, see *Dezza*, Beiträge, *Id.,* Kodifikationszeitalter (**Cisalpine Republic**, first Kingdom of **Italy**, Duchy of **Lucca**, Duchy of **Piombino**, Kingdom of **Naples**).

already took up their tasks in March 1808.[76] However, their activities suffered, as attempts to pass a new criminal code for the kingdom remained unsuccessful.[77] With the end of the Westphalian Kingdom, French law also lost its influence there—unlike in the Rhineland (on which see below). After 1815, the successor states of Brunswick, Hannover, Electoral Hesse and Prussia abolished French laws. Nonetheless, occasionally their subtle influence can be detected.[78]

Prussia was a special case. After its defeat in 1806 it had remained a state due to Russian intervention, if somewhat diminished in territory. The Stein-Hardenberg reforms[79] (which of course did not affect criminal law) set a process of "defensive modernisation"[80] in motion; this process was indebted both to the objective need for reform and a desire to become more aligned with Napoleonic reforms in the states of the Confederation of the Rhine, and in fact served to prepare for the so-called wars of liberation, which could only be won by calling up large parts of the population (introduction of compulsory military service!).[81]

French criminal and criminal procedure law remained in place even after 1815 in the territories left of the Rhine, that had belonged to France between 1797/1801 (Treaties of Campo Formio and Lunéville) and 1815 (Congress of Vienna).[82] The attempts of the new Prussian authorities to extend Prussian law (particularly the General Code of 1794 and the Criminal Code of 1805) to the new Rhine Province were foiled by the resistance of the Rhenish middle classes, who had learnt to value

[76] In greater detail *Christian zur Nedden*, Die Strafrechtspflege im Königreich Westphalen (1807 bis 1813). Frankfurt am Main. 2003. The author uses the example of a cause célèbre (p. 38 ff.) to detail the new criminal proceedings and show the practical difficulties faced in dealing with this new law.

[77] In detail on the reasons for this *zur Nedden*, Westphalen, S. 27 ff.; the text of the Westphalian Code Pénal, which was completed but did not become law, in *Werner Schubert* (Ed. and introduction), Der Code Pénal des Königreichs Westphalen von 1813 mit dem Code Pénal von 1810 im Original und in deutscher Übersetzung. Frankfurt am Main 2001.

[78] Individual details in *zur Nedden,* Westphalen, p. 134 ff.; *Knollmann,* Einführung, p. 98 ff.; the views of the Brunswick (temporarily Westphalian) jurist **Friedrich Karl vom Strombeck** (1771–1848) can be found in *Cipolla*, Strombeck, particularly p. 51 ff.

[79] On these, see *Eisenhardt*, Rechtsgeschichte, p. 299 ff.

[80] On this particular trait of German modernisation, a politics of "reform as a response to the challenges of the revolution" which was later to become characteristic of the whole of Germany, see *Hans Ulrich Wehler*, Gesellschaftsgeschichte. Vol. 1, p. 363 ff.

[81] That the wars of liberation were fought against the country of the "ideas of 1789" (however stunted these ideas had become) meant that the German nationalism emerging at this time had a strongly anti-libertarian element from the very beginning (*Heinrich von Kleist* wrote in a poem: "Kill him! You will not be asked why at the Last Judgment"). From quite early on, this also included anti-Semitic utterances, noted perceptively for example by Heinrich Heine; on this, see *Vormbaum*, Judeneid, p. 213 ff.; *Id.*, Einführung Heine, p. 27 ff.

[82] General information on the continued validity of French law in the Rhineland (Baden, Rhine-Hesse, the Bavarian Palatinate, Rhenish Prussia) in *Eisenhardt*, Rechtsgeschichte, p. 312 ff.

the French institutions.[83] The insight that Prussian law could not be transposed to the Rhineland led to a comprehensive revision of law that lasted for several decades and only reached its preliminary conclusion in regard to substantive criminal law in 1851, and in 1849 in regard to criminal procedure law.

Of particular importance, though not uncontroversial in Germany,[84] was the **three-part division of criminal offences** in French law *(crimes, délits, contraventions)*, which had its respective counterpart in court jurisdiction *ratione materiae*. Prussian legislation was the means by which this three-part division entered the Reich Criminal Code of 1870/71, subsequently becoming common across the Reich. The Code divided offences into *Verbrechen* (felonies), *Vergehen* (misdemeanours) and *Übertretungen* (transgressions). The Constitution of Courts Act of 1877/79 created a (somewhat modified) counterpart to this three-part division in relation to court jurisdiction *ratione materiae*.

2. *German Territorial Criminal Law*

a) Criminal Law Outside Prussia

There were several reasons for the wave of codifications in the area of criminal law that occurred in the states of the German Confederation in the course of the nineteenth century. This urge to codify, typical of Enlightenment thought, had already found expression in the *codifications of natural law* in Bavaria, Prussia and Austria,[85] and had remained acute in criminal law despite the objections raised by the German Historical School that had led to a delay in the willingness to engage in the codification of civil law. *Feuerbach's* theory of psychological compulsion

[83] *Hermann Conrad,* Preußen und das französische Recht in den Rheinlanden, in: Josef Wolfram/ Adolf Klein (Eds.), Recht und Rechtspflege in den Rheinlanden. Cologne 1969, p. 78 ff.; *Ernst Landsberg,* Die Gutachten der rheinischen Immediat-Justizkommission und der Kampf um die rheinische Rechts- und Gerichtsverfassung 1814–1819. (Publikationen der Gesellschaft für rheinische Geschichtskunde. XXXI) Bonn 1914.—That the Rhenish middle classes' high regard for French institutions was based not only on progressive ideals but had its self-interested side is shown in *Dirk Blasius*, Der Kampf um die Geschworenengerichte im Vormärz, in: Sozialgeschichte heute. Festschrift f. Hans Rosenberg. Göttingen 1974, p. 148 ff. The resistance of the Rhenish parliament to the draft criminal code of 1843 was directed against the lowering of the punishment for theft, which meant that this would no longer fall within the remit of jury courts, and which had led—due to the severe punishments threatened by French criminal law against property offences—to a drastic reduction in numbers. *Blasius*, p. 158: "the bitter edge [to the conflict regarding the jury courts] derived not from the political processes, which were nonexistent in the Rhine Province; the jury court seems to have been less the Palladium of civil liberty than the Palladium of bourgeois property rights".

[84] On its rejection by Saxon theory of criminal law, see e.g. *Weber*, Sächsisches Strafrecht, p. 172 ff.

[85] As already discussed in § 2 II.

demanded the positivisation of criminal law, a demand taken up by *legal positivism*, for which this positivisation provided the only true legitimation of criminal law. The aspect of legal certainty, providing protection against the authorities, was particularly important for political *liberalism*.

Besides the French Code Pénal, the **Bavarian Criminal Code of 1813**—significantly influenced by Feuerbach—served as a model for German territorial criminal codes. Following the French model, the code divided punishable acts into felonies, misdemeanours and police offences[86] to be sentenced by different courts and by the police in the case of police offences. Austrian influence (law of 1803) is evident in the punishments (Art. 4 ff.). Capital punishment is carried out publicly through beheading; severe capital punishment (*verschärfte Todesstrafe*) only means that "the criminal is exposed in the pillory for half an hour [. . .] immediately prior to the execution" (Art. 6).

Both the nature and extent of punishments remain very severe. This can be seen in Art. 215 (punishment of simple theft), which also serves as an example of how the judge's activity is restricted:

> If a thief has stolen the sum of twenty-five guilders of Bavarian Reich currency or above, either in money or in monetary value, he is to be sentenced to one year in the workhouse, and this sentence is to be extended by as many quarters of a year as the value of the stolen property contains the sum of fifty guilders; but the duration of the punishment may not be extended to longer than eight years.

Where the judge's discretion is less restricted (Art. 90: "in so far as the law does not determine the degree of punishment. . ."), he is to "take due consideration, partly of the nature of the act to be punished as such, partly of the extent of the unlawfulness of the criminal will". However, the law does not leave it at that, but subsequently provides the judge with guidelines in 28 articles (including some still common today on *concursus delictorum* and reoffending).

Even though over time it increasingly came to be seen as excessively harsh and doctrinaire, the Bavarian Criminal Code served as a model for other German criminal codes. In 1814, 1 year after its enactment, it was adopted in the **Grand Duchy of Oldenburg**, but revised in 1858.[87] By the 1860s all German territories, with the exception of Mecklenburg, possessed criminal codes.[88] In **Bavaria** itself a new criminal code came into force in 1861.[89]

---

[86] On the *legal-theoretical* importance of this differentiation, see I. 1. above.

[87] On this *Berner*, Strafgesetzgebung, p. 320 ff.; Text in *Stenglein*, Vol. 1, No. II.

[88] Overview over the territorial criminal codes in *Kesper-Biermann*, Einheit und Recht, p. 119 ff.; for a cross total of the procedures when enacting the codes ibid., p. 165 ff.

[89] On this *Berner*, Strafgesetzgebung, p. 324 ff.; *Müller*, Generalprävention, p. 273 ff.; Text in *Ludwig Weis,* Das Strafgesetzbuch für das Königreich Bayern sammt dem Gesetze vom 10. November 1861 zur Einführung des Strafgesetzbuchs und des Polizeistrafgesetzbuchs erläutert. 2 volumes. Nördlingen 1863/1865.

Criminal codes were enacted in the **Kingdom of Württemberg** 1839),[90] in the **Duchy of Brunswick** (1840),[91] in the **Kingdom of Hannover** (1840),[92] in the **Grand Duchy of Hesse** (1841),[93] and in the **Grand Duchy of Baden** (1845)[94]; the **Thuringian states** (Saxe-Weimar, Schwarzburg-Sondershausen, Schwarzburg-Rudolstadt, Anhalt-Dessau, Anhalt-Köthen, Saxe-Meiningen, Saxe-Coburg-Gotha, Reuss Younger Line) largely followed an 1850 draft model[95]; in the **Austrian Empire** (which was part of the German Confederation until 1866) the 1803 code was revised in 1852.[96]

The **Kingdom of Saxony** serves as an example of seemingly never-ending reforms in criminal law: in the nineteenth century it enacted no fewer than three criminal codes (1838, 1855, 1868)[97], each preceded by several drafts, all of them fully worded.[98] Saxony was one of the states of the Confederation in which the death penalty was abolished,[99] but had to be reintroduced following the enactment of the Reich Criminal Code, as a compromise—to retain the abolition of capital punishment in those states that had renounced it—had been rejected.[100] The position of Saxony, which had twice made the wrong political choice during the nineteenth century (it had clung to its alliance with Napoleon the longest during the wars of liberation, and it had allied itself with Austria in the 1866 Austro-Prussian War), proved weak here as in many other points in the face of opposing

[90] On this *Mittermaier*, Fortentwicklung, p. 47 ff.; *Berner*, Strafgesetzgebung, p. 107 ff.; Text in *Stenglein*, Vol. 1, No. IV. As early as 1829, the Brunswick jurist Friedrich Karl von Strombeck had published a "Draft of a criminal code for a North German state" which no longer included capital punishment; the code of 1840 did not follow this suggestion; for more detail, see *Cipolla*, Strombeck, p. 113 ff., 212.

[91] On this *Mittermaier*, Fortentwicklung, Vol. 1, p. 85 ff.; *Berner*, Strafgesetzgebung, p. 135 ff.; Text in *Stenglein*, Vol. 1, No. V.

[92] On this *Mittermaier*, Fortentwicklung, Vol. 1, p. 93 ff.; *Berner*, Strafgesetzgebung, p. 157 ff.; Text in *Stenglein*, Vol. 2, No. VI.

[93] On this *Berner*, Strafgesetzgebung, p. 172 ff.; Text in *Stenglein*, Vol. 2, No. VII.

[94] On this *Berner*, Strafgesetzgebung, p. 197 ff.; Text in *Stenglein*, Vol. 2, No. VIII.

[95] On this *Berner*, Strafgesetzgebung, p. 208 ff.; Text in *Stenglein*, Vol. 3, No. X.

[96] On this *Berner*, Strafgesetzgebung, p. 273 ff.; Text in *Stenglein*, Vol. 3, No. XII.

[97] On the drafts of 1838 and 1855 *Berner*, Strafgesetzgebung, p. 92 ff., 304 ff. Text of the 1855 criminal code in *Stenglein*, Vol. 3, No. XIII.

[98] On this *Berner*, Strafgesetzgebung, S. 135 ff.; for a detailed account, see *Judith Weber*, Sächsisches Strafrecht. Berlin 2009.

[99] King John had championed the abolition of capital punishment, which took place after a lengthy phase of experimentation and much debate in the parliamentary houses; for more detail, see *Weber*, Sächsisches Strafrecht, Chapter 7 B) I. 2.; besides Saxony, the main state in which it was abolished (except in martial law and maritime law for mutiny) as early as 1858 was **Oldenburg**, even though it followed the Prussian Criminal Code of 1851 in most other aspects (on this *Berner*, Strafgesetzgebung, p. 323); it was also abolished in **Anhalt** and **Bremen** (*Sten. Ber. des Reichstags des Norddeutschen Bundes*, Term I. Session 1870. Vol. 3. Printed matter no. 5. Attachment 2, p. VII ff., XVII ff.). Majorities in many German parliaments during the 1860s had declared themselves in favour of capital punishment, without these resolutions being acted upon; *Evans*, Rituale, p. 400 ff.

[100] In detail, *Weber*, Sächsisches Strafrecht, p. 161 ff.

Prussian demands. The proposals of the Saxon member of the committee for the North German criminal code, *Oscar von Schwarze,*[101] were usually voted down. The influence of Saxon criminal law on the later Reich Criminal Code can only be detected in a few individual points, such as the offence of mercy killing (*Tötung auf Verlangen*).[102]

The decades of legislative work in the states of the German Confederation provided material for refining criminal law doctrine, above all for defining the most important criminal offences in the forms still current today.[103]

During much of the nineteenth century, legislators were concerned with restricting judiciary discretion as much as possible. The official notes on the Brunswick Criminal Code of 1840 are typical in this regard[104]:

> It is an irrefutable demand that, in every well-ordered state, everyone should know in advance which acts are crimes and which punishment they are threatened with. [...] The freest nations have chosen to instruct the judge in carrying out laws to the letter, and suffer the severity and inconsistency this must inevitably result in rather than give arbitrariness any leeway.

Nonetheless, over the course of the century a relaxing of the range of sentences in the extreme example of the Bavarian Criminal Code of 1813 can be observed. These result partly from less than satisfactory practical experiences, partly from the theoretical and intellectual opposition to the "doctrinaire" criminal law described above.[105] However, on the whole the principle *nullum crimen, nulla poena sine lege* came to be included in all emergent criminal codes and constitutions in the course of the nineteenth century.[106]

---

[101] On Schwarze, see *Werner Schubert,* Die Kommission zur Beratung des Entwurfs eines Strafgesetzbuchs für den Norddeutschen Bund, in: Schubert/Vormbaum, Entstehung des StGB, p. XI ff., XXIV f.

[102] On this *Große-Vehne*, Tötung auf Verlangen, p. 28 ff.

[103] On **criminal offences against the state**, see *Schroeder*, Schutz von Staat und Verfassung, p. 56 ff.; on **fraud**, see *Schütz*, Betrugsbegriff, p. 162 ff., 247 ff.; on **the offence of omitting to effect an easy rescue** see *Gieseler*, p. 5 ff.; on **criminal and terrorist/anarchist organisations** see *Felske*, p. 62 ff.; on the **failure to report a crime** see *Kisker*, p. 17 ff.; on **duelling** see *Baumgarten*, p. 82 ff.; on **abortion** see *Koch*, p. 29 ff.; on **theft** see *Prinz*, p. 4 ff.; on **false accusation** see *Bernhard*, p. 13 ff.; on **arson** see *Lindenberg*, p. 6 ff.; on **assault** see *Korn*, p. 26 ff.; on the **unauthorised publication of official documents** see *Voßieck*, p. 22 ff.; on **perverting the course of justice** see *Thiel*, p. 31 ff.; on **mercy killing** see *Große-Vehne*, p. 13 ff.; on the **frustration of creditors' rights** see *Seemann*, p. 22 ff.; on **lèse majesté** see *Andrea Hartmann*, p. 59 ff.; on **prostitution and procurement** see *Ilya Hartmann*, p. 42 ff.; on **trespassing** see *Rampf*, p. 34 ff.; on **embezzlement and unlawful appropriation** see *Rentrop*, p. 19 ff.; on **forgery of documents** see *Prechtel*, p. 15 ff.

[104] Cit. in *Berner,* Strafgesetzgebung, p. 140, 142.

[105] *Hälschner*, Geschichte, p. 259 ff.; on how Feuerbach distanced himself from his strict views on how the judge should be bound by the law, see above footnote 61.

[106] *Schreiber*, Gesetz und Richter, p. 156 ff., who also points out that some provisions of the constitutions and laws could be interpreted in such a way that the application of law by way of analogy became permissible.

b) Prussia

aa) Codification Process

The development in the **Kingdom of Prussia** is of particular importance, not only because of its aforementioned particularities, but also in general terms.[107] The General Code of 1794 was very soon seen to be in need of revision. For various reasons (restriction of judicial discretion, deterrent effect of the threat of punishment), many of its offences did not meet the standards of specificity required. The first small corrections (rescripts, amendments, etc.) were soon attempted, but these only led to the General Code becoming even more confusing. As early as December 1799, a complete revision of the part relating to criminal law by *Ernst Ferdinand Klein* was therefore decreed.[108]

However, the aforementioned external impetus provided by the acquisition of the Rhenish territories was necessary in order to initiate a comprehensive reform of criminal law—which was of course to take over 30 years to complete. Given the resistance of the middle classes of the Rhineland[109], the Prussian heads of state realised that any standardisation of law required a new legal foundation.[110] The process of revision was to be speeded up by the creation of a special "Ministry for the Reform of Legislation and Judicial Organisation in the New Provinces" (3 November 1817–31 December 1819), headed initially by *v. Beyme*. After the two Ministries of Justice had been merged once more in 1825, the new Minister of Justice *Count Danckelmann* put together a Committee for the Revision of Criminal Law.[111] It was presented with a draft developed by supreme court justice *Bode* in **1828.**[112] On 22 May 1830 the Committee concluded its deliberations on *Bode's* draft, and Minister of Justice *Danckelmann* presented the State Ministry with a slightly altered draft version (**E 1830**; E here stands for *Entwurf*, draft).[113]

---

[107] *Wolfgang Naucke,* Hauptdaten der preußischen Strafrechtsgeschichte 1786–1806, in: Id., Zerbrechlichkeit, p. 49 ff.

[108] *Schubert/Regge*, Gesetzrevision, Vol. 1, p. XXIX.

[109] See footnote 81 above.

[110] For a description of the general process of legal reform up to 1842, see *v. Kamptz*, Aktenmäßige Darstellung der Preußischen Gesetz-Revision, in: Jahrbücher für die Preußische Gesetzgebung, Rechtswissenschaft und Rechtsverwaltung 60 (1842).

[111] The Commission was made up of: *Danckelmann*, *Kamptz*, *Sethe*, *Reibnitz*, *Köhler*, *Eichhorn*, *Sack*, *Müller*, *Savigny*, *Simon*, *Fischenich*, *Scheffer*, *Scheibler* and *Bötticher*; cf. *Schubert/Regge*, Gesetzrevision, Vol. 1, p. XVI f.

[112] Entwurf des Straf-Gesetz-Buches für die Preußischen Staaten, Berlin 1828, reprinted in: *Schubert/Regge*, Gesetzrevision, Vol. 1, p. 271 ff (302 f.).

[113] Entwurf des Straf-Gesetz-Buches für die Preußischen Staaten, Erster Theil. Criminal-Straf-Gesetze, Berlin 1830, reprinted in: *Schubert/Regge*, Gesetzrevision, Vol. 2, p. 467 ff. (500 ff.).—The changes compared to the draft of 1828 referred mainly to the abolition of corporal punishment, the preceding draft having retained these for the "lower classes"; *Hälschner*, Geschichte, p. 266.

After *Danckelmann's* death in late 1830, work on the reform was suspended and only resumed after *v. Kamptz* had been entrusted with continuing the legal reform process at the beginning of 1832.[114] In collaboration with *Bode*, v. Kamptz—who was now head of a separate "Ministry of Legal Reform" following yet another division of the Ministry of Justice—created the "Revised Draft of the Criminal Code for the States of the Kingdom of Prussia" (**E 1833**).[115] After a final thorough editing by *v. Kamptz* himself (**E 1836**)[116], this formed the basis of further deliberations. The revisions by Minister of the State v. Kamptz, who had infamously taken a hard line against all liberal tendencies during the period of the Restoration and the Vormärz,[117] mainly affected political criminal law.

> Not only was attempted treason classed as equal to the committed crime, but incitement to treason was also. In addition, there were detailed and severe punishments decreed for treasonous plots, banned organisations, the use of flags, symbols, ribbons and other signs of organisations and societies, as well for other acts leading to treason, and in such broad and vague terms, that those set on political persecution would not find it hard to characterise even the most inoffensive act as treasonous.[118]

The review of the new Immediate Committee led to the "Draft according to the Decrees of the Royal State Council" published in 1843 (**E 1843**),[119] which tempered the political exaggerations of v. Kamptz's draft. It was submitted to the eight provincial parliaments for consultation.[120] After a large number of written responses—including from the legal scholars who had been requested to evaluate the E 1843—had been received, *Savigny*, who had replaced *v. Kamptz* as Minister of Justice in 1842,[121] was entrusted with revising the material presented. This fresh revision resulted in the "Revised Draft of the Criminal Code for the Prussian States" of 1845 (**E 1845**)[122], which formed the basis for the negotiations of the Committee of the State Council. The Committee approved the draft with only minor changes. In the plenary of the State Council, the Rhenish lobbyists argued

---

[114] *Schubert/Regge*, Gesetzrevision, Vol. 1, p. XIII f.

[115] Reprinted in: *Schubert/Regge*, Gesetzrevision, Vol. 3, p. 1 ff. (35 ff.).

[116] Revidirter Entwurf des Strafgesetzbuchs für die Königlich-Preußischen Staaten. Berlin 1836, reprinted in: *Schubert/Regge*, Gesetzrevision, Vol. 3, p. 785 ff. (883 ff.).

[117] The poet and supreme court justice *E.T.A. Hoffmann*, who had himself suffered under v. Kamptz's persecution, made him an object of ridicule in his novella *Meister Floh* as the character of privy councillor Knarrpati; on this, see *Alfred Hoffmann,* E.T.A. Hoffmann. Leben und Arbeit eines preußischen Richters. Baden-Baden 1990.

[118] *Hälschner*, Geschichte, p. 268 (Readers will note that much of what Hälschner criticises [from the point of view of 1855, during the reactionary period itself!] is still contained in the federal German Criminal Code at the beginning of the twenty-first century.); see also *Schroeder*, Schutz von Staat und Verfassung, S. 73.

[119] Reprinted in: *Schubert/Regge*, Gesetzrevision, Vol. 5, p. 1 ff. (42 f.).

[120] *Schubert/Regge*, Gesetzrevision, Vol. 5, p. XIII; on one of the Rhenish provincial parliament's points of criticism, see footnote 81 above; on this also see *Hälschner*, Geschichte, p. 275 ff.

[121] On Savigny's part in the revisionary process, see *v. Arnswaldt*, Savigny, p. 104 ff.

[122] Reprinted in: *Schubert/Regge*, Gesetzrevision, Vol. 6, p. 1 ff. (32 f.).

that the draft was scarcely compatible with the judiciary of the Rhine Provinces and with jury trials.[123] Further consultation in the plenary of the State Council and the Committee produced the draft criminal code of 1847 (**E 1847**).[124] This draft, along with its *travaux préparatoires*, was submitted to the *Vereinigter Ständischer Ausschuss* (United Committee of the Estates), the representative of the Prussian United Parliament outside plenary meetings appointed to contribute and agree to matters of finance.[125] In its last meeting, the United Committee of the Estates voted not to continue work on a criminal code before the United Parliament had decided upon a new code of criminal procedure.[126] At least prior to this it had discarded severe capital punishment, confiscation of property and corporal punishment (corporal punishment had been temporarily re-adopted). For the first time, a three-part division of offences into felonies, misdemeanours and transgressions according to the French model was proposed, and the provisions on attempt and secondary participation were also strongly influenced by French criminal law. *Savigny* continued with his legal revisions, disregarding the Committee's decision to suspend them. In 1849, a further draft was produced (**E 1849**),[127] large sections of which[128] conformed to another earlier draft (**E 1848**).[129] This work was taken up once more after the failure of the Revolution and the German drive for unification; the "Draft of the Criminal Code for the Prussian States" of 10 December 1850 (**E 1850**)[130] was completed and, together with the appurtenant *travaux*, was submitted to the Upper and Lower Houses of the newly created Prussian Parliament as a "government bill". Deliberations lasted until 12 April 1851. On 14 April 1851, the new Criminal Code was signed by the King[131] and came into force on 1 July 1851.[132]

---

[123] *Schubert/Regge*, Gesetzrevision, Vol. 1, p. XLI.

[124] Entwurf des Strafgesetzbuchs für die Preußischen Staaten, nebst dem Entwurf des Gesetzes über die Einführung des Strafgesetzbuchs und dem Entwurf des Gesetzes über die Kompetenz und das Verfahren in dem Bezirke des Appellationsgerichtshofes zu Köln, reprinted in: *Schubert/Regge*, Gesetzrevision, Vol. 6 II, p. 735 ff. (765 f.)

[125] On the context of the formation of the Prussian United Parliament and the United Committee of the Estates, cf. *E.R. Huber*, Verfassungsgeschichte, Vol. 2, p. 488 ff.; cf. also *Bleich*, Verhandlungen des im Jahre 1848 zusammenberufenen Vereinigten Ständischen Ausschusses, Vol. 1, p. 2.

[126] *Schubert/Regge*, Gesetzrevision, Vol. 1, p. XLI.

[127] Cf. *Banke*, Entwurf, Vol. 2, Appendix p. 37 (65 f.).

[128] Entwurf des Strafgesetzbuchs für die Preußischen Staaten, Berlin 1848; cf. *Banke*, Entwurf, Vol. 1, Appendix p. 40 (60 f.).

[129] Cf. *Banke*, Entwurf, Vol. 1, p. 28 ff.

[130] Reprinted in: Stenographische Berichte über die Verhandlungen der durch die Allerhöchste Verordnung vom 2. November 1850 einberufenen Kammern, Berlin 1851, Lower House, Document No. 24.

[131] *Goltdammer*, Materialien zum Strafgesetzbuch für die preußischen Staaten, Vol. 1, p. XVI.

[132] Art. I of the Introductory Act of 14 April 1851 (Pr.GS., p. 93).

In 1869, when the North German Confederation was working on a new uniform criminal code, the Prussian **Criminal Code of 1851** formed the basis of their deliberation process and was later expanded with only slight changes into the Reich Criminal Code.

Similarly to the other territorial criminal codes, the Prussian Criminal Code reveals a level of legislative refinement that was the result of decade-long reform debates. This debate was reflected particularly strongly in property offences. It had the positive effect of creating clearly defined offences and thus an adherence to and confirmation of the principle of *nullum crimen sine lege*. § 2 of the Prussian Criminal Code (preußStGB) read as follows:

> No crime, no misdemeanour and no transgression can be subject to punishment unless it was defined by law before the act was committed.

The conservative turn in sexual ethics—already contained in the ideal of the family present in French legislation, and promoted by Romanticism and the Biedermeier Era—was supported in theory by the replacement of the doctrine of infringement of rights by the doctrine of infringement of legally protected interests, and had favoured an expansion (or rather, a non-reduction) of so-called offences against morality or "offences of the flesh".[133] In other respects, however, the liberal period achieved many reductions in offences.

For example, simple theft according to § 216 preußStGB was punishable with "imprisonment of no less than a month" (but according to § 14 was limited to a maximum of 5 years), compared to the punishment threatened in the Bavarian Criminal Code of 1813.

However, the frequent threat of capital punishment on the one hand and the system of mitigating circumstances on the other were subject to criticism.

bb) Individual Laws

Of course it would too simple to see the time of the "liberal state under the rule of law" as an era of continuous constitutional progress and leniency in criminal law. This would certainly present an oversimplification in the case of Germany, whose political progress was typically slow. An examination of criminal law beyond the codifications shows clearly that this kind of optimism regarding progress is unwarranted. The Prussian **Circular decree (*Zirkularverordnung*) on the punishment of theft and other similar crimes of 26 February 1799** shows not only remarkable severity, but also modern structures in a problematic sense. Its prologue already reveals its general bent; its function is cited there as "securing subjects' peaceful

---

[133] A critical evaluation of this can be found in *Holtzendorff*, Handbuch Vol. 1, p. 98 ff.; see also *Frommel*, Strafjustiz und Polizei, op. cit., p. 190. On the development of sexual offences, see *Andreas Roth*, Die Sittlichkeitsdelikte zwischen Religion und Rationalität. Strafrechtspraxis und Kriminalpolitik im 18./19. Jahrhundert, in: Schulze/Vormbaum et al., Strafzweck und Strafform, p. 195 ff.

possession of their property, preventing theft and robbery by setting deterrent examples, possibly reforming criminals, and if they are incapable of reform rendering them harmless to their fellow citizens".[134] A criminal convicted of repeated theft or violent robbery was to be released only once he had definitely reformed, could prove he was able to make an honest living and his release constituted no threat to public security.[135] The importance of this rule, which naturally had its precursors in the General Code,[136] can hardly be exaggerated. Here a current of development was preserved that remained weak during the development of Prussian and German criminal law, but was taken up once again at the beginning of the twentieth century.

At the same time it is evident that legal institutions which seem far apart in terms of doctrine often converge in reality. In terms of development, there is a connection between the extraordinary punishments of the criminal *ius commune*, the extraordinary punishments (on suspicion) issued after the abolition of torture, and the two-track model represented by the Prussian General Code and the Decree of 1799, both of which became the predecessors of the measures of rehabilitation and incapacitation introduced in 1933.[137] The Enlightenment thinker and "father" of the criminal law section of the General Code, *Ernst Ferdinand Klein*, was a major influence on the development of Prussian criminal law. He was the first to draw the theoretical distinction between "punishments" and "protective measures", using it to argue against extraordinary punishments, which he regarded as inexpedient.[138]

That a conflation of criminal law and police law occurs or is preserved here is evident in § 4 ALR II 20, the decree immediately preceding § 5 ALR II 20, which states that "beggars, vagrants and idlers are to be made to work; if they are foreigners, they are to be expelled from the country".[139]

In general history, the best remembered measures are the **Carlsbad Decrees of 1819** with their "combating of demagogues", prohibition of associations, restriction of press freedom and associated penal provisions.[140]

---

[134] Cit. according to *Hälschner*, Geschichte, p. 250.

[135] *Eb. Schmidt*, Einführung, p. 253; see also *Naucke*, Hauptdaten, op. cit., p. 52: "relapse into the pre-Enlightenment police state"; further information on problematic rules id. p. 52 f.

[136] For "thieves and other criminals", § 5 ALR II 20 stipulated, in addition to their punishment, the so-called *Erwerbsdetention*, "proof of income detention", i.e. further detention after the sentence had been served until the possibility of earning an honest income had been proven. § 1160 ALR II 20 went even further in the case of thrice convicted felons. These were to be "detained in a workhouse after serving their sentence and forced to labour [. . .] until they have reformed and have provided sufficient evidence of how they will earn their living honestly in future"; see *Eb. Schmidt*, Einführung, p. 252 f.

[137] It is no coincidence that *Mumme* (p. 52), writing in 1936, draws a connection between the regulations introduced in 1933 and the Decree of 1799, which he pays tribute to.

[138] *Mumme*, p. 35; *Thäle, p.* 72 ff.

[139] *Mumme*, p. 51.

[140] From the point of view of Heinrich Heine's struggle against censorship: *Vormbaum*, Einheit, op. cit.; on the prohibition of associations, enforced by punishment, that already had a predecessor in the Prussian Edict of 20 October 1798, see *Grässle-Münscher*, Kriminelle Vereinigung, p. 18 ff. (Text of the Edict of 1798 in ibid., p. 15).

When the common land was finally enclosed in Prussia in the 1820s and it became forbidden to gather wood, something which had been usual and permissible until then (and was extremely important for the livelihood of the "common people" in the countryside[141]), this prohibition was enforced by a harsh **punishment for the theft of wood**. For a long time, the theft of wood was one of the most frequently punished offences.[142]

In the reactionary period following the failed revolution of 1848 further special laws were added. The ***Vereinsverordnung* of 1850** (Decree to prevent an abuse of the rights to assembly and association such as might endanger lawful freedom and order, of 11 March 1850) is worthy of mention.

There were further special penal laws for the lower social classes. Well into the second half of the nineteenth century, **strikers** were subject to the punishment threatened in the law on associations and assembly and the *Gewerbeordnung* (Trade Regulation Act), and were often dispersed by force by the police. At least the Prussian trade regulation act contained not only penal provisions for trade workers on strike in § 181, but in § 182 also had provisions for employers who made agreements on lock-outs and redundancies. Both of these laws were abolished by § 152 of the Trade Regulation Act of the North German Confederation.[143] For *domestic servants* and *agricultural labourers*, the prohibition of strikes from the outset was directed only at the employees' side. The Prussian **Law on Breach of Contract of 1854** decreed:

> (Servants and agricultural labourers of the kind defined in § 2), that attempt to make either employers or authorities undertake certain actions or make certain concessions by refraining from work or agreeing to prevent work at one or more employers', or by inciting others to such an agreement, shall be liable to imprisonment not exceeding one year.[144]

This group of people, who failed to benefit from the slow, hard-won progress in the legal rights of industrial workers, were subject to a number of special provisions in criminal law. Their masters had the right to administer **corporal punishment**; the workers' **right to self-defence** was accordingly restricted vis-à-vis their masters; and there were special provisions for how offences of **defamation** were to be treated by employers. **Double letting, failing to take up a work position** and unauthorised **leaving a work position** as well as **unruliness and disobedience**[145] were punishable according to criminal, not just civil law. A special branch of the police, the *Gesindepolizei*, ensured preventatively that servants' behaviour stayed within the law.

---

[141] *Blasius*, Bürgerliche Gesellschaft p. 43 ff.

[142] In greater detail *Blasius*, Gesellschaft, p. 103 ff.; *Karl Marx* produced a well-known commentary on the Rhenish provincial parliament's debate of the draft of the law on the theft of wood (excerpt in: *Vormbaum*, MdtStrD, p. 155 ff.).

[143] More detail in *Vormbaum*, Politik und Gesinderecht im 19. Jahrhundert. Berlin 1980, p. 102 ff.

[144] The larger picture of course shows that this decree probably hardly had any importance in practice; on the basis for this speculation and reasons for it, see *Vormbaum*, Gesinderecht, p. 103.

[145] In detail on all of these points *Vormbaum*, Gesinderecht, p. 85 ff.; see p. 107 for a catalogue with 13 special groups of punishable offences.

Thus the nineteenth century is not only the age of liberalism, but also—particularly in the second half of the century—the time of the modernisation of the police.[146]

3. *The Reich Constitution of 1849*

The Reich Constitution of the Paulskirche of 28 March 1849, besides extensive regulations of criminal procedure[147] also contained some substantive rules. §§ 117 ff. regulated **immunity**, § 120 the **indemnity** of members of parliament; according to § 138 **capital punishment** was to be abolished, except in the case of a war and in maritime law for mutiny; the same applied to the punishments of the **pillory**, **branding** and **corporal punishment**.

4. *Reich Criminal Code*

Following victorious wars against Denmark (1864) and Austria (1866) the **North German Confederation** was formed under the presidency of Prussia. On 20 March 1867, following *Lasker's* petition, the Confederation was given responsibility for criminal legislation.[148] Saxony, whose fears for the "high standard"[149] of its criminal law were not unjustified, had objected.

After the Federal Parliament and the Federal Council had proposed and voted in favour of drafting a criminal code in the spring of 1868, *Friedberg*, a councillor in the Prussian Ministry of Justice (and later Prussian Minister of Justice), was given the task of drawing up a first draft. He used the Prussian Criminal Code of 1851 as the basis for his work, for the reason that most lawyers in Northern Germany were familiar with it and it had been worked through, clarified and elucidated through its practical implementation in the largest judicial system. Furthermore, it had "proved itself as a wholly competent work, which has certainly not been *surpassed* by any other legislation".[150] All of these arguments aside, power politics made it impossible

[146] *Frommel*, Strafjustiz und Polizei, p. 186, talks of a "modernisation of the police in the wake of lofty ideals of the rule of law".

[147] See III. below.

[148] The following is based on *Schubert*, Kommission (as in footnote 98). The most recent account of its creation in *Kesper-Biermann*, Einheit und Recht, p. 297 ff; an the relationship between the theory of criminal law and the process of codification ibid., p. 373 ff.

[149] *Schubert*, p. XIII.

[150] *Schubert*, p. XVI.

to proceed otherwise. The **Friedberg Draft** thus created was published in July 1869. Between 1 October and 31 December 1869 it was revised by a commission with seven members.[151]

After minor changes, this revised version was submitted by the Federal Council to the Reichstag on 14 February 1870, and debated there at first reading on 22 February. In order to speed up the process, only Sections 8–29 of the Special Part were submitted to the Commission for consultation; all other sections were discussed directly in plenary. After many motions, mainly by Saxony, most of which were rejected, the plenary debate focused primarily on the question of **capital punishment**. After the decision at second reading to abolish it had been rejected as unacceptable by the Federal Council, a compromise was reached according to which it was to be restricted to cases of murder or attempted murder of the Head of the Federation or the sovereign of one of the territories. A proposal to replace capital punishment in states where it had already been abolished by a sentence of penitentiary imprisonment for life was withdrawn as futile. The draft was approved on 25 May. After the victory in the Franco-German war of 1870/71 and the expansion of the North German Confederation to the German Reich, it was declared the Reich Criminal Code (with some changes).

For those federal states in which capital punishment had been abolished, its reintroduction was a step backwards. The same went for states in which the now extensive criminal law on moral offences had previously been cut back under the influence of the theory of criminal law of the Enlightenment and the Bavarian Criminal Code of 1813. On the whole however, the liberal age of criminal law with its constitutional achievements, but also with the typical restrictions of these achievements by authoritarian elements[152] had produced one of its last great works with this unified Reich Criminal Code. Above all, the **principle of legality** was now recognised across the Reich. § 2 Abs. 1 RStGB decreed:

> An act can only be subject to punishment if that punishment was defined by law before the act was committed.

Mitigation was *compulsory* for **attempt**. However, scholarship and the courts failed to draw the logical consequence of an objective theory of attempts; as early as the first half of the nineteenth century, subjective theories—i.e., focused on the perception of the offender rather than on the dangerousness of the act—on when an act became an attempt existed[153]; the Reich Court founded in 1878 was soon to

---

[151] The commission was made up of four Prussian jurists (besides the Prussian Minister of Justice *Leonhardt*, there were *Friedberg*, *Bürgers* und *Dorn*), one from Saxony (*Schwarze*), one from Mecklenburg-Schwerin (*Budde*), and one from Bremen (*Donandt*). For their biographies, see *Schubert*, p. XXI ff.

[152] These include the offences of political criminal law (with which the Special Part characteristically opens), in which the conviction for *laesae majestatis* constituted a mass phenomenon; cf. *Andrea Hartmann*, p. 90 ff.

[153] More detail in *Seminara*, Versuchsproblematik, op. cit., including many references.

adopt an extremely subjective position in its case law under the influence of its judge *v. Buri*.[154] The General Part made no mention of **derivative omission offences**. The issue of **principal offender and secondary participation** had been clarified, by transferring personal assistance after the fact[155] and material assistance after the fact, which had still formed part of this section in the Prussian Criminal Code of 1851 as "auxilium post delictum" (§ 37 preußStGB), to the criminal offences of the Special Part (§§ 257, 258 RStGB).

The General Part did not contain any explicit rulings on the conditions of **intent and negligence**; however, the conditions of intent were formulated both explicitly and implicitly in the offences of the Special Part; offences of negligence formed a rare exception, apart from in the area of transgressions. As intent and negligence (both then and far into the twentieth century) were viewed as **forms of *Schuld* (blameworthiness)** [Translator's note: This is a reference to the developing tripartite structure of offences in German law: *Tatbestand*, *Rechtswidrigkeit* and *Schuld*, which is different from, for example, the English dual model.], frequent references to them firmly anchored the **principle of blameworthiness** in the Criminal Code.

Of course, the term "*Schuld*" should be used with caution in reference to this time, for it only became established gradually towards the end of the nineteenth century, rather than the previously commonly used terms "*Inputabilität*" (imputability) or "*Zurechenbarkeit*" (attributability). Furthermore, "blameworthiness" was only developed into a firm category of the system of criminal offences towards the end of the nineteenth century, mainly by Binding.[156]

In the tradition of Kantian philosophy, it was assumed that the offender was autonomous, and thus the **psychological concept of blameworthiness** forms the basis of the Code. Accordingly, **responsibility** could only be ruled out in the case of unconsciousness or insanity (§ 51 RStGB). No provision was made for diminished responsibility. An offender who could not be held responsible was thus to be acquitted and was thus no longer the responsibility of criminal justice, but of administration.

However, the Code made an exception from the condition of intent and negligence, and thus from the principle of liability—at least in prevalent opinion's interpretation[157]—for **result-qualified offences** in regard to the causation of the extended result. Here, an element of **constructive liability** survived.

The **Special Part** contained a clear, but not doctrinaire, order of laws. That the law did not attempt a systematic arrangement of this part must be welcomed from the point of view of liberal criminal law, for a "system of protection of *legal*

[154] More detail in *H.J. Hirsch*, Versuchstheorie, op. cit., S. 65.

[155] In today's terminology, "Assistance in avoiding prosecution or punishment (*Strafvereitelung*)".

[156] A discussion of the fundamental issues can be found in the standard work of reference by *Achenbach*, Grundlagen, p. 20 ff.

[157] See e.g. explicitly *Rüdorff*, StGB, § 59 Note 1 et al.; *Geyer*, Verbrechen gegen die leibliche Unversehrtheit, in: Holtzendorf, Handbuch Vol. 3.2., p. 533, both including references; *Schwarze*, StGB, § 224 final part; for an early different opinion, see *Berner*, Strafrecht, p. 478.

interests"—unlike a system of protection of rights—would have led to the temptation to systematically "close loopholes", given the arbitrary nature of the idea of protected legal interests.[158]

Offences were mainly formulated so as to meet not only the criterion of specificity, but also the practical criterion of being able to be understood by the jury. Thus the **offence of aggravated murder** followed the so-called model of premeditation; it differed from the offence of simple murder in that the murderer must have acted not only with intent, but with *premeditation* (§ 211 RStGB). The tendency towards leniency continued in the punishment of **infanticide**, which 100 years earlier had been a case of qualified homicide. § 217 RStGB had been developed to a *mitigated offence* in the case of women killing their *illegitimate* child *during or immediately following birth*. Of course, punishment still consisted of a minimum 3-year penitentiary sentence, and imprisonment of no less than 2 years in the case of mitigating circumstances. The section on **duelling** contained a combination of punishable and mitigating offences (§ 202 ff. StGB); the punishment was always honourable imprisonment in a fortress (*custodia honesta*).[159] The offence of **coercion** had a variant, threat, which however postulated that this threat be of a *felony or misdemeanour*, thus the threat of any offence did not suffice (§ 240 RStGB). The offence of **omitting to effect an easy rescue** was formulated as a transgression and presumed that the offender had been requested to provide assistance by the police or its representatives in cases of accidents or a "common emergency" (§ 360 No. 10 RStGB). **False testimony** in court was only punishable if made under oath (§§ 153, 154 RStGB), which was of course regularly taken according to procedural rules. All the offences listed here were to undergo significant changes in the course of the twentieth century.

---

[158] On the order of laws in the Reich Criminal Code, see *Oehler*, Legalordnung, p. 186 ff.—The regulation of individual offences and groups of offences in the RStGB: on **criminal offences against the state**, see *Schroeder*, Schutz von Staat und Verfassung, p. 86 ff.; on **the offence of omitting to effect an easy rescue** see *Gieseler*, p. 21 ff.; on **criminal and terrorist/anarchist organisations** see *Felske*, p. 79 ff.; on the **failure to report a crime** see *Kisker*, p. 21 ff.; on **duelling** see *Baumgarten*, p. 97 ff.; on **abortion** see *Koch*, p. 43 ff.; on **theft** see *Prinz*, p. 30 ff.; on **false accusation** see *Bernhard*, p. 19 ff.; on **arson** see *Lindenberg*, p. 39 ff.; on **assault** see *Korn*, p. 42 ff.; on the **perverting the course of justice** see *Thiel*, p. 43 ff.; on **mercy killing** see *Große-Vehne*, p. 37 ff.; on the **frustration of creditors' rights** see *Seemann*, p. 33 ff.; on **offence against a sovereign** see *Andrea Hartmann*, p. 73 ff.; on **prostitution and procurement** see *Ilya Hartmann*, p. 51 ff.; on **trespassing** see *Rampf*, p. 47 ff.; on **embezzlement and unlawful appropriation** see *Rentrop*, p. 39 ff.; on **forgery of documents** see *Prechtel*, p. 43 ff.; on **demagoguery** ("incitement to class warfare") see *Rohrßen*, p. 45 ff.

[159] "Duelling" forms the main topic of the 5th volume (2003/2004) of the Jahrbuch der juristischen Zeitgeschichte; see also *Peter Dieners*, Das Duell und die Sonderrolle des Militärs. Zur preußisch-deutschen Entwicklung von Militär- und Zivilgewalt im 19. Jahrhundert. Berlin 1992.

III. Criminal Procedure

1. General Comments

The first half of the nineteenth century was a time of intense debate on the reform of criminal procedure. The eighteenth century had provided the topics of reform. It was mainly the French Code d'instruction criminelle of 1808 which served as the model for solutions; in part, reformers fell back on German legal institutions; considerations that went in the direction of the English procedural model[160] were mostly unable to establish themselves.

The influence of the French procedural model was due on the one hand to its modern elements, and on the other to the fact that French law, including criminal procedure, had remained in force in territories that had been French until the Congress of Vienna, mainly left of the Rhine. In addition, German governments gradually came to realise that the procedural model from the time of Napoleon's reign also contained structural elements that could be harnessed for their own purposes. This applied mainly to the structure of investigative proceedings and the role of the public prosecutor.

While substantive criminal law only touched on the interests of the authorities in a few politically and socially particularly controversial areas—political offences, associations, sexual offences—in criminal procedure law, the authorities' relationship to the citizen was the immediate focus of debate. Thus reforms in this area began somewhat more slowly than in the area of substantive law.

Apart from the demand to abolish torture, complied with everywhere during the first third of the nineteenth century, demands for reform were directed at abolishing the monocratic position of the judge[161] while maintaining the judge's independence and discretionary powers, at open justice[162] and oral presentation of evidence[163] at trial, as well as improving the legal position of the accused and strengthening of the right of defence. The political controversy of some of these demands is obvious, and partly explains why outdated procedures were clung to so stubbornly; however, it also explains why changes in legal affairs occurred over such a brief time span within the context of a political event—the Revolution of 1848/49.

The connections or correspondences between the political system and the system of criminal procedure were observed by most participants in this debate, even thought they did not always voice these observations openly for tactical reasons. Thus the demand for independence of the judges (and with it, judicial control over compulsory procedural measures) affected the state constitution directly. Furthermore, the demand to dissolve the inquisitorial judge's monocratic position in criminal procedure as the one raising

---

[160] See e.g. *C.J.A. Mittermaier*, Englisches Strafverfahren (from 1851).

[161] Subsequent demands were jury courts, the accusatory principle, and public prosecutors. More on these shortly.

[162] On this *Fögen*, Öffentlichkeit; *Alber*, Öffentlichkeit, and *Haber*, ZStW 1979, 590. More on this shortly.

[163] On this *Mittermaier*, Mündlichkeit. More on this shortly.

suspicion, accusing, investigating, presiding over the trial and often as the one handing down the judgment was often made plausible using the parallel of the state division of powers, and was thus met with scepticism on part of those in government.[164]

2. Procedural Model

The reception of Roman law and the influence of canonical law on the threshold of the modern era resulted in the inquisitorial procedure of the *ius commune* and, with it, the inquisitorial principle of the **ascertainment of material truth.**[165] Of course, from today's perspective this marked an improvement on medieval ordeals by fire, water and battle. Sentences based on irrationalism thus ceased; however, the principle also contained the danger of an idealisation of the ascertainment of truth and its implementation with no regard to the personal dignity and integrity of the accused.[166]

The tendency is to see *torture* as a particularly clear expression of this danger. However, this only holds partially true. It applies to torture used to discover the names of further accomplices after a sentence has already been pronounced. The answer must be differentiated further when it comes to torture used to force a confession, for torture was used not only when the accused was the only source of information in an individual case, i.e. if his statements alone could ascertain the truth. It was also used when other evidence existed and only the confession was lacking (as has already been discussed, a confession only became unnecessary if there were two eye-witnesses).[167] Thus torture was concerned with producing a *confession* as such, not necessarily with the ascertainment of material truth, which had perhaps already been successful. In this regard torture can be seen rather as following a "formal" rule, opposed to the ascertainment of material truth with its "deformalisation".[168] There is an indirect connection, for as the accused (the "*Inquisit*") tended to be made the object of the inquisitorial trials characterised by the search for material truth, torture can be seen as an expression of this position of the accused.[169]

---

[164] The idea that a change in form of government also changed criminal laws and criminal procedure was already widespread in the eighteenth century due to Montesquieu's influence; see e.g. the position of the Italian theorist of criminal law **Luigi Cremani** in *Dezza,* Beiträge Strafrecht, p. 10 f.

[165] *Eb. Schmidt*, Einführung, § 70, p. 86; *Rüping/Jerouschek*, p. 42, marginal note 84.

[166] After a thorough analysis of recent legal developments, *Ingo Müller* (Leviathan 1977, 522 ff.) comes to the conclusion that the principle of the ascertainment of truth is always used very rigidly when the aim is to gloss over the rights of the accused, whereas in other cases there is much more willingness to dispense with "exaggerated demands" of truth-ascertainment.

[167] However, some authorities preferred to use torture if the offender refused to confess even if sufficient evidence existed; *Günter Jerouschek*, Die Carolina—Antwort auf ein Feindstrafrecht? In: Hilgendorf/Weitzel, Strafgedanke, p. 79 ff., 90.

[168] Whether this "formal" requirement of conviction was intended to balance out the search for material truth, which is in itself opposed to formality, and to which extent a role was played by deeply rooted religiosity that linked confession with penance and repentance, is hard to determine; on this see § 2 footnotes 21, 22 above; see also *Edw. Peters*, Folter, p. 75 ff., and most recently, *Mathias Schmöckel*, Metanoia. Die Reformation und der Strafzweck der Besserung, in: Schulze/Vormbaum et al., Strafzweck und Strafform, p. 29 ff.

[169] One of the structural demands of the reform of criminal procedure was thus a recognition of the accused as the **subject of the trial**.

Establishing the principle of the ascertainment of material truth was only *one* possibility of overcoming medieval forms of evidence and judgment that can be seen as aiming at *formal* truth. It would also have been possible to replace these by another form of *ascertainment of formal truth,* in which the parties (prosecution and defence) carry out the hearing of evidence in an adversarial fashion *in front* of the court and are able to delimit the subject-matter of the proceedings (*Dispositionsmaxime*, maxim of delimitation of the subject-matter by the respective parties), so that their corresponding submission is taken as a (formally) true basis.[170] Such a procedure would be governed by the *Anklagemaxime*, the maxim of accusation (or the *accusatory principle*). However, no such development took place in continental Europe—unlike in English-speaking countries. When the reform of criminal procedure hit the legal-political agenda during the first third of the nineteenth century, there were a few individual voices calling for a replacement of the inquisitorial principle by the accusatory principle according to the British and American models[171]; however, these suggestions never had any serious chance of success in political reality.

The results of the reform debates and reforms was a form of procedure that can only cautiously be called a procedural "model", for at a closer glance it proves to be a **conglomeration** of various heterogeneous parts.[172] The procedural principle of the old inquisitorial procedure was preserved on the whole. The principle of the ascertainment of material truth—as a principle—dominates German criminal procedure to this day. Nearly all the progress achieved during the nineteenth century resulted in elements of procedure that would have developed organically from the *accusatory principle* in a procedure governed by this principle, but which formed heterogeneous parts—although functionally linked *amongst themselves*—in a procedure still dominated by the continued inquisitorial principle. The new procedural structure that was thus created, commonly referred to as the **reformed criminal procedure**, according to *Ignor* were better called the **reformed inquisitorial procedure.**[173] In this procedure, the position of the accused as a **subject of the trial** is not a result of the procedural model's structure, but only comes about as a result of the newly "added" elements. In the following, these new elements will be examined individually.[174]

---

[170] Despite the introduction of § 138 ZPO in 1933, the maxim of delimitation of subject-matter applies to civil procedure to the present day.—The assumption that the principle of the ascertainment of material truth plays no role in Anglo-American criminal procedure should of course not be exaggerated, for the simple reason that the vast majority of criminal proceedings do not take place in front of a jury; more details in *Herrmann*, Reform, p. 160 ff.

[171] On these voices, see *Herrmann*, Hauptverhandlung, p. 49 ff.

[172] I think this geological image is even more fitting than the architectural one adopted from Glaser by *Ignor*, Geschichte, S. 20, that compares the way the examination of the *ius commune* was combined with the new public trial with adding a new storey to an old building; *Glaser*, Handbuch Vol. 1, p. 182.

[173] *Ignor*, Geschichte, p. 16; the term "reformed" of course expresses that something old has been improved, but its substance has been retained.

[174] In contemporary literature, C.J.A. Mittermaier and H.A. Zachariae in particular wrote on the whole range of issues: *Mittermaier*, Mündlichkeit; *Zachariae*, Gebrechen. On **Heinrich Albert Zachariae** (1806–1875), Professor at the University of Göttingen and like Mittermaier a Member of the Frankfurt Parliament, see *Bandemer*, Zachariae.

3. Prosecution[175]

The fact that the separation of accusatory and judicial functions and thus the introduction of a prosecution service formed part of the reformatory demands of the nineteenth century for a long time led to the assumption that prosecution itself was an achievement of the liberal age of reform. This opinion was current particularly in the 1960s and 1970s, which themselves were seen as a period of reform,[176] and led to legislative slashes in 1975 that, by and large, abolished the judge's powers of investigation in preliminary proceedings and gave the prosecution additional coercive powers.[177]

The reality of how the prosecution was introduced in the nineteenth century is much more prosaic. The actual developments are virtually distorted by the aforementioned viewpoint.

One important reason for the introduction of the prosecution was that the accused was able to lodge an **appeal**, but there was no way of lodging an appeal *to his detriment*. As accuser and judge were one and the same person, and thus unable to challenge his own sentence, the prosecution provided an avenue for lodging such an appeal.[178]

It took some time for those in power to realise that the recognition of judicial independence, which was impossible to suppress in the long term, also gave them a new means of exerting **political influence** on the criminal procedure in the person of the prosecutor, who was subject to instructions. After the introduction of the prosecution service, the Prussian government—as *Collin* has shown[179] – made extensive use of this possibility.

The context of the **introduction in Prussia** is telling in this regard. It shows that utilitarian considerations were in fact ultimately the deciding factor. The introduction first occurred in 1846 in the criminal trials held at the Berlin Criminal Court and before the Supreme Court. The trial for treason of 250 participants in a Polish uprising in the Eastern Prussian provinces could no longer be managed with the cumbersome methods of the written inquisitorial procedure.[180] In 1849, during the time of the (so-far successful) Revolution, this new procedure was extended to all of

---

[175] Bibliographical references: *Collin*, "Wächter der Gesetze"; *Günther*, Staatsanwaltschaft; *Knollmann*, Einführung der Staatsanwaltschaft.

[176] Cf. the title of *Scheffler's* contribution in: Vormbaum/Welp, StGB, Suppl. I, p. 174 ff.

[177] More to follow in § 5; see also *Müller*, Rechtsstaat, p. 109; *Welp*, Zwangsbefugnisse, p. 5 ff., particularly p. 7.

[178] See (for Prussia) *Eb. Schmidt*, Einführung, § 289, p. 330; *Peters*, Temme, p. 98 ff.; in *Peters*, passim, a description of the positions taken by the Prussian judge, literary scholar and democratic politician **Jodocus Temme** (1798–1881) on all fundamental questions of (Prussian) of criminal procedure reform.

[179] *Collin*, Wächter, p. 247 ff.

[180] *Stölzel*, Rechtsverwaltung Vol. II, p. 586; *Günther*, Staatsanwaltschaft, p. 19 f.; *Ignor*, Geschichte p. 272; *Peters*, Temme, p. 100.—On *Savigny's* role in the creation of this decree, see *v. Arnswaldt*, Savigny, p. 249 ff.

Prussia. It is thus problematic to call the prosecution a "child of the revolution".[181] The progress that the introduction of the prosecution represented consisted in the fact that the judge was relieved of the functions of laying suspicion and accusation. However, these functions, which were particularly dangerous for citizens, now formed the remit of an authority subject to instructions from the Ministry of Justice. This result was not altered by the fact that the first Prussian prosecutor *Julius von Kirchmann*[182] was one of the revolutionaries of 1848 and was reprimanded during the reactionary period.

An examination of the prosecution reveals just how important it is to distinguish between the accusatory *principle* and the accusatory *procedure*. The introduction of the prosecution resulted in a separation of the functions of accuser and judge, turning the inquisitorial procedure into an **accusatory procedure**. However, the prosecution acted—in principle still acts today—according to the inquisitorial principle. Once it has a suspicion, it officially investigates matters with the aim of ascertaining the material truth. This reduction of the accusatory principle to the separation of an accusing and adjudicating authority is also called the ***Klageform-Prinzip*** **(principle of independent writ of prosecution)**.

The introduction of the prosecution[183] started in **Baden** (1832 for press offences; 1843 across the board), followed by **Hannover** (1841[184] in a law with the telling title of "Law on the permission of appeals against the findings of criminal courts in the interests of the state"), **Württemberg** (1843, the first state without restrictions) and **Prussia** (as described above, in 1846). The prosecution was introduced in most of the other German states, mainly in the context of general reforms of criminal procedure, with the **Revolution of 1848.**[185]

It may seem surprising from today's point of view that the prosecution, which once introduced proved a primarily conservative institution that represented the interests of the state, was only introduced by the German government after much resistance. This was probably caused by a combination of misunderstandings and correct conclusions. On the one hand, the prosecution was considered a French product and even though French criminal procedure law had been created during the Napoleonic era and was thus suspected of constituting revolutionary law—especially as its introduction was demanded by the liberals, who fell victim to their own misunderstandings. However, a greater part was played by the realisation that the isolated introduction of the prosecution was well-nigh impossible without a

---

[181] The title of a book by *Günther*.

[182] On Kirchmann, see *Rainer A. Bast* (Ed.), Julius Hermann von Kirchmann (1802–1884). Jurist, Politiker, Philosoph. Hamburg 1993; Kirchmann is remembered by (juristic) posterity less as the first prosecutor than as the author of his short work "Die Wertlosigkeit der Jurisprudenz als Wissenschaft", which contains the saying: "As science takes the arbitrary as its object, it becomes arbitrary itself; three corrective words from the legislator, and whole libraries become maculature".

[183] On the following, see *Elling*, Einführung; *Carsten,* Staatsanwaltschaft, p. 21 ff.

[184] More detail in *Knollmann*, Einführung.

[185] More detail in *Carsten*, p. 25 ff.

comprehensive reform of procedure.[186] Finally, there were also legal objections to the concrete form the prosecution took in French law, where it had the role of paramount guardian of the law and in some regards was even superior to the judges.[187]

The strong position of the prosecution on the one hand, and its dependence on instructions from the Ministry of Justice on the other gave rise to the question of whether a counterbalance was to be created in that the prosecution should have an *obligation* to intervene and prosecute where sufficient evidence existed (so-called **principle of mandatory prosecution**)[188]; this demand was only established in the Reich Code of Criminal Procedure.

The prosecution's monopoly on accusation was also taken from the inquisitorial procedure. Apart from a few instances of private prosecution, suspicions are followed up and matters investigated *qua officio* (so-called **maxim of public prosecution**).

4. Role of the Judge

In Prussia, the detachment of judicial activity from the person of the sovereign and from administration had begun comparatively early. Nonetheless, "the development of the judge from an official subject to instruction by the local ruler to an independent decision-maker [goes] in characteristic stages and can be described as an embittered rearguard battle fought by the monarchic executive powers".[189] In **Prussia**, for example, it was only the Decree of 1846 that ruled in § 23: "There is no confirmation of the judge's sentence by the Minister of Justice".

The unsuccessful Reich Constitution of 1849 guaranteed the judge's independence in several paragraphs of Article X. § 177 established that judges could not be removed or transferred. The abolition of patrimonial jurisdiction (§ 174) forms part of this context in its sense of a kind of private jurisdiction of major landowners; the criminal jurisdiction of the police was also to be abolished (§ 182(2)). The jurisdiction of the Cabinet and Ministry were expressly declared abolished (§ 175).

---

[186] *Carsten*, op. cit.

[187] *Carsten*, p. 16 f.

[188] Bibliographical references: *Hertz*, Legalitätsprinzip; most recently *Dr. Dettmar*, Legalität und Opportunität. Mittermaier—here as elsewhere happily accommodating the "needs of practice"—pronounced himself *against* the principle of mandatory prosecution and its counter model, the principle of discretionary prosecution, mainly for the reason that the introduction of the prosecution was intended to render opening criminal proceedings for every minor offence unnecessary; *Mittermaier*, ArchCrR 1842, 449 f.; *Id.*, Mündlichkeit, p. 319.

[189] *Fabian Wittreck*, Die Verwaltung der Dritten Gewalt. Tübingen 2003, p. 46; in general *Ogorek*, Richterkönig.

Between 1849 and the Reich Justice Laws, the principle of the judge's *independence* established itself throughout Germany. The same went for judicial control over compulsory procedural measures.[190]

5. Structure of the Trial

The separation of the offices of prosecutor and judge led to an institutional division of the procedure into two parts. For the prosecution to make and support an accusation, it needed to prepare the necessary materials. However, the extent to which this had to be done was not settled in advance. One possibility was that following a brief phase, during which only as much material as absolutely necessary to substantiate a suspicion was collected, the procedure passed into the hands of the court, which then first undertook further investigations ("preliminary investigation") before going on to an oral trial once charges had been brought. In reality, developments took another direction: an extensive investigation according to the French model emerged that continued to be structured as a non-public investigative procedure ("inquisitorial procedure"). Of course, according to the Prussian Decrees of 1846 and 1849 it was *possible* for the prosecution to request a preliminary investigation. But if it did not, it remained in control of the investigation. It was only in the Reichstag debates on the Reich Code of Criminal Procedure that a preliminary investigation was made *mandatory* for serious offences,[191] the results of which were binding on the prosecution. But the prosecution dominated the investigation in all other aspects until charges were brought. Only after charges were brought did a trial (*Schlussverhandlung* or *Hauptverhandlung*) in court ensue, to which the principles of open justice, oral presentation of evidence (*Mündlichkeit*) and its presentation before the deciding judges (*Unmittelbarkeit*) applied.

Although of all the elements added on to the inquisitorial procedure in the course of the nineteenth century, the trial with oral evidence was the one which contained the most "adversarial" features, its inquisitorial core was preserved. The inquisitorial maxim (sometimes referred to as the less suspicious-sounding "maxim of instruction") applied and still applies to the trial. The course of the trial is not determined by the parties; the judge is not only a moderator—like in Anglo-American law (at least in more significant trials)[192]—but the one responsible for carrying out the hearing of evidence and the one who, in the end, passes judgment. There was an exception only in the case of jury trials, where presiding over the trial (professional judge) and the decision on the guilt of the accused (jury) were divided between different organs.

---

[190] On the development up to 1848, see *Ollinger*, Richtervorbehalt.

[191] *Glaser,* Handbuch, Vol. 1, p. 195.

[192] On this, see *Herrmann*, Reform, p. 161.

6. Role of the Accused; Defence

The abolition of torture had removed the legal institution from the inquisitorial process that had expressed the position of the accused as an object particularly clearly. By the middle of the nineteenth century the judicial control powers had become established for arrests, most other sanctions and taking the oath (except in urgent cases). Codes of criminal procedure from the turn of the eighteenth to the nineteenth century—like earlier procedural codes—also gave the accused the right to contest the charges made against him from a certain phase of the trial onwards. From today's point of view, the possibility to make use of the assistance of a legally trained person (so-called *formal defence*) is vital to the defendant's legal position. Teachers and practitioners of criminal law of the early modern period took a similar view. Despite its severity, the criminal procedure of that time was by no means negatively disposed towards the formal defence.[193] In fact, it was precisely the Enlightenment period that saw the widely held view of *favor defensionis* as a hindrance in the ascertainment of material truth and thus of the fight against crime. Enlightenment thinkers such as *Klein* and *Beccaria* were particularly vocal in this regard. Beccaria, for example, considered a long preparation period for the defence as hindering effective crime control, viewing it as misguided philanthropy:

> Once the evidence has been collected and the crime established, it is necessary to allow the accused time and the means to clear himself. But the time should be brief so as not to compromise the promptness of punishment, which we have seen to be one of the main brakes on crime. Some have opposed such brevity out of a misguided love of humanity, but all doubts will vanish once it is recognised that it is the defects in the law that increase the dangers to the innocent.[194]

In line with this view, freedom of advocacy was abolished in 1780 in **Prussia** under Frederick II., and the profession of lawyer became regulated by the state. The designation "advocate" was explicitly abolished. The interests of the accused were to be supported by assistant councillors for civil procedure, by commissioners of justice for the cautelary jurisdiction—but only to the extent that they did not hinder the ascertainment of material truth.[195] The legal state of affairs in **Austria** was even more severe[196]: Emperor Joseph II.'s code of criminal procedure of 1788, in many respects "the first modern codification of criminal procedure law",[197] implemented

[193] *Ignor*, Geschichte, p. 110 ff.

[194] *Beccaria*, Of Crimes, Chap. 30, p. 76.

[195] *Gneist*, Freie Advocatur, p. 1–20; *Armbrüster*, Verteidigung, p. 90 ff.; *Weißler*, Rechtsanwaltschaft, p. 354; *Knapp*, Verteidiger, p. 27 f.; *Kern*, Gerichtsverfassung, p. 45. Certain abuses, particularly in civil justice, may have justified this manner of procedure; it should also be noted that the judges' profession had previously been reformed in the so-called Cocceian reform of justice and commissioners of justice were now required to have the same training as judges.

[196] Including the North Italian territories; on this, see dazu *Dezza*, JJZG 9 (2007/2008), S. 38 ff.; now also included in: *Dezza/Garlati*, Beiträge, p. 31 ff.

[197] *Dezza*, op. cit.; *Adriano Cavanna*, Storia del diritto moderno in Europa. Le fonti e il pensiero giuridico, Vol. 2, Milan (Giuffrè) 2005, p. 309.

the principle of the ascertainment of material truth with the utmost consequence.[198] Neither prosecution nor defence were permitted, even though the accused himself was granted certain rights of defence. Defence counsel was seen as an "enemy of the truth", and the judge was—as *Ettore Dezza* recently put it—to be a factotum,[199] a "jack of all trades", who was also meant to take care of the interests of the defence. This "system created by unswerving inquisitorial and state-centred logic" was retained in the *Gesetzbuch über Verbrechen und schwere Polizeiübertretungen* (Act on felonies and serious police law trangressions) of 1803.[200] Only in 1853 was the formal defence permitted once again in Austria.[201]

How current Beccaria's position still was as late as the 1820s is shown in the following observation by Mittermaier, who is himself regarded as one of the liberal nineteenth century reformers of criminal procedure:

> The nature of criminal procedure, directed at the ascertainment of the highest material truth, which could easily be hindered if representatives allowed it; the consideration that it usually arrives at punishments that can only be carried out on the convicted person; and that the behaviour of the guilty party can give rise to new suspicion and ways of ascertaining the truth; and that particularly in the inquisitorial process a prudent and expedient questioning of the accused can produce the desired result; all of these demand that a defendant should have no legal representative. A different matter is the right to use a trained defence lawyer, once the case has been closed, to present a written defence.[202]

This excluded any active rights of the defence during this phase of the trial, which experience had shown to be the stage when the course of the rest of the trial was set.

That the **Prussian Criminal Ordinance of 1805** regulated the defence extensively and thoroughly for its time (§§ 433–468 CrimO) was possibly due to the fact that no frictional losses in the operation of the administration of justice was anticipated due to the use of state-appointed commissioners of justice.[203] The

---

[198] § 82 contained the telling sentence: "The real purpose of the criminal investigation is: *Firstly*, to establish the true nature of the act, that is, either the proof of and the actual circumstances of the crime that the accused is charged with, or the proof of his innocence, to justify him in the face of the charges brought against him, so that the innocent individual is freed and the guilty individual is given the punishment he deserves, for the protection of general security."

[199] *Dezza*, op. cit.

[200] *Dezza*, op. cit., in footnote 14.

[201] *Dezza*, op. cit., Section V; on the struggle against "letting persons vanish without a trace", ascertainment of the conditions for imprisonment and the duty to notify a defence lawyer if the arrested person so desired, see *Cornelius*, Verschwindenlassen.

[202] *Mittermaier*, Strafverfahren in der Fortbildung (1827), § 45, p. 203; in 1813, Mittermaier had declared in the preface to the first edition of his "Vertheidigungskunst": "It could never have been my aim to give the defence advice aimed at undermining the law, and saving proven criminals from the sword of justice by artifice and rabulistic devices. Rather, I saw the defence itself as the sacred servant of the law and of justice, I saw it not as necessarily opposed to the judge, but as his ally on a joint quest for the truth. [. . .] All of the powers that the defence was *once permitted to hold, due to the excessive preferential treatment afforded it*, that could not stand up to the law, needed to be removed"; *Mittermaier*, Vertheidigungskunst, p. VI, cited according to the 2nd edition. (My emphasis—T.V.). The changes Mittermaier's point of view underwent in light of developments in the state of legal affairs are summarised in *Malsack*, Verteidigung.

[203] For individual details, see *Armbrüster*, Verteidigung, p. 109; *Manfred Hahn*, Die notwendige Verteidigung im Strafprozeß. Berlin 1975, p. 54 ff.

Bavarian Criminal Code of 1813 (which included a section on procedure) also included a number of rights of the defence.[204] But it was only with the shift in the structure of the procedure caused by the inclusion of accusatory elements around the mid-century that a number of rights of the defence became generally accepted.[205] The introduction of the prosecution in particular added a new aspect to the debate on the defence's position, for the increasing institutional independence of the accusatorial body demanded, with a certain logic, a procedural counterbalance—both in terms of legal policy and of psychology,[206] even though this did not follow the rationale of the inquisitorial principle. Therefore it is hardly a coincidence that the aforementioned Prussian **Decree of 1846**, which introduced the prosecution (first in the royal capital), stated in § 16 (1): "The accused may, in all cases, have the assistance of counsel".[207]

In detail, the modification of the procedural structure resulted in the following rights of defence counsel:

- The right to access to the prosecution dossier.[208]
- The right to private conversation with the accused.[209]
- Rights to participate actively in the trial, above all the right to examine witnesses[210] and the right to make evidential motions.[211]

However, the position of the defence (and thus of the defendant) remained weak during the pre-trial investigation procedure. Defence counsel had no right to participate. § 48 of the Prussian Decree of 1846 stated this clearly, even for cases where the prosecution had applied for a preliminary investigation: "Defence counsel must not be admitted during the preliminary investigation". Only during the trial, in front of the court, was defence counsel allowed to make full use of his rights.

7. *Open Justice*

An intensive struggle also developed around the issue of open justice. While familiar in the Germanic and medieval justice traditions, it had suffered retrenchment with the rise of inquisitorial procedure and its ex-officio character; "the

---

[204] Art. 141–149 bayStGB; *Armbrüster*, Verteidigung, p. 109 f.

[205] Overview of the regulations in individual territories in *Armbrüster*, Verteidigung, p. 110 ff.

[206] *Armbrüster*, Verteidigung, p. 104 ff.; *Knapp*, Verteidiger, p. 30.

[207] The Prussian Decree of 2 January 1849 (Prussian Statute Book 1849, p. 1) expressly retained the rules on "commissioners of justice and advocates", but for the first time introduced the term ("Amtskarakter") of *Rechtsanwalt* as an official title to refer to them.

[208] *Armbrüster*, Verteidigung, p. 116 f.

[209] *Armbrüster*, Verteidigung, p. 117 f.

[210] On this, with particular focus on the Baden procedure law of 1845/51, *Hettinger*, Fragerecht.

[211] *Armbrüster*, Verteidigung, p. 119.

written nature of the procedure made it a secret one".[212] In the *Carolina* of 1532, open justice remained in the truncated form of the "*endlicher Gerichtstag*" (Art. 70, 80, 81 CCC), when the verdict, which had already been decided upon, merely remained to be announced. In *territorial criminal law*, open justice only disappeared towards the end of the eighteenth century—at a time thus, when the demands for reform already went in the opposite direction.[213]

Many arguments were put forward both for and against open justice in court. Its **opponents** claimed that it meant further hardship for the defendant, revealed even the most closely guarded of family secrets and could contribute to the unsanctioned slander of absent state participants in the trial, could endanger the judges' health, served the defence's craving for admiration, compromised the ascertainment of truth, hindered confession, provided as yet unrevealed accomplices with important knowledge, inconvenienced witnesses, caused disturbances in court, wasted time, attracted idlers, turned the trial into a spectacle, caused unnecessary costs, was a school of crime, endangered morality, and revealed the weaknesses of justice; it was unsuited to the German people, who were not particularly freedom-loving, and promoted Jacobinism.[214]

Its **supporters** claimed that justice needed to be controlled and that open justice would be able to create a counterbalance to the jury's foolhardiness and lack of conscientiousness; it would reassure the defendant, provide a defence against the judges' whims and serve the protection of innocence, would restore the honour of the innocent party in the case of an acquittal, would motivate defence counsel and promote rhetorical skill; it would facilitate the ascertainment of truth, particularly the conviction of the criminal, give the public the impression that justice was being done, strengthen judicial independence and impartiality, act as a deterrent and as a warning against suspect persons, and it would disseminate knowledge about the law; it was furthermore in line with the idea of criminal justice, for it showed that criminal investigations were public matters, satisfied the justifiably strong public interest in important legal interests, was akin to the practice of legislation and raised the confidence of the citizenry.[215]

The Frankfurt National Assembly incorporated this principle in its Catalogue of Basic Rights (§ 178) without debate or providing any further reasons, obviously assuming it to be self-evident. Restrictions were only allowed "in the interest of morality" (§ 178 (2)). Territorial law followed suit. During the reactionary period, these regulations were restricted not only by rules for the protection of morality, but also by those for the protection of public security and order, but the principle itself was preserved.[216] These restrictions were included in the Reich legislation of 1877 (§ 173 RGVG), which however made it clear that the pronouncement of judgement had to be public in each and every case (§ 174 RGVG).

---

[212] *Alber*, Öffentlichkeit, p. 15.

[213] *Alber*, p. 17.

[214] On this list of topics, see *Alber*, p. 46 ff.

[215] On this list of topics, too, see *Alber*, p. 36 ff.

[216] References in *Alber*, p. 152 ff.

In a detailed analysis, *Fögen* has shown that participants' interests were slightly different from what public statements might lead one to assume. The open justice of courts was—according to Fögen—not gained in defiance of and opposition to the justice system and governments, but was rather promoted by the justice system (if with the exception of the deliberation and decision-making phases, precisely the phases of the greatest public interest; these remain shrouded in secrecy with an almost ethical dignity to the present day), in order to gain the support of public opinion in its struggle for independence from government intervention. "The open justice of courts was thus a means of establishing the (factual) independence of the justice system from the theoretically undivided power of the regent".[217]

Apart from the aforementioned exceptions during the trial, the principle of open justice also failed to apply to the *pre-trial investigation*, which still remained subject to the principle of secrecy. To speak of a victory of open justice must thus be subject to serious reservations.

8. Oral Presentation of Evidence and Presentation Before the Deciding Judges

The demands for oral presentation (*Mündlichkeit*) before the deciding judges (*Unmittelbarkeit*) in criminal procedure were closely linked to open justice.[218] At first they were not clearly terminologically distinguished from one another, but gradually the separation of the two principles and the further division between formal and material *Mündlichkeit*[219] emerged.[220]

For open justice at trial to work, the trial must be conducted orally, for it is impossible for the public to follow the proceedings if the participants merely exchange written documents. The problem was mirrored during the introduction of jury trials, for as the jury had no knowledge of the records, they were only able to gain a comprehensive picture of the evidence if all facts relevant to the decision were discussed orally. In this regard the principle of written procedure, which had emerged during the inquisitorial procedure of the early modern period, was first juxtaposed to the principle of *Mündlichkeit* through the French Code d'instruction criminelle (*oralité*).[221]

---

[217] *Fögen*, Gerichtsöffentlichkeit, p. 123.

[218] This is expressed in the title of the best-known pertinent work, *Feuerbach's* book "Öffentlichkeit und Mündlichkeit der Gerechtigkeitspflege". *Mittermaier's* 1845 book also combines *Mündlichkeit* and *Unmittelbarkeit* (with the accusatorial principle and jury courts) in its title.

[219] *Formal:* All evidence must be presented in the presence of the participants in the trial. Evidence taken during the investigation stage has to be reproduced during the trial. *Material:* Of all evidence accrued, the most immediate and direct source of evidence must be used ("best evidence"); a familiar associated problem is that of hearsay evidence.

[220] Represented in *Geppert*, Unmittelbarkeit, p. 68 ff.

[221] On this and the following, see *Geppert*, Unmittelbarkeit, p. 63.

The written nature of the inquisitorial procedure of the *ius commune* was also due to the fact that case files were often sent to the regional authorities, an appellate court or faculty of law once the taking of evidence was completed, in order for a decision to be made.[222] This decision was only made possible by documenting in writing the progression of the trial in detail. The difficulties in adhering to this precondition accurately did not only arise from the recorders' lack of skill, but were owed to the nature of the matter in question; for example, no record can exactly reproduce the facial expressions and gestures of examined individuals, whether they turn pale, blush and give any other signs of embarrassment. In addition, not all members of the panel of the appellate court or faculty involved in decision-making would read the files submitted, but were instead given information on them by a reporting member (*Referenten*). Thus the *Unmittelbarkeit* of the decision and the written nature of the trial were linked, and the struggle for *Mündlichkeit* necessarily also became a struggle for *Unmittelbarkeit*.[223]

A central point of the debate about *Unmittelbarkeit* was the requirement to reproduce the examinations conducted as part of the investigation, or, from the opposite point of view, the possibility of replacing informants' statements during the oral trial by reading out the records of examinations conducted during the investigation.

The breakthrough for *Mündlichkeit* (and open justice) came with the aforementioned **Prussian Decree of 1846** (§ 15[224]). The **Decree of 1849** confirmed this rule (§ 14[225]). The Constitution of the Paulskirche had decreed in § 178 (1): "The trial is to be public and oral".

As with the principle of open justice, those of *Mündlichkeit*/*Unmittelbarkeit* were recognised in the end, but had to suffer many exceptions and restrictions until the advent of and even within the Reich legislation (for individual details, see §§ 248 ff. RStPO; today—with modifications—§§ 249 ff. StPO).[226]

9. *Jury Courts*

In the debate about the reform of criminal procedure, the politically most controversial topic was the introduction of jury courts (*Schwurgerichte* or *Geschworenengerichte*).[227] They had been adopted by French revolutionary legislation from

[222] The reason for this was the lower courts' frequent lack of knowledge of (Roman) law; *Löhr*, Unmittelbarkeit, p. 26 f.

[223] *Löhr*, p. 30.

[224] "The pronouncement of judgement is to be preceded by an oral trial in front of the adjudicating court, during which the prosecutor and the defendant are to be heard, the evidence presented and the defence of the accused is to be conducted orally".

[225] "The pronouncement of judgement, on pain of invalidity, is to be preceded by an oral public trial in front of the adjudicating court, during which [. . .]" (continuing as in § 14 of the Decree of 1846).

[226] More detail in *Geppert*, Unmittelbarkeit, p. 77 ff. (on territorial criminal law), 106 ff. (RStPO).

[227] For basic information, see *Erich Schwinge*, Der Kampf um die Schwurgerichte bis zur Frankfurter Nationalversammlung. Wroclaw 1926; most recently, *Diana Löhr*, Zur Mitwirkung der Laienrichter im Strafprozess. Hamburg 2008, p. 55 ff.

Anglo-American law, including both an accusatory and an adjudicating jury. It regarded the jury court—in an oft-quoted metaphor—as the "Palladium of civil liberty".[228] It was seen as the criminal procedural equivalent of the parliament.[229] It was retained by Napoleon, if in a somewhat weakened form (only as an adjudicating jury responsible merely for deciding issues of fact), despite the way it had been abused during the Terror; however, he had not actively pursued its introduction in states dependent on him, and in some cases—for example in the Kingdom of Italy—had expressly objected to it.[230] The jury court was preserved in its French form in the Rhineland; here, too, French law took on the role of a catalyst, as it had in other areas of law.

For a long time, the position of German criminal law scholars towards jury courts was sceptical or even hostile.[231] In his analysis of jury courts, Feuerbach came to the conclusion that they must be evaluated differently from a legal and a political perspective; from a legal point of view nothing spoke in their favour, yet in political terms they were to be welcome in a constitutional body politic[232]; Mittermaier also demanded that these two areas be distinguished, and was sceptical regarding both.[233]

Towards the middle of the century, however, this view became increasingly relaxed, and support for jury courts became more frequent in scholarship, too.[234] One of the decisive factors—besides the political experience with professional judges during the Restoration period—was the link to other reformatory demands: we have already pointed out the connection between *Mündlichkeit* and *Unmittelbarkeit*; the connection with the question of evidence was even more crucial: the dispute between evidential rules theory and the principle of free evaluation of the evidence (discussed below under 10.) was conducted mainly by the supporters and opponents of the jury court[235]; it was thought necessary to bind professional judges with clear rules in their evaluation of the evidence, while the jury were intended to reach their decision based on an "overall impression"[236] not

---

[228] Reference in *Peters*, Temme, Chapter 8 A).

[229] *Ignor*, Geschichte, p. 249; *Peters*, Temme, Chapter 8 A).

[230] On Italy, see *Dezza*, Kodifikationszeitalter, p. 66; in 1805, Napoleon declared in a speech opening the session of the legislative body of the (first) Kingdom of Italy: "I did not think that the situation in which Italy finds itself at present allows me to consider the institution of the jury. Judges must however, as a jury does, reach a verdict based on their own conscience, without using that system of half-proofs that offends innocence itself far more frequently than him who is called to solve a crime. The most secure guiding principle of a judge who has led a trial is the conviction of his own conscience".

[231] Cf. the list in *Peters*, Temme, Chapter 8 B).

[232] *Feuerbach*, Geschworenengericht, p. 74 ff., 112 ff.; *Radbruch*, Feuerbach, p. 100 ff.

[233] *Mittermaier*, Mündlichkeit, p. 363 ff.

[234] This shift occurred at the Lübeck German Scholars' Assembly of 1847; on this, *Schwinge*, Schwurgerichte, p. 146 ff.; *Küper*, Richteridee, p. 219.

[235] *Schwinge*, Schwurgerichte, p. 74; see also *Küper*, Richteridee, p. 217.

[236] On this, see *Mittermaier*, Mündlichkeit, p. 364.

restricted by rules. As the sceptical attitude towards the feasibility of evaluating evidence according to rules gradually became more and more established, the development, at least as far as the adjudication of serious crimes was concerned, tended towards jury courts. Only a further (intellectual and chronological) step resulted in the free evaluation of evidence being extended to include the judge.[237]

During the course of the Revolution of 1848/49[238] jury courts were introduced nearly everywhere in the German states. In Prussia, Art. 93 of the constitutional charter decreed that for crimes carrying severe punishments, as well as all political crimes and press offences, the question of the defendant's guilt should be settled by a jury. The constitutional charter came into force with the **Decree of 3 January 1849**. An accusatory jury was not introduced; it would have been hard to reconcile with the secret, non-public, written nature of the investigation.

Unlike French law, the jury were responsible not only for deciding issues of fact, but for the entire question of guilt. It remained for the professional judges to determine the extent of the punishment.

10. Evaluation of Evidence and Reaching a Verdict

As described in § 2, the abolition of torture had removed a central element of the *factual* system of the inquisitorial procedure. It has already been mentioned above that torture was not a necessary element of the inquisitorial procedure, but a *historical* one added to it.[239] Presumably, it was a deeply rooted idea of the necessity of confession—except in cases with two eye-witnesses—that prevented the rules of evidence of the *ius commune* from being abolished at the same time as torture. Towards the end of the eighteenth century, the demand had already been voiced to allow the free judicial evaluation of evidence to decide in cases where torture would traditionally have been used.[240] However, in France this measure of evidence was introduced only for the jury,[241] for unlike professional judges, these were meant not to follow the often complicated rules of evidence, but their "instinct for truth", deciding on the basis of an "overall impression". It was considered too dangerous for the accused to allow professional judges the same measure. Thus the rules of evidence were maintained for decades, and with them punishments for lying and disobedience.[242] **Negative proof theory**, developed in scholarship and

[237] Thus e.g. *Mittermaier*, NArchCrimR 13 (1833), 120 ff., 139 ("Turn it whichever way you like,—there is only *one* solution: *to introduce jury courts*"; emphasis in the original text). More details on background context in *Küper*, Richteridee, p. 219 ff.

[238] The Constitution of the Paulskirche decreed in § 179 (2): "Jury courts are to sentence serious crime and all political misdemeanours".

[239] See this section under "Prison reform".

[240] E.g. in *Pietro Verri*, Betrachtungen über die Folter, op. cit., p. 68 f.

[241] *Nobili*, Überzeugungsbildung, p. 74; *Küper*, Richteridee, p. 174 ff.

[242] As already discussed in § 2, footnote 38 ff.

temporarily introduced into codes[243], according to which "the meticulous legal rules on the completeness of evidence and the value of evidence [were to be] used only for conviction, but not for acquittal",[244] did not last in the long run. Starting with the Prussian Decree of 1846—and here even before the introduction of jury courts—the principle of the free judicial evaluation of evidence became prevalent,[245] which had already been introduced at the beginning of the century by Napoleon in France and its dependent territories. There were several reasons for this system's success. Firstly, the conviction was generally accepted that it was impossible to set rules for dealing with all the problems of evidence that might arise; secondly, the free judicial evaluation of evidence was supplemented by the mandatory requirement that the professional judge set out the reasons for his judgment—here, the *conviction intime* was transformed into a *conviction raisonée* subject to scrutiny on appeal; and finally, progress in forensic science gave rise to the hope that the rational ascertainment of material truth could be improved. Of course, none of this changes the fact that the "price" for abolishing torture was the free judicial evaluation of evidence. The decade-long hesitation of both theory and practice to accept this consequence fully shows that there were widespread reservations both related to miscarriages of justice and the abuse of power by the judges—fears apparently no longer shared today, even though criminal law today gives the judge far greater leeway than in the nineteenth century.

11. Reich Code of Criminal Procedure

The factors described above resulted in their totality in the **reformed criminal procedure**, which was ultimately used as the basis for the provisions in the **Reich Code of Criminal Procedure of 1877/79**[246]. Open justice, *Mündlichkeit* and *Unmittelbarkeit* were introduced with some restrictions; jury courts were responsible for severe crimes, although precisely not for press offences and serious political crime. The central characteristic of the Reich Code of Criminal Procedure was also the so-called "principle of independent writ of prosecution": the demand for the separation of the functions of accusation and adjudication was fulfilled; however, the reform was limited to transferring the investigation to an institution separate from the court, the prosecution. The investigative judge remained in charge of some

[243] E.g. the Austrian Code of 1803 § 414, and the Baden Code of 1845, § 270; references to Bern in *Nobili*, Überzeugungsbildung, p. 157, to Bavaria in *Mittermaier*, Beweis, p. 84.

[244] *Nobili*, Überzeugungsbildung, p. 77, see also ibid. p. 154 ff.; *Küper*, Richteridee, p. 130. Exponents of this theory were, among others, *Feuerbach* (Betrachtungen über das Geschworenengericht, p. 132 f.), *Grolman* (Grundsätze der Criminalrechtswissenschaft, p. 611) und *Mittermaier* (Beweis, p. 92).

[245] On this, see *Nobili*, p. 149 ff., *Dezza*, Kodifikationszeitalter, p. 64 ff., 143 ff.

[246] For a detailed account of its creation, see *Schubert*, Die Entstehung der Strafprozessordnung von 1877, in: Schubert/Regge, StPO, p. 1 ff., 4 ff.

individual parts of this procedural stage, and, in cases of serious crime, retained his own investigative responsibilities within the preliminary investigation now mandatory for serious crime. The liberal model, where the two adversarial parties of prosecution and defence would have shaped the entire procedure, was not put into practice. In the first procedural stage, the defence's activity remained almost utterly ineffective. Here, the prosecution was not a party, but—in an expression commonly used to the present day—"*Herrin des Ermittlungsverfahrens* (the master of the pre-trial investigation)". Additionally, it was an institution dependent on the Ministry of Justice, assigned (with restrictions) the role of "guardian of the law" even beyond the criminal trial. Only during the trial did prosecution and defence face one another as parties; but here, too, there was no actual adversarial trial, but rather one governed by the inquisitorial maxim or maxim of instruction, where the judge presided over the trial, was responsible for the taking of the evidence as well as—apart from jury trials—reaching the verdict. The parties were left only with making minor corrections.

In the Reich Code of Criminal Procedure, following lengthy discussions[247] the activity of the prosecution was bound to the **principle of mandatory prosecution** (requirement to investigate and prosecute, § 152 (2) StPO). The procedure for compelling the prosecution to file an indictment (§§ 172 ff. StPO) was intended to safeguard this principle.[248]

The judge's **free conviction and free evaluation of the evidence** established itself in place of the abolished torture. More reluctant models, which wanted to retain at least the old rules of evidence *in favour* of the defendant, i.e. for sentencing, were unable to assert themselves.[249]

According to § 244 RStPO, the court was required to include all the witnesses and experts summoned and any other evidence collected in the **evaluation of evidence**. § 245 (1) RStPO expressly forbade a refusal to hear evidence on grounds of its late submission. However, this was not applicable in cases of first instance trials before a *Schöffengericht* (a mixed panel of professional and lay judges), as well as appeal hearings for transgressions and private prosecutions before the district courts; there the court decided the extent of the evaluation of evidence without being bound by motions, waivers or previous decisions (§ 244 (2) RStPO).

The Law on the Legal Profession of 1878 introduced **freedom of advocacy**, which Rudolf Gneist had called the "paramount demand of any reform of justice in Prussia"[250], throughout the Reich. This put an end to the time of the functionary commissioners of justice in Prussia.

---

247 *Hertz*, Geschichte, p. 40 ff.

248 More detail in *Dr. Dettmar*, Legalität und Opportunität, Chapter 7 A) IV. 6.

249 On the "negative proof theory" proposed by *Feuerbach* among others, see *Nobili*, Überzeugungsbildung, p. 154 ff.

250 Thus the subtitle of his book "Freie Advokatur".

IV. Sentences and the Prison System

1. Development of Penitentiaries

The nineteenth century is the period when state control over the human body gradually diminished. If legal systematic categorisations are left aside, the repression and abolition of torture also forms part of this secular development. **Corporal punishment** and **severe capital punishment** were also repressed and abolished; through the use of the guillotine, the execution of the death penalty itself was reduced to as brief a process as imaginable; **flogging** as a criminal punishment was abolished around the middle of the nineteenth century.

This can be seen as a further important element of the epochal threshold discussed in Chapter 1. **Michel Foucault** identified a change in discourse during the transition from pre-modernity to modernity, from a brutal, but often carelessly enforced penal justice system to a "thorough" one characterised by conformity and deviance[251]; **Richard Evans** summarises Foucault's analysis in the sentence: "The penal reform movement of the eighteenth century, in this view, aimed not to punish people less, but to punish them better",[252] thus adding a further facet to the ambivalence of the criminal law and politics of the Enlightenment that this book has repeatedly stressed.

This development's vanishing point should really have been the abolition of the death penalty. But this occurred only in very few individual cases during the nineteenth century. It was retained or reintroduced across Germany with the Reich legislation.[253] Though not abolished, its actual ambit of application was severely restricted—first through an increase in pardons,[254] and then by law; in the Reich Criminal Code it was only available in cases of murder and serious political crimes. Since the mid-century it was no longer carried out in public.[255]

The trend to abolish corporal punishment and severe capital punishment and the restriction of simple capital punishment brought **custodial sentences,**[256] particularly penitentiary sentences, to the fore.

---

[251] *Michel Foucault*, Überwachen und Strafen. Die Geburt des Gefängnisses. Frankfurt am Main 1976, p. 93 ff.

[252] *Evans*, Rituals, p. 10. Of course, Evans criticises that Foucault "remained effectively silent about the origins of discursive shifts and the mechanisms of historical change" (p. 12). This is of course a problem of all theories of discourse.

[253] See footnote 97 above.

[254] This development already started at the beginning of the nineteenth century; *Hälschner*, Geschichte, p. 252 f.

[255] In detail on this topic *Evans*, Rituals, p. 399 ff.; *Nicola Willenberg*, Das Ende des "Theater des Schreckens". Zum Wandel der Todesstrafe in Preußen im 19. Jahrhundert, in: Schulze/Vormbaum et al., Strafzweck und Strafform, p. 265 ff.

[256] *Eb. Schmidt*, Zuchthäuser, p. 10.

Penitentiaries and prisons have different origins and the development has only been parallel since the 19th century. While prison sentences were first only handed out for low-level crime and only for comparatively short terms (as they do not form a *peinliche Strafe*, i.e. a penalty involving corporal or capital punishment, they are hardly even mentioned in the Carolina of 1532),[257] penitentiaries at the beginning of the 19th century already look back on a long history, which can only be sketched briefly here. Calvinism rejected the medieval view of poverty as a welcome opportunity for giving alms and thus engaging in deserving works of charity, seeing it instead as an offence against work ethics. Under Calvinist influence, the "house of correction" and the "tuchthuis" had been established in England and Holland by 1600; the later German institutions derived their name, *Zuchthaus*, from the latter.[258]
These were not first and foremost penal institutions, but rather establishments where the inmates – consisting chiefly of prostitutes, idlers, vagrants, beggars, partly also of people with mental disabilities – were to be reformed by work and strict rules. Convicts remained a marginal phenomenon, primarily for the reason that they were mainly sentenced to "painful" punishments, i.e. corporal and capital punishment. Calvinist ideals of reform became merged with policing considerations; the mercantile attitude led to the consideration of how to exploit inmates' labour power.[259] The *Zuchthaus* arrived in Germany via the Hanseatic cities.[260] By the end of the 18th century, there were around 70 penitentiaries in Germany.[261]

The penitentiary's importance as an institution for *executing* punishment grew as a result of the repression of corporal punishment and of (both simple and severe) capital punishment, which it came to replace. During the second half of the eighteenth century it gradually gained recognition as a form of *punishment* and was built into the catalogue of sanctions.[262] This development was strengthened by the repression of further sanctions:

Galley slavery, in any event more apt as a punishment in seafaring nations, fell out of use once galleys were replaced with modern sailing ships; thus it was no longer possible to transfer convicts to states engaging in sea trade, such as Venice, Genoa, Naples or France.[263]

---

[257] *Krause*, Geschichte, p. 21 f., 57.

[258] *Eb. Schmidt,* Zuchthäuser, p. 6; *Krause,* Geschichte, p. 32 ff.—The most famous examples are Amsterdam's "spinhuis" for women and the "tucht- en rasphuis" for men; cf. the images in *Robert v. Hippel*, ZStW 18 (1898), 482 f.; *Eb. Schmidt*, Zuchthäuser (Appendix) und *Krause*, Geschichte, p. 35.

[259] *Krause*, Geschichte, p. 41.

[260] *Rüping/Jerouschek*, Grundriss, p. 95 (marginal note 209); *Krause*, p. 38 ff. The names "Zucht-, Armen- und Waysenhaus" ("house for correction, for the poor and for orphans", Waldheim/ Sachsen, 1716) und "Zucht- und Tollhaus" ("house for correction and for the insane", Celle, from 1717) are telling; *Krause*, p. 50. The craftsmen's guilds protested against work in the penitentiaries, *Eb. Schmidt*, Zuchthäuser, p. 13.

[261] *Krause*, Geschichte, p. 50.

[262] *Rüping/Jerouschek*, Grundriss, p. 94; *Krause*, Geschichte, p. 50.

[263] *Krause*, Geschichte, p. 30; *Rüping/Jerouschek*, Grundriss, p. 94; *Hans Schlosser*, Die Strafe der Galeere als poena arbitraria in der mediterranen Strafpraxis, in: ZNR 10 (1988), 19 ff.; *Id.*, Deportation und Strafkolonien als Mittel des Strafvollzuges in Deutschland, in: Mario Da Passano (Ed.) (see the following footnote), p. 41 ff., 44 f.

Deportation also only played a minor role in Germany, due to a lack of colonial territories and German islands that could have served as prison islands.[264] Around 1800, Prussia had made an attempt, based on an agreement with Russia, to send convicts to Siberia, but this attempt was unsuccessful.[265]

By contrast, the punishment of **public labour**, usually carried out in the construction of fortresses, gradually merged with penitentiary sentences.[266] On the other hand, the **workhouse** became distinct from the penitentiary and thus disappeared from the focus of the doctrine and history of criminal law.[267]

These last points touch on the general problem of the relationship between **criminal law and equality**, which was particularly evident when it came to punishments.[268] During the eighteenth century, (formal) equality was generally recognised with regard to *criminal offences,*[269] but was controversial when it came to *punishments*. The dominant opinion in legal theory and case law around the middle of the eighteenth century saw "the social status of the delinquent as a central aspect to be considered when selecting the type of punishment—and partly also the severity of the punishment".[270] During work on the Bavarian Criminal Code of 1813, the differentiation of punishments threatened according to status was still debated. The fact that new codifications from the beginning of the nineteenth

---

[264] This was markedly different in **Britain** and **France**, where convicts could be shipped off to the colonies (Britain: first North America, then Australia; France: Cayenne), and **Italy**, who was able to create prison colonies on its many islands; for more detailed information on France and Italy: *Mario Da Passano* (Ed.), Europäische Strafkolonien im 19. Jahrhundert. International Conference of the Dipartimento di Storia der Universität Sassari and the Parco Nazionale di Asinara. Porto Torres, 25 May 2001. Berlin 2006. Furthermore, Italy had the particular case of *forced relocation colonies*, where persons who were suspicious on political or other grounds could be banished to designated areas; on this, see *Daniela Fozzi*, Eine "italienische Spezialität": Die Zwangskolonien im Königreich Italien, in: ibid., p. 191 ff.

[265] On the reasons for this, *Eb. Schmidt*, Einführung, § 243, p. 254 f.; on this and other attempts, see also *Schlosser* (as in footnote 261), p. 46 f. with further references; this text also contains information on the revival of this discussion occurring after the acquisition of German colonies from 1884 onwards, and on the attempts to establish **transportation**, i.e. "emigration of criminals directed by the authorities" (*Schlosser*, p. 51 ff.), particularly to the USA, until this was prohibited by law by the US Congress in 1875.

[266] *Krause*, Geschichte, p. 55.

[267] This is rightly criticised by *Naumann*, Gefängnis und Gesellschaft, p. 13 ff.

[268] The following is based closely on *Sylvia Kesper-Biermann*, "Nothwendige Gleichheit der Strafen bey aller Verschiedenheit der Stände im Staat"? (Un)gleichheit im Kriminalrecht der ersten Hälfte des 19. Jahrhunderts; in: Geschichte und Gesellschaft 35 (2009), 603 ff. The quote in the title is taken from a written statement by Feuerbach made during the legislative consulation procedure.

[269] This did not preclude that certain offences, such as duelling (as a mitigated homicide offence), could in fact only be committed by members of certain social classes. As a marginal phenomenon, duelling carried its own grounds for punishment, e.g. for *challenging, accepting and taking part* (in detail *Baumgarten*, Zweikampf; on the issue of duelling as a whole see also the contributions to the special volume on this topic, "Duell/Zweikampf" in the Jahrbuch der juristischen Zeitgeschichte 5 (2003/2004).

[270] *Kesper-Biermann*, op. cit., p. 608.

century onwards dispensed with explicit references to social class was due to the influence of the principle of equality (which was in part constitutionally guaranteed). Its implementation was, of course, due less to a recognition of the individual's interest in equal treatment than to the enlightened, absolutist state's interest in "the 'equality' of its subjects in relation to itself".[271]

Therefore aspects of class do not appear in the new codes' rules for punishment, nor does a differentiation between the sexes[272] or between rich and poor. In the Bavarian Legislative Committee, *Feuerbach* prevailed with his suggestion of a compromise of *surrogate punishment*, where a prison sentence could be carried out in various locations, depending on the judge's decision; this is where the institutions of ***Festungshaft*** and ***Festungsarrest*** **(imprisonment in a fortress, considered *custodia honesta*)**, that became established over the course of the nineteenth century until the advent of the Reich Criminal Code, originated. Of course, this still allowed for differentiation, as the decision on surrogate punishment was to be dependent upon the convicted individual's "personal circumstances" or "living conditions", occasionally also upon his "level of education", his "personality" or "attitude",[273] which was to the advantage of members of the middle and upper classes. In today's terminology, this result was legitimated by the rule that what is different should be treated differently.

Custodia honesta was the intended privileged penalty for prohibited **duels** and **political offences**, yet it played no significant role in practice.[274]

2. *"Prison Reform"*

At the end of the eighteenth century, penitentiaries were in a dismal condition—and not only in Germany.[275] The most important structural reason for this was probably the subsiding of mercantile politics, which destroyed the economic foundation of the *Zuchthaus*.[276]

The Englishman **John Howard** (1726–1790) was the first to call for a reform of the prison system. Over many years, he visited penitentiaries first in England and Wales, then across the whole of Europe, reporting on their overwhelmingly poor condition in his works "The State of the Prisons" (1777, on England and Wales) and

[271] Ibid., p. 617.

[272] Of course there were sex-specific offences, such as infanticide, which only applied to women (and which in the nineteenth century was turned from a qualified to a mitigated offence), or homosexuality, which only applied to men.

[273] *Kesper-Biermann*, op. cit., p. 620 ff.

[274] *Christian Baltzer*, Die geschichtlichen Grundlagen der privilegierten Behandlung politischer Straftäter im Reichsstrafgesetzbuch von 1871. Bonn 1966; *Krause*, Geschichte, p. 73 ff.

[275] *Eb. Schmidt*, Zuchthäuser, p. 12; *Id.*, Einführung, p. 253; *Krause*, Geschichte, p. 52.

[276] *Rusche*/*Kirchheimer*, Sozialstruktur, p. 143.

"Account of the principal Lazarettos in Europe" (1789). His list of demands included better supervision of establishments, better hygiene and a system of progressively more lenient conditions for good behaviour, and furthermore called for the introduction of **solitary confinement** instead of the communal confinement common at the time (no separation of criminals and other groups, sometime no separation of sexes) in order to prevent criminal contagion.

These ideas were realised in Philadelphia, capital of the Quaker state Pennsylvania; the prison founded in 1790 was based on the principle of strict solitary confinement both day and night, with no work. This was meant to give the prisoner a chance for inner reflection and moral improvement. The prison of Auburn in New York State attempted to avoid the obvious flaws of the **Philadelphia System**. The so-called **Auburn System** only used solitary confinement in individual cells at night, while prisoners were together during the day, albeit subject to strict silence.[277]

In **Prussia**, the "**Generalplan** zur allgemeinen Einführung einer besseren Criminalgerichtsverfassung und zur Verbesserung der Gefängniß- und Strafanstalten" ("General plan on the general introduction of an improved criminal court organisation and the improvement of prison and penal institutions") **of 1804** developed by *Albrecht Heinrich von Arnim* represented an attempt at reform,[278] as it were, the flipside of the Decree on Theft of 1799.[279] He saw the task of penal institutions as: "separation of criminals from human society", to get inmates used to activity, order and cleanliness, as well as to improve and deter others by "the unpleasantness of imprisonment, which is partly an aspect of imprisonment as such, partly connected with forced labour and a hard lifestyle". Criminals were to be separated into three different classes dependent on their life and career so far and the "morality evidenced by these and their crimes".

This plan, based on "the ideals of the benevolent, patriarchal, enlightened police state", was not realised due to the Napoleonic Wars. By the end of Napoleon's reign, a new view of the task of penal institutions had spread throughout Germany. Prevailing opinion on punishment drew on the combination of retributive criminal law and criminal law based on general deterrence which dominated the nineteenth century. Based on a theory of purpose-free punishment (*Kant*) and a theory which saw punishment only as the confirmation of the seriousness of the threat of punishment (*Feuerbach*), the conclusion was that the execution of punishment must refrain from any attempt to morally improve or educate the criminal. As the function of the state lies only in establishing the juridical condition, the execution of punishment can only

---

[277] *Krause*, Geschichte, p. 69; *Rüping/Jerouschek*, Grundriss, p. 96 (marginal note 211); *Eb. Schmidt*, Einführung, p. 348 f.; on the discussion surrounding the introduction of the Philadelphia System in the Kingdom of Württemberg, see *Paul Sauer*, Im Namen des Königs. Strafgesetzgebung und Strafvollzug im Königreich Württemberg 1806 bis 1871. Stuttgart 1984, p. 138 ff.

[278] Excerpts reproduced in *Sellert/Rüping*, Volume 1, p. 451 ff.; the following quotes are based on these.

[279] *Eb. Schmidt*, Einführung, p. 254; *Id.*, Zuchthäuser, p. 15 ("can only be called great"); on the Decree on Theft see footnote 132 above).

be directed at instilling lawful behaviour in the prisoner. The consequence of this was strict disciplining, which was to make the punishment to be felt as an evil and promote the practice of clearly visible virtues. Corporal punishment remained as a disciplinary measure. "*Willkomm und Abschied*" ("welcome and farewell"), i.e. corporal punishment at the beginning and end of a prison sentence,[280] and annual floggings on the anniversary of the crime were practiced well into the nineteenth century.

This resulted in the accusation often levelled against these theories, that they had hindered or at least delayed a reform of punishment and a humane organisation of penal institutions.[281] In reality, this was not a necessary consequence. One can only derive from the theories of the authors mentioned that moral education could not be forced against the will of the prisoner. In the same way that Prussian bureaucracy reduced Kant's theory of duty to an abstract ideology of duty-fulfilment, the realisation of Kant's theory of punishment remained mechanic and clichéd. In an extensive study, *Sandra G. Müller-Steinhauer* has shown that a programme of voluntary rehabilitation can be compatible with Kant's notion of autonomy.[282]

However, as this new opinion dominated punishment for a long while, the number of those concerned with an improvement of prisons remained small at first. **Nikolaus Heinrich Julius** (1783–1862)[283]—tellingly, a doctor—shared the experiences of his extended research in England (later also in the USA) in his "Vorlesungen über Gefängnißkunde" ("Lectures on Prison Studies", 1827), which gave this branch of scholarship the name it was to carry for the next 100 years (today it is known as "*Strafvollzugskunde*", "Prison Studies"). As the later Prussian King Frederick Wilhelm IV. was among his audience, Julius was able to exert a certain influence on politics. Besides Julius, **Carl Joseph Anton Mittermaier**, whose empirical interests included a concern with punishment,[284] **Franz von Holtzendorff** (1829–1889)[285] and the theologian **Johann Heinrich Wichern** (1808–1881), founder of the Protestant "*Innere Mission*" and Director of the Penal Institution Berlin-Moabit between 1856 and 1872, are worthy of mention. The gradual emergence of prison studies and *prison societies*, based on the American model which, apart from the improvement of penal institutions, was also dedicated to the care of released prisoners, contributed to the gradual advance of the reform ideals.[286]

---

[280] *Krause*, Geschichte, p. 53.

[281] *Rüping/Jerouschek*, Grundriss, p. 97.

[282] *Müller-Steinhauer*, Autonomie, p. 234 ff.

[283] *Rüping/Jerouschek*, Grundriss, p. 96 (marginal note 124); *Krause*, Geschichte, p. 69; *Albert Krebs*, Nikolaus Heinrich Julius, "Vorlesungen über Gefängniß-Kunde", gehalten 1827 zu Berlin. Eine Studie, in: MschrKrim. 56 (1973), 307–315.

[284] *Jürgen Friedrich Kammer*, Das gefängniswissenschaftliche Werk C.J.A. Mittermaiers. Freiburg im Breisgau (Dr. iur. Dissertation) 1971; *Heinz Müller-Dietz*, Der Strafvollzug im Werk Mittermaiers, in: Küper (Ed.), Mittermaier, p. 109 ff.

[285] *H.J. Schneider*, Franz von Holtzendorff, seine Persönlichkeit und sein Wirken für den Strafvollzug, in: Zeitschrift für Strafvollzug 13 (1964), 63 ff.

[286] *Krause*, Geschichte, p. 70 f.; see more recently *Désirée Schauz*, Strafen als moralische Besserung. Eine Geschichte der Straffälligenfürsorge 1777–1933. Munich 2008.

The English penal institution of **Pentonville**, built in 1842, became one of the models most frequently imitated. Its structure, a central hall with five radiating wings of cells, is characteristic of prison construction to this day. The first German imitations of this "giant delusion made into stone" *(Eb. Schmidt)* were built in **Bruchsal** (1848) and **Berlin-Moabit** (1849).

3. Reich Criminal Code

After legislation in the various German territories had experimented with a number of models,[287] the **Reich Criminal Code** created a unified system of punishments across the Reich. Besides **capital punishment**, it contained **penitentiary sentences** of 1–15 years, **prison sentences** of 1 day to 5 years, life sentences and 1–15 year sentences of **fortress imprisonment**, and **detention** (for transgressions) from 1 day to 6 weeks. **Fines** played a less important role. Rules for the execution of punishment are sparse. At least § 22 (2) RStGB stated that **solitary confinement** in both penitentiaries and prisons was not permitted for more than 3 years without the prisoner's consent. The **provisional release** from prison or penitentiary after three quarters of the sentence (after a minimum of 1 year) set out in § 24 was innovative—even though it was only optional (§§ 23 ff.).[288] The flipside of this was the correctional further detainment in a **workhouse** which § 362 RStGB defined as an option for individuals sentenced for vagrancy, begging, gambling, drunkenness and idling, prostitution, refusal to work or homelessness under § 361 (3–8).

The piecemeal regulations of the Reich Criminal Code failed to satisfy the need for a nationwide regulation of the execution of punishments. After the draft of a unified Prison Act fell through in 1879, mainly because of financial obstacles, an agreement was reached between the governments of the German states in the so-called ***Bundesratsgrundsätze*** (**Basic Principles of the Federal Council**). However, these were restricted to unifying administrative regulations; they added nothing new in terms of content. At least the minimum requirements of a well-ordered execution of prison sentences were thus enforced throughout Germany.[289]

---

[287] *Krause*, Geschichte, p. 72 ff.

[288] *Saxony* had led the way in this regard in 1862, see *Weber*, Sächsisches Strafrecht, Chapter 6.

[289] *Hans-Dieter Schwind/Günter Blau*, Strafvollzug in der Praxis. 2nd edition. Berlin, New York 1988, p. 15.

V. Review

Looking at the situation in criminal law at the end of the liberal period, around the beginning of the last quarter of the nineteenth century, i.e. after the enactment of the Reich Criminal Code and the *Reichsjustizgesetze* (Reich Justice Laws), and comparing it to the situation at the beginning of the century, it is clear that liberalism succeeded in achieving some of its demands. Where governments' power and the bourgeoisie's economic interests were not compromised, criminal law became more lenient.

The relationship between criminal law proper and criminal police law remained unresolved. The Reich Criminal Code had integrated a large part of minor offences in a title of their own as the third and lowest category of **transgressions**. Other offences remained subject to police law.

The inquisitorial principle remained dominant in **criminal procedure law**, with the main additions however of the accusatorial elements of open justice, *Mündlichkeit* and *Unmittelbarkeit* in trials, freedom of advocacy, free choice of defence counsel, defence counsel's right to ask questions, make evidential motions and (with restrictions) access to dossiers, the court's duty to consider present evidence, and judicial control over compulsory procedural measures. Nonetheless, the position of the defence counsel was one of those individual aspects where the reform agenda had been the least successful.

Citizens' participation in the criminal administration of justice mainly took the form of ***Schöffen*** (lay assessors) responsible predominantly for matters of petty crime, and who were more easily supervised by professional judges. **Jury courts**, demanded by the revolutionary middle classes mainly for press offences and political crime, were excluded from trying exactly these offences. In this regard, the Reich Justice Laws marked a step back compared to the legal state of affairs already achieved in some German states.[290] The criminal chambers of the district court, the backbone of the criminal justice system, were made up only of professional judges; the Reich Supreme Court was responsible for serious political crime as a court of first and last instance.

All in all, some important elements of the accusatory model had been added to or embedded in the inquisitorial principle. That these hard-won elements remained alien to the procedural body can be seen in the rejection reactions that have repeatedly taken place even recently—and not all of these have been unsuccessful.

During the nineteenth century, **imprisonment** oscillated between custodial sentences invoking Kant (albeit without much justification) and welfare-oriented reforms. There was no constructive combination of Kantian-liberal and social prison theory. At least the Reich Criminal Code contained some innovative elements with its restriction of solitary confinement and the option of provisional

---

[290] In Prussia, for example, according to § 60 (2) of the Decree on Open Oral Trials and Juries of 3 January 1849, jury courts had been expressly responsible for political misdemeanours and press offences.

release. The *workhouse* connects the criminal policies of the eighteenth and the twentieth centuries. The tradition of police responsibility for social discipline following the Decree of 1799 was continued here, setting the scene for further increased demands.

Not withstanding some successes, liberal demands thus also failed in several substantial aspects. Whether this justifies talk of a failure of the liberal reform effort[291] depends on one's perspective on the word "liberal". If the successes gained in criminal procedure are measured against a purely accusatorial principle, understand as the model of a liberal criminal procedure governed by the rule of law, then of course there were certain frictional losses, which can be filtered down to create a formidable list of aspects in which the rule of law aspect has failed. However, if the word "liberal" is understood politically and sociologically in the sense of liberalism as a political form of expression of the middle classes, a different conclusion can be drawn, for the bourgeoisie lost much of its "liberal" verve in the course of the nineteenth century. The dogged political situation which had been restored in 1815, and which in line with "defensive modernisation" opened up no more than politics and economics demanded, was not the only reason for this loss of impetus. In addition, while the attempt at a revolutionary shift in politics had failed in 1849 and Germany's political unification, originally at least partially associated with democratic ideals, had been achieved through authoritarian intervention in Bismarck's foundation of the Reich, this had only delayed one half of the "double revolution": in terms of economy, Germany had experienced a wave of industrialisation, mainly from the mid-century onwards, that ensured it a place among the foremost industrial nations by the end of the nineteenth century. However, this development went hand in hand with the emergence of large and increasingly politicised masses of workers, which in the eyes of the (upper) middle classes were just as threatening as the authoritarian state. In the eighteenth century, the long-term protection of property was a central concern which no reform debate could transcend; in the course of the nineteenth century, the interests of bourgeoisie and nobility became increasingly amalgamated: the middle classes became more "feudal", the nobility shifted from feudal to capitalist economic activity.[292]

In this situation, achieving a radically liberal, constitutional criminal law and a consistently accusatorial principle in criminal procedure was no longer high on the legal political agenda of the middle classes, although they had formerly been the champions of liberal demands. Since the period of the Enlightenment, "effective crime control" had been not only part of the programme of the authorities and

---

[291] *Malsack,* Verteidigung, p. 187; this tendency can also be detected in *Frommel,* Implementation, op. cit., p. 561.

[292] On this process, see e.g. *Thomas Nipperdey*, Deutsche Geschichte. Volume 1 (1866–1918). Munich 1992, p. 414 ff., 418; in connection with social democracy, see *Thomas Vormbaum*, Die Sozialdemokratie und die Entstehung des Bürgerlichen Gesetzbuchs. 2nd edition Baden-Baden 1997, p. XLI ff., in connection with the *Gesinderecht*, see *Vormbaum,* Gesinderecht (as in footnote 140), p. 150 ff.—On this development's effects on or parallels in cultural history and history of thought, see § 4 I, II.

powerful conservative elites, but also part of the bourgeois reformers' agenda.[293] The so-called reformed criminal procedure can thus be regarded as a compromise between the powerful elite and the liberals (with clear advantages for the former). This view is confirmed by the fact that the progress in criminal procedure demanded in the Paulskirche Constitution and established during the year of the Revolution remained in force after 1849, albeit with some restrictions.

Bourgeois liberalism[294] thus embarked on a path that the workers' movement (both democratic and non-democratic), the Green movement and the women's movement were to follow on. Although originally sceptical of criminal law and rule-of-law oriented, all of these movements discovered criminal law as an effective governance tool once they hoped to or were given a chance to influence the enactment of criminal law and use it to achieve their political aims.

The subsequent exposition will show that the times in which reforms in criminal law automatically meant a more lenient criminal law and constitutional progress in criminal law and criminal procedural law were now a thing of the past. Towards the end of the nineteenth century, a school of criminal law theory emerged whose intellectual starting point was not the liberalisation or increased leniency of criminal law and the struggle against the severe aspects it still contained, but its inexpediency and the need to overcome it.

---

[293] *Ignor*, Geschichte, p. 290.

[294] The description given here does not apply to all liberal politicians. A smaller part of political liberalism remained committed to its liberal and constitutional demands. This division of the Liberals was evident in the political organisations of the Kaiserreich (*Nationalliberale* and *Freisinnige*) and the Weimar Republic (*Deutsche Volkspartei* and *Deutsche Demokratische Partei*); in the Federal Republic, depending on the political situation, Liberalism's dominant focus is either constitutional or economic.

§ 4 The Shift from the Nineteenth to the Twentieth Century

I. Background

During the last third of the nineteenth century, ongoing modernisation propelled society into a state of crisis. While other countries besides Germany were affected, this crisis was felt particularly strongly there. Industrialisation, urbanisation, and a population boom made the traditional means of governing society appear inadequate. Economic activity became ever more frantic. The big bank and stock exchange crash of 1873 put an end to the boom of the *Gründerjahre* (the years that had seen the birth of modern industry in Germany), triggering the economic "Long Depression" that lasted well into the 1890s.[1] This was accompanied by a shift from a liberal "night watchman state" to a social interventionist state. Increasingly, the state provided not only a framework system within which free economic agents could act, but developed means of controlling and steering economic processes. In legislative terms, this trend produced first spectacular results only a few years after the foundation of the Reich in the legislation on stock corporations, which formed a clear counterpoint to the laissez-faire views current up until that point.[2] Anti-usury legislation followed the same direction.[3] From 1879 onwards, an

[1] For basic information, see *H. Rosenberg*, Große Depression und Bismarckzeit. Wirtschaftsablauf, Gesellschaft und Politik in Mitteleuropa. 3rd edition, Berlin 1976; see also *Id.*, Wirtschaftskonjunktur, Gesellschaft und Politik in Mitteleuropa 1873–1896, in: H.U. Wehler (Ed.), Moderne deutsche Sozialgeschichte. 3rd edition, Cologne, Berlin 1970, p. 225 ff.; *Wolfgang Zorn*, Wirtschafts- und sozialgeschichtliche Zusammenhänge der deutschen Reichsgründungszeit 1850–1879, ibid. p. 254 ff.; *Karl Erich Born*, Der soziale und wirtschaftliche Strukturwandel Deutschlands am Ende des 19. Jahrhunderts, ibid. p. 271 ff.

[2] On changes to the laws governing stock corporations, especially the stock corporation amendment of 1884, see *Bernhard Großfeld*, Aktiengesellschaft, Unternehmenskonzentration und Kleinaktionär. Tübingen 1968, p. 143 ff.; *Thomas Vormbaum*, Die Rechtsfähigkeit der Vereine im 19. Jahrhundert. Berlin 1976, p. 121 ff.

[3] Law on usury of 24 May 1880, RGBl. 1880, 109; Law regarding amendments to the rules on usury of 19 June 1893, RGBl. 1893, 197.

T. Vormbaum and M. Bohlander, *A Modern History of German Criminal Law*,
DOI 10.1007/978-3-642-37273-5_4,

economic foreign politics of protective tariffs replaced free trade; its domestic counterpart can be seen in Bismarck's coalition shift from the Liberals to the Conservatives,[4] the Socialists Act (which we will return to shortly), and—not paradoxically, but rather complementarily—the social legislation that was to follow soon after. The intention was to domesticate the Fourth Estate using the carrot of social welfare and the stick of special laws. From a matter of religious and social charity, the "social question" thus became a matter for state regulation. The state increasingly took on the characteristics of the modern *Anstaltsstaat* (state of institutions). The liberal era was coming to an end.

Changes in the history of ideas and particularly the history of science went hand in hand with these economic and social shifts. (It is hard to identify what was cause and what effect; influences were certainly reciprocal.) In the same way that the rationalism promulgated by the Enlightenment had gained currency over the years and decades, eventually spreading to every aspect of social life (though increasingly mutating from a theoretical line of thought to an everyday attitude, thus becoming more trivial),[5] a similar development could be observed in the empirical sciences during the last third of the nineteenth century. An absolute trust in science spread to all circles of society. The zoologist **Ernst Haeckel** (1834–1919) thought the "mysteries of the world" could be solved.[6] Lay theories based on everyday experiences accompanied the triumphal march of these sciences (which themselves often overestimated their theoretical and practical potential) in the same way that Mr Hyde accompanied Dr Jekyll. The borders between science, popular science and charlatanry became blurred, as can be seen in the first beginnings of "racial theory" and incipient, pseudo-scientific "modern" racial anti-Semitism.

The phenomenal progress in natural sciences and technology was characterised by an emphasis on the empirical and a tendency to reject anything "transcendental", whether religious or philosophical. It was only a matter of time until this attitude was extended to include society as well. *Darwin's* theory of evolution provided a bridge for many political theories: **Karl Marx** and **Friedrich Engels**, for example, saw many points of contact between their thought and Darwin's. Hegel's influence meant they were familiar with the idea that world history developed according to certain laws, and they were attracted by the dialectics inherent in Darwin's theory.[7]

Closer to the other end of the political spectrum—though certainly not without influence on the social democrats—**social Darwinism** transferred the theory of the

---

[4] On this, incl. references, *Thomas Vormbaum*, Einführung, in: Id. (Ed.), Die Sozialdemokratie und die Entstehung des Bürgerlichen Gesetzbuchs. 2nd edition, Baden-Baden 1997, p. LI ff.

[5] On this, see *Rosenberg*, Rationalismus, p. 18 ff.

[6] *Ernst Haeckel*, Die Welträthsel. Gemeinverständliche Studien über Monistische Philosophie. First published Bonn, 1899.

[7] Friedrich Engels at Karl Marx's grave: "Just as Darwin discovered the law of development of organic nature, so Marx discovered the law of development of human history: the simple fact, hitherto concealed by an overgrowth of ideology, that mankind must first of all eat, drink, have shelter and clothing, before it can pursue politics, science, art, religion, etc."; *Karl Marx/Friedrich Engels*, Collected Works. Vol. 41. London 1985, p. 246.

"survival of the fittest" to society; as early as the end of the nineteenth century, suggestions on how to categorise human beings according to eugenic principles were made, and ideas on human selection and "grafting" were formulated. The theory of **racial hygiene**, at first applied to the human race in general, began to develop. First thoughts on "euthanasia" appeared, although they held no majority or political appeal yet.[8] The radical political manifestations and excesses of some of these theoretical considerations faded somewhat once the economic depression came to an end in the final years of the nineteenth century; however, a latent potential manifesting itself in "social codes" remained that only needed conditions to worsen once more (as they did with the First World War and its consequences) in order to revive.

All in all, the phenomenon that Max Weber termed the "disenchantment of the world" was accelerated during the period under discussion. This process had begun with the Enlightenment and now received fresh impetus. Its effect on art and literature can be seen in realism (*Wilhelm Raabe*) and naturalism (*Gerhard Hauptmann*).

Positivism was a central scientific term. *Auguste Comte* (1798–1857), the inventor of the word "sociology", had already published his seminal work *Plan de traveaux scientifiques nécessaires pour réorganiser la société* on the philosophy of positivism in 1822, but it had met with resistance during his lifetime. Comte differentiated between three stages of the human spirit: a theological, religious (childlike) stage, a metaphysical (adolescent) stage (under which he categorised philosophers and legal theorists), and the positivist (adult) stage. In this third stage, the human being dispenses with supernatural and metaphysical insights and is content to trace connections between phenomena through observation and experiment and discover laws through induction.

These new sentiments in state and society did not remain without effect on law and legal theory. **Legal positivism** was positivism's offshoot in the field of law. It rejected the ideas of natural and rationalist law—i.e. those based on speculative, transcendental, rationally determined insights into human and social existence—and based itself completely on empirical facts, whether taken from within the field of law or from without. In its narrower expression as *positivism of law*, it was based purely on the "positive" law enacted by the state legislator (this is the variant later embraced by the so-called "classical school"). In its more general form, it made reference to empirical (natural scientific, psychological or sociological) insights and demanded that positive law be restructured accordingly in a reform of criminal law (this is the variant later espoused by the "sociological" or "modern" school). Terms such as "justice", which cannot be expressed empirically through measuring, weighing, or counting, or sorted into terminological categories, were either rejected or given a new empirical definition.

The replacement of the doctrine of infringement of rights by the doctrine of infringement of *protected legal interests* was an early indication of this development in criminal law, for—as has already been demonstrated—this ultimately

[8] On this, see *Große-Vehne*, p. 48 ff.

referred the theory of criminal law back to positive laws.[9] However, the positivism it expressed—which was hardly self-aware, but grew out of criminal policy or court practice or (if presenting itself in theoretical terms) out of historicism—was, so to speak, a "naive" legal positivism. By contrast, the form of legal positivism dominant towards the end of the nineteenth century "originates in a deeply felt, militant conviction [...] far more self-assured [than earlier positivism] as it is intimately entwined with the *Zeitgeist*".[10] Ethnic-political statements or indeed any 'ought'--statements were regarded with suspicion. Legal philosophy became "general theory of law" and was to concern itself only with positive law. The codification of the legal matter, which had already been completed in the field of criminal law and was yet to be carried out for civil law, gave this new positivism materials it could work its way through while remaining within the system itself and "neutral".[11]

The tendency towards a purely formal understanding of the rule of law referred to at the end of § 2 also accommodated legal positivism. If the legal matter was at the disposal of the legislator as a matter of principle, then its contents depended on political decisions. However, in 19th century Germany these decisions were made within the context first of the Restoration, then of the failure of the bourgeois revolution and the reactionary period, then of the Wilhelminian authoritarian state. It was hard for generally recognised, unquestioned material preconceptions of civil liberties and human rights to develop. The "rule of law" was a feature of the Reich that Bismarck created; however, basically the rule of law was reduced to adherence to rules of procedure when creating laws, to adherence to law by the administration and the justice system, and to access to justice.

II. Changes in Criminal Law

As described at the end of § 2, the understanding of criminal law prevalent during the nineteenth century took the infringement of a right—defined as precisely as possible and according to objective criteria in the law—as its starting point. The only subjective factor taken into consideration (besides negligence, which was only seldom provided for) was intention (*Vorsatz*, which towards the end of the century had been termed *Schuld*, "blameworthiness", and prior to that *Zurechnung*, "attribution"). Responsibility for an offence was only ever questioned in cases of unconsciousness or insanity (§ 51 RStGB).[12] The subjective factor ("blameworthiness in the wider sense") was thus a purely psychological one; questions of character, attitude etc. played no role at all. This paradigm of a **criminal law**

[9] Cf. § 2 I.—The German Historical School, which in terms of legal policy originally had been an opponent of legal positivism, ended up merging with it, for that which has come to be (through legal history) ultimately coincides with that which is (in positive law); see for private law *Wieacker*, Privatrechtsgeschichte, p. 430 ff.

[10] *Amelung*, Rechtsgüterschutz, p. 53.

[11] Ibid.

[12] Here responsibility itself was not seen as forming *part* of blameworthiness, but as its *precondition*. On *Frank's* criticism, see below § 5 II. 2.

based strictly on the offence (*Tatstrafrecht*) (rather than the person of the offender) began to erode towards the end of the nineteenth century.

One important factor in this erosion was the impact that new lines of thought had on ideas of **free will** and thus on one of the central pillars of liberal criminal law, the offender's autonomy. "Naturalistically", as a purely empirical phenomenon, human beings—like all other phenomena within space and time—are subject to the law of causality, or in philosophical terms, the law of sufficient cause. Idealist philosophers were already familiar with this idea. Immanuel Kant had made the distinction between the empirical side of human beings as a part of nature (*homo phainomenon*) and their "intelligible" side independent of space and time (*homo noumenon*), thus declaring the parallel existence of both human subjection to nature and human freedom and autonomy. If a tendency to reduce human beings to their empirical side now existed, then it questioned freedom and autonomy, the ability to act in a self-determined manner, to "be able to act differently".

In criminal law as in the history of ideas in general, new ways of thinking only seldom manifest themselves suddenly (and if they do, it usually only seems to be that way). Usually they mature slowly within the "womb" of earlier conditions. Whether they are the catalysts of social change or are themselves driven by it, whether the nineteenth century academic theories of criminal law and criminal procedure were simply foam on the waves of political and social developments or whether their arguments were able to establish themselves in the face of political opposition is a question that requires further analysis, but that we have no space to pursue here. Some indication is provided by a development in the history of ideas and culture that, by virtue of its nature, can be more easily compared to the development in the theory of criminal law than can economic or social developments.

The philosophy of **Arthur Schopenhauer** (1788–1860), which had at first remained without much impact for several decades, experienced a surge in public interest and had a significant influence on art (e.g. *Richard Wagner's* "Tristan" and "Ring of the Nibelung"), literature (*Thomas Mann's* "Buddenbrooks") and philosophy (particularly in the early works of *Friedrich Nietzsche*). Schopenhauer's pessimistic philosophy, which saw the aim of a successful life in overcoming the *will* (to live) by (contemplative) *representation* (his philosophy of pity less so), resonated well with a cultural context in which a large part of the social class concerned with creating and promoting culture and art had lost its faith in the steady progress of liberty, due to the failure of the 1848/49 Revolution on the one hand and this class's inclusion in the authoritarian state and social system on the other.

In his key work of 1818, *The World as Will and Representation*, Schopenhauer adopts a theory of threat and general deterrence derived from Beccaria and Feuerbach and expressly opposed to Kant.[13] In his 1839 essay *On the Freedom of the Will*[14] he posits that human beings are free to *do* what they will, but not to *will* something other than they will; thus there is freedom of action, but no freedom of

[13] See the respective texts from 1818 (Vol. 1) and 1844 (Vol. 2) in *Vormbaum*, MdtStrD p. 110 ff. and 372 f.

[14] *Schopenhauer*, Freedom of the Will, Cambridge 1999. The following quotes are taken from pages 46–47, 94.

will: "Under the assumption of the freedom of the will, every human action would be an inexplicable miracle—an effect without cause". What human beings will depends on their unchanging *character*, and is thus determined by it: "A human being never changes; as he has acted in a given case, so will he always act again in exactly the same circumstances [and with the same level of knowledge]"; the only thing that can be changed is *knowledge*. Human beings carry responsibility not because they could have *acted* differently, but because they could not have *been* different. A deed "is regarded here merely as evidence of the character of the doer".[15] The result is certainly not that "no criminal may be punished". The execution of punishment—here Schopenhauer follows Feuerbach—only has the purpose of proving the threat of punishment, which is one of the factors influencing the will, to be a serious one.

By clearly locating criminal responsibility in the character—which is moreover seen as unchanging—Schopenhauer's theory proves itself the seismograph of a development and line of thought that the theory, policy and practice of criminal law (as well as criminology, which subsequently emerged) were soon to be confronted with and that they still grapple with to the present day. The liberal model of a criminal law that judged matters objectively and only used subjective factors to limit what was punishable was toppled by doubts of the freedom of the will and an interest in the offender's character. The **person of the offender** was "discovered". This will be discussed further (see IV. below).

III. Finality in Criminal Law

1. The "Marburger Programm"

The aim of the criminal law to achieve restitution of the legal condition was supplanted by the aim of achieving the purposes of criminal policy. The idea of **purpose (*Zweckgedanke*)** revived a tradition of thought that had already played an important role in the philosophy of the Enlightenment, but that had temporarily forfeited its leading position (at least as far as legal theory was concerned) at the beginning of the nineteenth century.

Beccaria had already made the connection between justice and expediency in his statement: "[i]f a punishment is to be just, it *may* be pitched *only* at that level of intensity which suffices to deter men from crime".[16] *Franz v. Liszt* now wrote in a

[15] The freedom of the will, that we experience as a sense of responsibility for the actions we have committed, according to Schopenhauer (who here refers to Kant) is "transcendental; i.e., it does not emerge in the appearance but is present only insofar as we abstract from the appearance and all its forms in order to reach that which, outside all time, is to be thought of as the inner essence of the human being in himself" (p. 86).

[16] *Beccaria*, Crimes p. 68.

similar vein: "Justice in criminal law consists in keeping to the extent of punishment demanded by its purpose".[17]

Rudolf v. Jhering (1818–1892) unmistakably alluded to Darwin's "struggle for existence" in the title of his work *Der Kampf ums Recht* (1872). In his two-volume work *Der Zweck im Recht* (1877/1884), he provided the keyword *Zweck* ("purpose") for this new line of thought's manifesto, the so-called *Marburger Programm* of **Franz v. Liszt** (1851–1918).[18] Liszt's essay *Der Zweckgedanke im Strafrecht* ("The Idea of Purpose in Law"), based on a paper given at the University of Marburg in 1882 and published in 1883, was a "polemic" in more ways than one: it both challenged current theory of criminal law and declared war on crime.[19] The challenge to the theory of criminal law targeted the theory of compensation or retribution, which had in the meantime taken a positivist turn, and whose main representative was **Karl Binding** (1841–1920). Thus Liszt triggered the so-called *Schulenstreit* in criminal law (see§ 5 II. 1. below).

Of course, *Liszt* was not the first to ground the study of criminal law in the new *Zeitgeist* and new lines of thought. As early as 1879, the chief prosecutor and later Reich Supreme Court justice **Otto Mittelstädt** (1834–1899) had attracted attention with his book "Gegen die Freiheitsstrafen", in which he denounced retributive punishments and called for them to be replaced by harsh, even brutal punishments aimed at general deterrence. In his response "Die Abschaffung des Strafmaßes" published a year later, the psychiatrist **Emil Kraepelin** (1856–1926) also took a rejection of the theory of retribution as his starting point, paying homage to a strict determinism. He developed a theory of reform that regarded the criminal offender as an invalid and therefore demanded that the psychiatrist play a central role in sanction and enforcement. Those incapable of reform were to be imprisoned for life or deported.[20]

With this theory of rehabilitation and incapacitation, which – as already evident in the book's title – aimed at abolishing punishment as retribution in favour of punishment as a means of securing incapacitation, Kraepelin had already pre-empted much of the thought behind the "Marburger Programm".

Introducing this programme, Liszt sees the current theory of criminal law as weakened above all by the "growing horror at the powerlessness of doctrinaire criminal law, as irrefutably proven by criminal statistics".[21] The thrust of his criticism, something often overlooked or blocked out, is thus not the harshness of the retributive criminal law practised during his time, but rather its insufficient success in combating crime; his starting point is by no means a liberal one.[22] He and

---

[17] *v. Liszt*, Zweckgedanke, p. 37.

[18] On Liszt's biography, see *Naucke*, Kriminalpolitik, p. 229 incl. references.

[19] *Köhler*, Einführung, p. VI.

[20] For more details on Mittelstädt and Kraepelin: *Schmidt-Recia / Steinberg*, ZStW 2007, 195 ff., especially p. 200 ff.; also including information on further participants in this debate: **Ernst Sichart** (1833–1908) and **Richard Sontag** (born 1835); see also *Arndt Koch*, Binding vs. Liszt.—Klassische und moderne Strafrechtsschule, in: Hilgendorf / Weitzel, Strafgedanke, p. 127 ff., 131.

[21] *v. Liszt*, Zweckgedanke, p. 6.

[22] *Vogel*, Einflüsse p. 92.

his followers are concerned less with protecting the individual from the state than protecting society from the criminal.[23]

This view is confirmed in his further elaborations. In the first section, v. Liszt develops a kind of natural history of punishment: originally, it is "society's blind, instinctive reaction, not driven by the idea of purpose, to external disruptions of its living conditions",[24] following the purpose of "preservation of the species".[25] In the next stage of development, the discovery of purpose turns punishment from an instinctive act to an act of will.[26] Human beings analyse their "living conditions" and fix them as protected legal interests; then they examine actions aimed at harming these protected legal interests and thus gradually develop definitions of individual crimes.[27] This leads to the postulate that "in an individual case, that punishment [be imposed] that is necessary to safeguard the protected legal interests through punishment. The right, i.e. the just punishment is the necessary one". Purpose thus also governs the principle of the extent of punishment.

Liszt develops his method of defining the punishment to be imposed in each individual case from this principle. Punishment is coercion directed against the will of the criminal. Coercion can be applied through encouraging and strengthening motives already present or through violence. Thus punishment has three effects:

---

[23] *Wetzell*, Inventing, p. 33.

[24] *v. Liszt*, Zweckgedanke, p. 8.

[25] Op. cit., p. 11.—A few years later (1887), **Friedrich Nietzsche** (1844–1900) was also to develop an evolutionary theory of punishment and purposes of punishment in his "Genealogy of Morality" (Cambridge 2007; excerpt in *Vormbaum*, MdtStrD, p. 238 ff.), which has both similarities and differences to Liszt's theory (it cannot be assumed that Nietzsche read Liszt; but it is well-known that he read Jhering): like Liszt, Nietzsche sees that a phenomenon extant in society, a procedure (the "stable"), is given meaning (the "fluid") by the term punishment; of course, he states that no one meaning of punishment can be defined: "Only something which has no history can be defined". He sees the sole purpose and effect of punishment—following Schopenhauer—as the "sharpening of intelligence, [. . .] a lengthening of the memory" (*Nietzsche*, Genealogy p. 56). He considers a (moral) reform of the offender unlikely, as "he sees the same kind of action practised in the service of justice and given approval, practised with a good conscience: like spying, duping, bribing, setting traps, the whole intricate and wily skills of the policeman and prosecutor, as well as the most thorough robbery, violence, slander, imprisonment, torture and murder, carried out without even having emotion as an excuse, all practices that are manifest in the various kinds of punishment,—none of which is seen by his judges as a depraved and condemned act *as such*" (ibid., p. 55).—For a closer analysis of punishment in Nietzsche's philosophy: *Knut Engelhardt*, Die Transformation des Willens zur Macht. Bemerkungen zum Verhältnis von Moral, Strafe und Verbrechen in Nietzsches Philosophie, in: ARSP 71 (1985), 499 ff.; *Lucas Gschwend*, Nietzsche und die Kriminalwissenschaften. Eine rechtshistorische Untersuchung der strafrechtsphilosophischen und kriminologischen Aspekte in Nietzsches Werk unter besonderer Berücksichtigung der Nietzsche-Rezeption in der deutschen Rechtswissenschaft; in: ZRG.GA 119 (2002), 919 ff.; *Jochen Bung*, Nietzsche über Strafe, in: ZStW 119 (2007), 120 ff.

[26] *v. Liszt*, Zweckgedanke, p. 21.

[27] Op. cit., p. 23.

1. *Reform*, i.e. "implanting altruistic, social motives",
2. *Deterrence*, i.e. "implanting and strengthening egoistic motives, whose effects coincide with those of altruistic motives".
3. *Neutralisation*: in this regard, punishment is

> sequestration of the criminal; temporary or permanent neutralisation, expulsion from society or imprisonment within it. It appears as an artificial selection of the socially unfit individual. 'Nature casts one who has committed an offence against her into the sickbed, the state casts him into prison (Jhering)'.[28]

Both these and other passages show that the language of the *Marburger Programm* contains "phrases that, even if they are due to the abruptness of the new beginning, appear disconcerting given the historical experiences that followed"[29]; much of the programme "can be seen as bureaucratic with problematic emotional undertones (particularly when using medical and military comparisons)".[30]

The elaborations on "neutralisation" are far from the only problematic passages. Liszt was thus in line with a time that thought little of "maudlin humanitarianism". In the following decades, a populist, coarse jargon, an ill-kempt language later to be reinforced by the brutalising influence of the World War became a familiar feature of criminal policy. Aspirations to humanity, which the philosophers of the Enlightenment had wished to combine with utilitarian thought, were abandoned in favour of a merciless "scientificity".

According to Liszt, the three categories of punishment correspond to three categories of offenders. The following features can be added to his three-part system:

1. Reform of those offenders capable of and in need of reform,
2. Deterrence of those offenders *not* in need of reform,
3. Neutralisation of those offenders *incapable* of reform.

Liszt uses the term *habitual offending* in connection with this third group,[31] a term which was to rise to prominence during the twentieth century and furnish the title of one of the first criminal laws of the National Socialist legislation. In a essay published 10 years later, Liszt demanded—in contrast to current opinion, which only considered the act to be judged and sentenced in meting out punishment—that "the attitude and intention of the culprit evident in the act committed be the decisive factor"[32]—a demand that is only consistent if the offender's personality was the key factor in determining the type and extent of punishment.

---

[28] Op. cit., p. 40.

[29] *Köhler*, Einführung, p. VII; similarly *Kubink*, Strafe, p. 94: what Liszt demands for the category of those incapable of reform, appears "at least at first glance as a precursor of later programmes of biological cleansing and 'special treatment'"; see also *Koch*, Binding vs. Liszt, p. 135 f.

[30] *Naucke*, Kriminalpolitik, p. 228.

[31] Op. cit., p. 42.

[32] *v. Liszt*, Die deterministischen Gegner, op. cit, p. 354.

Liszt's line of argument, based on evolution theory, viewed revenge as the absolute (retributive) *Ur*-form of punishment, which then progressed to utilitarian punishment; hence, he called his view of punishment **unification theory**.[33]

Liszt was unable to accept the traditional term ***Zurechnungsfähigkeit*, responsibility**, which attributed the crime to a decision freely made by the offender. For him, responsibility represented "normal determinability by motives"[34]—or put differently: "Someone who reacts to motives in a normal manner is responsible".[35] The term of free will as developed by Kant, which derived from rational judgement and was thus transcendental, and was supported by the dominant late nineteenth century view of the theory of criminal law,[36] was opposed by *Liszt's* empirical average measure for the influence of causal factors on the offender's consciousness.[37] A lack of responsibility was not longer a matter of *defective autonomy*, but of *defective determinability* (or *motivability*). The connection with punishment arose not only because punishment becomes constitutionally legitimated by ethical and other motives once motivability has been established, but also because the punishment inflicted is itself capable of preventing the offender from relapsing.[38]

This line of argument of course fails to take into account the fact that responsibility is not established comprehensively, but only *in reference to the offence*, so that one cannot make blanket statements on both sides of motivability. Here, too, criminal policy represses (or at least *op*presses) the structures of the doctrine of criminal law and the rule of law.

As an empirical factor, there are different grades of motivability. All followers of *Liszt's* modern school therefore demanded the introduction of the legal concept of **diminished responsibility**. In this regard, they agreed with exponents of the new discipline of criminology.[39]

While *Liszt* thus adhered to the demand of responsibility and the idea of blameworthiness, there was no question for him that blameworthiness itself could form a measure and limit for punishment. The most important aim of his deliberations was **punishment as protection**, i.e., punishment with the purpose of establishing security. This was to take the following form: while those

[33] This should not be confused with the various unification theories current today that attempt to combine different purposes of punishment, for example the so-called phase model, that sees each different stage of the criminal procedure as pursuing a different punitive purpose.

[34] *v. Liszt*, Die deterministischen Gegner, op. cit, p. 342.

[35] *v. Liszt*, Zurechnungsfähigkeit, op. cit., p. 219.

[36] Of course, the Reich Criminal Code had not yet taken a stance on the question of free will. The phrasing (misleading in this regard) "prevention of the free exercise of will" in § 51 RStGB was chosen as the "relatively best" one, without intending that the "various metaphysical views on free will in its philosophical sense be included in criminal trials"; see references in *Schwarze*, StGB, p. 83.

[37] *Bohnert*, Schulenstreit, p. 167: "Equating normal with average determinability uses statistics to gloss over the obvious question of evaluation".

[38] *v. Liszt*, Zurechnungsfähigkeit, op. cit., p. 221. *Schopenhauer* had referred to this thought as "correction of insight".

[39] *Chr. Müller*, Verbrechensbekämpfung, p. 40, 164.

"incapable of reform", the "habitual offenders"—which were to include "theft, dealing in stolen goods, robbery, blackmail, fraud, arson, criminal damage, violent fornication and fornication with children (this list may be extended on grounds of closer observation)"—were to be imprisoned for life (or an indefinite period) following a third conviction,[40] those "in need of reform" were to receive a custodial sentence of at least one and no more than 5 years in a reformatory institution—the length was not to be declared in the verdict. Depending on the degree to which he or she reformed, the convict could be released after 1 year.

Followed through to its conclusion, Liszt's idea of punishment as protection ultimately dispenses utterly with the concept of blameworthiness, for the culprit's attitude, the decisive issue, is less an expression of his *blameworthiness* than of his *dangerousness*. And the extent of punishment was supposed to be determined not by blameworthiness, but by the reform the criminal achieved and by his dangerousness. However, as we shall see, in this regard *Liszt* made a welcome, but inconsistent concession to the rule of law.

In an 1893 contribution, Liszt suggested where a line of compromise in practical criminal policy might be drawn:

> We should not be concerned with what name this child is given. That is the pleasant side of our opponents' behaviour, that they are content if time-honoured labels are retained. The 'proportion of guilt and atonement' must not be exceeded in the 'punishment' of the habitual offender; but our opponents have no objection to lifelong or very lengthy 'security measures' after a sentence has been served. 'Retributive' justice will not allow two years in prison for vagrants incapable of reform; but our opponents would probably allow five years of workhouse, which is considerably more unpleasant. So let us call it security measure and workhouse; let us take what we can get.[41]

The "dual track" of punishments and security measures was thus presented, and this was to form the so-called compromise in the so-called Schulenstreit—a conflict between two schools of thought, neither of which seemed to have a problem with rendering vagrancy punishable (an offence that, like begging, only disappeared from the Criminal Code in 1969 during a brief renaissance of liberal criminal theory).

2. The "Comprehensive Study of Criminal Law"

Liszt's (Figs. 13, 14, 15, and 16) typology of crimes and offenders resulted in calls for a scholarly investigation into the causes of crime. The study of criminal law was not supposed to exhaust itself simply in cultivating doctrine. New additions were made to it: **criminology**, the study of the causes of crime—encompassing on the one hand *criminal sociology* as the study of (social) environmental factors, criminal

[40] *v. Liszt*, Zweckgedanke, p. 45 f.

[41] *v. Liszt*, Gegner, p. 368.

Fig. 13 Franz von Liszt (1851–1919)

Fig. 14 Karl Lorenz Binding (1841–1920)

Fig. 15 Arthur Schopenhauer (1788–1860)

Fig. 16 Adolf Merkel (1836–1896)

anthropology, later criminal psychiatry and, above all, *criminal biology,*[42] and on the other the study of predisposition—as well as **criminalistics**, the study of the techniques of solving crime.[43] **Criminal statistics** established itself as a comparatively independent discipline. According to Liszt, the legal-political, practical task of *punishment* could "at best" only be to target the "individual factors of crime". This explains his criticism of politicians who believed they "could charm and control danger through a few new threats of punishment".[44]

The concept of the "comprehensive study of criminal law" also formed the basis for the *Internationale Kriminalistische Vereinigung* (IKV), which was co-founded by Liszt and significantly influenced by his programme.[45]

For Liszt, the question arose of what role **criminal law** still had to play within the comprehensive study of criminal law. In 1907, **Karl Birkmeyer** (1847–1920) summed up this problem in the oft-quoted phrase from the title of his lecture (and pamphlet) *Was läßt v. Liszt vom Strafrecht übrig?* ("What has Liszt left of criminal law?"). Followed through to its ultimate conclusion, his empirical approach left "only purposeful punishment, but not criminal law".[46] While *Liszt* only briefly touched on this question in the *Marburger Programm*, he gave his opinion on it elsewhere, coining one of his most frequently quoted phrases: criminal law is "the **Magna Charta** of the criminal", it is "an insurmountable barrier to criminal policy". Accordingly, the extensive access to the (convicted and) sentenced offender demanded by Liszt was only to occur once a legally defined offence fulfilling the principle of specificity had been committed and the offence had been proven in a criminal trial strictly subject to law. The principles of *nullum crimen sine lege* and *nulla poena sine lege* are "the citizen's bulwark against the absolute power of the state".[47] *Liszt's* construction of punishment as protection naturally paid far less attention to the second principle than to the first. From the above descriptions it already follows that this applied to those incapable of and those needing reform, and it clearly becomes applicable also to those not in need of reform when reading that *Liszt* there demanded a unified custodial sentence of 6 months to 10 years.[48]

---

[42] This last term, which was actually introduced by *Liszt* (see *Baumann*, Verbrechen, p. 12), fell out of use after 1945.

[43] On criminalistics at the turn of the century: *Miloš Vec*, Die Spur des Täters. Baden-Baden 2002.

[44] *v. Liszt*, Verbrechen, p. 236; see also *Holzhauer*, p. 182.

[45] *Elisabeth Bellmann*, Die Internationale Kriminalistische Vereinigung (1889–1933). Frankfurt am Main 1994.—The IKV forms part of a general internationalising trend in the theory and politics of criminal law; on this, see *Sylvia Kesper-Biermann / Petra Overath* (Eds.), Die Internationalisierung von Strafrechtswissenschaft und Kriminalpolitik (1870–1930). Deutschland im Vergleich. Baden-Baden 2007.

[46] *Naucke*, Kriminalpolitik, p. 233.

[47] *v. Liszt*, Gegner, p. 357; it remains unclear how the second principle fits in with Liszt's demand for indeterminate punishment. On other occasions, Liszt distanced himself from it, cf. *Liszt*, Die deterministischen Gegner der Zweckstrafe, op. cit, p. 365 (included in *Vormbaum*, MdtStrD, p. 233 f.).

[48] *v. Liszt*, Zweckgedanke, p. 49.

The perspective of *Liszt's* picture is skewed: "Magna Charta of the criminal" already assumes that there is a "criminal". But whether someone is a criminal can only be determined by applying definitions of offences and by a formal criminal trial, i.e. by criminal law. Ultimately, the basis of this picture is a material definition of crime, the idea of actions that can be referred to as "crimes" regardless of offence definitions and trial conditions. The metaphor of the "insurmountable barrier" only makes sense if it refers to a barrier limiting the *scope* of criminal policy, for once the criminal legal and procedural conditions of a conviction have been fulfilled, the barrier to criminal policy is lifted.

The *scope* of criminal policy—and this is where content criticism begins—lies in the hand of the legislator; he can extend it; *Liszt* states explicitly: "Criminal legislation is, without doubt, a matter of state criminal *politics*".[49] The position of this "bulwark" could thus be altered at any time.[50]

The force with which *Liszt* championed upholding the rule of law on this side of the bulwark,[51] the ambivalence of the idea of utility, which could lead to a restriction of criminal law in cases of inexpedient or counterproductive punishment (e.g. short-term custodial sentences), the fact that social democrats were among Liszt's followers (e.g. Gustav Radbruch), and finally his political dedication to liberalism (i.e. the left-wing liberals in the Reichstag)—all of this probably contributed to the long-held opinion that *Liszt's* theory was a liberal, constitutional one and was opposed and defended as such. As it also influenced plans for reform during the late imperial period and the Weimar Republic, it was rejected by the National Socialists. However, it was no great difficulty for Liszt's followers—most importantly, *Eberhard Schmidt* und *Eduard Kohlrausch*—to show his theory's compatibility with the "new way of thinking".

But here we are getting ahead of ourselves. Whether the barrier of criminal law was really to prove insurmountable was something only the future could tell—but what it told was mainly negative.

IV. Discovering the "Offender"

An empirical study of criminality in line with the *Zeitgeist* developed independently of Liszt, though it gained strength following the publication of the *Marburger Programm*, both in Germany and in Europe. The new discipline of criminology,

[49] *v. Liszt*, Gegner, p. 367.

[50] *Koch*, Binding vs. Liszt, p. 138.

[51] The fact that Liszt wants to make how habitual offenders are treated dependent on a specific number of relapses, i.e. a formal criterion, seems to point in the same direction, but could also be interpreted as an attempt to prevent psychiatry encroaching on the monopoly of jurists in upholding criminal law.

particularly German criminology, became caught up in an individual criminal etiology that focused on factors of predisposition.

For a long time, criminal *sociology* remained subordinate to criminal biology and criminal psychiatry, particularly in Germany. One obvious reason for this is that prison doctors and psychiatrists had their "individual" material directly at hand in penal institutions, and predisposition as a factor suggested itself to their professions. Social workers, "streetworkers" and other social professions that might have formed a counterbalance did not yet exist. Furthermore, opportunities for the practical prevention of crime were more likely to present themselves in influencing individual delinquents, whereas changes to the social causes of crime fell under the remit of politics, an area that criminologists and sociologists did not feel responsible for and could influence either only with difficulty or not at all. Thus the problem of crime remained too abstract to interest most sociologists.

Accordingly, it was a doctor and psychiatrist, the Italian **Cesare Lombroso** (1835–1909), who first formulated an explanation of criminal behaviour using scientific, empirical methods in his work *L'uomo delinquente* ("Criminal Man") first published in 1876. According to Lombroso, crime can be explained anthropologically: criminals belong to an atavistic race of humans, a peculiar anthropological type surviving from earlier times. This type can be recognised by its physical features: strong brow ridges, huge lower jaws, square chins, handle-shaped ears (in short, "a Mongolian or even negroid type").[52] Lombroso qualified his statements increasingly with every edition of his book in response to criticism, not least that of his student **Enrico Ferri** (1856–1929). In the end he declared his statements only applied to 30–40 % of all offenders.

From today's perspective, many objections can be raised to Lombroso's view of the "born criminal", due to historical experience and advances in criminology. The time that followed proved the inherent danger of "criminal anthropological" theories; objectively, Lombroso's theories can be seen in connection with racist theories of crime or even labelled "protofascist"—which once again shows (as with the philosophers of the Enlightenment) how differently objective or structural evaluations and individual evaluations of one person's behaviour can be. As the vast response to his work shows, Lombroso struck a chord with popular thought of the time that adulated the (natural) sciences and was as yet unmarked by the experiences of the twentieth century (Lombroso himself was Jewish and a socialist, according to his own description, and thus would have been anything but popular in National Socialist Germany). The enthusiasm of his time for the natural sciences also explains a mistaken categorisation which is obvious to a criminologist of today familiar with the *labeling approach*, but was also criticised then. The French criminal sociologist **Alexandre Lacassagne** (1843–1924) raised the objection that given the cultural, legally defined nature of the term crime, it was absurd to assume a specific biological type of crime.[53]

---

[52] *Albrecht*, Kriminologie. Munich 2002, p. 10 f. [including images]; *Wetzell*, Inventing, p. 28 ff.; *Id.*, Kriminologie; *Bernd-Dieter Meier*, Kriminologie. Munich 2003, p. 17.

[53] *Gadebusch Bondio*, Rezeption, p. 44.

Even if the definitions approach and the *labeling approach* are not accepted as passe-partouts for explaining crime, it cannot be denied that the legal canon of offences is *also* the result of political and social processes of definition. The decision whether a person and their actions remain in the dark field, so to speak, or whether they are investigated and adjudicated, is also a result of social labels and selection. Categories of the natural sciences or anthropology are unable to deal adequately with these dimensions.[54]

Of course, earlier times had also been familiar with "criminal psychiatry" and "criminal psychology". Even without going back to the "lively interest of jurists of the early Enlightenment in psychology", the Gießen philosopher **Johann Christian Gottlieb Schaumann** (1768–1821) can be mentioned, who was probably the first to use the compound term "criminal psychology" in his book *Ideen zu einer Kriminalpsychologie*.[55] If this development is seen from the point of view of discourse theory, then it becomes evident that two discourses emerge during the time period discussed in the previous chapter, whose key terms according to *Peter Becker* are "depravity" (*Verderbnis*) and "degeneracy" (*Entartung*).[56]

Both discourses share a "binary logic", a dichotomy between the bourgeois self and the criminal "other"; however, while definition was a matter for forensic practitioners (policemen, investigating judges) in the earlier discourse, in the new discourse it is a matter for doctors, psychiatrists, anthropologists and experts in criminal law. Practitioners increasingly make space for academic scholars. In the first discourse, interest is focused on the *behaviour* of the offender, in the second on the *person* of the offender. There, the offender is a "fallen human being", here an "impeded human being". The "moral history of evil" is replaced by the "naturalisation of crime".[57] The connection to the conditions described at the beginning of § 4 is clear.

The strong criticism of Lombroso[58] may have reduced the impact of his criminal-anthropological approach, but could not prevent the individualist explanation of criminality from remaining dominant in Germany. The "atavistic" offender

---

[54] This can be seen as a particular nub of legal positivism: one the one hand, it created a formal definition of wrong oriented at the positive legislator, and on the other, it examined the conditions of real, existing people—a "material" fact. Perhaps jurists' preference for factors of predisposition is due to the fact that any research into the social conditions of crime (and thus processes of criminalisation) would have threatened this closed system. Furthermore, social conditions were seen as unchanging anyway; *Chr. Müller*, Verbrechensbekämpfung, p. 77; cf. also *Wetzell*, Inventing, p. 36.

[55] *Miloš Vec*, Die Seele auf der Bühne der Justiz. Die Entstehung der Kriminalpsychologie im 19. Jahrhundert und ihre interdisziplinäre Erforschung (Literaturbericht), in: Berichte zur Wissenschaftsgeschichte 30 (2007), 235 ff. (also including a review of *Ylva Greve*, Verbrechen und Krankheit. Die Entdeckung der "Criminalpsychologie" im 19. Jahrhundert. Cologne 2004.

[56] *Peter Becker*, Verderbnis und Entartung. Eine Geschichte der Kriminologie des 19. Jahrhunderts als Diskurs und Praxis. Göttingen 2002; in-depth review in *Vormbaum*, JJZG 8 (2006/2007), 229 ff.

[57] All terms according to *Becker*, op. cit.

[58] Also *Liszt*, Gegner, p. 332, who advocated a comprehensive investigation into *all* causal factors of crime. Liszt distanced himself from Lombroso and vehemently objected to being placed close to him. Of course, the offender typology of his *Marburger Programm* had encouraged this view.

was replaced by the "inferior" offender.[59] The criminal "type", later a leading character in the doctrine of National Socialist criminal law, rose to prominence in criminology.[60]

Lombroso's rejection by German (criminal) psychiatry was due not to his theory of born criminals but to the fact that it took physical features as its starting point (which Lombroso himself qualified ever further from edition to edition). Morel's *degeneration theory* was close to Lombroso's line of thinking. Julius Koch used Morel to develop his term of *psychopathic inferiority*; Abraham Baer drew a connection between the characteristics of degeneration and their massed occurrence in the lower classes, thus regarding the social living conditions of offenders as the trigger of crime. He was supported strongly by Paul Näcke, while Hans Kurella and Robert Sommer defended Lombroso against them. Eugen Bleuer's 1896 work *Der geborene Verbrecher* significantly influenced the course subsequently taken by the criminal-biological paradigm. Hans Groß and Gustav Aschaffenburg proposed combinations of biological and sociological explanations. Aschaffenburg's textbook integrated criminal sociology and criminal psychiatry as reciprocal complementary approaches of criminal etiology; social factors could cause biological degeneration; resulting biological anomalies impeded those they affected in their social lives, and this impediment again caused some of them to become criminal. Aschaffenburg drew a connection to Liszt's demands in the title of the journal he founded, *Monatsschrift für Kriminalpsychologie und Strafrechtsreform* (its title changed several times, depending on the political situation).

---

[59] More detail in *Gadebusch Bondio*, JJZG 8 (2006/2007), 280 ff.; *Wetzell*, Inventing, p. 39 ff.; *Id.*, JJZG 2006/2007, 256 ff., especially on the leading criminology textbook by **Gustav Aschaffenburg** (born 1866, died 1944 in exile in the USA).

[60] Immediately prior to the beginning of the 20th century, concrete discourse on types of criminals emerged (*the* poisoner, *the* infanticide, *the* sex murderer), reaching its climax in the Weimar Republic. Academic and non-academic publications (including aesthetic literature) that reinforced and reproduced each others' content ensured that this discourse established itself as a firm part of the sociology of knowledge. On this topic, from the point of view of literary history and women's history, see *Hania Siebenpfeiffer*, "Böse Lust". Gewaltverbrechen in Diskursen der Weimarer Republik. Cologne, Weimar, Vienna 2005, p. 95 ff., 150 ff., 185 ff.; review by *Vormbaum* in JoJZG 1 (2007), 157 ff.; on the sociology of knowledge see § 1 II. 1. b) above.

§ 5 The Twentieth Century

I. Preliminary Remarks

The previous chapter described the shifts that took place at the end of the 19th and the beginning of the twentieth century. This account will now be continued and the developments of the twentieth century depicted. However, the "twentieth century" is not to be understood strictly according to the calendar; rather, we will first start by going back once more and giving an account of the developments occurring since the end of the nineteenth century. Given that this single chapter covers events from then nearly up to the present, implying a unified time period, we can anticipate one objection to proceeding in this manner which will need to be addressed at this stage. This objection is that the 12 years of National Socialist rule, with their perversion of the law and mass crimes supported and carried out by the state, represent a break in the unified line of development of criminal law and should thus not be included in an overall account of it. This objection, which also has implications for this book's understanding of time periods, concerns the question of the continuity or discontinuity of the history of criminal law in the twentieth century. Conveying this history in one single comprehensive chapter shows that this account takes the concept of continuity (which by now represents the predominant understanding of these events) as its basis. However, we will not debate this question theoretically in advance, but instead will make it plausible in the course of this account—the previous chapter already touched upon the subject—and will then summarise and discuss it in conclusion.

Naturally, even the continuity approach does not regard the period of National Socialist rule as a "normal" historical period. This chapter, divided into constitutional stages, therefore devotes a separate section to this period.

T. Vormbaum and M. Bohlander, *A Modern History of German Criminal Law*,
DOI 10.1007/978-3-642-37273-5_5, © Springer-Verlag Berlin Heidelberg 2014

II. The Period Before the First World War

1. Theory of Criminal Law: The So-Called "Schulenstreit"

Liszt's "*Marburger Programm*" and his indefatigable activity in the field of criminal policy—organising, publishing and public speaking—was the cause of the so-called "*Schulenstreit*" (doctrinal dispute) in criminal law. This label, which the history of law has adopted, expresses the self-perception of those involved, and can be deemed acceptable for use here given the unavoidable simplification that historiography applies to historical events and processes. However, we should also bear the limitations of such a juxtaposition in mind. The "*Schulenstreit*" was not really concerned with a dispute between a liberal and a "social" school of thought, for neither can the main exponent of the so-called classical school, **Karl Binding** (1841–1920),[1] be termed a liberal, nor **Franz v. Liszt** a socialist.[2] Liszt's line of thought is often referred to as "*Moderne Schule*", the modern school, an accurate enough designation if a school is called "modern" that is "in keeping with the times"; if standards as regards content are applied however, for example in the sense of an expansion of human liberty, then by no stretch of the imagination can either of the two main exponents of criminal law at the turn of the nineteenth to the twentieth century be termed "modern".

Both of them were positivists – *Binding* was purely a legal positivist, and *Liszt* was also a legal positivist as far as the doctrine of criminal law was concerned; as regards criminal policy, he also was a positivist with regard to empirical and criminological insights.

Binding's "theory of norms" is of central importance when attempting to classify him. According to Binding, criminal offences are not addressed to the citizen but to the judge, for an offending citizen does not infringe the definition of a criminal offence—in fact, he actually *conforms* to it—but rather infringes the *norm* that lies behind and conceptually precedes the defined offence. The criminal offence negates the part of the norm the observance of which is necessary to secure the norm. If a corresponding *norm* existed at the time a crime was committed, then in principle a retrospectively issued *definition of a criminal offence* could be applied; the only reason that this does not actually occur is the legislator's self-imposition of the principle of *nullum crimen sine lege*[3]; thus the task of positive law and its application is to *secure norms*. However, as a "norm" is not (or not necessarily) something

---

[1] On Binding, see *Westphalen*, Binding; *Naucke*, Staatsverbrechen.

[2] *Liszt* himself occasionally called himself a "socialist"—his claim to this is doubtful, but he appears to have impressed the Social Democrats with it; on this, see *Vormbaum*, Sozialdemokratie, p. LIVIII, footnote 5; even the post-1933 exile SPD (cf. *Deutschland-Berichte der SPD (SoPaDe)*, second year 1935 3rd edition Frankfurt am Main 1980, p. 245, 251) still praised Liszt as the progenitor of a "liberal understanding of criminal law".

[3] *Dannecker*, JJZG 3 (2001/2002), 125 ff., 170 ff.; *Westphalen*, p. 39 f.; *Naucke*, Staatsverbrechen, p. XIII ff.; on Binding's criticism of the "tyranny" of the principle of legality see *Schreiber*, Gesetz und Richter, p. 169 ff., and above § 3 I. 3. a).

fixed in law, but rather stands *behind* the law; it is laws that ultimately serve to secure society.[4]

When *Binding* defines a norm's objective as guaranteeing "the preconditions of a peaceful and healthy development and state of the law",[5] this still might seem to contain echoes of a Kantian definition of law (see above § 2. III. 1.). However, here "development and state of the law" does not refer to the realisation of a transcendental definition of law, based on a theory of mutually delimiting spheres of freedom; rather, it is the sum of those facts that the positivist legislator regards as the "preconditions for a healthy development and state of the legal community",[6] and these facts are *Rechtsgüter*, protected legal interests.[7] Thus the definition of the protected legal interest is just as devoid of content as the definition of wrong, for both are based on the positivist legislator's value judgements and decisions. These cannot be verified further,[8] and could turn out any number of ways.[9] Given his authoritarian understanding of the state,[10] *Binding* is anything but a representative of free and liberal thinking.

His dreadful book *Die Freigabe der Vernichtung lebensunwerten Lebens. Ihr Maß und ihre Form* ("Allowing the Destruction of Life Unworthy of Existence"), published in 1920, the last year of his life, with a contribution by the psychiatrist *Alfred Hoche*, was later used as the official sanction of National Socialist mass murder of people suffering from mental illness. Opinions on whether it can be linked to his theory of norms vary.[11]

In Binding's case the definition of the protected legal interest factually lies on the border between the "healthy preconditions" defined by the legislator and positive law; in Liszt's case it is borderline in a double sense (Liszt actually uses

[4] *Naucke*, Staatsverbrechen, p. XV.; cf. also *Id.*, "Schulenstreit?", in: Festschrift für Winfried Hassemer (2010), p. 559 ff., 563: "The dispute between classicists and moderns shows criminal law in the period where prevention technique reigned supreme. Classicism and modernity are two complementary, vicarious forms of policy, both of which indisputably demand a reduction in crime in order to ensure social security and stability"; *id.* p. 566: "The *Schulenstreit* remains of topical relevance to the question of the limitation of criminal policy. The beginnings of this theory in the constitutionally founded limitation of all criminal policy are discontinued; they are neglected, trapped by criminal policy and neutralised".

[5] *Binding*, Normen, 2nd edition, Vol. I 1, p. 339.

[6] Op. cit., p. 353; Binding later abandoned the wording "the preconditions for a healthy life", replacing it with an even more general phrase ("everything, the unaltered and unimpeded preservation of which positive law considers in its own interest"); on this and on further developments *Frommel*, Präventionstheorien, p. 118 f.

[7] Op. cit., p. 340; on this whole field see *Amelung*, Rechtsgüterschutz, p. 74.

[8] *Amelung*, Rechtsgüterschutz, p. 74; *Frommel*, Präventionsmodelle, p. 117.

[9] *Amelung*, p. 76.

[10] *Dannecker*, p. 172.

[11] A sceptical view is taken in *Frommel*, Präventionsmodelle, p. 75 f.; expressly in the affirmative, providing a detailed explanation, *Naucke*, Staatsverbrechen, p. XVIII ff.—Binding and Hoche's text was reprinted in 2006 as part of the series "Juristische Zeitgeschichte. Taschenbücher". In the spring of 2010, the city of Leipzig posthumously withdrew Binding's honorary citizenship because of this book.

the term "*Grenzbegriff*", "borderline concept"), and is characteristic of his ambivalent stance in between (formal) constitutional doctrine of criminal law and rigid criminal policy. As a *dogmatist of criminal law*, Liszt understands this concept in a positivist sense as determined by the legislator, but as a *maker of criminal policy* he also understands it as an expression of the "vital interests" to be secured.[12] As far as doctrine of criminal law is concerned, Liszt has more in common with Binding than there are in fact differences between them.[13]

In the end, the crux of this theoretical dispute was the criminal-political differentiation between punishment as retribution and punishment as a means of securing incapacitation; Binding's means of upholding punishment as retribution were strict or even brutal punishments and (*beyond* the ambit of criminal law) the protective measures of police law. This in fact already pointed towards the compromise, even though Binding remained in denial, which consisted—as in *Liszt's* offer—in the dual track model of punishment as retribution and measures *within* criminal law. The first criminal law reform draft, the preliminary draft of 1909, already included this dual track (more on this shortly).[14] Thus Liszt's school had prevailed, even though it had been forced to relinquish the label of "punishment" for its sanctions securing incapacitation. In November 1933, the National Socialist legislature passed the Habitual Offenders Act, thus encoding an important point of the "*Marburger Programm*" in law.

It was first and foremost **Adolf Merkel** (1836–1896) who endeavoured to take a position independent of either school with his theory, which is also – with greater justification than Liszt's – called "unification theory". He regarded the modern school as mistaken in its opposition to the theory of retribution; to his mind, the idea of retribution was based on a sense of justice which already in actual fact included a consideration of finality. Purpose and ideas of justice were not contradictory, but polar opposites. Merkel accuses Binding's theory of norms, which sees a criminal offence as an attack on the state's right to obedience, of forcing the norms of law into the role of Gessler's hat, "which the people are forced to

[12] Thus the interpretation in *Frommel*, Präventionsmodelle, p. 120 f., who in my opinion justifiably accuses *Amelung* (Rechtsgüterschutz, p. 82 ff.) of simplifying this ambivalence in Liszt's position.—On the distinction between protected legal interest (= protected interest) and the object of the action that "embodies" the legal interest, and the consequent abstraction and (increasing) intangibility of the concept of the protected legal interest, see *Amelung*, Rechtsgüterschutz, p. 86.

[13] This also qualifies the statement that Liszt was a proponent of a material definition of unlawfulness, that of the infringement of protected legal interests (as found for example in *Rüping/Jerouschek*, Grundriss, p. 110), for this definition only applies to criminal policy, while in regard to legal doctrine unlawfulness is defined by the formal aspect of an infringement of the law.

[14] With a high degree of certainty, the historic moment in which this compromise was reached can be identified: in 1904, Liszt presented the conference of the *Internationale Kriminalistische Vereinigung* with a draft law on the imprisonment of "mentally inferior individuals" and the elimination of the danger they posed. Besides this, there was also to be preventive detention for "those constituting a threat to public safety". This draft was later supported by the Deutscher Juristentag, the Conference of German Jurists; cf. *Wetzell*, Inventing, p. 90 ff.; *Chr. Müller*, Verbrechensbekämpfung, p. 149.

show submission to, for this point of view disregards the objective meaning that distinguishes norms from the hat on the pole"[15]; he criticises contemporary theories of finality, for in using "dangerousness" they take up a category that eludes judicial quantification and that, if applied systematically, leads on the one hand to unjustified reductions, and on the other to unmistakeable expansions of "the field of criminal law".[16] These theories "provide grounds for a profound change in our legal constitution and at the same time rob it of those features that up till now have been regarded both as particularly valuable and as intimately connected to the conditions of the life of our culture".[17]

2. Criminal Law Doctrine

While the many different regional criminal codes of the nineteenth century were the "laboratory" in which the development of the modern definitions of individual criminal offences was stressed, and less the advancement in the area of general legal theory, towards the end of the nineteenth century the focus of criminal legal doctrine shifted to the General Part of the Code and a refinement of the system of criminal offences.

A differentiation was made between blameworthiness and unlawfulness. Since *Liszt*, blameworthiness had been reduced to intent and negligence, in the sense of a "psychological theory of blameworthiness"—despite the problems that this definition of blameworthiness caused for negligence.[18] Responsibility (*Schuldfähigkeit*) is seen as the precondition, not yet a component of blameworthiness.[19] **Ernst Beling** (1866–1932) founded the modern theory of criminal offence characterisations (*Tatbestandslehre*) with the legal "description" of the actions for which punishment is threatened. This should be differentiated from the evaluation of an action as illegal.[20] Thus we arrive at the classic tripartite structure of criminal offences, where illegality and blameworthiness are equated with the objective and subjective sides of the criminal offence[21] and illegality itself is further divided into the definition of the offence (*Tatbestand*) and the individual act's unlawfulness (*Rechtswidrigkeit*).

However, once activities in the field of criminal legal doctrine were stepped up, this simple psychological definition of blameworthiness was questioned. In 1907 **Reinhard Frank's** (1860–1934) text *Der Aufbau des Schuldbegriffs* was published, which had a great impact on theories of blameworthiness in the following decades.

---

[15] *Merkel*, Lehrbuch, p. 9 f.

[16] *Merkel*, Vergeltungsidee und Zweckgedanke [1892], in: *Vormbaum*, MdtStrD, p. 248 ff., 254.

[17] Ibid., p. 522; for more detail on Merkel's theory of criminal law see *Achenbach*, Grundlagen, p. 44 ff.; *Frommel*, Präventionsmodelle, p. 43 ff., and the comprehensive study by *Gerhard Dornseifer*, Rechtstheorie und Strafrechtsdogmatik Adolf Merkels. Berlin 1979.

[18] *Achenbach*, Grundlagen, p. 38.

[19] *Achenbach*, Grundlagen, p. 40, 42 f..

[20] On this, see *Plate*, Beling, particularly p. 49 ff.

[21] Also cf. *Roxin*, Strafrecht AT (4th edition), p. 201.

Frank criticised the psychological concept of blameworthiness, as it only took account of intent and negligence but provided no explanation for duress under which offenders are driven to act with intent; furthermore, regarding responsibility as the precondition but not as a component of the concept of blameworthiness is contradictory, for a mentally ill individual might under certain circumstances also be acting with intent. The concept of blameworthiness is complex; it is made up of the components of a "normal mental condition", "a certain concrete psychological relation of the offender to the offence" and "normal attendant circumstances of the offence". At the centre of the concept of blameworthiness lies *Vorwerfbarkeit*, i.e. the concept of whether a person can be blamed for their actions.[22] Thus the psychological concept of blameworthiness became a **normative concept of blameworthiness**. The basic structure of objective (=unlawfulness)/subjective (=blameworthiness) began to dissolve; this dichotomy was replaced by a tendency towards the pairing general/individual.

Classifying this process depends on the point of view taken: from the "internal" perspective of the **history of doctrine**, the development from the psychological to the normative concept of blameworthiness without doubt led to a refinement in the way that the system of criminal offences was expressed, in the sense that some individual problems could be more easily integrated into the system. From the perspective of the **history of ideas**, this transition can be seen as part of the gradual supplanting of positivism by *neo-Kantianism* (for more details, see the beginning of IV. 1. below), which however left the foundations of legal positivism undisturbed; in terms of the **history of law**, it marks a first step towards an *ethicisation* of criminal law, i.e. the abolition of the separation between law and ethics that had been maintained throughout most of the nineteenth century.

Only when these three perspectives are distinguished can an appropriate overall picture emerge. The dogmatist (Frank) will hardly have considered whether his structural suggestions helped doctrine to move beyond positivism; while this is the case for the neo-Kantian philosopher of law, he in turn will hardly have thought about whether his theory contributed to the dilution of the constitutional tradition of criminal law. Separating out these levels is only possible in retrospect.

3. Penal Legislation

The Criminal Code of the North German Confederation was passed in 1870 and expanded to become the Reich Criminal Code following the founding of the German Kaiserreich. It marked the external end of a legislative era for substantive criminal law, much as the Code of Criminal Procedure and the procedural part of the Constitution of Courts Act, both passed in 1877 and coming into effect in 1879, did for criminal procedure law. During the deliberations of the North German

[22] *Frank*, Aufbau des Schuldbegriffs, p. 11; the 2009 reprint contains an introduction and analysis by *Hans Joachim Hirsch*.

Reichstag on the Criminal Code, the Prussian Minister of Justice *Leonhardt* had of course already held out the prospect that the code would soon be revised.[23]

Nonetheless—or perhaps precisely because of this—only few changes were made to the Reich Criminal Code until 1914.[24] Of the more than 200 amendments made and new publications added to the body of laws up to 2010, a period of around 140 years, only 18 date to the 45-year period up to 1914. The following were most important:

The *Kulturkampf* ("culture struggle", Bismarck's attempt to subject the Catholic Church to state control) produced—alongside other repressive measures against the Catholic Church—the so-called ***Kanzelparagraph*** ("pulpit paragraph", Section 130a StGB),[25] the first change to the Criminal Code, creating a public speech offence. The central phrase used in the offence was "disturbing the public peace", which was to become familiar in drafts and laws from then on. The **StGB Amendment Act of 1876**[26] ushered in important innovations (besides changing the currency of fines from Thaler to Mark) that mainly served to extend what was punishable and to increase the intensity of prosecution. The introduction of the offence of *causing bodily harm by dangerous means* (Section 223a RStGB, cf. today's Section 224 StGB) and Section 49a RStGB (cf. today's Section 30 StGB), which became known as the so-called *Lex Duchesne*, are worthy of mention. The latter for the first time made the (unsuccessful) attempt to induce another to commit or attempt to commit a felony as well as abetting a felony punishable, likewise the declaration of willingness to accept the offer of another or the agreement with another to commit or abet the commission of a felony—though there were at first some restrictions (subsection 3). Both regulations are still preserved today in slightly or more strongly expanded versions.[27] The so-called **Lex Heinze**, published in 1900 after an approximately 10-year consultation period, toughened and expanded the so-called "criminal law on moral offences" in the areas of prostitution, procuring and pandering.[28] That the principle of *nullum crimen sine lege* was still taken seriously can be seen in the offence of **withdrawal of electricity**, introduced by law on 9 April 1900 (RGBl. p. 228), as the Reich court had declared that this action could not be subsumed under the offence of theft.[29]

---

[23] Stenographische Berichte über die Verhandlungen des Reichstages des Norddeutschen Bundes, 1. Legislaturperiode, Session 1870, Vol. 1, p. 47.

[24] All changes to the Criminal Code since it came into effect listed in *Vormbaum/Welp*, StGB, Vols. 1–4 and Suppl. 3, p. 7 ff.; short descriptions of changes to the StGB during the various political phases of development in the contributions by *Roth*, *Rasehorn*, *Buschmann*, *Welp*, *Scheffler* and *Hilgendorf* in: Vormbaum/Welp, StGB, Suppl. 1; the overall development sketched in *Vormbaum*, ibid.; on the development of legislative technique *F.-C. Schroeder*, ibid.; individual information on all amending laws in the contributions by *Asholt*, *Werle/Jeßberger* and *Utsch*, ibid. Suppl. 3, p. 97 ff.

[25] *Vormbaum/Welp*, StGB, No. 2.

[26] *Vormbaum/Welp*, StGB, No. 3.

[27] On Section 49a *Busch*; on Section 224 StGB *Korn*, p. 93 ff.

[28] *Vormbaum/Welp*, StGB, No. 14; in detail *Ilya Hartmann*, p. 72 ff.

[29] RGSt 29, 111; 32, 165.

The regulations on **lèse majesté** were moderated in the Amendment Act of 1908.[30] In this context it should be pointed out that the common notion that lèse majesté was an offence committed primarily by artists, writers and journalists is probably mistaken. Much evidence suggests that it was above all a mass offence common in the working class, and that was also prosecuted on a massive scale.[31] The **Amendment Act of 1912**[32] opened up the alternative of punishing a number of criminal offences with fines, and introduced the offences of theft and fraud committed out of necessity because of one's common circumstances.[33]

The low number of—nonetheless important—changes to the Reich Criminal Code should not cause us to forget that a deluge of criminal laws were passed beyond the codification of criminal law. Thus began the triumph of the so-called ***Nebenstrafrecht***, the supplementary penal provisions, that has lasted until today. While its "supplementary" name had seemed apt for much of the nineteenth century (though of course it was not common at the time), now the quantitative relation of criminal laws shifted increasingly in its favour. Criminal law—and in parallel to it, police law and administrative criminal law, which later became the "law on regulatory offences"—extended to wide areas of society.

Between 1871 and 1914, supplementary penal regulations were passed in the following areas: copyright law, patent law, law on utility models, trademarks and competition, property, offences constituting public danger, defence, emigration, the press and associations, security, morals and the family, the economy, the social system, railways, shipping, communications, finance, the military and colonies.[34]

While the *objective* reason for this expansion can be found in the development towards state interventionism sketched out in the section above, the *positioning* of the regulations outside the codification of criminal law can be explained by the structure of most of the supplementary criminal offences: the definitions of offences in the Criminal Code are usually formulated in such a way that they contain the characteristics of the offence; by contrast, most of the supplementary criminal offences threaten punishment for infringements of the civil or administrative norms of a special law. On the one hand, this makes it difficult to integrate them into the Criminal Code, and on the other renders it expedient to include the punishments threatened in the factual context of the special law itself. The simultaneous expansion of punishments threatened for negligence is characteristic of the content of the expansion of the supplementary penal provisions. Thus criminal law and police law draw ever closer to one another.

The significance of this development cannot be overestimated; it influenced many areas of criminal law—and not to the benefit of its constitutional character: the beginning of the expansion of supplementary penal provisions also marked the beginning of an expansion of criminal law as a whole. This expansion affected not only the number of defined offences, i.e. the *breadth* or *horizontal* level, but also the

---

[30] *Vormbaum/Welp*, StGB, No. 16; *Andrea Hartmann*, Majestätsbeleidigung, p. 173 ff.

[31] *A. Hartmann*, Majestätsbeleidigung, p. 109 ff.; *Id.* JoJZG 1 (2007), 49 ff.

[32] *Vormbaum/Welp*, StGB, No. 18.

[33] On this, cf. *Prinz*, Diebstahl, p. 42 f.

[34] *R. Weber*, Nebenstrafrecht, passim; on commercial law cf. *Werner*, p. 30 f.

chronological *longitudinal* axis: as the supplementary penal provisions mainly standardise special areas, the prohibitions they enforce through punishment usually refer to infringements of technical norms, expressed through marginal values. Therefore supplementary offences usually standardise *offences of endangerment*, and more to the point of *abstract* endangerment, thus shifting liability towards the preparatory stage.

With the criminal law's expanding "colonisation of life worlds" (*Habermas*), the number of "non-moral" criminal offences grew: offences which did not target behaviour that simultaneously constituted a transgression of morals (mala per se) and which everyone under normal conditions would regard and understand as punishable. The increase in these norms could not fail to affect the doctrine of mistake, as it became increasingly impossible to assume knowledge of the prohibited norm in this area[35]; there was, however, a certain degree of compensation, in that large sections of the supplementary penal provisions referred to specialised areas and were thus directed at specialists who could be assumed to possess knowledge of the law.[36]

The effects on criminal procedure were particularly strong. The increase in offences produced a level of "input" that placed an ever greater strain on criminal justice. Strategies to relieve this were the necessary consequence, and consisted of reducing the size of judicial panels, simplifying proceedings (e.g. order of summary punishment) and simplifying the termination of proceedings (discretionary discontinuance). Under certain unusual economic and/or political conditions (war, economic crises) these tendencies were updated and intensified, and gradually established themselves.[37] At first, however, they remained unsuccessful. In fact, prior to 1914 there were actually attempts to bring the three-tier structure of criminal procedure to completion (see below).

There were also effects on the punishments themselves. To punish offences that were not a matter of morals invariably with imprisonment appeared inappropriate. (However, there was always the temptation for politicians to populistically "charge" these offences with moral content. On occasion this actually worked, for example during the period after the First World War with the character of the "profiteer", which often connoted anti-Semitic stereotypes; we can observe similar tendencies today for "moonlighters" and "speeders".)

It was also impossible to increase the number of prison cells along with the expansion of supplementary penal provisions. It would be interesting to examine the thesis that this material fact was actually a more effective factor in the complete turnaround of the ratio of custodial sentences to fines during the course of the 20th century, rather than theoretical considerations ("harmfulness of brief custodial sentences", "humanisation of criminal law").

---

[35] On this, cf. *Löw*, Erkundigungspflicht; *Id.*, JJZG 4 (2002/2003), 312 ff.

[36] For a contemporary discussion of this issue, cf. *Donini*, Strafrechtstheorie p. 131, 135.

[37] On the debate on orders of summary proceedings without trial: *Elobied*, Entwicklung, p. 57 ff.; on the debate on the principle of mandatory prosecution and grounds for termination cf. *Dettmar*, Legalität und Opportunität, p. 109 ff.

The supplementary provision of the Kaiserreich best known today was the so-called **Socialists Act** (Law against the public danger constituted by social democratic endeavours). Bismarck used two anarchist assassination attempts on Wilhelm I. as an excuse to push through a special law to suppress the emergent Social Democrats, against the initial resistance of the Liberals. This law was characterised by the structure typical of supplementary provisions described above. It prohibited associations, assemblies and printed matter "that seek to overthrow the existing state and social order through social democratic, socialist and communist endeavours" and extended this prohibition to include associated assemblies and printed matters as well as collecting subscriptions, and thus was primarily an administrative law. In Sections 17 ff. StGB violations were made punishable with constant reference to the prohibited offences of administrative law.[38]

Passed in October 1878 and extended in May 1880, April 1886 and February 1888, the Socialists Act expired in 1890; a further extension ultimately failed due to the Conservatives, who did not want to support the Liberals' suggestion to relax the law and indeed hoped for a completely new, stricter law. Then again, following Bismarck's resignation the Reich government's social and political initiatives aimed to reduce social democratic influence on the working class. After this plan proved unsuccessful, new attempts to repress social democracy were launched in the mid-1890s. A number of anarchist plots across all of Europe provided an excuse to call for drastic measures against the "revolutionary party". Towards the end of 1894, the so-called ***Umsturzvorlage*** (Revolution Bill)[39] was introduced in the Reichstag. In order to avoid a new political special law which the Liberals would not have agreed to, this time a change in the Criminal Code was envisaged. Among the many suggestions for changes was a change to Section 130 StGB, which was to render the person punishable "whosoever in a manner capable of disturbing the public peace publicly attacks religion, the monarchy, marriage, family or property through defamatory utterances". After a social democratic press campaign between the first and second reading and disagreements between the Centre Party, the Conservatives and the Liberals, the Bill was already rejected in the second reading.

Colonial criminal law should be mentioned separately. We know now that the way Germany exercised power in its "protectorates"[40] was anything but idyllic. It is undisputed today that the way German protection forces suppressed the Herero revolt of 1907 constituted genocide. Whether it is going too far to see German colonial politics, particularly in southwest Africa (Namibia), as a prelude to the

[38] On the Socialists Act, cf. *Pack*, Sozialistengesetz; *Vormbaum*, Sozialdemokratie, p. LII ff.; *Wehler*, Gesellschaftsgeschichte Vol. 3, p. 902 ff.—On the attempts of criminal law to combat **anarchism**, equated with the socialist workers' movement by the leading powers of the Reich and the main political parties (whether on purpose or as the result of autosuggestion), cf. *Wagner*, Terrorismus, especially p. 325 ff.; cf. also *Blasius*, Geschichte der politischen Kriminalität in Deutschland 1800–1980. Frankfurt am Main 1983, p. 55 ff.

[39] On this, cf. *Felske*, p. 87 ff.; *Vormbaum*, Sozialdemokratie, p. 133; *Grässle-Münscher*, Kriminelle Vereinigung, p. 53 f.

[40] On general legal questions, cf. *N.B. Wagner*, Schutzgebiete.

Holocaust,[41] or whether German colonial law should be seen, as *Naucke*[42] does, as one possible embodiment of modern criminal law, is still open to debate. At any rate, colonial criminal law had some shockingly modern traits[43]: legislation took place by imperial decree (Section 1 of the protectorate law[44]), thus beyond the constraints of constitutional law and the rule of law. As colonial (criminal) law applied to native peoples, but not to whites, there were regulations on the distinctions between these groups that are actually reminiscent of later race laws (Section 2 of the Decree on Legal Affairs in the German Colonies: "The Japanese do not count as belonging to coloured tribes"). As the Reich Criminal Code did not apply to native peoples, these were punished as the colonial administration thought fit. There were no legal definitions of offences. Even simply "lying in court" (i.e. before the colonial administration) was punishable (it only became so in the Reich in 1943); punishment on suspicion and kin liability were practiced; beating and caning were allowed; and unlike in the Reich the principle of discretionary prosecution applied in criminal procedure; there was no independent justice system.

4. The Beginnings of Penal Reform

The shifts in social, intellectual and criminal law theory described in § 4 above resulted in a general willingness to reform the criminal law. However, in the years leading up to the turn of the century, legislative capacity to a great extent was taken up with work on other projects (the revision of the Commercial Code and, above all, the creation of the Civil Code). Once the intense and productive reform efforts in the field of civil law had been completed, it was possible for legislative focus to return to criminal law and criminal procedure law. Thus the so-called reform of criminal law began, that was to last several decades.

In 1902 a free scholarly committee made up of eight professors was established, whose task it was to create a **comparative legal account** of all possible materials of criminal law. This account was then to be used to put forward suggestions for the reform of the Reich Criminal Code.

The committee, made up of the professors *Karl Birkmeyer* (Munich), *Fritz v. Calker* (Strasbourg), *Reinhard Frank* (Tübingen), *Robert v. Hippel* (Prussia), *Wilhelm Kahl* (Prussia), *Karl v. Lilienthal* (Heidelberg), *Franz v. Liszt* (Berlin) and *Adolf Wach* (Leipzig), was convened on 16 July 1902 by the State Secretary of the Reich Justice Office *Nieberding*, who also presided over the committee. By 1909, after enlisting the services of fifty further staff, a total of 16 volumes (six on the General Part, nine on the Special Part and one register volume) had been published.

---

[41] Cf. *Melber*, Kontinuitäten, p. 91 ff.

[42] *Naucke*, Kolonialstrafrecht, p. 285.

[43] On the following, cf. *Naucke*, Kolonialstrafrecht, and *Zimmerling*, Entwicklung.

[44] On this, cf. *Czeguhn*, JJZG 8 (2006/2007), 174 ff.

In May 1906, a commission made up of five jurists appointed by the Reich Justice Office to create a preliminary draft for a Criminal Code (Vorentwurf—VE) began their work, only a short time after the first volumes of the comparative account had been published. In April **1909** they presented a **preliminary draft** for a German Criminal Code, including comprehensive draft reports. This draft was not intended to be presented to legislative bodies, but was only for the purposes of general public consultation. In October 1910 it was sent to the governments of all German federal states with a request for comments. These responses were printed as a book. Furthermore, a compilation created by the Reich Justice Office, the *Zusammenstellung der gutachtlichen Äußerungen über den Vorentwurf zu einem Deutschen Strafgesetzbuch*, was also published in 1911. The 1910 two-volume work *Die Reform des Reichsstrafgesetzbuchs*, edited by *Aschrott* and *v. Liszt*, is worthy of being singled out from among the critical literature.

Only a few supplementary provisions were incorporated into this preliminary draft. Police law was not separate, but was placed in a special Fifth Book in the Special Part and was simplified. The draft failed to make any conclusive statements on the theories of punishment. Looking at individual aspects, it distinguished more strongly between custodial sentences in penitentiaries and prisons by including regulations on the enforcement of these custodial sentences (Sections 14 ff.). It reformed fines, particularly by allowing time for payment, payments by instalment and the working off of debt by unpaid work (Sections 30–35), and extended official warnings to include adults (Section 37).

The effects of the compromise in the "*Schulenstreit*" became visible, as for the first time "**security measures**", imposed instead or in addition to punishment, were listed explicitly in the General Part next to the punishments. These included workhouse sentences (Section 42)[45]; for alcohol abuse being banned from public houses and being sent to a sanatorium (Section 43); the custody of mentally ill individuals constituting a public danger was regulated in connection with blameworthiness (Section 65).[46] There were as yet no regulations on detention for the purposes of incapacitation.

Further innovations were: introduction of the **power of the judge to suspend sentences**[47] (conditional sentence; Sections 38–41) and the power of the judge to order rehabilitation (restoration of civil rights; deletion of previous criminal record), special sections on debt (Sections 58 ff.), detailed regulations on sentencing (Sections 81 ff. including regulations on reoffending), expansion of juvenile criminal law (age of criminal liability only from the age of 14), restriction of the limitation

[45] It is worth reproducing the text of Section 42 (1) here: "If a criminal offence is committed due to dissoluteness or laziness and is punishable by a custodial or prison sentence of at least 4 weeks, the court may in such special cases as defined by law place an offender capable of work in a workhouse for a period of 6 months to 3 years in addition to this sentence or, if the sentence does not exceed 3 months, instead of it, if this measure is deemed necessary to remind the offender to live a law-abiding and industrious life".

[46] For more details, cf. *Karl Meyer*, DJZ 1909, col. 1283.

[47] For more details, cf. *Meyer-Reil*, Strafaussetzung, p. 77 ff.

period, discontinuation of police supervision (replaced by restrictions on freedom of movement, Section 53), **provisional release** (Section 28; collaboration with welfare authority). Capital punishment was only threatened unconditionally for an attempt on the life of the ruler, but not for murder (Section 212). Constructive liability for **result-qualified offences** was abandoned; an increase in punishment was only allowed if the offender could at least have foreseen the possibility of the extended result (Section 62). In accordance with the demands of criminal psychiatry (see above), the preliminary draft contained the legal concept of **diminished responsibility** with compulsory mitigation (except in cases of voluntary drunkenness; Sections 63, 65, 70).[48] The definition of necessity (Section 67) was changed and expanded (to include threats to property and the defence of any third party). The right to file a request to prosecute was to be transferrable to next of kin. *Custodia honesta* (*Festungshaft*) was to be merged with the general category of custodial sentences (cf. Sections 19 and 20). All in all, many aspects of Liszt's programme had prevailed.[49]

Strong **criticism** was directed at two aspects of the preliminary draft in particular: the failure to separate police offences from criminal offences and the failure to take criminal supplementary laws into account.

Following the publication of several individual critical reviews, in **1911** the professors *Kahl*, *v. Lilienthal*, *v. Liszt* and *Goldschmidt* wrote an **alternative draft** ("Gegenentwurf"—GE) to the preliminary draft of a German Criminal Code. This alternative draft, conceived as a supplement to the preliminary draft rather than as its antithesis, according to its authors was to "make the continuation of the great and important reformatory work—drawing on the preliminary draft—easier and faster", as well as to summarise the many points of criticism in a legal format.[50]

Consequently, the alternative draft gave transgressions a book of their own, with a General and Special Part, which was only connected to the draft "proper" by the continuous numbering of sections. Therefore, the latter was restricted to felonies and misdemeanours, which again meant that those offences that the preliminary draft had classed as minor summary offences were now upgraded to misdemeanours.

---

[48] The phrasing of the respective law was at the expense of previous cases of insanity (*Chr. Müller*, Verbrechensbekämpfung, S. 164).

[49] An overview of important suggestions for the Special Part of the preliminary draft in *Meyer*, op. cit.—More details on **criminal offences against the state**, see *Schroeder*, Schutz von Staat und Verfassung, p. 106; on **the offence of omitting to effect an easy rescue** see *Gieseler*, p. 25 ff.; on **criminal and terrorist/anarchist organisations** see *Felske*, p. 119 ff.; on the **failure to report a crime** see *Kisker*, p. 37 ff.; on **duelling** see *Baumgarten*, p. 152 ff.; on **abortion** see *Koch*, p. 88 ff.; *Putzke*, p. 77 ff.; on **theft** see *Prinz*, p. 44 ff.; on **false accusation** see *Bernhard*, p. 37 ff.; on **arson** see *Lindenberg*, p. 61 ff.; on **assault** see *Korn*, p. 153 ff.; on **perverting the course of justice** see *Thiel*, p. 59 ff.; on **mercy killing** see *Große-Vehne*, p. 59 ff.; on the **frustration of creditors' rights** see *Seemann*, p. 58 ff.; on **lèse majesté** see *Andrea Hartmann*, p. 185 ff.; on **prostitution, procuring and pandering** see *Ilya Hartmann*, p. 108 ff.; on **trespass** see *Rampf*, p. 62 ff.; on **embezzlement** and **unlawful appropriation** see *Rentrop*, p. 74 ff.; on **forgery of documents** see *Prechtel*, p. 87 ff.; on **road traffic law**, see *Asholt*, p. 42 ff.; on **incitement to hatred** see *Rohrßen*, p. 59 ff.

[50] *Kahl*, Gegenentwurf zum Vorentwurf eines deutschen Strafgesetzbuchs, in: DJZ 1911, col. 501.

Section 1:(1) An offence punishable by death or imprisonment in a penitentiary (*Zuchthaus*) shall be a felony.

(2) An offence punishable by a imprisonment in a regular prison (*Gefängnis*) shall be a misdemeanour.

The new (third) book accordingly began with the regulation:

Section 343:An offence punishable by a fine shall be a transgression.

Due to time constraints, the alternative draft did not include the supplementary penal provisions, although it considered this possible in principle. Furthermore, it cut the 116 different punishments threatened in the preliminary draft down to a mere 16, and rendered them flexible through a comprehensive system of general regulations. The most important were Section 87, which has a similar structure to today's Section 49 StGB, and—as its counterpart—Section 89, which set out the rules for increasing punishments in particularly severe cases. In many aspects, the alternative draft's system used in the Special Part differed from the preliminary draft: unlike its predecessor, it did not divide the Special Part into four books (felonies and misdemeanours against the state, felonies and misdemeanours against state institutions, felonies and misdemeanours against persons, felonies and misdemeanours against property); rather, it divided it directly into 24 chapters and thus returned to the regulation technique employed by the Reich Criminal Code.[51]

On 17 June 1911 Reich Chancellor *v. Bethmann-Hollweg* petitioned the Kaiser to appoint a commission to continue the reform of criminal law. This commission was to take account of the preliminary draft of 1909 and the criticism of it,[52] and to produce a new draft. This commission, consisting of 16 full members and two associate members, commenced its work on 4 November 1911.

The members of the commission were: for the Reich, *v. Tischendorf*, *Joël*, *Ebermayer* (Reich Supreme Court justice, later Senior Reich Prosecutor); for Prussia: *Lucas* (Chair of the Commission), *Schulz*, *Cormann*, *Lindenberg* (State Supreme Court justice), *Kleine* (State Supreme Court justice) and *Friedmann* (barrister); for Bavaria: *Meyer*; for Saxony: *v. Feilitsch*; for Württemberg: *v. Rupp*; for Baden: *Duffner*; for Hesse: *Rüster*; for Alsace-Lorraine: *Pfersdorff*; for Hamburg: *Niemeyer*. Thus all larger states with a seat on the Judiciary Committee of the Federal Council and the legal profession were represented.

---

[51] For more details on the Special Part of the alternative draft: on **criminal offences against the state**, see *Schroeder*, Schutz von Staat und Verfassung, p. 106 f.; on **the offence of omitting to effect an easy rescue** see *Gieseler*, p. 29 ff.; on **criminal and terrorist/anarchist organisations** see *Felske*, p. 127 ff.; on the **failure to report a crime** see *Kisker*, p. 41 ff.; on **duelling** see *Baumgarten*, p. 157 ff.; on **abortion** see *Koch*, p. 101 ff.; *Putzke*, p. 87 ff.; on **theft** see *Prinz*, p. 54 ff.; on **false accusation** see *Bernhard*, p. 52 ff.; on **arson** see *Lindenberg*, p. 68 ff.; on **assault** see *Korn*, p. 174 ff.; on **perverting the course of justice** see *Thiel*, p. 63 ff.; on **mercy killing** see *Große-Vehne*, p. 64 ff.; on the **frustration of creditors' rights** see *Seemann*, p. 62 ff.; on **lèse majesté** see *Andrea Hartmann*, p. 189 ff.; on **prostitution, procuring and pandering** see *Ilya Hartmann*, p. 115 ff.; on **trespass** see *Rampf*, p. 69 ff.; on **embezzlement** and **unlawful appropriation** see *Rentrop*, p. 82 ff.; on **forgery of documents** see *Prechtel*, p. 102 ff.; on **road traffic law**, see *Asholt*, p. 48 ff.; on **incitement to hatred** see *Rohrßen*, p. 94 ff.

[52] Cf. Zusammenstellung der gutachtlichen Äußerungen über den Vorentwurf zu einem Deutschen Strafgesetzbuch, compiled by the Reich Justice Office, 1911.

Legal academia was represented by professors *Kahl*, *Frank* and *v. Hippel*, all supporters of the mediatory view in the "Schulenstreit". After the original Chair of the Commission *Lucas* retired due to old age, *Kahl* became Chair at the second reading.

A first commission draft was presented at the beginning of 1913, but was not published. It took the Commission six further meetings to complete the second reading, concluded at the beginning of September. On 27 September 1913 the final (third) **1913 draft** was passed and printed as a manuscript; it was to be presented to the Federal Council as a government bill. However, due to the outbreak of the First World War it was only published later together with another version that had been revised in the meantime, E 1919. The completed draft was far more extensive than the preliminary draft, which was partly due to the fact that the area of minor summary offences had been given its own General Part, and could in fact easily have been taken out of the Criminal Code. The draft once again extended the powers of the court. It closely followed the preliminary draft. At a quick glance through its content, it is already noticeable in particular that the alternative draft's sanctions system had not been adopted. Instead, the system of the preliminary draft had been adhered to in general and—probably partly due to the suggestions made in the alternative draft—developed further. The Commission also followed the suggestions made in the preliminary draft with regard to including a rule on compensation as a regulation of the General Part as well as by introducing an increase in punishment for offences committed with intent by state officials.[53]

5. *Criminal Procedure*[54]

At first, criminal procedure was affected less strongly by the new developments than substantive criminal law. While demands for the reform of the Code of Criminal Procedure and the procedural part of the Constitution of Courts Act had begun shortly after both laws were passed in 1879, they tended in the opposite

[53] For more details on the Special Part of the Commission draft: on **criminal offences against the state**, see *Schroeder*, Schutz von Staat und Verfassung, p. 107 f.; on **the offence of omitting to effect an easy rescue** see *Gieseler*, p. 30 ff.; on **criminal and terrorist/anarchist organisations** see *Felske*, p. 129 ff.; on the **failure to report a crime** see *Kisker*, p. 44 ff.; on **duelling** see *Baumgarten*, p. 160 ff.; on **abortion** see *Koch*, p. 103 ff.; *Putzke*, p. 91 ff.; on **theft** see *Prinz*, p. 56 ff.; on **false accusation** see *Bernhard*, p. 55 ff.; on **arson** see *Lindenberg*, p. 70 ff.; on **assault** see *Korn*, p. 192 ff.; on the **perversion of the course of justice** see *Thiel*, p. 66 ff.; on **mercy killing** see *Große-Vehne*, p. 64 ff.; on the **frustration of creditors' rights** see *Seemann*, p. 64 ff.; on **lèse majesté** see *Andrea Hartmann*, p. 190 ff.; on **prostitution, procuring and pandering** see *Ilya Hartmann*, p. 116 ff.; on **trespassing** see *Rampf*, p. 75 ff.; on **embezzlement** and **unlawful appropriation** see *Rentrop*, p. 85 ff.; on **forgery of documents** see *Prechtel*, p. 104 ff.; on **road traffic law**, see *Asholt*, p. 50 ff.; on **incitement to hatred** see *Rohrßen*, p. 99 ff.

[54] On the development of separate institutions of procedural law (up to today), cf. *Rieß*, Festschr. AG Strafrecht, p. 773 ff. (defence); *Id.*, Festschrift Volk, p. 559 ff. (distribution of tasks in the pre-trial investigation procedure); *Id.*, Festschrift Volk, p. 661 ff. (*Unmittelbarkeit*).

direction; the *Internationale Kriminalistische Vereinigung* (IKV) demanded a liberal criminal procedure in addition to social criminal law.[55]

Whether the legal condition in substantive law aspired to by the IKV can really be called "social criminal law" is of course debatable; Eb. Schmidt[56] interprets this demand as stating that criminal procedure must be equipped with many protective formal structures, precisely because

> the modern social state must adopt measures against the convicted criminal that are, if necessary, much more drastic than the retributive punishments of traditional liberal criminal law, precisely because his civil rights and liberties must to a great extent be sacrificed for the greater good.

It also seems doubtful whether the coexistence of a (in this sense) social substantive criminal law and a liberal criminal procedure law called for is actually possible without friction.[57] Indeed, to the present day, the further development of criminal procedure has not been one of liberalisation.

The body of laws of 1877/79 contained not only the friction following more or less "organically" from adopting the so-called Reformed Criminal Procedure, but also inconsistencies in its details—the distribution of first instance jurisdiction and staffing of the courts are particularly clear examples of this. Therefore it was seen early on that criminal procedure and the organisation of the courts were in need of reform. The Reichstag was presented with drafts in the years 1885, 1894 and 1895[58] that made suggestions for changes to individual aspects, particularly in regard to employing lay judges in criminal chambers and introducing appeals against all first instance verdicts, but these produced no legislative results. Other Reich government bills and petitions from the midst of the Reichstag with suggestions for improvements on individual fundamental aspects, that "changed in swift succession",[59] remained unsuccessful.[60]

After these attempts to improve and modernise existing laws had failed, the idea of a *comprehensive reform* gained increasing attention. Several years of commission consultations finally produced drafts of a StPO (Strafprozessordnung—Code of Criminal Procedure)and a GVG (Gerichtsverfassungsgesetz—Organisation of Courts Act) that were published in 1908 and submitted to the Reichstag in 1909 (*E 1908*). Following the first reading and a thorough consultation of the commission in the Reichstag, the drafts fell through on the issue of appointing lay judges at courts of appeal.

---

[55] Cf. *Eb. Schmidt*, Einführung, § 339, p. 414.

[56] Ibid.

[57] On this, cf. *Krauß*, Wahrheit.

[58] List of official documentation in *Bolder*, p. XVIII ff.

[59] *Bumke*, p. 2.

[60] A list of the most important official documentation on the reform of the organisation of courts between 1861 and 1920 in *Zacharias*, Reformversuche p. X ff. On the debate on orders of summary punishment, cf. *Elobied*, Entwicklung, p. 64 ff.; on the debate on the principle of mandatory prosecution and grounds for a discontinuance cf. *Dettmar*, Legalität und Opportunität, p. 114 ff.

Now the view gained ground that a comprehensive reform of criminal procedure would have to wait until the reform of the substantive criminal law had been completed. Therefore, apart from two individual—though significant—changes during the Great War,[61] no further changes to criminal procedure and the organisation of courts were made until the end of the Kaiserreich, nor did any plans to change them become apparent.

III. First World War and Postwar Period

1. Penal Legislation

Although not one change was made to the Criminal Code during the First World War, the number of criminal laws rose significantly during this time. This was because criminal laws that had been created prior to the outbreak of hostilities for the case of war, entered into force once the war had started ("*Schubladengesetze*" or "ready-made/pre-fabricated laws"). They authorised the issuing of decrees, insofar as they did not regulate content themselves.[62] As these laws were not regarded as sufficient, a further flexible, quick and easy to use arsenal was created.[63] The basis for this was an **Enabling Act** passed 4 days after the outbreak of war, which enabled the Federal Council to "impose those legal measures that prove necessary to relieve commercial damage".[64] On this basis, martial commercial criminal law was created as a supplementary penal provision; the term "commercial" was interpreted loosely.[65] Although it was created because of the war, this criminal law actually continued a trend visible since the end of the nineteenth century. State control of the economy, underpinned by criminal law, spread to almost every sphere of life. Non-moral norms had become too many to keep in mind, and the problem caused by a lacking sense of wrongdoing led the Federal Council to issue a special **Mistake of Law Decree**[66] in 1917. This decree was to have substantial after-effects, for in large parts it anticipated today's regulation in Section 17 StGB

[61] VO des Bundesrates über die Zulassung von Strafbefehlen bei Vergehen gegen Vorschriften über wirtschaftliche Maßnahmen vom 4. Juni 1915 (Decree of the Federal Council on the authorisation of orders of summary punishment for misdemeanours against the economic measures of 4 June 1915; RGBl. p. 325), replaced by BundesratsVO vom 7. Okt. 1915 (Decree of the Federal Council of 7 October 1915; RGBl. p. 631); Gesetz betreffend die Vereinfachung der Rechtspflege vom 21. Okt. 1917 (Law on the Simplification of the Administration of Justice of 21 October 1917; RGBl. p. 1037). For more detail, including evidence of contemporary reactions, cf. *Klingebiel*, p. 41 f.; more critically, *Naucke*, Weltkrieg p. 294 f.

[62] *Riechstein*, p. 61 ff.

[63] On this and the following, *Naucke*, Weltkrieg, p. 290.

[64] More detail in *Riechstein*, p. 84 ff.

[65] *Naucke*, p. 293.

[66] *Riechstein*, p. 96 ff.

with its "avoidability formula" that gave the citizens the responsibility for the failure to convey knowledge of the vast jumble of criminal laws. The citizen—thus the core of the rule—was responsible for keeping up to date with current laws.

The fact that this regulation, now included in the Criminal Code, is accepted without any further question, shows that the authoritarian view of the relationship between state and citizen—supported by the doctrine of criminal law—has become firmly established in this area. Even the term "mistake" itself is deceptive, for in actual fact—as textbooks usually aptly show—we are dealing with *a lack of knowledge* of unlawfulness; or, even more accurately, "a lack of intent to commit unlawful acts" That this intent should be accorded different treatment than intent relating to mistakes of fact (Section 16 StGB) is not obvious in itself, and was contested by the theory of intent that formerly dominated the literature on this topic. Indeed, the draft of 1922 still took a different point of view.[67]

The authoritarian commercial criminal law created during the War was to be used readily by both democratic and, subsequently, totalitarian governments; it did not disappear. The style of legislation also caught on. When the **Bavarian Soviet Republic (*Räterepublik*)** was proclaimed in Munich in 1918, the provisional Revolutionary Central Council issued a "Notification on the Appointment of a Revolutionary Tribunal" that included the sentence:

> Every infringement of revolutionary principles will be punished. The method of punishment shall be at the judge's discretion.

The (justified) outrage that followed this notification did not extend to the martial criminal law that preceded it. The latter also served as a model for the Munich Soviet Republic insofar as it issued a flood of criminal laws during the brief period it was in existence, using criminal law as an instrument of control *by* the state rather than control *of* the state. The war and postwar period thus marked a surge in the instrumentalisation and functionalisation—i.e., the politicisation—of criminal law.[68]

2. *Penal Reform*

Following the outbreak of war, work on the reform of the Criminal Code had come to a standstill. However, once the peace treaty of Brest-Litovsk with Soviet Russia in the spring of 1918 had freed up additional forces for the Western Front and territory was gained there in the short-term, appearing to promise a successful end to the war, the Reich Ministry of Justice took up the plans for a reform of criminal law once more. A small commission of five members convened in April 1918,[69] and

[67] See below § 5 IV. 3.

[68] On this as a whole: *Barreneche*, Räterepublik, incl. references.

[69] Members: *Joël* (Director in the Reich Justice Office), *Ebermayer* (President of the Senate of the Reich Court), *Cormann* (OLG President), *Bumke* (*Geheimer Oberregierungsrat* [Privy

between 15 April 1918 and 21 November 1919 produced a draft based mainly on the decisions of the criminal law commission of 1913.[70] Thus the drafts of 1909 (VE) and 1913 (KE) formed the material starting point on the one hand, while on the other hand they themselves were reviewed to see to which extent the decisions contained in them needed to be adapted to the postwar situation. One of the lessons of the War, the Revolution and the time that followed was that "nothing is more harmful to upholding criminal law than an excess of threats and punishments".[71] This insight led to the suggestion to dispense with a number of punishments threatened—particularly for political offences—and to restrict individual offences, such as coercion and blackmail for example, more closely.[72]

The phase of reform to follow also aimed to defend this insight against the diverse political interests of the parties. During the time of the Weimar Republic – following the increasing political polarisation of the extreme right and left wings – this was to become an obstacle with drastic consequences for parliamentary collaboration. Early on – when structuring the Criminal Code – the aforementioned small commission was faced with the question of whether it was possible to sharply demarcate police offences and criminal offences. It considered expressing the special nature of minor summary offences by only threatening fines, with prison sentences only in cases of default of payment or for recidivist offenders. The upper limit of fines, which at the time was five hundred Marks, was to be raised. Furthermore, the commission planned to deal with police offences in a separate book. At first, a resolution was suspended on 17 December 1918; however, a predisposition towards separating criminal and police offences along the lines suggested above during the review of the Special Part of the Second Book (summary offences) could already be noted.

The E 1919 was only published in 1920, together with the commission draft of 1913 and an explanatory "memorandum". Even though little attention was paid to the draft of 1919 in Germany following its publication, it gained particular importance in comparison to predecessor drafts as it was used as a model in the Austrian reform of criminal law: its publication was used as an opportunity to force the German-Austrian harmonisation of laws first encouraged in 1916 by *Count*

Councillor]) and *Krause* (Secretary of State of the Reich Justice Office), further staff: judges *Schäfer* and *Kiesow*.

[70] Cf. *Bumke*, Die neuen Strafgesetzentwürfe, in: DJZ 1921, col. 11, 16.

[71] *Bumke*, DJZ 1921, col. 14.

[72] For more details on the Special Part of the Draft of 1919: on **criminal offences against the state**, see *Schroeder*, Schutz von Staat und Verfassung, p. 137 f.; on **the offence of omitting to effect an easy rescue** see *Gieseler*, p. 43 ff.; on **criminal and terrorist/anarchist organisations** see *Felske*, p. 186 ff.; on the **failure to report a crime** see *Kisker*, p. 53 ff.; on **duelling** see *Baumgarten*, p. 180 ff.; on **abortion** see *Koch*, p. 130 ff.; *Putzke*, p. 212 ff.; on **theft** see *Prinz*, p. 61 ff.; on **false accusation** see *Bernhard*, p. 71 ff.; on **arson** see *Lindenberg*, p. 81 ff.; on **assault** see *Korn*, p. 277 ff.; on **perverting the course of justice** see *Thiel*, p. 74 ff.; on **mercy killing** see *Große-Vehne*, p. 69 ff.; on the **frustration of creditors' rights** see *Seemann*, p. 74 ff.; on **lèse majesté** see *Andrea Hartmann*, p. 194 ff.; on **prostitution, procuring and pandering** see *Ilya Hartmann*, p. 129 ff.; on **trespass** see *Rampf*, p. 79 ff.; on **embezzlement** and **unlawful appropriation** see *Rentrop*, p. 93 ff.; on **forgery of documents** see *Prechtel*, p. 127 ff.; on **road traffic law**, see *Asholt*, p. 81 ff.; on **incitement to hatred** see *Rohrßen*, p. 105 ff.

Gleispach.[73] Following the end of the War, the standardisation of laws between Germany and Austria in the area of criminal law was promoted primarily by the *Österreichische Kriminalistische Vereinigung* (ÖKV), founded in 1906 following the example of the German branch of the *Internationale Kriminalistische Vereinigung* (IKV), on the basis of the E 1919.

IV. Weimar Republic

1. Criminal Law Theory

Even before the turn of the century, the natural sciences' exclusive claim to scientificity had been contested by counter-movements. The one with the most philosophical significance and the most long-term influence on criminal law was the so-called **Neo-Kantianism.**[74] Natural sciences investigated general, repetitive phenomena capable of being subsumed under laws and regularities, without bias or rather blind to bias; neo-Kantianism contrasted these with the humanities and cultural sciences. Thought "linked to values and judgements" (not identical with "judgemental" thought) was to be characteristic of the latter.[75]

This new school of thought called itself "neo-Kantianism" partly because it took as its starting point the proposition taught by Kant (and first posited by **David Hume** [1711–1776] before him) that no conclusion can be drawn as to what ought to be from what is, and that both spheres must therefore be kept separate ("methodological dualism"; rejection of the "naturalistic fallacy"). The main exponent of southwest German neo-Kantianism, **Heinrich Rickert** (1863–1936), defined the difference between the two branches of science as the contrast between value and reality, validity and actuality. At the centre of neo-Kantian philosophy stands the *theory of value*: "Values are neither physical nor mental realities. As entities, they consist of their validity, not their actuality".[76]

This school of thought was significant for the theory of criminal law in that it regarded jurisprudence not as based on actual facts, but as a normative science aiming to interpret the meaning of laws as objectifying the collective will. This led at first to a **teleological definition of the *Rechtsgut***, i.e. to an understanding of a legal interest as a *value*, the protection of which is the purpose (the *telos*) of the legal catalogue of offences. Thus a clear differentiation was made between the *Rechtsgut* and the *Handlungsobjekt*, the *object* of the punishable action performed.

---

[73] Cf. *Gleispach*, DStrZ 1916, p. 107 ff.; cf. also *Schubert* I 3.1, p. XXIX.

[74] On neo-Kantianism and its influence on criminal law, cf. *Ziemann*, Neukantianisches Strafrechtsdenken (2009).

[75] The following according to *Amelung*, Rechtsgüterschutz, p. 125 ff.

[76] *Heinrich Rickert*, Kulturwissenschaft und Naturwissenschaft. 1st edition 1899, p. 89. Cf. also the major work of **Max Ernst Meyer** (1875–1932): "Rechtsnormen und Kulturnormen" (1903); on M.E. Meyer, cf. *Sascha Ziemann*, JJZG 4 (2002/2003), 395 ff.

The differentiation between these two terms, which can already be found in Liszt,[77] is still current today, as is the understanding of the protected legal interest as the central point of the teleological method of interpretation focused upon the meaning and purpose of legal regulations.[78] In structural terms, the differentiation between *Rechtsgut* and *Handlungsobjekt* repeated the process initiated by *Birnbaum*. While he had differentiated between "interest" and "(subjective) right", it was now the concept of the legal interest that became increasingly cerebral, and the "object of action" became its tangible substratum. The material definition of crime was thus back at its old level of abstraction, but there had been a fundamental change: while the theory of infringement of rights had been based on a small circle of subjective rights that could only be widened to a limited extent,[79] the new cerebral idea of the protected legal interest is related to positive law and is thus subject to shifts in politics and the *Zeitgeist*; its power to limit and contain is thus comparatively weak. The fact that one authoritarian branch of criminal law theory influential mainly during the National Socialist period denounced even this minimal capacity as liberalist, was due less to actual fact than to scientific strategy and politics.

In terms of the **theory and doctrine of criminal law**, the influence of neo-Kantianism (which incidentally was not uniform throughout, but included various branches or movements[80]) led to several lasting "discoveries" that have left a mark on the doctrine of criminal law to the present day: reference has already been made to *Reinhard Frank's* "pioneering" contribution to the concept of blameworthiness (see § 5 II. 2. above)[81]; the new trend produced the following individual points:

1. The efforts to create a law of causality that defined the success of criminal law not purely in terms of natural science (the starting point for the theory of adequate causation and the theory of relevance; going beyond these and still influential today in the theory of objective ascription);
2. The "discovery" of intentions and other subjective criteria formulated in legal definitions of offences that led to the understanding that unlawfulness could also contain subjective elements[82];

[77] See footnote 12 above.

[78] *Amelung*, Rechtsgüterschutz, p. 133, with reference to *Richard Honig*, Die Einwilligung des Verletzten (1919), *Erich Schwinge*, Teleologische Begriffsbildung im Strafrecht (1930) and *Max Grünhut*, Methodische Grundlagen der heutigen Strafrechtswissenschaft (Festgabe für Frank Vol. 1, 1930); cf. also *Schünemann*, Systemdenken, p. 25, 30.

[79] A good example of this is furnished by Section 823 (1) BGB. In over a century, only the general right to privacy and the right to an established and functioning commercial enterprise have been added to its canon of (absolute) rights; one might also think of the right to "informational self-determination" (i.e. data protection) inferred from the constitution by the Federal Constitutional Court.

[80] For individual detail, cf. *Ziemann*, Neukantianisches Strafrechtsdenken, p. 40 ff.

[81] On the development of the concept of blameworthiness under the influence of neo-Kantianism, cf. *Achenbach*, Grundlagen, particularly p. 75 ff.

[82] It was probably *Edmund Mezger* who "discovered" the *subjective elements of unlawfulness* in *Mezger*, Die subjektiven Unrechtselemente, in: Gerichtssaal 1924, 207 ff.

3. The further "discovery" already made by Frank that duress also includes objective elements[83];
4. The "discovery" of the mistake of law, also in connection with the normative concept of blameworthiness from a systematic point of view (on the historic point of view, see II. 1. above).

The characteristics of this so-called **neoclassical system** are:

1) Relaxing the equation of unlawfulness with the objective and blameworthiness with the subjective side of the offence, thus rendering the system of criminal offences more *flexible*;
2) The advance of *normative elements of criminal offences* into the doctrine of criminal law; Liszt and Binding had assumed that all value judgements had already been made by the legislator, and the doctrine of criminal law could thus proceed impartially. As the system of criminal offences became increasingly normative, it also came closer to becoming *moralised*, i.e. the separation between law and morals recognised since Kant was in danger of breaking down.

As with Frank's theory of blameworthiness, we must here distinguish between the perspectives of doctrine and history of law when attempting to classify these developments.

In terms of the **doctrine of criminal law**, this development could be seen as beneficial as it made it clear that those implementing the law not only already use their own value judgements—whether consciously or unconsciously—when making decisions, but in fact are legally bound to make value judgements or at least to understand them. Some problems of doctrine could only be solved once this differentiated, more flexible system had been created.

In terms of **legal history**, going beyond the categories of doctrine, this development caused the disintegration of the "particularly clear and simple theory of crime" of the late nineteenth century,[84] which in its clarity and simplicity had also guaranteed some legal certainty. Even though positivism had watered down the material definition of crime over the course of the nineteenth century, it had at least on a *formal* level set standards for the rule of law by strictly binding judges to clearly defined criminal offences. Even though one might welcome the fact that the neoclassical structure of offences had reclaimed territory wrongfully annexed by positivism from the point of view of the system of criminal offences, these new insights were negligible if not indeed counterproductive for constitutional liberal criminal law. From the perspective of criminal policy, *Liszt* had already advocated an orientation towards the offender and his or her attitude and thus the related

[83] The point at which duress became included in the concept of blameworthiness was the discovery of the aspect of "*Unzumutbarkeit*" (i.e. whether a person might legitimately be expected to suffer a certain harm). This enabled the differentiating addition of duress to unlawfulness and blameworthiness that began with the decision RGSt 61, 242 ff. (see footnote 132 below); *Schünemann*, Systemdenken, p. 29.

[84] *Roxin*, Strafrecht AT, p. 201.

extension of judicial discretionary powers. In both points, the old and new lines of thought converged. The new aspect was of course that with these new insights these points could more easily be included in the doctrine of criminal law.

Another anti-positivist line of thought already foreshadowed the future: the irrationalism and anti-liberalism, beginning with **vitalism**, which was most popular after the loss of the First World War under the influence of conservative anti-republicanism. This line rejected the neo-Kantian separation of being and value and demanded that existence be examined in its entirety. This questioned precisely that aspect of the rule of law that legal positivism had provided for and preserved, namely the clear definition of what was punishable. This line achieved its fullest expansion and domination during the period of National Socialist rule.[85]

Here, too, we must differentiate between the perspective of criminal law doctrine from within the system and the "external" perspective of legal history. A view from within the system of course tends to enlarge differences in doctrine, for these are its main focus. In this regard, it is certainly accurate to state that the comprehensive perspective "ultimately would have led to irrationalism and decisionism and thus to the theory of criminal law abolishing itself".[86] An external point of view puts this more in perspective, for the irrational comprehensive view itself follows the trend of the development of criminal law since the beginning of the century, even though it does make it more radical. An orientation towards the offender and a criminal law focusing on offenders' attitudes become increasingly prevalent; the principle of *nullum crimen, nulla poena sine lege*, already disregarded by Binding and unable to establish itself as an unquestioned part of the achievements of the rule of law during the Weimar Republic, fitted in even less well with a comprehensive ideology that rejected subversive, formalistic patterns of thought and a formal definition of crime.

Overall, **anti-liberalism** dominated the theory of criminal law during the Weimar period.[87] In the old conflict between state punishment as protection *by* the state and criminal *law* as protection *from* the state, the latter was constantly forced into a defensive position. Even individuals like Gustav Radbruch, who supported the republic and advocated a humane criminal law, did not shrink from drastically toughening criminal law, as the description of the reform draft of 1922 will show.

This already shows that it is not always easy to determine which lines of thought individuals fall under. Liszt's disciple *Gustav Radbruch* professed himself to be a neo-Kantian, but was also one of the most pronounced exponents of legal positivism. The following utterance of his became famous (and indeed infamous after 1945):

> We despise the priest who preaches against his conscience, but we admire the judge who despite his sense of justice remains unswervingly loyal to the law.[88]

---

[85] Still unsurpassed on anti-liberalism, irrationalism and their influence on the theory of criminal law: *Marxen*, Kampf, p. 47 ff.

[86] *Schünemann*, Systemdenken, p. 33 f.

[87] For basic information, see Marxen, op. cit.

[88] *Gustav Radbruch*, Rechtsphilosophie. 4th (posthumous) edition, edited and introduced by Erik Wolf. Stuttgart 1950, p. 182.

During the Weimar Republic Radbruch became a Social Democrat politician, and for some time was Reich Minister of Justice. After 1933 he was ousted from his university position due to the "*Berufsbeamtengesetz*" (Civil Service Restoration Act). Liszt's followers *Eduard Kohlrausch*[89] and *Eberhard Schmidt*[90] came to terms with the NS regime and put much effort into showing how Liszt's theory could be reconciled with National Socialist criminal policy. As late as 1937, the neo-Kantians *Erich Schwinge* und *Leopold Zimmerl* were still defending their line of thought against the dominant irrational school.[91] However, Schwinge himself even in his old age defended National Socialist military justice – not least because of his personal involvement with it.[92] Biographies and political developments are not always consistent with developments in scholarly theory.[93]

Criticism of Liszt's now hegemonic criminal policy and the StGB draft of 1925 that it influenced (on this, see § 5 IV. 3. below) led to the foundation of the ***Deutsche Strafrechtliche Gesellschaft*** (German Society of Criminal Law) on 6 June 1925. The Würzburg teacher of criminal law *Friedrich August Oetker* (1854–1937) may have been the one to initiate its foundation.[94] In its preliminary meeting, the society passed the following resolution:

> The publication of the draft (sc. the draft of 1925) [. . .] gives rise to the serious concern that the Reich legislature is determined to break with the tradition of our national criminal law and its development. The idea of justice, as expressed in punishment under law that is firmly regulated and applies equally to all citizens, is harmed if measures are suggested that in some cases must result in reverting to the conditions of a police state, and the uniform practice of law is thrown into question by well-nigh unlimited judicial discretionary powers.[95]

The society's profile was as ambiguous as that of the German branch of the Lisztian *Internationale Kriminalistische Vereinigung* (IKV). The view that the latter of the two groups is the more liberal is utterly refuted if one undertakes a

---

[89] On Kohlrausch, cf. *Karitzky*, Kohlrausch; *Vormbaum*, Opportunismus.

[90] Even after the recent substantial monograph by *Simone Gräfin von Hardenberg*, Eberhard Schmidt. Ein Beitrag zur Geschichte unseres Rechtsstaats, Berlin 2009, there is still no critical biography of **Eberhard Schmidt** (1891–1977).

[91] *Erich Schwinge/Leopold Zimmerl*, Wesensschau und konkretes Ordnungsdenken im Strafrecht. 1937.

[92] *Erich Schwinge/P. Schweling*, Die deutsche Militärjustiz in der Zeit des Nationalsozialismus, 2nd edition 1978; *Erich Schwinge*, Verfälschung und Wahrheit, 1988; *Id.*, Die Urteile der Militärstrafjustiz „offensichtlich unrechtmäßig"? In: NJW 1993, 368 f.

[93] This is not to say that political developments had no influence on developments in scholarly theory. One attempt to relate both lines of development to one another is made by *Kubink*, JJZG 5 (2003/2004), 517 ff. (cf. particularly p. 520). However, the limitations of such outlines of parallels must always be borne in mind.

[94] *Schubert*, Reform Division I Vol. 1.1, p. LXIV; Other founding members were among others the teachers of criminal law *Philipp Allfeld, Ernst Beling, August Finger, Heinrich Gerland, August Hegler, Paul Heilborn, Eduard Kern, Karl Klee, Adolf Lobe, Edmund Mezger, Johannes Nagler, Richard Schmidt, August Schoetensack, Ludwig Träger, Adolf Wach* and *Friedrich Wachenfeld*. The name of all founding members are listed in *Friedrich August Oetker*, Die Deutsche Strafrechtliche Gesellschaft, in: Gerichtssaal 91 (1925), 321 ff., 322.

[95] *Oetker*, op. cit; cf. also *A. Graf zu Dohna*, Die Deutsche Strafrechtliche Gesellschaft, in: DJZ 1925, col. 1100 ff. From 1926 onwards, the *Deutsche Juristenzeitung* reported annually on multiple conferences and statements of the *Deutsche Strafrechtlichen Gesellschaft*.

close reading of the draft reform of 1922, strongly shaped by the IKV protagonist Gustav Radbruch (even though he was counted as a member of its liberal wing). While the *Deutsche Strafrechtliche Gesellschaft* became caught up in authoritarianism more quickly than the IKV towards the end of the 1920s, some of its objections to the hegemonic IKV policy were motivated by the rule of law. Some individuals were members of both associations. The IKV in turn had a major quarrel at its Frankfurt conference of 12–13 September 1932, where only a superficial compromise could be reached[96] between those who supported a continuation of the criminal law reform one the one hand and the NS sympathiser and teacher of criminal law **Wenzeslaus Count Gleispach** (1876–1944)[97] and his followers on the other; the latter included young scholars such as **Friedrich Schaffstein** (1902–2001), **Karl Engisch** (1899–1990) and **Erik Wolf** (1902–1977). At the turn of the following year, Schaffstein together with **Georg Dahm** (1905–1963) published the text "Liberales oder autoritäres Strafrecht?" (Liberal or Authoritarian Criminal Law?), the programme of which is already evident in its title.[98]

The Weimar period saw a vast increase in criminal-biological research activity in the field of **criminology.**[99] Although the development of crime during the First World War and the time immediately following had proven the importance of environmental influences for crime, sociologists remained uninterested in questions of criminality; thus criminology basically could only draw on statistical data from the field on chronological developments and the distribution of crime according to geographical location and age. Even so, **Moritz Liepmann** (1869–1928) and **Franz Exner** (1881–1947) were able to develop remarkable criminal-sociological interpretations that they linked to the "gigantic field of experimentation" of the First World War.[100]

Research in criminal biology was conducted nearly exclusively by psychiatrists (Gustav Aschaffenburg, Kurt Schneider, Karl Birnbaum, Johannes Lange, Hans Gruhle). In Bavaria, the psychiatrist **Theodor Viernstein** (1878–1949) designed

---

[96] Separately, with different majorities, the two sentences of the following resolution were passed: "In regard to the continuation of the reform of criminal law, the German branch of the IKV adheres to its previous aims in criminal policy (unanimously accepted)—notwithstanding its recognition of the influence of new lines of thought and significant changes in the relationship of political forces" (accepted with 25 to 23 votes and 7 abstentions); more detail in *Eb. Schmidt*, Einführung, § 345, p. 426; in greater detail *Marxen*, Kampf, p. 91 ff.; cf. also the description of events from the point of view of *Schaffstein*: Erinnerungen an Georg Dahm, in: JJZG 7 (2005/2006), 173 ff.

[97] On Gleispach, cf. *Eduard Rabofsky/Gerhard Oberkofler*, Verborgene Wurzeln der NS-Justiz. Strafrechtliche Rüstung für zwei Weltkriege. Vienna, Munich. Zurich 1985, p. 111 ff.; *I. Müller*, Furchtbare Juristen, p. 76 ff.

[98] *Georg Dahm/Friedrich Schaffstein*, Liberales oder autoritäres Strafrecht? Hamburg 1933; in detail on this text, *Mario A. Cattaneo*, Strafrechtstotalitarismus, p. 194 ff. *Marxen*, Kampf, p. 103 ff.; on the debate, rejection and reception of these theories in *Italian* theory of criminal law, cf. *Giorgio Marinucci*, Giuseppe Bettiol und die Krise des Strafrechts in den 30er Jahren, in: JJZG 10 (2008/2009), p. 173 ff.; also including information on further texts by these authors.

[99] *Wetzell*, Inventing the criminal, p. 107, 125.

[100] *Wetzell*, op. cit., p. 109 ff.

criminal-biological questionnaires for new prison inmates aimed to differentiate between those capable and those incapable of reform. The collected questionnaires in 1925 resulted in the ***Kriminalbiologische Dienst*** (Criminal Biological Service),[101] which Viernstein himself regarded as a contribution to race hygiene, for he considered criminal behaviour to be rooted in criminal character. Viernstein's methods of collecting data were strongly criticised by prison reformers.[102] Most researchers regarded the hereditary factor as merely influencing *disposition* or as one factor of many. In 1932, 30 years after his textbook first appeared, Gustav Aschaffenburg was forced to admit that criminal biology was still in its infancy.[103] Nonetheless, there was a noticeable trend towards the increasing prevalence of the paradigms of criminal biology.[104]

The debate on the reform of criminal law in the Weimar Republic was constantly accompanied by **demands for sterilisation**; their connection to criminal biology – as well as to the ideas of exclusion espoused by many criminal reformers following Liszt (detention for the purpose of incapacitation) – is obvious. "Eugenics" or "race hygiene" was not the exclusive preserve of one particular school of politics – this impression only arose as the political (extreme) right wing was later ready to follow it through to its last, deadly consequence with its "euthanasia" programme. Neither were they a purely German obsession – even though the propensity for "merciless" systematic consistency particularly pronounced in Germany[105] may have encouraged the realisation of its deadly potential. The First World War with its "negative selection" encouraged the demand for compensatory measures.[106] Particularly hotly debated were the questions of whether only voluntary sterilisation or also enforced sterilisation should be allowed, and whether delinquency should constitute grounds for sterilisation. Scholarship replied to the latter question with a resounding yes,[107] while politicians were undecided; several parties changed their stance from approval to rejection over time. The Social Democrats and the National Socialists expressed approval throughout – with the big difference of course that the Social Democrats only wanted to permit voluntary sterilisation.[108]

---

[101] *Wetzell*, op. cit., p. 131 ff., particularly p. 135; *Christian Müller*, Verbrechensbekämpfung, p. 241 ff.; *I. Baumann*, Verbrechen, p. 55 ff.; *Wachsmann*, Gefangen, p. 44 ff.

[102] In detail *Wetzell*, op. cit., p. 137 ff. "Viernstein's unsophisticated methodology and crude hereditarianism were not representative of psychiatric research on the causes of crime, most of which presented a far more complex picture of the interaction of biological and social factors in criminal behaviour" (op. cit., p. 142).

[103] *Wetzell*, op. cit., p. 178.

[104] *I. Baumann*, Verbrechen, p. 66 ff.

[105] There are historical reasons for this—besides the unlimited possibilities open to a dictatorship capable of and prepared to do anything—that *Heinrich Heine* was probably the first to prophetically note (as noted in § 2 footnote 74).

[106] *Wetzell*, op. cit., p. 237; Karl Binding and Alfred Hoche had coined the key word in 1920; see § 5 II. 1. above; cf. also *Große-Vehne*, Tötung auf Verlangen, p. 89 ff.; *Christian Müller*, Verbrechensbekämpfung, p. 150 ff., especially p. 173.

[107] *Wetzell*, op. cit., p. 241 ff.

[108] *Wetzell*, op. cit., p. 250 ff.; *I. Baumann*, Verbrechen, p. 73 ff.; on social democracy cf. *Michael Schwartz*, Sozialistische Eugenik. Eugenische Sozialtechnologien in Debatten um Politik der deutschen Sozialdemokratie 1890–1933. Bonn 1995; *Id.*, Medizinische Tyrannei: Eugenisches

2. Penal Legislation

With the **Weimar Constitution**, the first catalogue of fundamental rights for the whole of Germany came into force. Germany became a democratic republic. The principle *nullum crimen sine lege* was made law in **Article 116** of the Constitution, though phrased in such a way that—as was to be seen—allowed it to be interpreted in ways that excluded its application to the kind and extent of punishment (nulla-*poena*-principle):

> An act can only be subject to punishment if its punishability was defined by law before the act was committed.

Section 2 (1) RStGB, dating from the time of the Kaiserreich, was clearer:

> An act can only be subject to punishment if that punishment was defined by law before the act was committed.

Art. 136 (3) WRV determined that nobody could be forced to take a religious form of oath. Following a petition by the Deutsche Volkspartei, the transitional provision of **Art. 177 WRV** was added, according to which the words "I swear" could be used to take a legal oath instead of the religious oath.[109] This at least defused the old quarrel on whether there could actually be a non-religious oath.[110]

Despite the radical changes on the level of state and constitutional law, the lower-level legal order by and large remained unchanged. Except the Constitution of 1871, **Art. 178 WRV** declared that all existing laws remained in force unless they contradicted the new Constitution. This was a particularly thorny issue when it came to offences against the state. Regulations on treason against the person of the Kaiser were not applied to the Reich President.[111] As the adaptation of offences against the state—which actually became important in practice during the time of the Weimar Republic, unlike during the Kaiserreich[112]—to the republican context

---

Denken und Handeln in international vergleichender Perspektive (1900–1945), in: JJZG 7 (2005/2006), 37 ff., especially p. 38 f.; *Christian Müller*, Verbrechensbekämpfung, p. 209 and passim.

[109] For more details and information on further developments, cf. *Vormbaum*, Eid, p. 97 ff.

[110] This quarrel was only settled in 1975 after a decision of the Federal Constitutional Court (BVerfGE 33, 33) opened up the possibility to make an affirmation instead of an oath; more detail in *Vormbaum*, Eid, p. 164 f.

[111] *Gusy*, Weimar, p. 108; *Id.*, Der Schutz des Staates gegen seine Staatsform. Die Landesverratsrechtsprechung in der Weimarer Republik, in: GA 1992, 195 ff.; *A. Hartmann*, Majestätsbeleidigung, p. 196.

[112] *Gusy*, Weimar, p. 126; *Rasehorn*, Justizkritik, p. 159 ff.; contemporary criticism: *Emil Julius Gumbel*, Vier Jahre politischer Mord und Denkschrift des Reichsjustizkommissars zu "Vier Jahre politischer Mord". Berlin 1924. Reprint Heidelberg 1980 with an introduction by Hans Thill. Gumbel, a mathematician and associate professor of statistics at the University of Heidelberg, had first published his book "2 Jahre politischer Mord" in 1920, in which he presented his calculation that "the German justice system let over 300 political murders go unpunished". In the sequel he calculated that 22 murders by left-wingers stood in opposition to 332 murders by the right, and that the average prison sentence was 15 years per left-wing murder, and 4 months per right-wing murder. In a memorandum, the Reich Ministry of Justice basically confirmed Gumbel's numbers. There was no reaction on part of the justice system (the Reich Supreme Court had jurisdiction in

was unsuccessful up to 1933, its application was left to the judiciary. While the courts developed a technically detailed interpretation, its application tended to be biased, treating the Communist Party far more strictly than the NSDAP.[113]

Similarly to the later period of occupation and the early years of the Federal Republic, the democratisation of the justice system was impeded by the fact that it had to make do with the personnel from the earlier political system.[114]

In general, the legislative trend of the years before and during the war continued. The brutalisation caused by the war and the economic symptoms of crisis common after a war (particularly a lost war: shift from a wartime economy to a peacetime economy; black market; "war profiteers"), the inflation that had already begun during the last years of the war due to the misguided policies for financing it (war bonds instead of raising taxes) and which was aggravated by Allied (primarily French) demands for reparation, culminating in the hyperinflation of the crisis year 1923, all resulted in a remarkable level of **economic crime**. "Organised crime" became topical, though not yet under this name ("rings of thieves and handlers of stolen goods", "traffickers", crime syndicates).[115]

On the one hand, this level of crime was combated by extensive legislation controlling the economy and appurtenant supplementary provisions, but on the other hand also was created by the very fact of its definition.[116] The form in which laws were enacted followed the pattern familiar from the Great War. Thus the *Gesetz über eine vereinfachte Form der Gesetzgebung für die Zwecke der Übergangswirtschaft* (Law on a simplified form of legislation for the purposes of a transitional economy) of 17 April 1919 authorised the Reich government, the State Committee and a 28-member committee elected by the National Assembly to pass legislative decrees "deemed necessary and urgent in regulating the transition from a wartime economy to a peacetime economy".[117] Further enabling acts followed up until 1924.[118]

first and last instance over political murders). However, in 1924 Gumbel was prosecuted for treason no less than three times, as he had reported on the so-called "Schwarze Reichswehr" and the links of the Bavarian state government to right-wing hit squads in essays in the "Weltbühne" and a further book titled "Verschwörer".

[113] *Gusy*, p. 109 ff., 127.

[114] Differentiating and emphasising the particular situation in Baden, *Kißener*, p. 52 ff.; on political justice in general and the bias against the "Left" in judicial practice: *Hannover/Hannover-Drück*, Politische Justiz.

[115] Examples of art that deals with this phenomenon, if sometimes in a time-displaced manner, are *Bertolt Brecht's* Threepenny Opera (1928), *Norbert Jacques's* novel "Dr. Mabuse the Gambler" (1922) and the final scene in *Fritz Lang's* film "M" (1931; Fritz Lang also made a film of Jacques's novel). Further significant works are discussed in *Hania Siebenpfeiffer*, Böse Lust. Gewaltverbrechen in Diskursen der Weimarer Republik. Cologne, Weimar, Vienna 2005; this also includes a discussion of gender-specific discourses of crime (the female poisoner; the female infanticide).

[116] More detail in *Werner*, Wirtschaftsstrafrecht, p. 34 ff.

[117] *Richstein*, Das belagerte Strafrecht, p. 148.

[118] The so-called Emminger Decree on the organisation of courts and criminal procedure was also passed on the basis of such an enabling act (see IV. 4. below).

The so-called *Kapp putsch* and the assassination attempts on republican politicians (Matthias Erzberger, Walter Rathenau), both preceded by articles inciting to downright murder in the extreme right-wing press, led to several stages of a **Legislation for the Protection of the Republic**[119] from 1921 onwards that included a toughening of the press laws and laws on the right to association and assembly. According to a statement by Reich Chancellor Wirth, the main political purpose of these regulations was "to protect the state, the republic and the lives of its representatives threatened by political assassination squads".[120] After several emergency decrees had been lifted after having been in force for a short period, these efforts culminated in the *(Erstes) Gesetz zum Schutze der Republik ((First) Law for the Protection of the Republic)*. Its first section contained "Criminal Laws for the Protection of the Republic".

The *participation in associations or meetings* whose aim it was to "eliminate members of the republican government of the Reich or a federal state by murder" was punishable by a penitentiary sentence, and in the case of successful or attempted murder was punishable "by death or a penitentiary imprisonment for life" (Section 1). Section 5 of the Law rendered the *failure to report* such an association or meeting punishable. There were exceptions for information revealed under the seal of confession and for close relatives, but the latter were only excused if they had to the best of their ability attempted to dissuade the offender from committing the offence; there was an ex post facto exception to this if a murder or attempted murder had been carried out. *Assisting* an offender in committing an attempted or successful murder was punishable according to the law with a penitentiary sentence; there were no exceptions for relatives in this case.

Besides these offences which were similar to those included in earlier decrees, the law also included regulations on the slander or denigration of the Republic, its symbols and its representatives (Section 8).[121] These regulations were certainly problematic, as the incriminated behaviour was very close to—legally and constitutionally acceptable—mere criticism. For the sake of supporting a worthy political aim, the Republic was willing to apply criminal law at far earlier stages and to make it stricter, too; particularly the additional offences included in the Law had a great practical impact during the time the Law was in force up until 1929 (although of course this declined in the quieter years of the Republic).[122]

An especially controversial topic that was subject to particular criticism following 1945 was the judicial practice related to someone calling the Republic a "*Judenrepublik*" (Jews' Republic). This was particularly precarious for the main parties of the Weimar Republic, for interpreting this name as derogatory or denigrating meant accepting the same system of reference as the anti-Semitic and anti-republican parties.[123] Of course, in this regard the

[119] On the individual laws, cf. *Gusy*, Weimar, p. 128 ff.; *Grässle-Münscher*, Kriminelle Vereinigung, p. 71 ff.

[120] *Gusy*, Weimar, p. 135.

[121] More detail in *Gusy*, Weimar, p. 142 ff.

[122] Numbers available in *Gusy*, p. 169.

[123] *Gusy*, Weimar, p. 161 ff.

judiciary behaved hypocritically in adopting – at least at first – a naive position.[124] When evaluating these events, we need to consider on the one hand that it is possible to objectively (and retrospectively) see these events and their judicial assessment as stages on the road to the Holocaust. On the other, even those who criticised anti-semitism and the aforementioned court practice did not imagine that the end point of this development would take the form it did and as it is generally known today.

The Law was extended in 1926 and 1927, and lapsed in 1929. In 1930 a—much weaker—Second Law for the Protection of the Republic was passed.[125] Several emergency decrees "to combat political riots", not aimed primarily at protecting the Republic, were passed towards the end of the Weimar Republic.[126]

Even making allowances for the necessity of defending the beleaguered Republic, it must be stated clearly that the Legislation on the Protection of the State made criminal law a political tool to an extent that the Weimar Republic was all too easily forgiven after 1945. The style of penal legislation that had established itself no later than in 1914 and was continued after 1918 was adhered to readily. The **State Constitutional Court for the Protection of the Republic** on a formal level at least served as the predecessor of the People's Court (*Volksgerichtshof*), and the frequent enabling acts and emergency decrees formed a legislative model for the later transfer of power to the Nazi Party. It is the task of the historian to make these observations independently of personal sympathies and antipathies (it is of course clear in this case where they lie).

These observations would be incomplete if no reference was made to the numerous, mainly politically motivated **amnesties** of the Weimar Republic. Here the criminal law, which the Republic had toughened as a means of combat for political reasons, lost some of its effect, but in this way it created a flexible political arsenal—that could now also be applied in the opposite direction. In this regard, too, it served as a model for the subsequent political system.[127]

Similarly to Liszt's criminal policy, the initial motivation for the **juvenile court movement** had been aspects of combating crime.[128] Accordingly, state powers of intervention and control formed this movement's context as they had for general criminal law; the level of flexibility that characterises juvenile criminal law to this day is required for the purpose of expediency, and draws its justification from the idea of education, or, in terms of criminal law theory, the idea of reform. Here, too, decriminalisation was largely a retrospective effect of criminal policy deliberations on expediency and making the law fit for purpose. The **Juvenile Court Act** of 1923 primarily created a "special law of sanctions".[129] It made it possible for juvenile

[124] For more detail, cf. *Gusy*, p. 160 ff.; *Angermund*, p. 34.

[125] On this, cf. *Gusy*, p. 171 ff.

[126] More detail in *Gusy*, Weimar, p. 193 ff.; *Nobis*, Strafprozessgesetzgebung.

[127] On the early amnesties cf. *Max Alsberg*, Die Reichs-Amnestiegesetze. Berlin 1919; cf. also *Marxen*, Rechtliche Grenzen der Amnestie. Heidelberg 1984, p. 11 ff.

[128] *Kubink*, Strafen, p. 127.

[129] *Kubink*, Strafen, p. 190.

criminal law to choose "modes of reaction derived from juvenile welfare law"[130]; the consequences were the first regulation of conditional suspension of sentences and the first exception to the principle of mandatory prosecution[131] (of course, the latter occurred here only a short time before it did in general criminal law; on this, see IV. 4. below).

During the time of the Weimar Republic, only comparatively few changes were made to the **Criminal Code**, namely 13 altogether[132]; with only one exception, we are dealing throughout with editorial changes following on from other acts of legislation or with individual additions, some of which were of course quite significant:

The *Legislation on the Protection of the Republic* resulted in a 1922 addition to **Section 49a RStGB**. Besides attempted abetting and acting on another's incitement to commit a felony, both punishable since the introduction of the Lex Duchesne (see § 5 II. 2. above), conspiracy to commit murder became an offence; if the reason for the conspiracy to murder a person lay in the position they held in public life, the punishment was qualified further. The original punishment was a prison sentence of no less than 1 year, while the qualified punishment was a penitentiary sentence—a significant threat of punishment for behaviour that in the original Reich Criminal Code had not been subject to prosecution at all.[133]

A further addition that was also transferred from the Legislation on the Protection of the State to the Criminal Code was made to this area in 1932 with **Section 49b**, added by the *Decree of the Reich President for the Preservation of Domestic Peace*.[134] According to paragraph 1, whosoever took part in an association or conspiracy "that aim[ed] to commit crimes against life or use[d] them for other purposes, or who support[ed] such an association" became subject to prosecution.[135] The punishment was a prison sentence of no less than 3 months, and in particularly severe cases a penitentiary sentence not exceeding 5 years.

An amendment of 1926[136] downgraded abortion—except in cases when it was carried out against the will of the pregnant woman—to a misdemeanour.[137] In the following year, on the basis of the medical indication for abortion, the Reich Supreme Court developed the legal concept of **supra-legal duress.**[138] This was

---

[130] *Kubink*, Strafen, p. 192.

[131] *Kubink*, Strafen, p. 197.

[132] *Vormbaum/Welp*, StGB, Nos. 20–32; *Rasehorn*, Weimar, in: Vormbaum/Welp, Suppl. 1, p. 38 ff.

[133] In order to evaluate this it should be mentioned that according to today's law, the punishment for conspiracy to commit a felony is based on the basic rules for attempted felonies, and thus in theory may encompass the maximum punishment for the completed offence (Section 30 (2) StGB).

[134] *Vormbaum/Welp*, StGB, No. 32.

[135] On this and its background, cf. *Felske*, Vereinigungen, p. 185.

[136] *Vormbaum/Welp*, StGB, No. 26.

[137] More detail in *Putzke*, Abtreibung, p. 273 ff.

[138] RGSt 61, 242 ff., decree of 11 March 1927; more detail in *Putzke*, Abtreibung, p. 25 ff.

derived from the principle of weighing conflicting interests and was later generalised. The Second Criminal Law Reform Act later made this into law under the heading of **necessity** (Section 34 StGB), and as such it came into force in 1975.

Incidentally, work on the reform of criminal law (see IV. 3. below) seems to have delayed individual changes to laws in the core area of criminal law during the period of the Weimar Republic as well.

However, this time did produce a significant change to one aspect of the Criminal Code. Since 1921, several laws and decrees had already extended the area of application of fines. The **Sanctions against Assets and Fines Decree** of 6 February 1924[139] transferred this legislation into criminal law and subsequent regulations provided the necessary detail.[140] The central regulation of this amendment was the new Section 27b (1) StGB:

> If a custodial sentence of less than 3 months is forfeit for a misdemeanour or a transgression not usually punishable by a fine alone or only in addition to a custodial sentence, the court shall impose a fine instead of a custodial sentence, if the purpose of the punishment can be achieved by a fine

This regulation encoded a trend in penal legislation and criminal justice that had begun in judicial practice already at the beginning of the twentieth century and that with some interruptions was to last throughout the century: the constant expansion of the proportion of fines at the cost of custodial sentences, which has led to the preponderance of fines in present day practice.[141] Of course, this trend was somewhat qualified by the comparatively high number of custodial sentences for default of payment (again lasting throughout this entire period). This development was encouraged by the simultaneous expansion of the criminal law, particularly the supplementary penal provisions, which created offences where the sanction of a custodial sentence was inappropriate in the first place.[142] This regulation was characteristic also in that it enforced, to a large degree, Liszt's demand to abandon short custodial sentences, although the phrasing "if the purpose of the punishment can be achieved by a fine" left the judge a wide discretion at the cost of legal specificity—thus corresponding to Liszt's criminal policies in this regard as well.

3. *Continuation of Penal Reform*

Under the new government of Reich Chancellor Josef *Wirth*, the reform of criminal law continued, led by the professor of criminal law and Liszt disciple *Gustav Radbruch*, now appointed Minister of Justice. Together with his collaborators *Bumke*, *Kiesow*, *L. Schäfer*, *Joël* and *Koffka* and the Austrian *Hofrat* [privy

---

[139] *Vormbaum/Welp*, StGB, No. 24.

[140] For more detail and an interpretation, cf. *Stapenhorst*, p. 39 ff.

[141] *Kubink*, Strafen, p. 103.

[142] On the development as a whole, cf. *Stapenhorst*; also *Kubink*, Strafen, op. cit.

councillor] *Kadečka*, he created the **Draft of 1922** later named after himself.[143] It was submitted to the Reich government on 13 September 1922 as a cabinet bill.

This draft, which was only published 30 years later with an introduction by *Eberhard Schmidt*, is considered a "highlight of the work on the reform of criminal law"—not least because of the way it is evaluated in Schmidt's introduction.

When creating the draft, Radbruch and his colleagues were moving in a force field between the poles of the preceding draft of 1919, the desire to harmonise legislation between Germany and Austria, Radbruch's own background as a student of Liszt, and lastly Radbruch's own ideas. These various influences make it difficult and indeed ultimately impossible to pinpoint the decisive factor of influence on each of the important aspects.[144] But the desire to harmonise the laws of Germany and Austria doubtlessly played a significant role.

Outwardly, the draft's **structure** differs from that of its predecessors in its tripartite division into "felonies and misdemeanours", "transgressions" and "behaviour harmful to the public"; the latter two groups were regulated completely separately; the section on transgressions, sanctioned by fines and custodial sentences, had its own General Part; "behaviour harmful to the public" as "unsocial behaviour" was differentiated from the "antisocial behaviour" of criminal law and was punishable by workhouse. Both Parts were later to be severed and allocated to a separate branch of the law. Special rules for young offenders were not included, because the Juvenile Court Act was about to be passed.

When trying to identify the legal theory upon which the draft is based, it becomes clear that Franz v. Liszt's thought also dominated Radbruch's ideas on criminal policy. At least his ideas tend towards a philosophical consolidation of this thought; his concept of the state in particular shows evidence of consideration in depth (and in a way that is, in principle, liberal). Especially since the end of the Kaiserreich, Radbruch, despite his dislike of the idea of retribution, was nonetheless aware of its constitutional and liberal aspects.[145]

The most remarkable and today best-known feature of this draft is that it no longer contained **capital punishment**. However, in his comments on the draft Radbruch explicitly left it open whether it should be included in decrees of the Reich president according to Art. 48 WRV. The Austrians had emphatically demanded the abolition of the death penalty during the consultation process, as it was forbidden in the Austrian constitution.[146]

Both these facts raise questions on the significance of the abolition of the death penalty in the StGB draft on the one hand, and the threat of capital punishment in the Legislation on the Protection of the Republic on the other hand. One might assume that the abolition of capital punishment in the draft – similarly to Beccaria – hinged on peaceful political conditions; then again, the threat of capital punishment in the Law on the Protection of the Republic might have referred to the still extant death penalty in the RStGB in order to

---

[143] For details of the genesis of this draft, cf. *Goltsche*, Entwurf Radbruch (2008).

[144] Thus also the summary of *Goltsche*, Entwurf Radbruch, p. 394, who has studied all available (German and Austrian) sources on the draft's genesis.

[145] More detail in *Goltsche*, Entwurf Radbruch, p. 110 ff.

[146] More detail in *Goltsche*, Entwurf Radbruch, p. 252 ff.

avoid giving a privilege to "murderers' clubs".[147] This last suggestion is not convincing, for when "murderers' clubs" attempted a murder they became subject to the death penalty anyway according to the RStGB; there could be no danger of any privilege. Then again, the clause for presidential decrees (and thus for supplementary provisions) could have been conceived of as a loophole in order to limit the abolition of the death penalty (demanded categorically by the Austrians) to the Criminal Code.

The second innovation of the draft that is often emphasised was the replacement of penitentiaries by "**strict imprisonment**". In order to evaluate this innovation, it is important to answer two questions: 1) Did this new name actually change anything about the sentence, or were there—apart from the fact it lasted longer than a simple prison sentence—no longer any differences between the two kinds of prison? 2) Were the dishonourable consequences connected to having served a penitentiary sentence abolished? The sentencing law which was intended to be passed with the new StGB was not developed, rendering it impossible to provide a precise answer to the first question. In regard to the second, we can note that the draft no longer contained the loss of civil rights by law; however, as a *measure* the judge could withdraw the eligibility to hold public office and the right to vote. Here, at least, *Radbruch* had emancipated himself from his teacher *v. Liszt*, who had wanted to "designate the unconditionally dishonourable character of the penitentiary sentence as 'severe'"[148]; it speaks in Radbruch's favour that apparently there was no support (if no resistance either) from the Austrians for his decision.[149] It is problematic that judicial discretion was to decide on the measure based on the "particular trust" that the offender had earned.

That Liszt's non-liberal starting point came through in Radbruch's draft in spite of the latter's more relaxed stance on some points is also evident in the consistent **implementation of the principle of blameworthiness** publicised in the draft's explanatory reports. With this aim—which was becoming more and more accepted in literature and was consistent with the E 1919—in mind, Radbruch not only abolished strict liability for result-qualified offences (§ 15 E 1922),[150] but also developed a subjective theory of attempt focusing on the offender's attitude with an accordingly optional mitigation of punishment (23 (2) E 1922)[151]; it is here that the conflation of abetting and principal by proxy and the basically equal treatment of aiding and abetting (with only optional mitigation of punishment for the former) occurs,[152] as well as the removal of the different treatment of *Realkonkurrenz*

[147] Radbruch hints at this in a letter to his wife; cf. *Goltsche*, Entwurf Radbruch, p. 258.

[148] *Liszt*, Zweckgedanke, op. cit., p. 46 f.; *Goltsche*, Entwurf Radbruch, Chapter 6 A) II. 1. b) cc).

[149] *Goltsche*, Entwurf Radbruch, p. 264 ff.

[150] "A more severe punishment prescribed by law for a particularly defined consequence of the offence shall be imposed on the offender only if he caused this consequence at least through negligence."

[151] "The attempt may be punished more leniently than the completed offence."—Section 23 (4) made impunity compulsory for cases of gross ignorance.

[152] Sections 25, 26 E 1922. Section 27 separated the liability of the abettor and the aider from the liability (not only from the blameworthiness) of the principal. The regulation of Section 28 E 1922

[where the same offender commits several separate acts punishable under the criminal law], and *Idealkonkurrenz* [where one and the same act is an offence against several laws].[153]

Judges' discretionary powers were extended particularly when it came to **sentencing**, as they were expected to assess social, psychological and medical aspects in detail—the judge as a kind of "social officer, diagnostician and social therapist". According to the guidelines for sentencing laid out in Sections 67–77 E 1922, a "reprehensible attitude" (Section 67 (1)) and the "criminal will" of the offender (Section 76) as well as reoffending twice (Section 77) were the main criteria upon which decisions were to be based. In the case of reoffending, this was meant to emphasise whether the offences showed that "the offender was a habitual offender who posed a threat to public security". Then again, the possibilities for mitigation meant the judge had substantial discretion.

One particularity of the draft and a special concern of its creator was the particular treatment accorded **offenders who committed crimes for political or religious reasons**. According to Section 71 of the draft, "if the offender's decisive motivation consisted of feeling obliged to commit the offence due to his moral, religious or political convictions", then instead of prison or strict prison, confinement of the same length was to be applied. Confinement, which replaced *Festungshaft* as *custodia honesta*, was thus to be placed on a new footing. However, Radbruch's attempt to take the offender's convictions positively into account was widely rejected.[154]

The regulation on **detention for the purpose of incapacitation** (Section 45 E 1922) marked a quantum leap in the tightening of criminal law sanctions in the context of measures of rehabilitation and incapacitation (Sections 42 ff.); it tied in with the aforementioned rule on reoffending in Section 77, and was already triggered after two severe sentences of imprisonment (Section 45 E 1922). For this, as for all other forms of confinement (hospitals and care institutions, institutions for alcoholics), the rule was that detention should last as long as the purpose of the sentence required (Section 46 (1) E 1922). While the maximum detention in an institution for alcoholics was 2 years, it was 3 years for all other kinds of detention; however, the court could extend the term prior to its expiry. For the first time, the draft included the possibility of **substituting** punishment and

on personal characteristics or situations *establishing liability* was stricter than the regulation in today's Section 28 (1) StGB (that both have the identical numbering is coincidental): it was to apply to both abettors and aiders if these characteristics were present in their case *or* in the case of the principal; in the case of the abettor, their absence meant that mitigation was merely *optional*.

[153] In the cases of both kinds of *Konkurrenz*, only one punishment was to apply (Section 63). The punishment was to be determined according to the strictest law; the maximum punishment could be raised again by half (Section 64 I, II E 1922); more detail in *Goltsche*, Entwurf Radbruch, p. 182 ff.

[154] More detail in *Markus Thiel*, Gustav Radbruch und die Rechtsfigur des Überzeugungsverbrechers, in: JJZG 3 (2001/2002), 259 ff.; *Schroeder*, Schutz von Staat und Verfassung, p. 134 f.; *Goltsche*, Entwurf Radbruch, Chapter 6 A) II. 3. b).

measure (Section 47, 48 E 1922), relaxing the strict regulations on incapacitation detention; taken together with the simultaneous option of conditional remission of punishment (Sections 35 ff.), an undefined punishment as demanded by Liszt had been achieved to a large extent.

Given all of these factors, evaluations of the draft should be more differentiated than the one written by Eberhard Schmidt—who like Radbruch was a follower of Liszt—which has dominated the draft's reception since the 1950s.

After both the General and the Special Part[155] had been completed in September 1922, *Radbruch* submitted the draft to the cabinet in its meeting on 5 October 1922, which Reich Chancellor *Wirth* did not attend. However, *Wirth* sent instructions by telegram on 6 October that any discussion was to be postponed until after his return on 5 November. In November 1922, the *Wirth* cabinet resigned because of problems of foreign policy. A week later, the independent *Wilhelm Cuno* (1876–1933) was appointed Reich Chancellor, and *Karl Rudolf Heinze* (1865–1928) made Reich Minister of Justice. Both neglected to continue the reform of criminal law.

Radbruch—who became Reich Minister of Justice for a few months in 1923—reminded the *Stresemann* government in cabinet that the draft needed to be passed, as otherwise there was a danger that the plans for a unified German-Austrian criminal law might fail. In a letter to Radbruch of 25 May 1927, *Bumke* later explained to Radbruch that neither the French invasion of the Ruhr region nor the inflation had been the reason for delaying the criminal law reform; rather, this had been due to "inner inhibitions of the cabinet members". In the end, *Stresemann* was deposed by a vote of no confidence in the Reichstag on 23 November 1923, so that any continuation of the criminal law reform had temporarily failed.

After *Radbruch* had failed to push his draft through cabinet and work on the reform had come to a standstill for the time being, Secretary of State *Joël*, who held the office of Minister of Justice from April 1924 to the beginning of 1925, undertook a revision of the E 1922. This revision made changes mainly to the system of sanctions. Thus modified, *Radbruch's* draft was passed by the cabinet on 12 November 1924, and was presented to the Reich Council for approval by *Joël* as the "Official Draft of a General German Criminal Code, including draft reports" on 17 November 1924.

[155] Literature on individual offences and groups of offences in the draft of 1922: on **the offence of omitting to effect an easy rescue** see *Gieseler*, p. 55 ff.; on **criminal and terrorist/anarchist organisations** see *Felske*, p. 193 ff.; on the **failure to report a crime** see *Kisker*, p. 57 ff.; on **duelling** see *Baumgarten*, p. 183 ff.; on **abortion** see *Koch*, p. 222 ff.; *Putzke*, p. 136 ff.; on **theft** see *Prinz*, p. 72 ff.; on **false accusation** see *Bernhard*, p. 75 ff.; on **arson** see *Lindenberg*, p. 85 ff.; on **assault** see *Korn*, p. 294 ff.; on **perverting the course of justice** see *Thiel*, p. 75 ff.; on **mercy killing** see *Große-Vehne*, p. 71 ff.; on the **frustration of creditors' rights** see *Seemann*, p. 76 ff.; on **defamation of the head of state** see *Andrea Hartmann*, p. 217 ff.; on **prostitution, procuring and pandering** see *Ilya Hartmann*, p. 167 ff.; on **trespass** see *Rampf*, p. 83 ff.; on **embezzlement** and **unlawful appropriation** see *Rentrop*, p. 98 ff.; on **forgery of documents** see *Prechtel*, p. 132 ff.; on **road traffic law**, see *Asholt*, p. 86 ff.; on **incitement to hatred** see *Rohrßen*, p. 110 ff.

After 20 years' of reform work, the first official draft—i.e. the first draft supported by the Reich government—of a criminal code thus appeared. It corresponded with the current law of the RStGB particularly with regard to sanctions. Following the Draft of 1922, the **Draft of 1925** also encoded transgressions in a separate book with a General Part of their own, and regulated "behaviour harmful to the public" in a third book. The main instances of such behaviour listed were begging, vagrancy and certain kinds of prostitution. Capital punishment[156] and penitentiary sentences were included once more; by contrast, the Draft of 1922's regulations on attempt, secondary participation and *Konkurrenz* were retained, including the optional mitigation of punishment for attempt. The lower threshold set by the previous draft for incapacitation detention was also retained. As in the E 1922, judges had a great deal of freedom in sentencing; in particular, they were authorised to a far greater degree than previously to counter particularly offensive behaviour with "the necessary severity". Then again, the aim in practice was to abolish the increased minimum sentence, as the generally valid assumption of "mitigating circumstances" always made it possible to go down to the system's lowest sentencing level. Thus the E 1925 took account of both the demands to toughen the punishments threatened, as well as the need resulting from criminal statistics to abolish short-term custodial sentences by introducing fines. In these aspects, too, the E 1925 drew on the central points of *Radbruch's* draft.[157]

---

[156] The 1923 statement of the Social Democrat Home Secretary *Stollman* shows what a defensive position even those sceptical of capital punishment were placed in (cit. in *Chr. Müller*, Verbrechensbekämpfung, p. 189): "Where there is a state emergency, particularly when organised resistance to the power of the state arises, it will perhaps be necessary in future to allow the death penalty to be imposed"; but there is "no reason to retain a kind of punishment perhaps necessary in cases when the state is particularly threatened during normal times, when it really can be done without". This is a detailed repetition of the main argument against capital punishment put forward by **Cesare Beccaria** at the end of the 18th century. The abolition of capital punishment with the caveat of political expediency is one of the Enlightenment's most ambivalent legacies to the modern era.

[157] Literature on individual offences and groups of offences in the Reich Council Bill: on **the offence of omitting to effect an easy rescue** see *Gieseler*, p. 55 ff. (including E 1922); on **criminal and terrorist/anarchist organisations** see *Felske*, p. 195 ff.; on the **failure to report a crime** see *Kisker*, p. 60 ff.; on **duelling** see *Baumgarten*, p. 184 ff.; on **abortion** see *Putzke*, p. 304 ff.; *Koch*, p. 165 ff.; on **theft** see *Prinz*, p. 74 ff.; on **false accusation** see *Bernhard*, p. 75 ff. (including E 1922); on **arson** see *Lindenberg*, p. 85 ff. (including E 1922); on **assault** see *Korn*, p. 294 ff. (including E 1922); on the **perverting the course of justice** see *Thiel*, p. 76 ff.; on **mercy killing** see *Große-Vehne*, p. 75 ff.; on the **frustration of creditors' rights** see *Seemann*, p. 77 ff.; on **defamation of the head of state** see *Andrea Hartmann*, p. 217 ff. (including E 1922); on **prostitution, procuring and pandering** see *Ilya Hartmann*, p. 171 ff.; on **trespass** see *Rampf*, p. 84 ff.; on **embezzlement** and **unlawful appropriation** see *Rentrop*, p. 98 ff. (including E 1922); on **forgery of documents** see *Prechtel*, p. 136 ff.; on **road traffic law**, see *Asholt*, p. 86 ff. (including E 1922); on **incitement to hatred** see *Rohrßen*, p. 112 ff.

On 27 November 1924 the Bill was submitted to the United Committees VII, VIII and V of the Reich Council,[158] whose deliberations over its details, presided over by *Bumke*, were to last from 8 October 1926 to 22 December 1926. The draft of 1924/25 formed the basis of the Committee discussions in the Reich Council, including editorial changes made following the petitions of individual state governments. The plenary meetings of the Reich Council took place on 5 and 13 April 1927. The newly prepared draft was submitted to the Reichstag by the Reich Justice Minister on 14 May 1927. The draft aimed to retain the division of the Criminal Code into three books. Although by and large it conformed to the Draft of 1925, the **Draft of 1927** also differed from it in some significant points; for example, the privileged treatment of persons who committed offences based on their moral or political conscience (*Überzeugungstäter*) based on Radbruch's idea[159] was given up and the definition of necessity narrowed down[160]; mitigation for attempt once again became compulsory (Section 26 (2)).

The E 1927 was transferred to the newly created 32nd Criminal Law Committee following a two-day plenary debate on 21 and 22 June 1927. This Committee began its deliberations on details, chaired by *Wilhelm Kahl*, on 21 September 1927. These lasted until 2 March 1928. During this period of time, the 32nd Committee succeeded in debating the regulations as far as Section 202 E 1927 before the reform process threatened to founder prematurely due to the dissolution of the Reichstag in mid-May 1928. The Law on the Continuation of the Reform of Criminal Law of 31 March 1928 (RGBl. I 1928, p. 135) made it possible to transfer the results of the discussion so far to the new term, without tabling the Bill anew. Section 1 of the Law ran as follows:

> The drafts of a General German Criminal Code submitted to the Reichstag for approval on 14 May and 19 September 1927 (Printed matter of the Reichstag Nos. 3390 and 3628), are subject to approval by the Reichstag of the following term without being tabled anew if the Reichstag does not discuss them during the third legislative period. The drafts count as a new bill.

---

[158] The Reich Council Bill was published as a book in 1925. In 1926, a "Critical Review of the Official Drafts of a General German Criminal Code, commissioned by the German Branch of the *Internationale Kriminalistische Vereinigung*", edited by *Aschrott* and *Kohlrausch*, was published.

[159] On this, see

[160] Literature on individual offences and groups of offences in the Reichstag Bill: on **the offence of omitting to effect an easy rescue** see *Gieseler*, p. 64 ff.; on **criminal and terrorist/anarchist organisations** see *Felske*, p. 218 ff.; on the **failure to report a crime** see *Kisker*, p. 62 ff.; on **duelling** see *Baumgarten*, p. 187 ff.; on **abortion** see *Koch*, p. 304 ff.; *Putzke*, p. 156 ff.; on **theft** see *Prinz*, p. 88 ff.; on **false accusation** see *Bernhard*, p. 82 ff.; on **arson** see *Lindenberg*, p. 90 ff.; on **assault** see *Korn*, p. 318 ff.; on **perverting the course of justice** see *Thiel*, p. 82 ff.; on **mercy killing** see *Große-Vehne*, p. 77 ff.; on the **frustration of creditors' rights** see *Seemann*, p. 78 ff.; on **defamation of the head of state** see *Andrea Hartmann*, p. 219 ff.; on **prostitution, procuring and pandering** see *Ilya Hartmann*, p. 174 ff.; on **trespass** see *Rampf*, p. 92 ff.; on **embezzlement** and **unlawful appropriation** see *Rentrop*, p. 116 ff.; on **forgery of documents** see *Prechtel*, p. 145 ff.; on **road traffic law**, see *Asholt*, p. 95 ff.; on **incitement to hatred** see *Rohrßen*, p. 116 ff.

The newly elected Reichstag once again transferred the E 1927 to the Commission for deliberation on 11 July. The Commission took up its work as the (now) 21st Committee on 12 July 1928: the work on the details—once again chaired by Kahl—commenced on 9 October 1928 and lasted until 11 July 1930.

The last meeting of the 21st Criminal Law Committee took place on 11 July 1930. The continuation of these discussions planned after the summer recess was at first prevented by the renewed dissolution of the Reichstag of the fourth legislative period on 18 July 1930. Attempts to pass a law to continue the reform failed. In collaboration with the Reich Ministry of Justice, *Kahl* managed to continue the criminal law reform in the following fifth legislative period of the Reichstag. On 6 December 1930 he petitioned the Reichstag to accept the "Draft of a General German Criminal Code". In terms of content, this petition reproduced the decisions of the first reading of the 21st Criminal Law Committee in the form developed by the German and Austrian parliamentary conferences on criminal law.[161] In the Reichstag elections of 14 September 1930, the NSDAP had entered the German Reichstag as the second strongest party after the SPD with 18.3 % and 107 MPs. Due to this result, the NSDAP was also given 5 votes on the Criminal Law Committee, which was made up of 28 members. As it soon became evident that the NSDAP (like the KPD before them) refused to cooperate constructively and for the most part conducted political propaganda, reform work stagnated. This was due to the death of *Kahl*, who had been the reform's driving force, on 14 May 1932 on the one hand, and to yet another dissolution of the Reichstag on 4 June 1932 on the other. The last meeting of the (now) 18th Committee took place on 18 March 1932. Given the lack of any parliamentary efforts worth mentioning and of any willingness to continue *Kahl's* work, attempts to reform criminal law first flagged, then came to a complete standstill.

4. Criminal Procedure

After the Revolution of 1918/19, the desire arose to develop a new comprehensive concept of criminal procedure and of the organisation of courts that matched the

[161] Literature on individual offences and groups of offences in the "Kahl Draft": on **the offence of omitting to effect an easy rescue** see *Gieseler*, p. 66 ff.; on **criminal and terrorist/anarchist organisations** see *Felske*, p. 235 ff.; on the **failure to report a crime** see *Kisker*, p. 65 ff.; on **duelling** see *Baumgarten*, p. 192 ff.; on **abortion** see *Koch*, p. 328 ff.; *Putzke*, p. 164 ff.; on **theft** see *Prinz*, p. 104 ff.; on **false accusation** see *Bernhard*, p. 85 ff.; on **arson** see *Lindenberg*, p. 96 ff.; on **assault** see *Korn*, p. 349 ff.; on **perverting the course of justice** see *Thiel*, p. 93 ff.; on **mercy killing** see *Große-Vehne*, p. 78 ff.; on the **frustration of creditors' rights** see *Seemann*, p. 80 ff.; on **defamation of the head of state** see *Andrea Hartmann*, p. 229 ff.; on **prostitution, procuring and pandering** see *Ilya Hartmann*, p. 179 ff.; on **trespass** see *Rampf*, p. 98 ff.; on **embezzlement** and **unlawful appropriation** see *Rentrop*, p. 123 ff.; on **forgery of documents** see *Prechtel*, p. 153 ff.; on **road traffic law**, see *Asholt*, p. 98 ff.; on **incitement to hatred** see *Rohrßen*, p. 117 ff.

new constitutional and political conditions in the Republic—before the reform of substantive criminal law, if necessary. At the beginning of 1920, Reich Minister of Justice Schiffer (DDP) published a *Draft Law to amend the Constitution of Courts Act and a Law on Criminal Procedure* with draft reports, both of which had been written mainly by James Goldschmidt (**Drafts Goldschmidt/Schiffer**). These drafts by a Professor of Criminal Law (and a leading member of the IKV) under the aegis of a liberal Reich Minister of Justice[162] according to their authors' concept aimed to achieve a "democratisation of the criminal justice system".[163] Eberhard Schmidt,[164] who himself had always regarded the drafts rather sceptically, stated of them[165] as late as 1965 that they were the first that had been evidence of a really "major thread". Their characteristics:

> The participation of lay persons in the first instance, particularly the jury courts in their old form, should be retained. Appeals in all legal matters were regarded as a self-evident political necessity [...] The judicial investigation (*gerichtliche Voruntersuchung*) was abolished, as was the decision to transmit the case for trial (*Eröffnungsbeschluss*)". The principle of mandatory prosecution was retained (Section 176 (2) E 1920). "A significant expansion of the rights of defence counsel was to improve the possibilities of defence. Like the accused himself, defence counsel was to have the right to be present at all examinations during the preliminary proceedings – not only those conducted by the judge, but also those led by the prosecution – with the full right to ask questions. The rights of access to the prosecution dossier and to private conversation with the accused were expanded. Custody on remand was made subject to far stricter conditions. The pre-trial investigation was left entirely in the hands of the prosecution, and any bias of the investigation thus removed from the main proceedings. The prosecution and the defence were given significant influence on the evaluation of the evidence during the main proceedings by granting them the right to individually examine witnesses.

That the judicial investigation was seen as a remainder of the old inquisitorial process shows just where a line of argumentation with little historical awareness can lead. The principle of the independent writ of prosecution which had established itself in the nineteenth century was by now taken for granted as an expression of the accusatory principle to such an extent that the involvement of an independent court (differing from the adjudicating court) in the preliminary proceedings was not regarded as a means of relativising the dangerous powers of the prosecution, but as a last remainder of the inquisitorial process, the abolition of which was the logical continuation of the idea of the accusatory trial. Fifty-five years later, this line of argument was then used to abolish the judicial investigation.

The drafts, published by the Reich government, did not reach the National Congress as they already met with opposition in the Reich Council. The Prussian

[162] For a detailed study of the drafts, cf. *Wolfgang Rentzel-Rothe*, Der "Goldschmidt-Entwurf". Inhalt, reformgeschichtlicher Hintergrund und Schicksal des Entwurfs eines Gesetzes über den Rechtsgang in Strafsachen. Pfaffenweiler 1995.

[163] Thus *Löwenfeld*, Sozialistische Monatshefte 1920 II, 810.—On the principle of mandatory prosecution and the reasons for discontinuing its application, cf. *Dettmar*, Legalität, p. 179 ff.

[164] *Eb. Schmidt*, Einführung, p. 417.

[165] In agreement with *Kohlrausch*, DtStrRZ 1920, col. 138.

government in particular expressed its concern to the Reich Ministry of Justice in an advisory opinion, and not just regarding the basic concept, which assumed the coexistence of a social criminal law and a liberal law of criminal procedure; it was also of the opinion that the constitution of courts in the drafts was "too complicated and [. . .] far too expensive, given the conditions created by the outcome of the War", thus rendering the drafts unsuitable for further discussion. The objection that it would be better "first to complete the new construction of substantive criminal law" also played an important role. There is a certain tragedy about the Drafts of Goldschmidt/Schiffer, the last ones to date that attempted to create a constitutional, liberal procedure law completely from scratch, in that individual ideas were taken from them and put into a practice which, however, gained a different function and significance as a result of being removed from the context of other elements of the regulations.

The following period saw some issues about details of criminal procedure being settled, including important ones such as the **involvement of women as lay assessors and members of the jury**[166] and **juvenile criminal procedure.**[167] If the failed Goldschmidt drafts and the two aforementioned laws were proof of reformatory activity, then the "Courts (Reduction of Workload) Law" of 11 March 1921 continued along the path already taken by the *Law on the Simplification of the Application of Criminal Law*, passed in the war year 1917, expanding summary proceedings without trial and extending the jurisdiction of courts with lay assessors at the *Amtsgericht* (*Schöffengericht*) at the expense of the criminal chambers at the *Landgericht.*[168] Since then, "reducing the workload of the courts" has been a constant theme in the history of German procedural law, with only a few interruptions; the solutions found for this problem during successive cycles were regularly at the expense of the forms of constitutional safeguards.

A new step towards a change in criminal procedure in more than just isolated points was the *Draft Law on a New Constitution of Criminal Courts*, written with draft reports in January 1922 in the Reich Ministry of Justice under Gustav Radbruch in his first term of office as Reich Minister of Justice (in the Wirth cabinet). This draft—similarly to the Draft of 1920—planned a massive extension of the jurisdiction of the *Schöffengericht*, while at the same time reducing first instance jurisdiction of the criminal chambers [of the *Landgericht*] and introducing the differentiation between small and large *Schöffengerichte*; furthermore, it continued regulations on the democratisation and streamlining of the procedure of selecting lay assessors and members of the jury, but otherwise left regulations on the jury court unchanged (apart from a reduction of the number of persons on the list of the selected main jurors [*Spruchliste*]).

The draft was approved in cabinet in the meeting of 28 April 1922. On 16 May, Radbruch submitted a revised version which took account of the suggestions and

---

[166] Law of 25 April 1922, RGBl. I, p. 465.

[167] Juvenile Courts Act of 16 February 1923, p. 135, 252.

[168] On this, cf. *Elobied*, Entwicklung, p. 93 ff.

concerns of state representatives. On 14 July 1922, the cabinet also approved this version. One month later, it was published (without the Draft Report) in the *Reichsanzeiger* ("Radbruch Draft"). From June 1922, the draft was debated in the relevant committees of the **Reich Council**. Several changes were suggested, motivated partly by financial and partly by political concerns. Some came from the Reich Council itself, others from Heinze (DVP), the new Reich Minister of Justice of the Cuno cabinet, who had succeeded Radbruch in November 1922. The suggestions for change referred mainly to the number of lay judges and their selection procedure, as well as the organisation and jurisdiction of the jury courts. The draft was then once again revised in the Reich Ministry of Justice. The Cuno cabinet approved the new draft version on 16 February 1923. The draft was submitted to the Reichstag on 29 May ("Heinze Draft").

Unlike its predecessors, this draft made it as far as being deliberated in the Reichstag. Radbruch—who was involved this time as the MP speaking for the Social Democrats—told the Reichstag that he was not happy to see the draft again. He rejected any "paternity" of this draft.[169]

> Reich Minister of Justice Heinze urged a speedy deliberation – not least in order to be able to prove in a legally unimpeachable manner the illegitimacy of the Bavarian people's courts (one of which was to provide a particularly scandalous spectacle in the following year with the Hitler/Ludendorff trial).

The Draft Heinze was passed to the Justice Select Committee of the Reichstag, which began its deliberations but then postponed and failed to continue them. After passing an enabling act on 13 October 1923, the Reichstag went on recess. Now the Reich Ministry of Justice saw its chance to achieve the reform of the organisation of courts via an emergency decree [*Notverordnung*].

The new draft version was the result of a complete restructuring. According to Bumke, the consultant in the Reich Ministry of Justice, the changes to its content were influenced by the fact that the financially precarious situation of the Reich meant that the aspect of cost efficiency had come to the fore, and the old idea of "completely avoiding pointless proceedings by restricting the principle of mandatory prosecution" had become more important. At the same time, as Radbruch once again held the office of Minister of Justice, jury courts were to be retained in line with the SPD's position. It was this *Draft of a Decree for the Simplification of the Application of Criminal Law* that the new Reich Minister of Justice Emminger found upon taking up office, and which was passed to the audit committees of the Reichstag and Reich Council for consultation, as provided in the enabling act. A petition to change the jury courts to *Schöffengerichte* with three professional judges

---

[169] The individual points criticised by Radbruch were the complexity of first instance jurisdiction, which he regarded as too flexible, the majority of professional judges in the large *Schöffengericht*, and the selection procedure of lay assessors and members of the jury; he demanded that if these revisions were approved, appeals against jury court verdicts should be permitted or at least the option of repeating the trial before a different jury retained.—The speakers of the bourgeois parties viewed the draft more favourably than Radbruch.

and six lay assessors was made in the committee of the Reich Council, along with other petitions. These petitions were approved in the Reichstag committee, which deliberated on the Bill on 23 December 1923; a petition to request the Reich government to maintain the separation between the bench and the jury box in jury courts was rejected with a slim majority.[170] The demands of the Reich Council committee were thereupon worked into the text of the decree.

With its **abolition of the jury courts,**[171] a massive downward **shift of first instance jurisdiction**[172] and the first **inroads into the principle of mandatory prosecution,**[173] the Emminger Decree represented a significant leap, perhaps even a turning point in the modern development of criminal procedure: if the nineteenth century, with its so-called reformed criminal procedure, had produced a compromise between the accusatory and the inquisitorial principle, the legislative intervention of 1924 can be seen as the return of a preponderance of the bureaucratic, inquisitorial element over the accusatorial, adversarial element of criminal procedure.[174]

While the state of affairs in criminal procedure had remained largely unchanged during the middle—the so-called "golden"—1920s of the Weimar Republic, the Republic's last years were characterised by a continuation along the path set by the Emminger Decree.[175] Like the domestic economic crisis during the early period, the Great Depression produced social and political disruption during the Republic's later period. As it had previously, the Republic created flexible means of regulation to combat the crisis, this time mainly through the Reich president's emergency decrees. The Reichstag was for the most part rendered ineffective and was dissolved repeatedly; the Reich chancellors Brüning, v. Papen and v. Schleicher ruled with so-called presidential cabinets. Once again, the "strain" on the criminal justice system was "relieved" with the excuse of cost cutting. Several decrees interfered in the organisation of courts, with severe and long-lasting consequences. Further exceptions to the principle of mandatory prosecution and the expansion of the possibility of rejecting appeals on points of law (*Revision*) as "obviously unfounded" had a long-term effect on the State Supreme Courts. The significance of the last of these decrees, the *Decree of the Reich President on Measures for the Administration of Justice and the Administration* of 14 June 1932, was hardly less than that of the Emminger Decree—as was already noted by contemporaries. In order to deal with so-called "monster proceedings", it reintroduced the first instance

---

[170] On the context, and especially on the unclear role played by Gustav Radbruch in the abolition of jury courts, cf. *Vormbaum*, Lex Emminger, Chapter 10.

[171] *Vormbaum*, Lex Emminger, p. 109 ff.

[172] Ibid. p. 85 ff., with a diagram on p. 98.

[173] Ibid. p. 153 ff., with a diagram on p. 168; more detail in *Dettmar*, Legalität und Opportunität, Chapter 5, particularly (B) and (C).

[174] *Vormbaum*, p. 84, 174 ff.

[175] For more detail on the following, cf. *Frank Nobis*, Die Strafprozessgesetzgebung der späten Weimarer Republik (1930–1932). Baden-Baden 2000.

jurisdiction of the large criminal chambers that had been abolished by the Emminger decree. This jurisdiction was in part not triggered by criteria set out in the law itself, but by prosecutorial motion.[176] This led to a reduction in appeals, because there was no more second instance for a re-trial on the facts available. In all cases subject to the first instance jurisdiction of the Amtsgericht, the three-tier model was reduced to two instances by introducing a choice between appeals (*Berufung*, i.e. trial de novo or *Revision*, i.e. appeal on points of law only). Except for first instance criminal chamber matters, the courts were given free discretion about which evidence to hear, and were thus freed from the general requirement to hear evidence which was present in court.

5. Sentences and the Prison System

During the first two decades of the twentieth century, the prison sentences in the German federal states took on the more or less unified appearance of solitary confinement, which meant that it became possible to think of uniform legislation across the whole of the Reich. But as the prison reform had been planned to coincide with the reform of substantive criminal law, Reich-wide legislation was not at first put in place, even though **Section 7 (3) WRV** expressly granted the Reich the (concurrent) legislative authority and control over this area. Therefore the states became active once more on the initiative of Reich Minister of Justice Gustav Radbruch, and in 1923 replaced the Basic Principles of the Federal Council (cf. the end of § 3. IV. 3. above) by the "***Reichsratsgrundsätze***" (Basic Principles of the Reich Council),[177] which went beyond their predecessors in that they defined the aim of custodial sentences in more concrete terms on the one hand, and improved the legal status of the prisoner on the other. The *Reichsratsgrundsätze* came into force over the following year through the states' service and prison regulations. Section 48 of the *Reichsratsgrundsätze* read:

> Through the enforcement of custodial sentences, the prisoners shall become accustomed to order and work to the necessary extent, and their morals shall be strengthened, to prevent them from reoffending.

In this way the **idea of reform** had entered into the definition of the aim of imprisonment—even if it was not spelled out explicitly. With regard to organisation, the Reichsratsgrundsätze assumed a progressive or **staggered system of prison sentences,** akin to the British and Irish models,[178] intended to prepare the prisoner for a life at liberty on the one hand, while on the other, and under the

[176] More detail in *Nobis*, Strafprozeßgesetzgebung, p. 33.

[177] Grundsätze über den Vollzug von Freiheitsstrafen. Vom 7. Juni 1923, RGBl. II 1923, 263 ff.; also reproduced in *Schubert/Regge*, Reform, Section 1 Vol. 5, p. 113 ff.

[178] *Krause*, Geschichte, p. 85; *Laubenthal*, Strafvollzug, p. 41 incl. further references; *Eb. Schmidt*, Einführung, § 344, p. 422.

influence of Liszt's thought, identifying those habitual offenders incapable of reform.

Juvenile criminal law, which was particularly closely linked to the idea of education and reform, had a strong influence on initiating the reform of prison sentences. As early as 1912, an independent juvenile prison in Wittlich on the Mosel put a concept based on staggered levels into practice[179] and the **Juvenile Court Act** of 1923 prescribed the creation of separate juvenile prisons.

The **Fines Act** (see § 5 IV. 2. above) had great potential to relieve the strain on custodial sentences; however, this potential was eaten up by the increase in criminalisation and crime in economic periods of crisis and through custodial sentences in default of payment.[180]

Dedicated reformers (Otto Krebs, Albert Krebs, Lothar Frede, Curt Bondy, Walter Herrmann, Siegfried Rosenfeld among others) put significant effort into practical steps for prison reform, mainly in Thuringia, Hamburg and Prussia.[181]

From 1925 onwards, prison reform plans from most states of the pilot phase with staggered and progressive systems were rolled out across the prison system as a whole.[182] However, it became evident that during the second half of the 1920s the number of those considered "capable of reform" dwindled more and more.[183] From around 1929, resistance towards the supposedly excessive leniency of the Weimar criminal justice system became entrenched. Professional associations of prison staff (fearing the competition of pedagogic experts), the press, political instrumentalisation and the objection of the *Deutsche Strafrechtliche Gesellschaft*, whose criticism also targeted plans for a rehabilitative function of the prison, made matters ever more difficult for the reformers. The expert staff required were only employed in insufficient numbers.

Prison-related legislation for the greater part did not progress beyond drafts.[184] In the Law on Vagrants passed in 1926 (one of the few planned laws realised during this time), Bavaria decreed workhouse sentences of up to 2 years for persons above the age of 16 who "wandered about in the manner of gypsies". Similar plans for a "detention law" on the level of the Reich, supported by Radbruch and the German branch of the IKV, did not come to fruition. Plans for a Prison Act to be passed together with the new criminal code petered out towards the end of the Republic, just like the plans for the new criminal code.[185]

---

[179] *Krause*, Geschichte, p. 83 f.; *Laubenthal*, Strafvollzug, p. 41 f.

[180] *Krause*, Geschichte, p. 84.

[181] More detail in *Naumann*, Gefängnis, p. 64 ff.

[182] *Naumann*, Gefängnis, p. 62.

[183] *Naumann*, op. cit., p. 72.

[184] *Naumann*, Gefängnis, p. 96 ff.

[185] *Naumann*, op. cit., p. 99 ff.

V. The National Socialist Period

1. Preliminary Remarks

On 30 January 1933, power passed to the National Socialist German Workers' Party (NSDAP) and the German National People's Party (DNVP). *Hitler* was appointed Reich Chancellor. The beginning of the National Socialist regime also marked the end of the parliamentary, democratic system (if the presidential cabinets of the two final years of the Weimar Republic can be called such). The NS regime cemented its legal standing, bringing legislative and executive powers into line through the Enabling Act passed soon after the change in government by the Reichstag (voted against by the Social Democrats). (This Enabling Act was preceded, in a slightly less severe form, by the Acts of the First World War and the Weimar Republic [see § 5 III. 1., IV. 1. and IV. 4. above].).[186]

The agreed-on version in general historiography seems to be: the 12 years of National Socialist rule are 12 dark years that represent a rupture in German history—the term "*Zivilisationsbruch*" has recently become common.[187] This understanding is certainly correct in that events took place during this time that single out this period from the course of German history in a catastrophic manner. Indeed, the logically planned and factory-style extermination of millions of human beings of "foreign race", conducted not because of political opposition (which in itself would be dreadful enough), but in the name of a supposedly scientific racial theory, were and have been unheard of in Germany before 1933 and since 1945, and the same goes for the murder of hundreds of thousands of humans allegedly "unfit to live" within the framework of a project euphemistically called "euthanasia", the motivation of which derived from the same source.[188] Nonetheless, in recent years historic research has identified many "normal aspects" that pervade the time of NS rule. On the one hand, they result from the trivial fact that human beings in any political system continue to love and hate, marry, bring up children, succeed or fail at school or in their profession, fall ill, recover or die, celebrate or mourn. The persistence of naturally given or long-term established lifestyles and customs often proves resistant to political influences.

However, of greater relevance for the continuities alleged in historical research on National Socialism is the identification of many modernising factors during the time of its rule. Resistance to this statement is due in large part to the positive associations connected with the term "modern". Therefore—as emphasised in the

---

[186] On the "Enabling Act" (official title: "Law to Remedy the Distress of People and Reich" of 24 March, 1933, RGBl. I 1933, p. 141), cf. the documentation in the "Kleine Reihe" of the series "Juristische Zeitgeschichte". Berlin 2003.

[187] See e.g. *Dan Diner* (Ed.), Zivilisationsbruch. Denken nach Auschwitz. Frankfurt am Main 1988.

[188] A reconstruction of the euthanasia project using the prosecution investigations of the post-war period includes the Hessian Prosecutor-General **Fritz Bauer's** (1903–1968) indictment of the euthanasia doctor Heyde alias Sawade; published in: *Institut für juristische Zeitgeschichte Hagen*, Euthanasie vor Gericht.

preceding chapters—it should be stated clearly here that our study is not informed by this understanding. The bureaucratic, technical perfecting of mass murder, down to the timetabling of the trains headed for the death camps, is a terrifying manifestation of modernity. Even the earliest attempts to review National Socialism thematised the use of modern technology in the NSDAP's election campaign (use of modern means of communication, increasing mobility by using aeroplanes); in addition, there was the modernisation of war technology, including the rocket technology that was not ready to be put into practice in time. But less technological elements can also be observed: using the insights of modern mass psychology for the purpose of propaganda; using social security and benefits to maintain the loyalty of the masses.[189] That race theory and ideas of social hygiene were the waste products of the trust in science emerging in the nineteenth century has already been mentioned.[190]

Thus National Socialist rule, its criminal exorbitance notwithstanding,[191] fits into a line of development that existed prior to 1933 and continued after 1945. Modern elements can be identified in law, too.[192] This also goes for criminal law, where on the one hand structures and tendencies from before 1933 are followed, and on the other some structures introduced under National Socialist rule are taken over after 1945. When the specific characteristics of criminal law under National Socialism are described in what follows, we must therefore remain aware of the extent to which they fit into the developments prior to 1933 and after 1945. The problem of continuity will be summarised in a later chapter of this book (§ 7 below).

2. *Criminal Law Theory*

As described above (§ 3 I. 1.), the concept of infringement of protected legal interests was not initiated by a desire to restrict state punishment, but rather by a desire to relax the doctrine of infringement of rights as represented by Kant and Feuerbach. If handled liberally and cautiously, the concept of protected legal interests can of course—notwithstanding its origins in the *expansion* of criminal law—support a reduced criminal law. It adopted the condition that basically only *external*, **objective** processes could provide the points of contact where criminal

---

[189] For a recent study of this topic, cf. *Götz Aly*, Hitlers Volksstaat. Raub, Rassenkrieg und nationaler Sozialismus. 3rd edition. Frankfurt am Main 2005.

[190] Further modern elements are described in *Michael Prinz/Rainer Zitelmann* (Eds.), Nationalsozialismus und Modernisierung. 2nd edition. Darmstadt 1994.

[191] On what we term the "specific pathology" of National Socialism, see § 5 V. 8. below.

[192] Examples can be found in the contributions to the colloquium of the Institut für Zeitgeschichte *NS-Recht in historischer Perspektive*. Munich, Vienna 1981; also in the contributions to the symposium "Justiz und Nationalsozialismus" of the Justizakademie NRW: *Pauli/Vormbaum*, Justiz und Nationalsozialismus.

law could intervene, from its predecessor, the doctrine of *protected rights* (the inner components, particularly intent and blameworthiness, followed later as *limitations*). In other words, the interface for the criminal law debate is not the offender's attitude, but the *offence* as formally defined by law. Furthermore, the concept of protected legal interests—even though it is less strict than the concept of protected rights –is capable of demarcating distinct groups of punishable offences from each other and from legitimate behaviour.

These practical consequences—liberal handling, a tendency towards an objective view of criminal law, thinking in separate, demarcated interests—were not a necessary consequence, and they had been weakened by the way the concept of protected legal interests had become increasingly cerebral since the turn of the century; nonetheless, like the Liszt school and the reform of criminal law that followed its ideals, the doctrine of protected legal interests was exposed to attacks from National Socialist legal theorists who disputed all three positions. NS legal theorists took the increased leniency that was *also* possible as a result of the purposive approach (*Zweckgedanke*) as pars pro toto, and branded it as a "taking a soft stance on crime" (*Erik Wolf*).[193] An authoritarian view of criminal law opposed the liberalism supposedly inherent to the concept of protected legal interests; according to this view, a national community was an organism made up of homogenous beings (i.e. beings of the same race). Crime was an indicator that the respective member of the nation was not true to type. Thus the primary goal of criminal policy and criminal law should not be to react to **offences**, but to eliminate dangerous elements of the community. Accordingly, this doctrine takes as its starting point the **offender** who fails in his duties to his community. In legal terminology, this approach produces the **doctrine of infringement of duty**; criminal law shifts from *Tatstrafrecht*, a criminal law focusing on the offence, to a ***Täterstrafrecht*** that focuses on the offender, or on attitudes and convictions. However, if the aim is to identify harmful attitudes, then a formal definition of behaviour harmful to society is dysfunctional. The formal offence is only of interest as an **indicator** of an **attitude** harmful to the community. Of course, these thoughts were not entirely new, for not only had irrationalism and a holistic view been promoted by some legal theorists during the Weimar period, but Liszt's "*Marburger Programm*" had also included offender-orientated thinking and evaluation of attitude as some of its main points.

Further consequences of this view of criminal law are an expansion of the liability for attempt and the purely optional mitigation of punishment for attempted offences (cf. today's Section 23 (2) StGB), bringing the threshold of liability for secondary participation forward (cf. today's Section 30 StGB), and creating definitions of offences that rendered even the preparation of the actual harmful act punishable (cf. today as an extreme example: Section 129a StGB).

The rejection of a *Tatstrafrecht* simultaneously led to a **material definition of crime**. In itself, this term simply means that behind the formal definitions of

[193] *Kubink*, Strafen, p. 250.

offences lies a perception of what makes certain behaviour appear punishable. In the theory of criminal law of the Enlightenment, this was the breaking of the social contract, for Kant and Feuerbach it was the (differently derived) infringement of rights, and since Birnbaum, Mittermaier, Binding and Liszt it was the infringement of legal interests. This material definition of crime is routinely linked to the idea that it can be used to derive a measure for limiting the creation and interpretation of formal criminal offences.[194] However, when National Socialist teachers of criminal law invoked the material definition of crime, their aim was a different one—in the end, quite the opposite. For them, what was meant was that criminal law should not make itself dependent on the criminal offences formally defined by law, but rather should realise "obvious substantial justice per se" and bring it to pass,[195] to penetrate to the "reality" of life as manifested in the **concrete order** of life in the community[196]; there was thus a tendency to liberate those who administered justice from the formal written law. No behaviour "harmful to the nation" was to go unpunished.

In this regard, National Socialist doctrine sometimes countered the "liberalist" principle *nullum crimen sine lege* with the phrase *nullum crimen sine poena* (no crime without punishment). This then gives rise to the question of which measuring stick is applied to *crimen*, i.e. what is "criminal". This question was never explained, apart from the aforementioned references to the concrete order of the community and the "healthy common sense of the people" (*gesundes Volksempfinden*) mentioned in the new Section 2 StGB introduced in 1935 (see § 5 V. 3. below).[197]

[194] More detail in *Marxen*, Kampf, p. 172 ff.

[195] *Carl Schmitt*, Nationalsozialismus und Rechtsstaat, in: JW 1934, 714. On Schmitt's theory of criminal law, see also *Mario A. Cattaneo*, Strafrechtstotalitarismus, p. 181 ff.; in regard to the basic principle *nullum crimen sine lege*, there is an interesting difference between the development of German criminal law and that in Fascist Italy, where the new criminal code passed in 1930/31, the so-called *Codice Rocco*, despite its authoritarian and even totalitarian traits adhered to the prohibition of analogy; cf. *Cattaneo* op. cit., p. 257 ff., who also points out that this prohibition was subverted by the option of indeterminate detention for incapacitation purposes; the statements of *Alfredo Rocco* cited in op. cit., p. 259 f. can of course already be found in Section 46 (2) of Radbruch's Draft of 1922: "Detention lasts as long as necessary to achieve the purpose for which it was decreed".

[196] On "concrete-order-oriented thought", cf. *Carl Schmitt*, Über die drei Arten des rechtswissenschaftlichen Denkens. Hamburg 1934, that differentiates between three types of thought: regulation- and law-oriented thought, decision-oriented thought and concrete-order- and design-oriented thought (op. cit., p. 8).

[197] The phrase *nullum crimen sine poena* can already be found in *Feuerbach* (Lehrbuch, § 20), but of course refers to something else, namely that no crime (as defined by law) should remain unpunished. As we know today, this is an illusion and may not even be desirable in certain circumstances (on this, cf. *Heinrich Popitz*, Über die Präventivwirkung des Nichtwissens [1968]. Re-publication with an introduction by Fritz Sack and Hubert Treiber in the series "Juristische Zeitgeschichte. "Kleine Reihe". Berlin 2003), but it has a different meaning than the same phrase during the National Socialist period; on this, cf. *Vormbaum*, ZNR 2000, 259. Furthermore, in Feuerbach the phrase was "... *sine poena legali*", showing clearly that the exact opposite of the phrase used by the National Socialists was meant.

The shift to the idea of the infringement of duty and the *Täterstrafrecht* also led to a rejection of the terminological and systematic "dissecting" of crimes; instead, a comprehensive and essentialist terminology and system of crimes was called for[198]; the "liability loopholes" that necessarily follow from a formal definition of crime based on language were unacceptable. The necessary consequence is a **rejection of the prohibition of analogy**.

This subjectivisation was given a particularly characteristic slant by the doctrine of ***Willensstrafrecht*** (a criminal law focusing on the "criminal will"). Here, too, familiar ideas were radicalised; after all, Liszt had stated explicitly that the offender's attitude was the deciding factor when determining the punishment. The so-called ***Tätertypenlehre***, a theory of specific "types" of criminal,[199] also has its predecessors in Liszt's three types of offenders (though his focus was on criminal policy, not on the doctrine of criminal law). *Liszt* had considered it possible to create a barrier between the spheres of criminal policy and law; now this barrier was—where it was still in existence—broken down.[200]

The shift in the focus of criminal law from the offence to the offender, which had been taking place since the end of the nineteenth century, reached its fullest expansion in the *Willensstrafrecht* and *Tätertypenlehre*.

Of course, the hidden pitfall of a criminal law based on "criminal types" and a "criminal will" was that these could actually result in a limitation of punishment if the offender did not conform to the required "type" of criminal, despite having committed a (formally defined) offence. However, where this possibility occurred, it never had any practical consequences.[201]

The polemic rants of National Socialist theorists of criminal law against the doctrine of protected legal interests, particularly the attacks by NS teachers of criminal law such as **Georg Dahm** (1904–1963) and **Friedrich Schaffstein** (1905–2001)—later members of the Kiel "Stoßtruppfakultät" ("storm trooper faculty")[202] which also included **Karl Michaelis** (1900–2001), **Ernst Rudolf Huber** (1903–1990), **Wolfgang Siebert** (1905–1959) and **Karl Larenz** (1903–1993)—show that the doctrine of protected legal interests and the Liszt school could be criticised as too "liberal"; but basically these attacks were ideologically motivated,

---

[198] More detail in *Marxen*, Kampf, p. 214.

[199] Cf. *Marxen*, Kampf, p. 189 ff.

[200] Interestingly, as shown by *Marxen* (Kampf, p. 167 ff.), this did not occur as one might think by an overspill of criminal policy into the law, but in fact by a shift in debate from questions of criminal policy to those of doctrine—so quite the opposite course.

[201] For example, during the debate of the NS criminal law committee on bankruptcy laws, the theorists of criminal law (*Gleispach*, *Mezger*, *Nagler*) invoked the *Willensstrafrecht*, suggesting that the objective condition of punishment of what was then Section 209 KO (today's Section 283 (6) StGB) should be replaced by an objective offence characteristic including intent; more detail in *Seemann*, Vereitelung von Gläubigerrechten, p. 92 f., 176; on a similar situation when debating laws on sex crimes, cf. *Müting*, Vergewaltigung und sexuelle Nötigung, Chapter 7A) I.

[202] On this, cf. *Eckert*, Stoßtruppfakultät, p. 21.

for if "used correctly", the authoritarian, expansive criminal law aimed for by National Socialist theory could also be achieved by applying the doctrine of protected legal interest. This is shown in *Erich Schwinge* and *Leopold Zimmerl's* 1937 critical work on "Wesenschau und konkretes Ordnungsdenken im Strafrecht", which as far as is known caused its authors no political difficulties.[203] *Liszt's* disciple *Eberhard Schmidt* was quite justified in stating in 1942 that Liszt's concept of punishment was completely misunderstood if seen as a "soft, yielding theory of 'reform'".[204] The Habitual Offenders Act of November 1933 (on which more shortly) fulfilled "Liszt's old demand to step up the fight against habitual crime".[205]

Of course, a historic perspective also requires an appropriate quantification. *Liszt's* call to "incapacitate" those incapable of reform does not mean they should be "exterminated". Structurally, however, these thoughts are part of a tradition in which Liszt's understanding of criminal law forms one stage. In *Kubink's* phrasing, "the negative aspects of the efforts to reform criminal law" had now come to the fore,[206] "an application of criminal law that is hardly bound by law anymore – the radical line of Liszt" had become dominant.[207] Unlike in the case of the theory of constitutional law,[208] one cannot say of the theory of criminal law that it had experienced a "radical change".

This observation does not preclude the fact that German criminal law theory experienced a moral and intellectual decline during the time of the NS regime that reached its lowest point[209] in the 1936 conference organised by **Carl Schmitt**

---

[203] Incidentally, there was also no "duty" to favour criminal-biological approaches in criminology; on this, cf. *Richard F. Wetzell*, Der Verbrecher und seine Erforscher: Die deutsche Kriminologie in der Weimarer Republik und im Nationalsozialismus, in: JJZG 8 (2006/2007), 256 ff.

[204] *Eb. Schmidt*, Anselm von Feuerbach und Franz von Liszt, in: Monatsschrift f. Kriminologie 1942, 205 ff., 221 f. Other followers of Liszt, such as *Eduard Kohlrausch*, made similar statements; on this, cf. *Vormbaum*, Kohlrausch, including the references to *Karitzky's* biography of Kohlrausch.

[205] Ibid.; more detail in *Kubink*, Strafen, p. 254.

[206] *Kubink*, Strafen, p. 233.

[207] Op. cit., p. 249; *Muñoz Conde*. Liszt, p. 558, is of the opinion that "if National Socialism had never existed, [...] today not a shadow of doubt would be cast on the theories of Franz von Liszt". It is certainly correct that National Socialism was an extremely strong catalyst in bringing out the problematic aspects of Liszt's theories. Incidentally, it is difficult to discuss hypothetical historical developments; if one wished to follow up this line of thought, then one would have to ask whether the problematic aspects of modern criminal law shaped by Liszt in the form that can be seen today (on this cf. § 7 below) would also be evident and invite criticism of Liszt without the NS period; the *heuristic* significance of that period (on this cf. the end of § 7 II. 4. below) would of course not apply.

[208] On this, cf. *Kroeschell*, 20. Jahrhundert, p. 74.

[209] As we now know, the discipline of law was not alone in its eagerness to serve the NS regime; cf. e.g. *Till Bastian*, Furchtbare Ärzte. Medizinische Verbrechen im Dritten Reich. München 1995; *Ernst Klee*, Auschwitz, die NS-Medizin und ihre Opfer. Frankfurt am Main (Fischer-TB) 2001; *Norbert Frei* (Ed.), Karrieren im Zwielicht. 2nd edition. Frankfurt am Main 2002 (with contributions on doctors, businessmen, officers, lawyers and journalists); on psychoanalysis *Hans-Martin Lohmann* (Ed.), Psychoanalyse und Nationalsozialismus. Beiträge zur Bearbeitung eines unbewältigten Traumas. Paperback edition, Frankfurt am Main 1994; on the discipline of history *Winfried Schulze/Otto Gerhard Oexle*, Deutsche Historiker im Nationalsozialismus.

together with the "*Reichsrechtsführer*" ("Reich Law Director") **Hans Frank** with the theme "Jews in Legal Academia".[210] Thus the generalising statement by Eberhard Schmidt (which is also a judgement in his own case) that "the continuity of the true discipline of criminal law was not broken" during the period of the NS regime, seems in need of revision[211]; it is obvious that this understanding of continuity is not to be confused with the understanding of continuity that has already been mentioned and will be touched on once again in the last chapter of this book.[212]

That judgements about the significance of scholarly theories can support judgements about individuals only to a limited extent has already been mentioned several times, starting with *Beccaria* (see § 2 I. 4. above). It is usually easy to make the former – particularly in retrospect – even if these judgements are subject to the slight vagueness typical of the Humanities; the latter however must be *fair*, which they can only be if the person judging is able to put him- or herself in that individual's position. If this is done successfully, then a differentiated spectrum emerges *on this level*. Of course, an established university professor such as *Carl Schmitt* did not have to publish such a vile piece of work as the aforementioned one,[213] as indeed hardly anyone was forced to publish.[214] On the other hand, many a

3rd edition. March 2000; on classical philology: *Volker Losemann*, Nationalsozialismus und Antike. Studien zur Entwicklung des Faches Alte Geschichte 1993–1945. Hamburg 1977; on the natural sciences most recently *John Cornwell*, Forschen für den Führer. Deutsche Naturwissenschaftler und der Zweite Weltkrieg. Bergisch Gladbach 2004 (the book covers far more than suggested in its subtitle). "In all fields of activity and all disciplines related to ideology, in schools and universities, in newspapers and on the radio, in magazines and with writers, even in subjects as neutral as mathematics, physics, chemistry, music and industry the National Socialist rulers' strategies of leadership and control became prevalent. Their influence was not only noticeable in, but even partly dominated a significant portion of church organisations"; *Bernd Rüthers*, Entartetes Recht. Rechtslehren und Kronjuristen im Dritten Reich. Munich 1988, p. 213.

[210] On this, cf. *Rüthers*, Carl Schmitt im Dritten Reich. Wissenschaft als Zeitgeist-Verstärkung? Munich 1989, p. 53 ff.

[211] *Eb. Schmidt*, Einführung, p. 451. In his biography of **Eduard Kohlrausch**, Karitzky shows that he can be invoked in support of this statement only to a limited extent: *Holger Karitzky*, Eduard Kohlrausch—Kriminalpolitik in vier Systemen. Eine strafrechtshistorische Biographie. Berlin 2002. (An attempt to conduct a secondary analysis and evaluation following Karitzky's work in *Vormbaum*, Kohlrausch, op. cit.; in his much-used StGB commentary, which included the most important supplementary provisions, *Kohlrausch* left the comments on the race laws up to his student **Richard Lange** [1906–1995], who was later to become one of the leading teachers of criminal law in the Federal Republic. Lange's commentary cannot by any means be seen as attempting to limit these problematic regulations). However, *Eb. Schmidt* (op. cit., § 46, p. 428) explicitly and critically mentions the conference organised by **Carl Schmitt** and "Reichsrechtsführer" **Hans Frank**.

[212] On the continuities in the theory of offences which persist throughout the NS period, cf. also *Klaus Marxen*, Die rechtsphilosophische Begründung der Straftatlehre im Nationalsozialismus. Zur Frage der Kontinuität strafrechtswissenschaftlichen Denkens, in: Hubert Rottleuthner (Ed.), Recht, Rechtsphilosophie und Nationalsozialismus (ARSP supplement No. 18). Wiesbaden 1983, p. 55 ff.

[213] But he did expect that it would give him a better position in the struggle between factions within the system; on this, cf. *Bernd Rüthers*, Carl Schmitt im Dritten Reich. Munich 1989, p. 74 ff.; *Id.*, Entartetes Recht, p. 125 ff.

[214] *Rüthers*, Carl Schmitt im Dritten Reich, p. 40.

publication that in retrospect forms part of a disastrous development is something produced by the writer more or less innocently, convinced of their own intellectual originality, without any awareness of being embedded in a longer-term development or of their political role.[215] And of course there is also the "portion of normality" that occurs, for example, in an essay on the problematic doctrinal details of a non-political offence.

However, the fields of **criminal policy** and **criminology** show just how closely the discipline of criminal law and politics are interwoven. Although it remained possible to conduct research in criminal sociology between 1933 and 1945,[216] there was yet again a clear shift in focus towards hereditary factors and, within these, towards genetics[217]; furthermore, there was a surge in the institutionalisation of criminal biology in the mid-1930s.[218] The Nazis criticised the "softness" of the Weimar criminal justice system (despite having profited from it themselves); their preference for biological approaches—to the extent that they were interested in scientific explanations at all—naturally led them to criminal biology. Prominent criminologists saw both the opportunities and dangers of the Nazis' accession to power. All sides declared that criminal-biological research did not support softness of any kind. Particularly as far as individuals deemed incapable of reform were concerned, certain points of contact arose. Some criminologists immediately offered the new rulers their services.

The question of continuity also applies to the criminology of the National Socialist period.[219] Given the stages of development already described here, this question cannot be negated; however, here too we can assume that the period of NS rule led to a *radicalisation* of this development (Fig. 17).[220]

[215] For example, **Hans Welzel** (1904–1977) in his 1944 essay "Über den substantiellen Begriff des Strafrechts" (excerpt in *Vormbaum*, MdtStrD, p. 291 ff.) speaks in favour of seeing the substance of criminal law not simply in protecting legal interests, but in maintaining a law-abiding attitude (p. 564), He does not mention completely removing the separation between criminal law and morals explicitly, but he certainly advocates relativising this difference (p. 562). Here his subjective aim is to rehearse a problem of legal philosophy, but objectively he forms part of the trend towards an moralisation of criminal law that persisted throughout the 20th century (on this, see § 7 below).

[216] In this, cf. *Wetzell*, Inventing, p. 295 ff.

[217] *I. Baumann*, Geschichte, p. 93.

[218] Ibid., p. 94; *Baumann* bases this interpretation on the work of *Edmund Mezger* (op. cit., p. 98 ff.).

[219] On this, cf. *I. Baumann*, op. cit., p. 91 ff.

[220] In the same vein *I. Baumann*, Geschichte, p. 91 ff.

Reichsgesetzblatt

83

Teil I

1933	Ausgegeben zu Berlin, den 28. Februar 1933	Nr. 17

Inhalt: Verordnung des Reichspräsidenten zum Schutz von Volk und Staat. Vom 28. Februar 1933 .... S. 83

Verordnung des Reichspräsidenten zum Schutz von Volk und Staat. Vom 28. Februar 1933.

Auf Grund des Artikels 48 Abs. 2 der Reichsverfassung wird zur Abwehr kommunistischer staatsgefährdender Gewaltakte folgendes verordnet:

§ 1

Die Artikel 114, 115, 117, 118, 123, 124 und 153 der Verfassung des Deutschen Reichs werden bis auf weiteres außer Kraft gesetzt. Es sind daher Beschränkungen der persönlichen Freiheit, des Rechts der freien Meinungsäußerung, einschließlich der Pressefreiheit, des Vereins- und Versammlungsrechts, Eingriffe in das Brief-, Post-, Telegraphen- und Fernsprechgeheimnis, Anordnungen von Haussuchungen und von Beschlagnahmen sowie Beschränkungen des Eigentums auch außerhalb der sonst hierfür bestimmten gesetzlichen Grenzen zulässig.

§ 2

Werden in einem Lande die zur Wiederherstellung der öffentlichen Sicherheit und Ordnung nötigen Maßnahmen nicht getroffen, so kann die Reichsregierung insoweit die Befugnisse der obersten Landesbehörde vorübergehend wahrnehmen.

§ 3

Die Behörden der Länder und Gemeinden (Gemeindeverbände) haben den auf Grund des § 2 erlassenen Anordnungen der Reichsregierung im Rahmen ihrer Zuständigkeit Folge zu leisten.

§ 4

Wer den von den obersten Landesbehörden oder den ihnen nachgeordneten Behörden zur Durchführung dieser Verordnung erlassenen Anordnungen oder den von der Reichsregierung gemäß § 2 erlassenen Anordnungen zuwiderhandelt, oder wer zu solcher Zuwiderhandlung auffordert oder anreizt, wird, soweit nicht die Tat nach anderen Vorschriften mit einer schwereren Strafe bedroht ist, mit Gefängnis nicht unter einem Monat oder mit Geldstrafe von 150 bis zu 15 000 Reichsmark bestraft.

Wer durch Zuwiderhandlung nach Abs. 1 eine gemeine Gefahr für Menschenleben herbeiführt, wird mit Zuchthaus, bei mildernden Umständen mit Gefängnis nicht unter sechs Monaten und, wenn die Zuwiderhandlung den Tod eines Menschen verursacht, mit dem Tode, bei mildernden Umständen mit Zuchthaus nicht unter zwei Jahren bestraft. Daneben kann auf Vermögenseinziehung erkannt werden.

Wer zu einer gemeingefährlichen Zuwiderhandlung (Abs. 2) auffordert oder anreizt, wird mit Zuchthaus, bei mildernden Umständen mit Gefängnis nicht unter drei Monaten bestraft.

§ 5

Mit dem Tode sind die Verbrechen zu bestrafen, die das Strafgesetzbuch in den §§ 81 (Hochverrat), 229 (Giftbeibringung), 307 (Brandstiftung), 311 (Explosion), 312 (Überschwemmung), 315 Abs. 2 (Beschädigung von Eisenbahnanlagen), 324 (gemeingefährliche Vergiftung) mit lebenslangem Zuchthaus bedroht.

Mit dem Tode oder, soweit nicht bisher eine schwerere Strafe angedroht ist, mit lebenslangem Zuchthaus oder mit Zuchthaus bis zu 15 Jahren wird bestraft:

1. Wer es unternimmt, den Reichspräsidenten oder ein Mitglied oder einen Kommissar der Reichsregierung oder einer Landesregierung zu töten oder wer zu einer solchen Tötung auffordert, sich erbietet, ein solches Erbieten annimmt oder eine solche Tötung mit einem anderen verabredet;
2. wer in den Fällen des § 115 Abs. 2 des Strafgesetzbuchs (schwerer Aufruhr) oder des § 125 Abs. 2 des Strafgesetzbuchs (schwerer Landfriedensbruch) die Tat mit Waffen oder in bewußtem und gewolltem Zusammenwirken mit einem Bewaffneten begeht;
3. wer eine Freiheitsberaubung (§ 239) des Strafgesetzbuchs in der Absicht begeht, sich des der Freiheit Beraubten als Geisel im politischen Kampfe zu bedienen.

§ 6

Diese Verordnung tritt mit dem Tage der Verkündung in Kraft.

Berlin, den 28. Februar 1933.

Der Reichspräsident
von Hindenburg

Der Reichskanzler
Adolf Hitler

Der Reichsminister des Innern
Frick

Der Reichsminister der Justiz
Dr. Gürtner

Herausgegeben vom Reichsministerium des Innern. — Gedruckt in der Reichsdruckerei, Berlin.

Fig. 17 Extract from the 1933 *Reichsgesetzblatt* (Reich Law Gazette). Decree of the President of the Reich for the Protection of People and State. 28 February 1933

3. Penal Legislation Before the Outbreak of the War [221]

The founding "basic law" of the National Socialist system of government was the so-called **Reichstag Fire Decree** *(Decree for the Protection of People and State of 28 February 1933)*. It was this emergency decree passed by Reich president **Hindenburg**, and not only the later Enabling Act, that suspended important civil rights, introduced the death penalty for a number of offences, and legitimised the SA's system of terror.[222]

The NS regime's first legislative acts regarding the constitution of courts and criminal procedure were contradictory. On the one hand, the Reich Supreme Court's verdict in the Reichstag Fire Trial (the death penalty was applied retrospectively to defendant *van der Lubbe*, while his fellow defendants *Torgler*, *Dimitroff*, *Popoff* und *Taneff* were acquitted due to lack of evidence) triggered the **Decree on the *Volkgerichtshof* (People's Court) of 12 June 1934**, which established the *Volksgerichtshof*, initially as a provisional institution; the law of 18 April 1936 transformed it into a "full court according to the Constitution of Courts Act". Thus the Reich Supreme Court lost jurisdiction over crimes against the state. Following the outbreak of war, the jurisdiction of the *Volksgerichtshof* was gradually extended. In the trial hearings, the senates of the *Volksgerichtshof* sat with a panel of five judges, of whom only three were required to be qualified lawyers. Honorary and professional judges were nominated by Hitler on the recommendation of the Reich Ministry of Justice.[223]

---

[221] It is not possible here to give an individual account of the plethora of emergency decrees and laws passed in the field of criminal law during the period of National Socialist rule. All important criminal laws of the NS state are described in *Werle*, Justiz-Strafrecht, p. 65 ff.; the changes to the Criminal Code in *Arno Buschmann*, Das Strafgesetzbuch in der Zeit von 1933 bis 1945—Die Novellierungen des Strafgesetzbuchs in der Zeit des Nationalsozialismus, in: *Vormbaum/Welp*, StGB, supplementary volume 1, p. 53 ff.; the most important texts in *Arno Buschmann*, Nationalsozialistische Weltanschauung und Gesetzgebung 1933–1945. Vol. II (Dokumentation einer Entwicklung). Vienna, New York 2000, p. 199 ff., 699 ff.; *Heribert Ostendorf*, Dokumentation des NS-Strafrechts. Baden-Baden 2000. In the following, the laws essential for an understanding of the development of criminal law will be described. On *penal provisions outside the Criminal Code (Nebenstrafrecht*; hereafter: *supplementary penal provisions)*, cf. the references in footnote 237.

[222] *Eisenhardt*, Rechtsgeschichte, p. 438 f.; *Kroeschell*, 20. Jahrhundert, p. 70 f.; *Werle*, Justiz-Strafrecht, p. 65 ff.; *Thomas Raithel/Irene Strenge*, Die Reichstagsbrandverordnung. Grundlegung der Diktatur mit den Instrumenten des Weimarer Ausnahmezustands, in: VfZ 2000, 413 ff.—On the **Enabling Act**, cf. the documentation published in the series "Juristische Zeitgeschichte. Kleine Reihe": *Das Ermächtigungsgesetz* ("Gesetz zur Behebung der Not von Volk und Reich") vom 24. März 1933. Reichstagsdebatte, Abstimmung, Gesetzestext. With an introduction by Adolf Lauf. Berlin 2003.

[223] For more detail on the *Volksgerichtshof*, cf. *Heinz Hillermeier* (Ed.), "Im Namen des Deutschen Volkes". Todesurteile des Volksgerichtshofes. Darmstadt, Neuwied 1980; *Klaus Marxen*, Das Volk und sein Gerichtshof. Eine Studie zum nationalsozialistischen Volksgerichtshof. Frankfurt am Main 1994; *Holger Schlüter*, Die Urteilspraxis des Volksgerichtshofes. Berlin 1995; *Klaus Marxen/Holger Schlüter* (Eds.), Terror und "Normalität". Urteile des nationalsozialistischen

By contrast, from the beginning the regime appointed only professional judges to the special courts (*Sondergerichte*) created by the **Creation of Special Courts Act** of 21 March 1933. Special courts were created at a district court in every State Supreme Court District. Originally their jurisdiction was only over offences included in the Reichstag Fire Decree, but then was gradually expanded until ultimately, during the war, it went far beyond its original ambit and special courts also always had jurisdiction when "the prosecuting authority is of the opinion that the severity or reprehensibility of the crime, the public outcry caused or the severe endangering of public order and security warrants immediate sentencing by the special court" (Section 14(1) of the Decree on Jurisdiction of 21 February 1940). The number of special courts also rose during the war. The ideal of the brief trial characterised proceedings: The judicial investigation and the decision to transmit the case for trial were abolished (Sections 11, 12(2) of the Decree of 21 March 1933); the rejection of evidential motions was made easier (Section 13 op. cit.); mandatory requirements to keep a record of proceedings were relaxed (Section 15 op. cit.); there were no appeals (Section 16 op. cit.).

The *Law for the Imposition and Execution of the Death Penalty of 29 March 1933*, the so-called **Lex van der Lubbe**, provided for capital punishment for the offences cited in Section 5 of the Reichstag Fire Decree, and applied it retroactively to crimes committed after 31 January 1933. This meant it became possible to sentence the alleged Reichstag arsonist Marinus van der Lubbe to death, which the Reich Supreme Court proceeded to do.

This retroactive decree was in turn made possible by the Enabling Act that had been passed only a few days earlier. Even before the Enabling Act had been passed, three teachers of criminal law – **Johannes Nagler** (1876–1951), **Friedrich August Oetker** (1854–1937) and **Hellmuth von Weber** (1893–1970) – had already affirmed the retroactive law's legitimacy in a report requested by the Reich Ministry of Justice; this point of view seemed to go too far even to the Ministry, and it held fast to its objections.[224]

National Socialist legislature gave a first clear sign of continuity in the area of substantive law with the **Law against dangerous habitual offenders and on measures of reform and incapacitation** of 24 November 1933.[225]

As a close connection between criminal policy and eugenics had already existed during the time of the Weimar Republic, the new rulers were able to draw on plans from the Weimar period for the eugenic measures that they pronounced immediately and implemented quickly (1933 Genetic Health Act; 1935 Marital Health Act). These plans included a draft law of the Prussian State Health Department.

Volksgerichtshofs 1934–1945. Eine Dokumentation (Juristische Zeitgeschichte NRW. 13). Recklinghausen 2004; further texts on the *Volksgerichtshof* are presented and reviewed in *Thomas Vormbaum*, Strafjustiz im Nationalsozialismus. Ein kritischer Literaturbericht, in: GA 1998, 1 ff.

[224] More detail in *Manfred Seebode*, Streitfragen des strafrechtlichen Rückwirkungsverbots im Zeitenwandel. Das Rechtsgutachten für den Reichstagsbrandprozeß, in: JJZG 3 (2001/2002), p. 203 ff.; a facsimile of the report is included in ibid. p. 229 ff.

[225] On this, cf. *Chr. Müller*, Gewohnheitsverbrechergesetz (1997); *Werle*, Justiz-Strafrecht, p. 86 ff.

Thus it was racial policy rather than criminal policy that provided the actual incentive for the Habitual Offenders Act.[226] The reform and incapacitation measures, now enshrined in law for the first time, included forced castration ("emasculation", Section 42k StGB n.F.). However, the stubborn resistance of the jurists in the Reich Ministry of Justice succeeded in preventing the inclusion of sterilisation of offenders *as such* in legal regulations.[227]

The new law's central aspect was *detention for the purpose of incapacitation* for dangerous habitual offenders. Following Liszt's criminal policy, the Draft of 1919 and—on a somewhat larger scale—the Radbruch Draft of 1922 had already included this measure (see § 5 IV. 3. above). The preliminary draft of 1909 had already included measures besides punishment as retribution. The toughening of punishment for repeat offences and incapacitation detention for dangerous habitual offenders conformed to National Socialist *Täterstrafrecht*, but also referred back to the categories of offenders coined by *Liszt*. Reading the new Sections 20a and 42e of the new version of the StGB of November 1933 against Sections 45 and 77 of the Radbruch Draft of 1922, the two versions correspond in their treatment of this category of offender under normal circumstances; they even match in details of the language used. However, the Act also included more severe measures that went beyond the Radbruch Draft; in its simultaneous continuity and radicalisation, it is representative of many laws of the NS regime. The judiciary played its part in expanding the application of detention for the purpose of incapacitation.[228]

With its introduction of the category of *diminished responsibility*, the draft fulfilled an old demand of the Lisztian school and offender-focused criminology. Furthermore, the law also introduced the offence of *committing an offence in a senselessly drunken state* (Section 330a, today Section 323a StGB).

This law remained in force after 1945, and it remained valid with only a few changes until 1968 as far as habitual offenders were concerned; the remainder of the law is still valid today [Editor's note: The Federal Constitutional Court declared the entire law in this area in its present shape unconstitutional on 4 May 2011; it is currently being reformed.].

The **Treachery Act of 20 December 1934** (preceded by the Treachery Decree of 21 March 1933) rendered "atrocity propaganda" punishable. The judiciary interpreted this broadly by introducing the term of "indirect publicity". The Act's enforcement was subject to an application order by the Reich Minister of Justice and the Deputy Führer, thus allowing it to be handled flexibly according to political requirements.[229]

---

[226] More detail in *Chr. Müller*, Verbrechensbekämpfung, p. 279 ff.

[227] *Wetzell*, Inventing, p. 260 ff.

[228] *Chr. Müller*, Verbrechensbekämpfung, p. 282.

[229] For more detail on how this law was put into practice, cf. *Werle*, Justiz-Strafrecht, p. 139; *Bernward Dörner*, "Heimtücke": Das Gesetz als Waffe. Kontrolle, Abschreckung und Verfolgung in Deutschland 1933–1945. Paderborn 1998.

The so-called **Analogy Amendment of 28 June 1935** went to the very heart of substantive criminal law. It served to "carefully pre-empt some of the thought behind the comprehensive reform [of criminal law]" and aimed to "take the adaptation of criminal law to the spirit of the new state one step further".[230] Art. 1 (= Section 2 RStGB n.v.) allowed the "analogous application of criminal laws",[231] Art. 2 (= Section 2b RStGB n.v.) allowed *Wahlfeststellung*, conviction in the alternative, in cases where it was unclear which of a number of offences the accused had committed.[232] This law firmly established the *material definition of crime*, which to a certain extent can be seen as the substantive counterpart of the procedural term of the ascertainment of material truth (cf. § 5 V. 2. above).

There is always the possibility that laws which are general and abstract but precisely formulated will, in individual cases, shoot wide of material justice ("fragmentary character of criminal law"); the liberal understanding of criminal law calms these doubts by noting that the principle *nullum crimen sine lege* can only result in injustice *in favour* of the accused citizen. However, if criminal law follows a completely material concept of justice that is determined afresh in each individual case, then the idea of the judge must change accordingly: the judge is no longer the servant of justice as given concrete shape in law, but its designer; he becomes—as already mentioned when first introducing National Socialist criminal law—an understanding partner of the legislator. This view did not necessarily follow from a National Socialist or fascist understanding of law. The 1930 Criminal Code passed in fascist Italy (the *Codice Rocco*) adhered to the principle of *nullum crimen* in spite of—or perhaps precisely because of—its authoritarian character, as it aimed to bind all subordinate points to the fascist legislator's will.

At least NS legislature did not follow more radical suggestions that wanted to sever nearly every tie that bound the judge to the law. The new Section 2 StGB held the judge to the "ideas fundamental to a [sc. *already existing*] criminal law" *and* [cumulatively] to the "healthy common sense of the people"—not a particularly strict tie by any means, but at least one that required the effort of giving reasons for going beyond the wording of the law in concrete cases. It would be interesting to examine whether a comparison between cases in which analogy was applied according to Section 2 StGB 1935 and the generous interpretation practice of the

[230] Cited according to *Werle*, Justiz-Strafrecht, p. 141.

[231] "Whosoever commits an offence declared punishable by law or that merits punishment according to the ideas fundamental to criminal law and according to the healthy common sense of the people, shall be punished. If no criminal law applies specifically to the offence, it shall be punished according to that law the fundamental idea of which best fits the offence".

[232] "If it is clear that an individual has infringed one of several criminal laws, but the offences in question exclude one another so that only one alternative can be selected, then the offender is to be punished according to the most lenient law".

criminal courts of the Federal Republic would produce any marked differences between them.[233]

As the principle of *nullum crimen sine lege* had already been qualified in pre-1933 legal theory, as pointed out by *Naucke*[234] (the three criminal law teachers' report on the planned Lex van der Lubbe mentioned at the beginning of this chapter is symptomatic of this), this change in the law – so spectacular at first glance – in the end amounts to little more than a symbolic act. "The nulla-poena-principle becomes the 'trophy' of a victory over liberal-constitutional criminal law".[235]

The **Law on Amending Provisions on Criminal Procedure and the Constitution of Courts**, also of 28 June 1935, introduced new grounds for detention—the danger of repeat offences and the severity of the offence—to criminal procedure.[236]

The number of **supplementary penal provisions** increased further, once again particularly in commercial criminal law, which served not least to secure the preparations for war; besides this, it also furthered the exclusion of Jews from the public and economic spheres.[237]

The most famous—and indeed infamous—supplementary penal provision was of course the *Law for the Protection of German Blood and German Honour* (the so-called ***Blutschutzgesetz*** **or Blood Protection Law of 15 September 1935**), that rendered "extramarital intercourse" between Jews and "citizens of German or kindred blood" a punishable offence.

Section 5 (2) in conjunction with Section 2 of the *Blutschutzgesetz* threatened prison or penitentiary sentences for "extramarital intercourse" between Jews and "citizens of German or kindred blood" for the male partner. Section 11 of the Decree on the Implementation of this Law of 14 November 1935 states clearly that according to the Blood Protection Law intercourse is to be understood "only as sexual intercourse" – a clear definition, one would think, of coitus. However, the Grand Senate of the Reich Supreme Court soon had to clarify the question of what the term "sexual intercourse" actually covered. It decided that the term did not cover "every indecent act", but neither was it restricted to coitus; it included "all sexual acts with a member of the opposite sex, that according to the way they are conducted serve to satisfy the sex drive of at least one partner as an alternative to coitus".[238] The reason given by the court was that the legislature was familiar with the word coitus, but had not used it here, and that the *Blutschutzgesetz* also included other regulations that did not

[233] A first attempt at this was made by: *Jens-Michael Priester*, Zum Analogieverbot im Strafrecht, in: Hans-Joachim Koch (Ed.), Juristische Methodenlehre und analytische Philosophie. Kronberg/Ts. 1976, p. 155 ff.

[234] *Naucke*, Aufhebung, op. cit, p. 324 ff.

[235] *Werle*, Justiz-Strafrecht, p. 143, taking up a phrase by *Carl Schmitt*.

[236] Art. 5 of the law also allowed pre-trial detention if evidence suggested that the accused "will abuse his liberty to commit further punishable offences, or if a consideration of the severity of the offence and the public outcry caused renders leaving the accused at liberty unacceptable".

[237] For greater detail on National Socialist supplementary penal provisions, cf. *Schmitzberger*, Nebenstrafrecht; also see *Werner*, Wirtschaftsstrafrecht, p. 124 ff.; *Joseph Walk*, Das Sonderrecht für die Juden im NS-Staat. Eine Sammlung der gesetzlichen Maßnahmen und Richtlinien—Inhalt und Bedeutung. Heidelberg 1981 (and further editions); on this, cf. *Vormbaum*, GA 1983, 372 f.

[238] Judgment ratio summary (*Leitsatz*) in *RGSt* (Gr. Senate) 70, 375.

aim at preventing mixed-race offspring. This supreme art of judicial interpretation reached its pinnacle in a methodically artful procedure that remains highly popular to the present day and that significantly weakens the doctrine of protected legal interests' delimiting potential (which was never strong at the best of times), namely the criterion of so-called "dual protective function".[239] According to this, the definition of an offence is able to protect several legal interests, and these legal interests are to be protected – using linguistically incorrect terminology – "alternatively"; this means that the act in question needs to infringe only *one* of the legal interests in order to constitute an offence. In this concrete example, the Reich Supreme Court based its verdict on the dual protective function of the Law ("German blood" *and* "German honour").[240]

4. Continuation of Penal Reform

The NS regime also soon turned its hand again to the reform of criminal law. In doing so, they propagated a rejection of earlier reform work and of the liberal Reich Criminal Code of 1871.[241] Official and academic accounts repeatedly listed the new criminal law's aims as abolishing the prohibition of analogy to the disadvantage of the accused, thus replacing formal unlawfulness based on definitions of offences with the concept of "material unlawfulness", an orientation towards *Willensstrafrecht*, "integrating moral judgement as a compulsory mode of interpreting elements of offences in need of further definition" and, finally, the "complete restructuring of the Special Part".[242] As early as the summer of 1933, the Reich Ministry of Justice developed a draft bill (**Draft 1933**)[243] that was submitted to the state administrations of justice as the draft of a general criminal code on 25 September 1933. This draft bill was in fact the Reichstag Bill of 1927, which had only been partially reworked. It was to serve as a basis for consultation in the debate on a "renewal of criminal law" by a commission appointed by Reich Minister of Justice *Gürtner* on *Hitler's* orders.

---

[239] This is occasionally taken even further, increasing the number of interests to be protected to as many as *eight*; *Friedrich-Christian Schroeder*, NJW 1993, 2581, 2582, with reference to an example from the law on sexual offences.

[240] RGSt 70, 377; on this topic as a whole, cf. *Gerhard Werle*, "Das Gesetz ist Wille und Plan des Führers"—Reichsgericht und Blutschutzgesetz, in: NJW 1995, 1267–1271; *Regina Ogorek*, "Rassenschande" und juristische Methode. Die argumentative Grammatik des Reichsgerichts bei der Anwendung des Blutschutzgesetzes von 1935, in: KritV 3 (2003), 280 ff.; numerous examples taken from judicial practice can be found in *Majer*, "Fremdvölkische", p. 600 ff.; *Hans Robinsohn*, Justiz als politische Verfolgung. Die Rechtsprechung in "Rassenschandefällen" beim Landgericht Hamburg 1936–1943. Stuttgart 1977.

[241] *Monika Frommel*, Von der Strafrechtsreform zur Rechtserneuerung, in: Hubert Rottleuthner (Ed.), Recht, Rechtsphilosophie und Nationalsozialismus (ARSP supplement No. 18). Wiesbaden 1983, p. 45 ff.

[242] References in *Schubert*, Reform, Vol. II 1.1, p. XII.

[243] Reproduced in *Vormbaum/Rentrop*, Reform, Vol. 2, p. 265 ff.

The commission's working materials also included (albeit only as a secondary source) the Prussian Minister of Justice *Kerrl's* **memorandum "National Socialist Criminal Law"**, which had been developed by his criminal law department and was also published in September 1933. This memorandum aimed to utilise experiences from the practice of criminal law in Prussia and to make suggestions on the design of the new criminal code. Generally, according to the demand to create a "*Willensstrafrecht*", the "undertaking" of the criminal act formed its primary focus.

The **Academy of German Law** founded by **Hans Frank** (1900–1946) in the autumn of 1933[244] and the **Reich Justice Office of the NSDAP** also contributed materials to the meetings of the criminal law commission: on the one hand, the memorandum of the Academy's criminal law panel, "Basic features of a general German criminal law", of June 1934; and on the other, the "National Socialist Principles for a new German criminal law" of the Reich Justice Office of the NSDAP of 1 May 1935. The "Official commission to debate the renewal of criminal law"[245] began its consultation process on 3 November 1933, presided over by *Gürtner*.[246]

After the first reading, the draft was passed to various sub-committees for further consultation. These submitted their suggestions to a drafting committee, which then drew up a bill. In an adaptation to popular sentiment, the Special Part was moved to the beginning of this bill, so that the numbering was completely changed. After these results had also been passed to a sub-committee made up of *Mezger*, *Reimer*, *Leopold Schäfer* and *Karl Schäfer* for further consultation, yet another "Draft of a Criminal Code" in which the General Part was once more placed at the beginning was finally presented by the RJM on 15 July 1935. The draft was edited several more times. The last version of 1 July 1936 formed the basis for a revised version

[244] On Frank, cf. *Dieter Schenk*, Hans Frank. Hitlers Kronjurist und Generalgouverneur. Frankfurt am Main 2006.

[245] The Commission was made up of: Reich Minister of Justice *Gürtner* as chair, the Ministers of Justice of Prussia and Bavaria *Kerrl* and *Frank* as deputy chairs, two secretaries of state (*Freisler* und *Schlegelberger*), five representatives from the ranks of practitioners (including *Reimer* and *Klee*), and as university representatives *Kohlrausch*, *Nagler*, *Dahm*, *Count Gleispach*, and *Mezger* among others.

[246] More details included in *Schubert/Regge*, Quellen, Abt. II Vol. 1.1, p. XV ff.; on the commission's deliberations on the offences in the Special Part, cf. on **the offence of omitting to effect an easy rescue** *Gieseler*, p. 74 ff.; on **criminal and terrorist/anarchist organisations** see *Felske*, p. 241 ff.; on the **failure to report a crime** see *Kisker*, p. 93 ff.; on **duelling** see *Baumgarten*, p. 208 ff.; on **abortion** see *Putzke*, p. 344 ff.; *Koch*, p. 185 ff.; on **theft** see *Prinz*, p. 114 ff.; on **false accusation** and **misleading the authorities about the commission of an offence** see *Bernhard*, p. 112 ff.; on **arson** see *Lindenberg*, p. 117 ff.; on **causing bodily harm** see *Gröning*, p. 10 ff.; on the **perverting the course of justice** see *Thiel*, p. 103 ff.; on **mercy killing** see *Große-Vehne*, p. 109 ff.; on the **frustration of creditors' rights** see *Seemann*, p. 89 ff.; on **defamation of the head of state** see *Andrea Hartmann*, p. 229 ff.; on **prostitution, procuring and pandering** see *Ilya Hartmann*, p. 201 ff.; on **trespass** see *Rampf*, p. 101 ff.; on **embezzlement** and **unlawful appropriation** see *Rentrop*, p. 141 ff.; on **forgery of documents** see *Prechtel*, p. 165 ff.; on **road traffic law**, see *Asholt*, p. 111 ff.; on **incitement to hatred** see *Rohrßen*, p. 125 ff.

created by the criminal law commission. On 1 December 1936, the draft thus produced was submitted to the Chancellery of the Reich and the departmental ministers as a cabinet bill **(E 1936)**, and on the following day was tabled in the Reich cabinet along with a comprehensive draft report. The book *Das neue Strafrecht—Grundsätzliche Gedanken zum Geleit*, edited by *Gürtner* und *Freisler*, and the two-volume work *Das kommende deutsche Strafrecht—Bericht über die Arbeit der Amtlichen Strafrechtskommission* edited by *Gürtner*, both commented on this Draft of 1936.

According to Minister *Gürtner's* plans, the Draft of a German Criminal Code was already to be passed in its entirety in the Reich cabinet's meeting on 26 January 1937. *Gürtner* explained in a letter to the Reich Chancellery and the Reich Ministries accompanying the Draft that it was the will of the Führer and Reich Chancellor that the German Criminal Code be proclaimed on 30 January 1937, the fourth anniversary of the "*Machtergreifung*", the Nazis' usurpation of power. However, Reich Minister *Frank*, the other Reich Ministries and the Party Chancellery intervened in this plan. As a result, *Hitler* had *Gürtner* informed on 22 December 1936 that detailed consultations on the Draft Code could not be avoided, and that it was impossible for the Reich Cabinet's consultations to be completed by the envisaged date. The Cabinet was therefore first to study the Draft and its basic principles in the first reading. In the meeting of 26 January 1937 it was thus only decided to put the Draft on the agenda of the subsequent meetings.

As a result of this decision, various drafts that took the changes envisaged so far into account were drawn up for the following cabinet meetings (Meetings of the Reich Cabinet of 9 March, 5 May, 22 June and October/December 1937). The cabinet meeting planned for June 1938 did not take place, and the following months showed that *Gürtner's* attempt to complete the draft in the cabinet meetings had failed. Thus the Chancellery of the Reich, at the request of the Reich Minister of Justice, ordered that consultation should take place by written circulation procedure. By 31 September 1938, various institutions had submitted detailed comments; the draft was revised in April 1939, taking these into account.

The commentaries include that of Reich Minister *Frank*. He criticised above all the draft's language, the splitting of offences, superfluous casuistics as well as flaws in its overall structure and order. He stated that completing the draft in circulation as initiated by the Reich Ministry of Justice could certainly not replace the Führer and Reich Chancellor's clarifying and decisive verdict on the draft's individual regulations. *Gürtner* rejected these allegations.

After the Second World War had broken out, *Gürtner* tried to have the Draft passed by the "Ministerial Council for the Defence of the Reich". This Council had been set up 2 days prior to the outbreak of war by *Hitler* to relieve the pressure on his person by dealing quickly with the legislative tasks that arose from adapting the administration and economy to the demands of war. In December 1939, *Gürtner* was able to gain *Göring's* support for further consultations on the Draft in the Ministerial Council for the Defence of the Reich by drawing his attention to a number of criminal law regulations important for the war. A new Draft was compiled for these consultations in December 1939. However, these consultations in the Ministerial Council for the Defence of the Reich did not take place: on 18 December 1939, *Hitler* had Reich Minister of Justice *Gürtner* informed that the German Criminal Code would have to be passed using ordinary legislative procedure, and furthermore, that he had his doubts whether the time for a new Criminal Code really had come. Thus the reform of criminal law by the Third Reich foundered due to *Hitler's* reluctance to pass basic laws in a time of war.

Nonetheless, further plans for "reform" emerged in 1944 and 1945, culminating in the draft of a **Law on the Treatment of Persons Alien to the Community (*"Gemeinschaftsfremde"*).**[247]

This draft, long disregarded or ignored in the history of law, brought a line of development to its most extreme (and extremely horrible) point: the new definitions of the offences of murder and voluntary manslaughter (Sections 211, 212 StGB) had introduced the personalised terms "murderer" and "manslaughterer", which had ultimately seemed purely a matter of inconsequential cosmetics; now, however, they took on concrete form.[248] The name of the Law already shows that the aim was not to combat concrete criminal offences, but instead to "weed out" dangerous persons from society; this image is not only used as a botanical metaphor here, but transfers the ideas of botany in concrete terms into an ideology of "eradication" and "grafting". It is easiest to see what this meant in concrete terms if some of the regulations are reproduced verbatim: according to Section 1 of the Draft Law, a "person alien to the community" was:

> 1. whosoever in their personality or conduct, particularly due to exceptional flaws of intellect or character, proves themselves incapable of meeting the minimum requirements of the national community through their own effort,
> 2. whosoever
> a) leads a worthless, wasteful or disorderly life due to work-shyness or licentiousness, thus becoming a burden to or endangering others or the general public, or displays a habit of or tendency towards begging or vagrancy, to idling at work, thieving, fraud or other minor offences, or to drunken excess, or grossly neglects to provide maintenance or
> b) due to cantankerousness or belligerence persistently disturbs the peace of the general public,
> 3. whosoever shows, through their personality and lifestyle, that they are disposed towards committing serious offences (criminals inimical to the community [*gemeinschaftsfeindlicher Verbrecher*] and criminals by inclination [*Neigungsverbrecher*]).

Besides police measures (surveillance, referral to welfare authorities, detention in a police camp—Section 4: "The community alien shall refund the costs of his

[247] On the draft procedure cf. *Werle*, Justiz-Strafrecht, p. 621 ff.; on this subject, cf. also *Francisco Muñoz Conde*, Edmund Mezger. Beiträge zu einem Juristenleben. Berlin 2007. (This volume summarises sections from the 4th edition of the work "Edmund Mezger y el Derecho penal de su Tiempo. Estudios sobre el Derecho penal en el Nacionalsocialismo". Valencia 2003); on the background to the crackdown on "persons alien to the community", cf. *Wolfgang Ayass*, "Asoziale" im Nationalsozialismus. Stuttgart 1995; *Detlev Peukert*, Volksgenossen und Gemeinschaftsfremde. Anpassung, Ausmerze und Aufbegehren unter dem Nationalsozialismus. Cologne 1982.

[248] "Editor's note: § 211 and § 212 StGB are usually translated by "aggravated murder" and "murder". This has been deviated from here for reasons of style and expression."

detention"), measures of criminal law applied. Sections 6 and 7 speak for themselves:

> Section 6
>
> (1) Whosoever shows, through repeated criminal activity or through their lifestyle and their personality, that they have a deeply rooted propensity towards serious crime, shall be given an indefinite penitentiary sentence, unless the offence itself warrants a more severe punishment or that the offender be handed over to the police as incapable of reform. The judge shall determine the minimum penitentiary sentence in the verdict; it shall be no less than 5 years.
>
> (2) The criminal inimical to the community shall be sentenced to death if this proves necessary to protect the national community or to satisfy the need for just atonement.
>
> (3) If the judge is convinced that a criminal inimical to the community cannot be expected to integrate into the national community, he shall refer them to the police as incapable of reform, unless the death penalty is applied.
>
> Section 7
>
> (1) Whosoever shows, through repeated criminal activity or through their lifestyle and their personality, that they have a propensity towards serious crime, shall be given an indefinite prison sentence as a criminal by inclination; if however a penitentiary sentence is warranted as punishment, they shall be given an indefinite penitentiary sentence, unless the offence itself warrants a more severe punishment.
>
> (2) The judge's verdict determines the minimum custodial sentence; it shall be no less than 1 year, including for prison sentences.

The end of the war prevented this Draft from being enacted.

The German discipline of criminal law is disgraced by the fact that two of its exponents, *Edmund Mezger* and *Franz Exner*, stooped so low as to work on this legislative concoction. They did so by no means in order to prevent something even worse, but were actively supportive, as the correspondence between the Central Office of Reich Security and these two academics published by Francisco Muñoz Conde shows.[249]

> Further correspondence with the Central Office of Reich Security took place due to Mezger's desire to visit Dachau concentration camp in order to "observe certain types of humans *in situ* in the concentration camps" – a request gladly granted this prominent professor, who was always so highly cooperative.

Naturally, the personal component should not be overemphasised in the debate about continuity vs. discontinuity—after all, one cannot dissolve a nation and appoint a new one at the end of a regime. Nonetheless, it is striking that an author who had actively participated in creating such a body of laws, had undertaken such activities in his free time, had published statements on "measures of racial hygiene to eliminate criminal lines" and in support of the "eradication of segments of the population harmful to the nation and the race"[250] and who had declared criminal law a tool of racial struggle in Gürtner's Commission for the Reform of Criminal

---

[249] *Muñoz Conde*, Mezger, p. 95 ff.

[250] References in *Klaus Rehbein*, Zur Funktion von Strafrecht und Kriminologie im nationalsozialistischen Rechtssystem, in: MschrKrim 1987, 193 ff., 201.

Law,[251] could play such an important role in the Federal Ministry of Justice's Commission for the Reform of Criminal Law during the 1950s.

The NS regime also had plans to reform **criminal procedure**. A *Small Commission*, whose deliberations took place between December 1933 and February 1936, produced drafts of a code of criminal procedure, a code on justices of the peace and on arbitrators, and a constitution of courts act.[252] These were submitted to a number of institutions for review, but not to the public. A *Grand Commission*, also appointed by the Reich Ministry of Justice, met from December 1936 onwards and completed their work in February 1939.[253] The finished drafts became available in May 1939.

The basic ideas of the draft code of criminal procedure included strengthening the position of the prosecution and clearly differentiating between the prosecution and the court; the prosecution was truly to become the master of the pre-trial proceedings—an idea regarded as a consistent realisation of the accusatory principle at the beginning of the Weimar period, but now valued as contributing to overcoming the "so-called adversarial trials".[254] The prosecution was to be given the right to issue an arrest warrant and to order searches as well as physical examinations. The principle of mandatory prosecution was to be abolished for cases of petty and medium-scale crime; offences prosecuted only on the request of the injured party (*Antragsdelikte*) were also to be scrapped. Court proceedings were to be relaxed by reducing the requirement that the defendant be present, by making it easier for fresh charges to be added to an existing accusation and for a different law to be applied, by increasing the discretionary margin for rejecting evidential motions, and by making it possible to limit the object of the proceedings;

[251] 37th meeting of 5 June 1934, (in: Schubert/Regge, Quellen, Abt. II, Vol. 2.2, p. 297): "...I emphasise particularly: in the racial struggle; for I am of the opinion that we are dealing with a struggle here... It is a struggle between races in the German *Lebensraum*, and I personally am forced to admit that I am far better able to bear the hardships and injustices of the struggle if I tell myself clearly that we are dealing here with a struggle with two opposing fronts, in which conflict is fierce. And I think that fundamentally criminal law can be a suitable, effective, in some cases even a devastating weapon in such a struggle". This passage is toned down markedly in the corrected version of the minutes (op. cit., p. 239). The question must be asked of whether nobody in the Federal Ministry of Justice, which had access to the minutes of that Criminal Law Commission and used the documents of the NS period as working material for the reformatory work of the 1950s, skimmed over them before Professor Mezger of Munich was appointed the deputy chair of the Grand Criminal Law Commission of democratic post-war Germany. Or was this common knowledge and simply not regarded as an issue? On Edmund Mezger cf. also *Gerit Thulfaut*, Kriminalpolitik und Strafrechtslehre bei Edmund Mezger (1883–1962). Baden-Baden 1999.

[252] *Schubert/Regge*, Reform Abt. III Vol. 1, p. VIII ff.; also the following.

[253] Minutes and drafts are reproduced in *Schubert/Regge*, op. cit., Vols. 1 to 3.

[254] Thus the official Principles of the Reform of Criminal Procedure; cited according to *Schubert/Regge*, op. cit., Vol. 1, p. XI.

within the court itself, the *Führerprinzip* or "leader principle" was to apply, giving the chairperson greater power.[255]

As the Reich Ministry of Justice's consultations with various committees left some basic questions unresolved, Reich Minister of Justice *Gürtner* did not table the Draft in cabinet, so as not to place additional strain on the discussions of the StGB Draft. Ultimately, this meant that plans for codification failed both in criminal procedure and substantive criminal law.

5. *Penal Legislation After the Outbreak of the War*

a) Military Penal Legislation

After the Second World War had begun, a brutal martial criminal law came into force. Its main aim was to stabilise the "home front". The so-called "*Dolchstoßlegende*" ("stab-in-the-back myth"), completely internalised by those who invented it, formed this law's background: according to the myth, the German army had been close to achieving final victory in World War I when it was stabbed it in the back by the revolution at home.

The **Special Martial Criminal Law Ordinance** of 17 August 1938/26 August 1939 issued regulations to prevent *Wehrkraftzersetzung*, subverting the war effort ("whosoever [. . .] publicly attempts to weaken or subvert the will of the German people or its allies to defend and assert themselves by force"). The vague definition of this offence, deprived of even the last vestiges of clarity by the expanded definition of "public" used here as in the Treachery Act, meant it could be applied flexibly in such a way that anything from a conviction for causing a public nuisance up to the death penalty was possible.[256]

The **Decree on Extraordinary Broadcasting Measures** of 1 September 1939 made it an offence to listen to enemy radio stations and disseminate foreign stations' news.[257] According to Section 1, it was a punishable offence to "intentionally listen to foreign radio stations", thus including not only enemy, but all non-German stations. The punishment threatened was a penitentiary sentence, or prison "in less severe cases"; judicial practice also applied this regulation directly or analogously to listening to enemy stations *indirectly*, i.e. the noting of content by middlemen.[258] Section 2 prohibited the intentional dissemination of the news of foreign stations if this news "was capable of endangering the German nation's powers of resistance"; this regulation aimed to combat "subversive word-of-mouth propaganda".[259] Passing news even to one individual was sufficient to count as

---

[255] Ibid., p. XI f.

[256] More detail in *Werle*, Justiz-Strafrecht, p. 210 ff.

[257] More detail in *Werle*, op. cit., p. 217 ff.

[258] References in *Werle*, Justiz-Strafrecht, p. 216.

[259] *Werle*, op. cit., p. 217, *Schmitzberger*, Nebenstrafrecht, both including references.

dissemination. This was punished by penitentiary, and in particularly severe cases even by death. The special courts had jurisdiction over trying such acts according to the Decree. Section 5 made the prosecution of offences according to Sections 1 and 2 dependent on the request of the Secret State Police, in order to ensure that the Decree could be applied flexibly.

The **War Economy Penal Decree** of 4 September 1939 threatened punishment for whosever "destroys, hides or withholds natural resources or products vital to the population, thus maliciously risking that this need may not be covered".[260]

The **Decree against Elements Harmful to the Nation** ("Volksschädlingsverordnung"—VVO) [Translator's note: "*Volksschädlinge*" literally means "vermin of the nation".] of 5 September 1939 achieved particular significance. Both in terms of criminal policy and the theory of criminal law, it is one of the central norms not only of martial criminal law, but of National Socialist criminal law as a whole. Accordingly, its authors hoped it would also set a precedent for the future development of German criminal law.[261] The title itself revealed that the theory of offender types had here been advanced to the fundamental principle of a piece of criminal legislation. In terms of regulatory technique, it contained a combination of its own definitions of criminal offences and general rules for rendering punishments more severe.

Section 1 made "Plundering in liberated territory" a punishable offence.[262] Mandatory capital punishment was threatened. It was a matter of some debate whether the offender type of the "plunderer" should be read into the interpretation of this offence in line with the decree's title, which would mean positive proof of this "type" would have to be provided at the trial (which in theory would lead to a restriction of the decree's remit of application), or whether the presence of the offence characteristics irrebuttably proved this "type". The Reich Supreme Court took the former point of view. Given the broad phrasing of the offence and its wide interpretation of the "plunderer" characteristic, the difference between these two points of view remained, however, more or less irrelevant in practice.[263]

Section 2 threatened persons who "took advantage of measures against aircraft raids to commit a felony or misdemeanour against life, limb or the property of others" with penitentiary not exceeding 15 years, lifelong penitentiary, and even with capital punishment in particularly serious cases. The nature of this offence was disputed. The opinion that it constituted a reason for increasing the punishment for the basic offence against life, limb or property, which cited the decree's wording in support, was opposed by the (dominant) view which considered it a special offence

---

[260] *Werle*, op. cit., p. 220 ff.

[261] *Gruchmann*, Justiz, p. 906; *Schmitzberger*, Nebenstrafrecht, p. 138; *Werle*, Justiz-Strafrecht, p. 233 ff.

[262] More detail in *Irmtraud Eder-Stein*, Plünderung im saarländischen Freimachungsgebiet 1939/40. Ein Straftatbestand in Strafrecht und Rechtsprechung des NS-Staates, in: Franz Josef Düwell/Thomas Vormbaum: Themen juristischer Zeitgeschichte (1). Schwerpunktthema: Recht und Nationalsozialismus. Baden-Baden 1998, p. 116 ff.

[263] References in. *Schmitzberger*, Nebenstrafrecht, p. 142; *Werle*, Justiz-Strafrecht, p. 237 ff.; *Marxen*, Kampf, p. 209; *Gribbohm*, „Geführte“ Strafjustiz, p. 21 ff.

overlapping with the basic offence. This latter opinion's consequence was that the provision applied also in cases where the basic offence had merely been attempted. The main area to which this decree applied was the exploiting of blackout measures. Here, too, the question arose of whether the offence should be reduced to a type of offender ("air raid criminal"); due to the broad phrasing of the offence, even broader than in Section 1, this view was even more popular in the literature on Section 2 than that on the former.[264]

Section 3 threatened capital punishment for whosoever "commits arson or any other such felony constituting a public danger and thus weakens the resistance of the German nation"; unlike in Sections 1 and 2, the controversial question of whether the offender type of the "saboteur threatening public safety" needed to be proved specifically was of no real importance, as the offence itself characterised the offender.

In practice, the catch-all offence in Section 4 VVO gained great significance. According to this definition, whosoever "with intent and taking advantage of the extraordinary circumstances created by the state of war commits any other offence" was to be "punished more heavily than provided for by the ordinary sentencing frame, with penitentiary not exceeding 15 years, lifelong penitentiary or death", if required "by the healthy common sense of the people due to the particularly heinous nature of the offence". Here it was clear that this boundless offence definition, which did not even exclude transgressions as relevant offences, could not be grasped at all without taking recourse to the offender type of the "*Volksschädling*".

It was not necessarily the special courts which held jurisdiction over the offences defined in sections 2 and 4 VVO that proved particularly important in practice, although their jurisdiction could be established under certain circumstances. If this occurred, then according to Section 5 (as in Section 1, where their jurisdiction was mandatory) special court proceedings were accelerated. The verdict was to be pronounced immediately, ignoring any time limits, if the offender "is caught in the act or his guilt is otherwise obvious".[265]

The **Young Felons Ordinance** of 4 October 1939 and the **Violent Offenders Ordinance** of 5 December 1939 were also based on criminal types.

The **Violent Offenders Ordinance** (RGBl. 1939 I, p. 2378),[266] like the VVO issued by the "Ministerial Council for the Defence of the Reich", aimed to fill the gaps left by the *Volksschädlingsverordnung*. Section 1 threatened mandatory capital punishment for whosoever "when committing a serious violent offence makes use of firearms, clubs or thrusting weapons or other equally dangerous weapons, or

---

[264] References with the authors listed in the previous footnote.

[265] References as above; on the various approaches to the definition of offender types, cf. *Werle*, Justiz-Strafrecht, p. 244 ff.

[266] Text in *Buschmann*, Weltanschauung, p. 745; on the Violent Offenders Act, cf. *Schmitzberger*, Nebenstrafrecht, p. 177 ff.; *Klaus Marxen*, Juristische Vergangenheitsbewältigung am Beispiel der Versuchsbestrafung im deutschen Strafrecht, in: Staatsverbrechen vor Gericht. Festschrift for Christiaan Frederik Ruter. Amsterdam 2003, p. 138 ff.; on the judicature of the Reich Supreme Court, cf. *Gribbohm*, "Geführte" Strafjustiz, p. 42 ff.

uses such a weapon to threaten limb or life of another person" (Subsection 1); the same punishment was to apply to the "offender who attacks or fights off pursuers using armed violence" (Subsection 2). Section 2 granted whosoever "when pursuing a felon makes a personal effort to capture them [. . .] the same protection under criminal law as police or justice officers".

The Act also granted a particularly momentous consequence of the *Willensstrafrecht* legal status. While Section 44(1) RStGB had made **mitigation for attempt** compulsory since 1870, Section 4 of the Violent Offenders Ordinance downgraded this mitigation to a purely optional one. The new regulation

> For the punishable attempt of a felony or misdemeanour or for aiding it, the same punishment may be applied as for the completed offence

made it possible—thus the official reason—"to determine the punishment for attempt and aiding according to the extent of the offender's criminal will".[267] It applied not only to the offences regulated in the Ordinance, but to criminal law in its entirety. Furthermore—like the whole Ordinance—it had retroactive effect according to Section 5.[268] This factual abolition of Section 44 RStGB succinctly expressed one of the central aims of National Socialist criminal policy—to strike "as early and with as much might as possible" on a "pre-emptive battlefield". The new regulation was included in the Reich Criminal Code 4 years later in a slightly altered form, and proved long-lasting, both in the GDR and the Federal Republic.[269] There may be doctrinal reasons worthy of consideration for a purely optional mitigation in the case of attempted offences,[270] but it is nonetheless surprising that, in its obliviousness to history, Federal German criminal law doctrine has failed to take account in its considerations of the circumstances under which the current regulation came about.[271]

b) Further Laws

Besides martial criminal law, changes were also made to the Criminal Code. While plans to reform the criminal law had failed (due to Hitler's objections according to current research) and been postponed at least until the "*Endsieg*", it seemed apposite to extract at least those sections that the Reich Ministry of Justice

---

[267] *Roland Freisler*, Gedanken zum Kriegsstrafrecht und zur Gewaltverbrecherverordnung, in: DJ 1939, 1849 ff.

[268] However, the Decree on the Implementation and Supplementation of the Violent Offenders Act of 9 December 1939 (RGBl. 1940 I, p. 17) restricted this retroactive effect: it was not to apply if the offence had been committed prior to the outbreak of war, i.e. prior to 1 September 1939; any exceptions required the consent of the prosecution.

[269] *Marxen*, op. cit., p. 139 f., who also notes that it has not been investigated to date how many people were sentenced to death for a merely attempted crime due to this new regulation.

[270] On this, cf. *Marxen*, op. cit., p. 142; also *Vormbaum*, Aktuelle Bezüge, p. 78.

[271] Thus also *Marxen's* criticism, op. cit., p. 141.

considered politically enforceable and to enact them by way of amendment legislation. Besides some minor laws that mainly resulted in toughening punishments, the following are worthy of particular mention, as a large part of them remained valid far into the period of the Federal Republic, and indeed some of which remain valid today.

The **Decree of 2 April 1940** (*Decree on changes to the rules for punishing negligent manslaughter, causing bodily harm and leaving the scene of a traffic accident without cause*) qualified the requirements for simple bodily harm and bodily harm caused through negligence by making prosecution possible also in cases of particular public interest. Furthermore, this Decree transferred the punishment for *hit and run driving* from automotive law to the Criminal Code (Section 139a StGB o.v.), while simultaneously drastically increasing the punishment threatened.[272]

The Decree on Criminal Jurisdiction of 6 May 1940 introduced the **personality principle** to German **international criminal law** (Sections 3 ff. StGB); accordingly, German criminal law applied to Germans anywhere in the world, even in places where the actions in question did not constitute offences. The idea behind this is shown clearly in *Richard Lange's* contemporary commentary[273]:

> One of the main purposes of our new norms on ambit is to train Germans to feel and behave like Germans everywhere. [. . .] In their comments on the new decree, *Freisler* and *Rietzsch* highlight that thought on criminal law to date focused on the offence, while the new line of thought focuses on the offender, and that this emphasis on the principle of personality rather than on the principle of territoriality is an example of the application of the general turn towards a *Täterstrafrecht*. [. . .] Even if the German citizen's offence abroad affects no real interests of the German national community and infringes no German protected legal interests, the infringement of duty must be punished for its own sake, and the citizen is punished as he has violated a bond.

As well as increasing several punishments, the **Law to Change the Reich Criminal Code** of 4 September 1941[274] extended the application of **capital punishment**. Section 1 decreed:

> Dangerous habitual offenders (Section 20a StGB) and sex offenders (Sections 176–178 StGB) shall be sentenced to death if this proves necessary to protect the national community or [!] to satisfy the need for just atonement.

In principle, capital punishment could thus be imposed for any offence at all in case of three convictions (Section 20a (2) RStGB).

Section 2 changed the definitions of aggravated **murder** and murder (Sections 211, 212 StGB), which until then had been differentiated according to whether the offender had acted with or without premeditation, producing the versions essentially still valid today. Not only was the subjectivisation introduced in the first and

[272] More detail in *Werle*, Justiz-Strafrecht, p. 306 ff.

[273] *Lange*, Die grundsätzliche Bedeutung der neuen Bestimmungen über den Geltungsbereich des Strafrechts, in: GA 1941, 6 ff.

[274] *Vormbaum/Welp*, StGB, No. 47.

third groups of characteristics of aggravated murder typical; so was the addition of the offender types "murderer" and "manslaughterer" "(Editor's note: See note on p. 189)". As far as can be seen, these labels were, however, not understood or used as additional characteristics (of offender types) which would have resulted in a limitation of what was punishable.[275]

A particularly dreadful example of National Socialist criminal legislation—though not a first[276]—was furnished by the **Decree on the Application of Criminal Law to the Poles and Jews in the annexed Eastern territories** of 4 December 1941. It summarised similar regulations issued up until that point,[277] creating a unified special criminal law and criminal procedure law.[278] In substantive criminal law, Poles and Jews were threatened with capital punishment if they "committed a violent crime against a German citizen because of their membership of the German nation".[279] Capital punishment, or custodial sentences in less severe cases, was threatened for persons who

> express an anti-German attitude through malicious actions or actions that incite hatred, particularly making anti-German statements, tearing down or damaging the public notices of German authorities or offices, or whose behaviour otherwise disparages or damages the reputation or wellbeing of the German Reich.[280]

The same sentence applied to those Poles or Jews who met the offence criteria described in a five-part catalogue. Furthermore, they were subject to punishment "if they infringe German criminal laws or commit an offence that merits punishment in line with the fundamental ideas of German criminal law according to the necessities of the state in the annexed Eastern territories".[281] Thus the prohibition of analogy was relaxed to an even greater extent than allowed in the "Analogy Amendment" of 1935.

The principle of discretionary prosecution applied to criminal procedure[282]; jurisdiction lay with special courts or judges at the Amtsgericht—depending ultimately on the choice of the prosecution.[283] Sentences could be carried out at once. Only the prosecution had the right of appeal and objection. Defendants were not permitted to challenge judges on ground of bias. Where strong cause for suspicion existed, arrest and provisional arrest were "always permitted". During the pre-trial

[275] More detail in *Sven Thomas*, Die Geschichte des Mordparagraphen. Eine normgenetische Untersuchung bis in die Gegenwart. Bochum 1985. p. 239 ff.; *Katharina Linka*, Mord und Totschlag, Chapter 7 B) I.

[276] As emphasised by *Werle*, Justiz-Strafrecht, p. 371, contradicting *Majer*, "Fremdvölkische", p. 753.

[277] On these, cf. *Werle*, Justiz-Strafrecht, p. 351 ff.

[278] The text is reproduced in *Hirsch/Majer/Meinck*, Nationalsozialismus, p. 496 ff.

[279] Section 1 I, subsection 2.

[280] Section 1 I, subsection 3.

[281] Section 1 II.

[282] Section 2 IV.

[283] Section 2 IV.

proceedings, the prosecution was also able to order "arrests or other permitted sanctions".[284] Poles and Jews did not take an oath ("*beeidigt*"); instead, regulations on perjury and false oaths were applied to unsworn testimonies. Thus false unsworn testimony became punishable under German law for the first time since 1871.[285] Giving false unsworn testimony was declared a general offence 2 years later in the Decree on the Alignment of Criminal Law, which will be introduced shortly.

This decree only applied to Jews until the **13th Decree on the Reich Citizenship Law** of 1 July 1943 entered into force. Its first Section states succinctly: "The police shall have jurisdiction over offences committed by Jews". This regulation can be seen as the Holocaust's criminal law side, for it meant—now also in formal terms—"abandoning [the Jews] completely to the lawless police system (i.e. death or concentration camp)".[286]

The so-called **Decree on the Alignment of Criminal Law** (*Decree on the Alignment of the Criminal Law of the Old Reich and the Alpine and Danube Foreign Sections of 29 May 1943*[287]) introduced the NS regime's most comprehensive and, in the long term, most drastic changes to the Criminal Code. This Decree marks a more or less forgotten focal point in the history of German legislation. It was probably motivated by the desire to put at least some fragmentary aspects of the failed comprehensive reform into practice. However, the Reich Ministry of Justice emphasised another point, namely the differences in the law of the "Old Reich" and annexed Austria (which appeared in the Decree neither under the name "Austria" nor "Ostmark", but was subsumed under the plural phrase "Alpine and Danube Foreign Sections"). For this reason, the Decree's title emphasised the aspect of aligning the state of criminal law in both parts of the Reich.

In order to assess this decree's importance (including the decrees on its implementation) it will suffice to list those regulations that took on the more or less final form they still have today:

1. Only optional mitigation for attempt (today Section 23(2) StGB),
2. Limited dependence for acts of secondary participants (today Section 28(1) StGB),
3. Generalisation of liability for the attempt to induce another to commit a felony and for other preparatory actions (today Section 30 StGB),
4. Misleading the authorities about the commission of an offence (Section 145d StGB),[288]

[284] Section 2 V–VIII.

[285] Section 2 IX. The language of German law does not recognise the word "*beeidigt*", only statements that are "*beeidet*" (i.e. made under oath) and the person that is "*vereidigt*" (i.e. who has taken an oath) making the statement; on this regulation's significance within the history of false testimony offences, cf. *Vormbaum*, Eid, p. 138 ff.

[286] *Hirsch/Majer/Meinck*, Nationalsozialismus, p. 535.

[287] *Vormbaum/Welp*, StGB, No. 53.

[288] More detail in *Bernhard*, Falsche Verdächtigung, p. 132 ff.

5. False testimony offences (particularly the introduction of the offence of false unsworn testimony; today Section 153 StGB),[289]
6. Dishonouring the memory of the dead (Section 189 StGB),
7. Using threats or force to cause a person to do, suffer or omit an act (Section 240 StGB), and
8. Forgery of documents (Section 267 StGB).[290]

Generally speaking, it can be observed that where the adoption of German or Austrian laws was concerned, the more extensive or stricter law was selected in each case. Further changes resulted from the developments in criminal law theory, some of which had been discussed prior to 1933 but were radicalised during the NS period. The legislative line of development evident since the beginning of the century continued: purely optional mitigation for **attempt** increased judicial control powers; **limited dependence** rendered punishment and sentencing more flexible; the generalisation of Section 49a (today **Section 30 StGB**) increased liability for actions taken prior to a given offence; the offence of **misleading the authorities about the commission of an offence** closed the "gap" discovered in Section 164 StGB, particularly concerning liability for false self-incrimination; the offence of **false unsworn testimony** was intended to close the "gaps" produced by the restriction of oaths in civil and criminal procedure; the regulation thus ultimately reacted to the increased flexibility and informality of court proceedings; a further "gap" was closed by the offence of **dishonouring the memory of the dead**; the new formulation of the **offence of using threats or force to cause a person to do, suffer or omit an act** in the section on threats no longer required the threat of a felony or misdemeanour, the threat of "serious harm" sufficed, thus corresponding to the "dilution" of the term "force" in judicature.

It is interesting to see how early Federal Court of Justice (*Bundesgerichtshof* – BGH) case law (by judges that necessarily received their training or gained experience during the NS period) dealt with the new Subsection 2 of Section 240, that based the judgement of unlawfulness on the "healthy common sense of the people".[291] – According to BGHSt 5, 154, 256 the change of the characteristic *gesundes Volksempfinden* (healthy common sense of the people) to the characteristic *Verwerflichkeit* (inappropriateness) made in 1953 "was in essence only a matter of language".

Juvenile Criminal Law was toughened by the **Revised Juvenile Court Act of 1943**, without any basic changes.[292] This toughening culminated in the introduction of juvenile detention in 1943—a sanction still (problematically) popular today with makers of criminal policy.[293]

---

[289] More detail in *Vormbaum*, Eid, p. 138 ff.

[290] More detail in *Prechtel*, Urkundendelikte, p. 178 ff.

[291] BGHSt 1, 84 ff.; more detail in *Vormbaum*, Festschrift StA Schleswig-Holstein; *Dencker*, Kontinuität und Diskontinuität; *Id.*, NS-Justiz vor Gericht.

[292] More detail in *Kubink*, p. 280 ff.

[293] More detail in *Meyer-Höger*, Jugendarrest; on the police surveillance of juveniles during World War II cf. the third part of *Franz's* study, Curfew; on juvenile criminal law under National

6. Criminal Justice

The National Socialist state's legislation tended to **strengthen the role of the judge**—as became particularly evident in the analogy amendment (cf. § 5 V. 3. above). In line with its own ideology, the NS regime understood the judge as a leader, a kind of "*Führer*"; moreover, this understanding continued the line along which criminal theory had developed since the turn of the century: since then, the idea of the judge had shifted even further. During the nineteenth century, judges were distrusted both by the authorities and by the heirs of Enlightenment philosophy, and accordingly the principle *nullum crimen, nulla poena sine lege* and particularly the principle of specificity had been followed strictly. Now, however, two factors once again came together—but this time factors that led in the opposite direction. On the one hand, Liszt's criminal policy automatically led to a demand for greater freedom for the judge, who was to pronounce the sentence most appropriate for each individual offender, and on the other hand the experiences of the authorities of the Kaiserreich and the Weimar Republic with German judges made it seem acceptable or even desirable to treat the judge as an "understanding partner of the legislator".

On the whole, judges lived up to the expectations placed in them. The list of scandalous verdicts is a long one.[294] Thousands of death sentences in general criminal and military courts[295] speak eloquently for themselves. In fact, courts were even repeatedly reprimanded by the Party and the Central Office of Reich Security for overly harsh sentences.[296]

Socialism in general: *Christian Amann*, Ordentliche Jugendgerichtsbarkeit und Justizalltag im OLG-Bezirk Hamm von 1939 bis 1945. Berlin 2003; *Frank Kebbedies*, Außer Kontrolle. Jugendkriminalität in der NS-Zeit und der frühen Nachkriegszeit. Essen 2000.

[294] For individual details of these, we must here refer to the relevant literature. Verdicts in political law are listed in: *Wolfgang Form* (Ed.), Literatur- und Urteilsverzeichnis zum politischen NS-Strafrecht. Baden-Baden 2001; all works noted and accessible until 1997 are presented and discussed in *Thomas Vormbaum*, GA 1998, 1 ff.; more recent additions are: *Robert Bohn/Uwe Danker*, Standgericht der Inneren Front: Das Sondergericht Altona/Kiel 1932–1945. Hamburg 1998; *Hans-Ulrich Ludewig/Dietrich Kuessner* Es sei also jeder gewarnt: Das Sondergericht Braunschweig 1933–1945. Braunschweig 2000; *Holger Schlüter*, "für die Menschlichkeit im Strafmaß bekannt ...". Das Sondergericht Litzmannstadt und sein Vorsitzender Richter. (Juristische Zeitgeschichte NRW. 14). Recklinghausen 2005. *Justizministerium NRW* (Ed.), "... eifrigster Diener und Schützer des Rechts, des nationalsozialistischen Rechts ...". Nationalsozialistische Sondergerichtsbarkeit. Ein Tagungsband. Recklinghausen n.d. (2006).

[295] On **Wehrmacht jurisdiction**, cf. *Günter Gribbohm*, Das Reichskriegsgericht. Die Institution und ihre rechtliche Bewertung. Berlin 2004; *Id.*, Selbst mit einer "Repressalquote" von zehn zu eins? Über Recht und Unrecht einer Geiseltötung im Zweiten Weltkrieg. Münster 2006; *Norbert Haase*, Das Reichskriegsgericht und der Widerstand gegen die nationalsozialistische Herrschaft. Berlin 1993; *Manfred Messerschmidt/Fritz Wüllner*, Die Wehrmachtsjustiz im Dienste des Nationalsozialismus. Zerstörung einer Legende. Baden-Baden 1987; *Manfred Messerschmidt*, Was damals Recht war ... NS-Militär- und Strafjustiz im Vernichtungskrieg. Essen 1996.

[296] *Angermund*, Richterschaft, p. 142, 199, 209.—**Navy jurisdiction** later came under particular public scrutiny, as in 1978 the author *Rolf Hochhuth* called the Prime Minister of

More recent research[297] has of course shown that the image presented by the horrible film recordings of the People's Court trial against the would-be assassins of 20 July 1944 are not representative of the everyday judicature of the **People's Court**[298] and the special courts. For those who wish to see the People's Court as nothing other than an instrument of terror, repressing the German people, the results are surprising. Despite the Court's undoubted terrorist nature, particularly in its later phase, the authors are able to discover "many traits of judicial normality".[299] The recruitment of professional judges, for example, was based mainly on their aptitude, the region they came from, and their length of service[300]; accused individuals were all represented by a defence counsel; the percentage of acquittals was the same as usual at other times (in fact, this percentage even increased towards the end of the war, as the percentage of death sentences shrank[301]). "Even during the late phase, the practice of the People's Court (thus)...includes vestiges of judicial behaviour".[302]

The response expected, namely that such a view of and approach to the topic plays down the actions of NS criminal jurisdiction, misses the point; in fact, it contradicts what we can suppose may be the critics' intention. Two quotes by the authors suggest the direction that critical questions should take: "The task—as yet unsolved—consists in...discovering and explaining a complicated link between terror and normality"[303]; "the fact that terror, with thousands of death sentences, was spread by an institution that exhibited many traits of normal judicial practice is particularly alarming".[304]

There are several—in part mutually related—explanations as to why it was possible to cast the justice system as a victim of the NS regime for some time after 1945:

1) **Hitler** himself despised and hated jurists (even though his own experiences during the Weimar period had given him little reason to do so). His statements

Baden-Württemberg, *Hans Filbinger*, a "dreadful jurist" because of his work as a navy judge. In 1987, this remark became the keyword of *Ingo Müller's* eponymous and highly regarded book on jurists' entanglement with the regime of National Socialism.

[297] *Marxen*, Gerichtshof, *Schlüter*, Volksgerichtshof, op. cit. respectively.

[298] Verdicts of the People's Court are collected in *Heinz Hillermeier* (Ed.), "Im Namen des Deutschen Volkes". Todesurteile des Volksgerichtshofes. Darmstadt, Neuwied 1980; more representatively: *Klaus Marxen/Holger Schlüter*, Terror und "Normalität". Urteile des nationalsozialistischen Volksgerichtshofs 1934–1945. Eine Dokumentation. (Juristische Zeitgeschichte NRW. 13). Recklinghausen n.d. (2004).

[299] Schlüter, op. cit., p. 231.

[300] *Marxen*, Gerichtshof, p. 58.

[301] *Marxen*, op. cit., p. 89.

[302] *Marxen*, op. cit., p. 90.

[303] Ibid.

[304] *Schlüter*, Volksgerichtshof, p. 232.—On the connections of both traditional forms of justice and judicial practice in line with measures to political justice, cf. also *Niermann*, Strafjustiz, p. 375 ff.

on the topic—in particular his exclamation that he would not rest until every German had realised that being a jurist was a disgrace—are a firm part of the inventory of legal-historical literature to this day. Because of its regularity, those in power often see the justice system as throwing a spanner in the works. Neither the legal practitioners nor the justice system of the NS period can use Hitler's viewpoint to claim any merit.

2) As described above, the Reich Supreme Court's verdict in the **Reichstag Fire Trial** led to the founding of the People's Court; retrospectively, it was thus possible to present this verdict as an unfriendly act directed against the regime.
3) The criminal courts increasingly lost ground to the prosecution,[305] the police and the SS.[306] If verdicts did not suit the regime or its local representatives, acquittals could be subject to **verdict corrections**, i.e. the acquitted individual was arrested and transferred to a concentration camp. Verdicts considered too lenient could also be subject to similar correction once the offender had been released from prison. (Some harsh verdicts may actually have been passed to avoid this kind of correction. On the whole, however, the rivalry between the police and the SS on the one hand and the courts on the other can certainly be seen as a factional struggle for the resource of "criminal law". But we should not ignore that there were wide areas in which the two factions collaborated closely.)[307]
4) Hitler's infamous Reichstag speech of 26 April 1942, from which the above quote is taken, expressed his outrage at the supposedly overly lenient Oldenburg verdict in the **Schlitt case**. In this speech, *Hitler* demanded and was granted the power to remove any German citizen from office, including judges.[308] This will certainly have cowed many a judge, stifling any inclination to pass verdicts that were not in line with the regime. Incidentally, this process shows that judicial independence was not formally abolished until that point, even though official meetings, recommendations and "judge's letters" were used to exert pressure on judges.[309]

---

[305] On the shift in balance in the justice system from the courts to the prosecution, cf. in detail *Ulrich Schumacher*, Staatsanwaltschaft und Gericht im Dritten Reich. Zur Veränderung der Kompetenzverteilung im Strafverfahren unter Berücksichtigung der Entwicklung in der Weimarer Republik und in der Bundesrepublik. Cologne 1985.

[306] On the introduction of a separate jurisdiction of the police and the SS, cf. *Bianca Vieregge*, Die Gerichtsbarkeit einer "Elite". Nationalsozialistische Rechtsprechung am Beispiel der SS- und Polizei-Gerichtsbarkeit. Baden-Baden 2002.

[307] *Rüping*, Staatsanwaltschaft, p. 113 ff.; *Naumann*, Gefängnis, p. 145.

[308] Individual details in *Jens Luge*, Festschrift OLG Oldenburg, p. 244 f.; on the consequences, cf. *Günter Gribbohm*, Die dem Richter gebührende Sühne—Zur rechtlichen Stellung des Richters im Dritten Reich nach dem Reichstagsbeschluss vom 26. April 1942, in: JoJZG 2 (2008), 1 ff.

[309] On the "judge's letters" distributed from 1942 onwards by the Reich Ministry of Justice, cf. the documentation in *Heinz Boberach* (Ed.), Richterbriefe. Dokumente zur Beeinflussung der deutschen Rechtsprechung 1942–1944. Boppard 1975.

5) The introduction of the possibility of launching **extraordinary objections** and **nullity appeals** against final verdicts in 1939 and 1940 respectively[310] created yet another tool to get rid of politically unpopular verdicts. Of course, we cannot deduce any distrust of the justice system from this, for the new remedies were also referred to the Reich Supreme Court (although the extraordinary objection was to a particular criminal law senate of the Reich Supreme Court, and the nullity appeal could not be launched against verdicts of the People's Court).
6) Lastly, the fact that **everyday business** predominated, as it did in many other spheres of life, may have played a role in the justice system also, at any rate after the Law for the Restoration of the Professional Civil Service had been implemented. As described above, this even went for the People's Court in the Freisler era and for the special courts. After 1945, criticised verdicts could thus be presented as "aberrations" or exceptional cases.

7. Sentences and the Prison System[311]

The development of prison sentences under National Socialist rule also shows both continuity and ruptures side by side.[312]

The 1934 "*Verreichlichung der Justiz*", the "Reichisation" of the justice system, gave the Reich Ministry of Justice supervision over prisons throughout the Reich. The aim of prison sentences, as formulated in Section 48 of the Prison Regulations of 14 May 1934, reveals that prisons were to be dominated by more authoritarian rules as a matter of principle:

> By serving a custodial sentence, the prisoners are to atone for the wrong they have committed. The imprisonment shall be of such a kind as constitutes a serious negative

[310] The **nullity appeal**—introduced in Section 34 of the *Decree on the jurisdiction of criminal courts, special courts and other criminal procedural regulations* of 21 February 1940—could be launched to the Reich Supreme Court by the Supreme Reich Prosecutor against final sentences issued by an Amtsgericht, the criminal chambers of the Landgericht and special courts, "if the verdict is unjust due to an error in the application of law to the facts proved".—The **extraordinary objection**, introduced as early as 16 September 1939 by the *Law to change the regulations on general criminal procedure, Wehrmacht criminal procedure and the Criminal Code*, gave the Supreme Reich Prosecutor the power to launch this remedy to the Special Senate of the Reich Supreme Court; this appeal could also be made after rejection of the nullity appeal; cf. the example in *Werle*, Justiz-Strafrecht, p. 320 f.

[311] It is only recently that research on sentencing during the period of NS rule has been significantly improved. A survey from 1988: *Heinz Müller-Dietz*, Der Strafvollzug in der Weimarer Zeit und im Dritten Reich. Ein Forschungsbericht, in: Id., Recht und Nationalsozialismus. Gesammelte Beiträge. Baden-Baden 2000; cf. also *I. Baumann*, Geschichte, p. 91 ff. *Naumann*, Gefängnis, p. 113 ff.

[312] For a comprehensive study of prisons in the NS state: *Nikolaus Wachsmann*, Hitler's Prisons. Legal Terror in Nazi Germany. New Haven 2004.

> experience for the prisoner and that creates long-term inhibitions towards the temptation to commit new offences, even in those incapable of inner reform.
>
> Prisoners are to be encouraged to show discipline and order, to grow accustomed to work and the fulfilment of duty, and to be strengthened in their morals.

The phrasing referred back to the *Reichsratgrundsätze*, but added the aspect of atonement and individual deterrence.[313] Prisoners' rights as documented in the *Reichsratsgrundsätze* were nearly completely abolished.[314]

For the National Socialist era, more than for any other period of course, reducing our focus to "regular" prison constitutes a significant abridgement, for forms of imprisonment were varied and became increasingly interlinked.[315] Offenders and prisoners were also among the victims of National Socialism—irritating as this observation might seem given the millions of "innocent" victims of this regime.[316]

Beginning with the Reichstag Fire Decree, police crime fighting escalated. Even before the Habitual Offenders Act was passed, "professional criminals" were taken into "preventive police custody". The "detention" of non-offenders propagated during the Weimar period even by "left-wing liberal" proponents of the Lisztian school was continued, and was applied to homeless people, prostitutes, vagrants, beggars and alcoholics from 1937 onwards—at first with no legal basis. The link between police crime fighting and National Socialist politics of annihilation became ever closer; internment measures were expanded to include "antisocial elements" and "Yeniche", youths "impossible to educate" and "incapable of reform", as well as "Jews, Gipsies, Russians and Ukrainians".[317] From 1941 onwards, the euthanasia-murder campaign spread from psychiatric institutions to workhouses, care homes and concentration camps and became linked to the programme "*Vernichtung durch Arbeit*", "annihilation through work".[318] The "rivalry" over the jurisdiction over imprisonment between Himmler's Home Office and Gürtner's Ministry of Justice began. This rivalry is overwhelmingly represented in the literature as an antagonistic struggle which the justice system ultimately lost; however, as already mentioned, over long periods this rivalry in reality was actually a collaborative relationship in which each party assisted the

---

[313] The 1940 Official Regulations of the Reich Ministry of Justice heightened this tendency further; however, Section 48(2) stated the aim that "prisoners capable of reform are to be strengthened in such a way that they become useful members of the national community upon their return to freedom".

[314] *Krause*, Geschichte, p. 86.

[315] *Laubenthal*, Strafvollzug, p. 44.

[316] Cf. *Chr. Müller*, Verbrechensbekämpfung, p. 13 ff.; of course, these "innocent" victims also include those sentenced unjustly and those "turned into" criminals by the regime's decisions on criminalisation.

[317] *I. Baumann*, Geschichte, p. 110 f.—The godfather of this policy was the "Gipsy and Antisocials researcher" Dr. med. Robert Ritter (ibid.).

[318] *I. Baumann*, Geschichte, p. 288; *Institut für Juristische Zeitgeschichte Hagen*, Euthanasie vor Gericht. Die Anklageschrift des Generalstaatsanwalts beim OLG Frankfurt/M. gegen Dr. Werner Heyde u.a. vom 22. Mai 1962. Ed. Thomas Vormbaum. With a commentary by Uwe Kaminsky and Friedrich Dencker. Berlin 2005, p. 17 ff. (so-called campaign "Sonderbehandlung 14 f 13").

other. Under Gürtner's successor Schlegelberger, the justice system for the first time handed prisoners over to the police before their sentence had been fully served, and under Thierack the police were for the first time officially given powers in relation to regular prison sentences.[319]

During the NS period, the number of those in incapacitation detention rose above that predicted during the Weimar Republic. From 1937 onwards, most of them were transferred to concentration camps. Taking up ideas from before 1933, the justice system also began to use prisoners first to clear wasteland, then to work in the arms industry.[320] There was a dramatic drop in food quality in prisons, particularly during the War. Race ideology led to chances of survival becoming a matter of hierarchy. The concept of staggered sentences was not abandoned for German citizens during the NS period; indeed, it was pursued even more strongly in the area of juvenile prisons, but with a "downward" shift in focus, i.e. towards "elimination".[321]

8. Specific Pathology of the NS System

Preceding sections have shown that earlier lines of development became increasingly more radical under NS rule, and that many normal elements continued to have an effect—or, seen another way, that many problematic aspects that had already taken root prior to 1933 continued to have an effect. This realisation is based mainly on structural characteristics, marking a first step towards gaining an insight into the question of continuity. In order to avoid misunderstandings, these elements of continuity should not lead us to forget the general and particular pathology of the NS regime that is evident primarily in the areas of politics and constitutional law.

By *general pathology*, I understand the regime's inherent anti-constitutional, authoritarian and totalitarian character, evinced in the area of criminal law above all in race and war legislation, and in its politics of revision and conquest in foreign policy, culminating in the World War and millions of deaths—in numbers far greater than during the First World War—through war and displacement. However, these traits alone would distinguish the NS regime from many other dictatorships of world history and the modern era only by degree at best, and even the particularly high number of victims could be seen more as a characteristic of modern warfare than a specific trait of the NS regime (Fig. 18).

However, there is a *pathology specific* to the NS regime that goes beyond this. I include in this a summary of all processes whose special traits *Herbert Jäger*

---

[319] On the topic as a whole, cf. *Naumann*, Gefängnis, p. 143; an overview is given in *Helmut Kramer*, Der Beitrag der Juristen zum Massenmord an Strafgefangenen und die strafrechtliche Ahndung nach 1945, in: KJ 2010, 89 ff.

[320] *Naumann*, op. cit., p. 161 ff.

[321] *Naumann*, op. cit., p. 175 ff.

Heft 15 Berlin, den 1. August 1934 39. Jahrgang

Deutsche Juristen-Zeitung

Organ
der Reichsfachgruppe Hochschullehrer
des Bundes Nationalsozialistischer Deutscher Juristen

Unter Mitwirkung der Mitglieder des Reichsfachgruppenrates

Dr. V. BRUNS, Professor in Berlin
Dr. G. DAHM, Professor in Kiel
Dr. Dr. C. A. EMGE, Professor in Jena, Direktor des Nietzsche-Archivs in Weimar
Dr. W. GRAF GLEISPACH, Professor in Berlin
Dr. J. HECKEL, Professor in Bonn
Dr. E. R. HUBER, Professor in Kiel
Dr. W. KISCH, Geh. Justizrat, Professor in München, stellv. Präsident d. Akademie f. Deutsches Recht
Dr. F. KLAUSING, Professor in Frankfurt a. M.
Dr. H. LANGE, Professor in Breslau
Dr. J. POPITZ, Preuß. Finanzminister, Staatsrat, Professor in Berlin
Dr. P. RITTERBUSCH, Professor in Königsberg

herausgegeben vom Reichsfachgruppenleiter
Dr. CARL SCHMITT
Staatsrat, Professor in Berlin

C. H. Beck'sche Verlagsbuchhandlung München und Berlin

Hauptschriftleitung: Berlin W 35, Tiergartenstr. 20 — Schriftleitung und Geschäftsstelle: Berlin W 57, Potsdamer Str. 96

Bankkonto: Deutsche Bank u. Disconto-Ges., Kasse P, Berlin
Postscheckkonto: Nr. 45561 Postscheckamt Berlin NW 7

Die „Deutsche Juristen-Zeitung" erscheint am 1. und 15. jeden Monats. Ueber die Bezugspreise und die Preise für einzelne Hefte vgl. die Angaben auf der 2. Umschlagseite. Bestellungen werden durch den Buchhandel und die Postanstalten sowie unmittelbar durch die Geschäftsstelle Berlin W 57, Potsdamer Str. 96, entgegengenommen.

Alle redaktionellen Sendungen nur an die Schriftleitung Berlin W 57, Potsdamer Str. 96 erbeten. Jeder Einsendung bitte Rückporto beizufügen. Anzeigen-Annahme der DJZ., Berlin W 57, Potsdamer Str. 96, u. bei allen Anzeigenstell. Anzeigenpr.: die 4gesp. Millimeterzeile (Großspalte: 46 mm breit) 22 Pf. Fernspr. B 7 Pallas 2403 u. 2564.

Der Führer schützt das Recht

Zur Reichstagsrede Adolf Hitlers vom 13. Juli 1934

Von Staatsrat, Professor Dr. Carl Schmitt, Berlin

I. Auf dem Deutschen Juristentag in Leipzig, am 3. Okt. 1933, hat der Führer über Staat und Recht gesprochen. Er zeigte den Gegensatz eines substanzhaften, von Sittlichkeit und Gerechtigkeit nicht abgetrennten Rechts zu der leeren Gesetzlichkeit einer unwahren Neutralität und entwickelte die inneren Widersprüche des Weimarer Systems, das sich in dieser neutralen Legalität selbst zerstörte und seinen eigenen Feinden auslieferte. Daran schloß er den Satz: „Das muß uns eine Warnung sein".

In seiner an das ganze Deutsche Volk gerichteten Reichstagsrede vom 13. Juli 1934 hat der Führer an eine andere geschichtliche Warnung erinnert. Das starke, von Bismarck gegründete Deutsche Reich ist während des Weltkriegs zusammengebrochen, weil es im entscheidenden Augenblick nicht die Kraft hatte, „von seinen Kriegsartikeln Gebrauch zu machen". Durch die Denkweise eines liberalen „Rechtsstaats" gelähmt, fand eine politisch instinktlose Zivilbürokratie nicht den Mut, Meuterer und Staatsfeinde nach verdientem Recht zu behandeln. Wer heute im Band 310 der Reichstags-Drucksachen den Bericht über die öffentliche Vollsitzung vom 9. Okt. 1917 liest, wird erschüttert sein und die Warnung des Führers verstehen. Die Mitteilung der damaligen Reichsregierung, daß Rädelsführer der meuternden Matrosen mit Reichstagsabgeordneten der Unabhängigen Sozialistischen Partei verhandelt hatten, beantwortete der Deutsche Reichstag in lauter Entrüstung damit, daß man einer Partei ihr verfassungsmäßiges Recht, im Heere Propaganda zu treiben, nicht verkürzen dürfe und daß schlüssige Beweise des Hochverrates fehlten. Nun, diese schlüssigen Beweise haben uns die Unabhängigen Sozialisten ein Jahr später ins Gesicht gespien. In beispielloser Tapferkeit und unter furchtbaren Opfern hat das Deutsche Volk vier Jahre lang einer ganzen Welt standgehalten. Aber seine politische Führung hat im Kampfe gegen die Volksvergiftung und die Untergrabung des deutschen Rechts und Ehrgefühls auf eine traurige Weise versagt. Bis zum heutigen Tage büßen wir die Hemmungen und Lähmungen der deutschen Regierungen des Weltkriegs.

Alle sittliche Empörung über die Schande eines solchen Zusammenbruchs hat sich in Adolf Hitler angesammelt und ist in ihm zur treibenden Kraft einer politischen Tat geworden. Alle Erfahrungen und Warnungen der Geschichte des deutschen Unglücks sind in ihm lebendig. Die meisten fürchten sich vor der Härte solcher Warnungen und flüchten lieber in eine ausweichende und ausgleichende Oberflächlichkeit. Der Führer aber macht Ernst mit den Lehren der deutschen Geschichte. Das gibt ihm das Recht und die Kraft, einen neuen Staat und eine neue Ordnung zu begründen.

II. Der Führer schützt das Recht vor dem schlimmsten Mißbrauch, wenn er im Augenblick der Gefahr kraft seines Führertums als oberster Gerichtsherr unmittelbar Recht schafft: „In dieser Stunde war ich verantwortlich für das Schicksal der deutschen Nation und damit des Deutschen Volkes oberster Gerichtsherr". Der wahre Führer ist

Fig. 18 Extract from the 1934 Deutsche Juristen-Zeitung. The *Führer* protects the law. An essay by Carl Schmitt on Adolf Hitler's Reichstag speech of 13 July 1934

analyses as "macrocrime".[322] The conventional object of studies in the history of criminal law, which to a large part consists of (state) criminal laws, is turned upside down by these processes, for we are here concerned not with the state as the creator of laws, but with the state as the breaker of laws, with "state-encouraged crime" (*Naucke*). Although this aspect thus forms part of general historiography, it needs at least to be mentioned here, for after 1945 this process was reversed: precisely these state crimes were—if sometimes reluctantly—subjected to prosecution and became the trigger for new state laws. To name only the most important[323]:

1. Murders carried out in connection with the so-called **Röhm-Putsch**[324];
2. the so-called **euthanasia project**, the systematic murder of hundreds of thousands of mental patients[325];
3. **"Einsatzgruppen" murders** in Poland and the Soviet Republic[326];
4. The systematic murder of around 6 million Jews (the so-called **Holocaust**, "final solution to the Jewish question")[327];

---

[322] *Herbert Jäger*, Makrokriminalität. Studien zur Kriminologie kollektiver Gewalt. Frankfurt am Main 1989. *Id.*, Verbrechen unter totalitärer Herrschaft. Studien zur nationalsozialistischen Gewaltkriminalität (1967). 2nd edition. Frankfurt am Main 1982.

[323] A complete list is included in *Rückerl*, NS-Verbrechen.

[324] These murders, which were declared legal in the retrospectively issued *Law on Measures of State Self-Defence of 3 July 1934* (more detail in *Gruchmann*, Justiz, p. 433 ff.), were justified only a month later by the professor of law *Carl Schmitt* in the journal "Deutsche Juristenzeitung" which he edited in an essay called "The Führer protects the law" (DJZ 1934, col. 945 ff.: "In actual fact, the action taken by the Führer constituted true jurisdiction. It was not subject to the justice system, but was itself the highest form of justice"); on this, *Bernd Rüthers*, Entartetes Recht. Rechtslehren und Kronjuristen im Dritten Reich. Munich 1988, p. 120 ff.; *Id.*, Carl Schmitt im Dritten Reich. Wissenschaft als Zeitgeist-Verstärkung? Munich 1989, p. 53 ff.; also *Gruchmann*, "Dummheiten eines Genies?", in: JZ 2005, 763 ff. (the author counters post-1945 attempts to represent Schmitt's activities as atypical aberrations by pointing out his elaborate and consistently upheld National Socialist theorems on criminal procedure).

[325] On this, cf. the description given in the indictment of the "euthanasia" doctor Dr. Heyde (who after 1945 practised medicine in Schleswig-Holstein for years under the name of "Dr. Sawade" in more or less open anonymity): *Institut für Juristische Zeitgeschichte Hagen*, Euthanasie vor Gericht.; also cf. the contributions to the symposium "NS-Euthanasie" in the Justizakademie NRW in October 2005 by Hans Schmuhl, Petra Fuchs et. al, Michael Schwartz, Uwe Kaminsky, Klaus-Detlev Godau Schüttke, Friedrich Dencker, Helia-Verena Daubach und Heinz Holzhauer, in: Jahrbuch der Juristischen Zeitgeschichte 7 (2005/2006), as well as the conference report by *Helia-Verena Daubach*, in: JoJZG 1 (2007), 30 ff.; *Große-Vehne*, p. 125 ff.; on the role played by the Reich Ministry of Justice and the justice system *Gruchmann*, Justiz, p. 497 ff.—NS medical studies' human experiments also belong in this context; on these, cf. *Ernst Klee*, Auschwitz, die NS-Medizin und ihre Opfer. Revised new edition. Frankfurt am Main 2001; on the text by *Binding/Hoche* that furnished the murder campaigns with their catchphrase, cf. § 5 II. 1. above.

[326] On this, cf. *Christopher Browning*, Ordinary Men. Reserve Police Battalion 101 and the Final Solution in Poland. New York 1992.

[327] In the plethora of literature on this topic, the standard work of reference remains: *Raul Hilberg*, Die Vernichtung der europäischen Juden. 3 volume paperback edition. Frankfurt am Main 1994; more recently *Christopher Browning*, The Origins of the Final Solution. The Evolution of Nazi Jewish Policy, September 1939-March 1942. Lincoln, NE 2004. Historian and antisemitism

5. The systematic murder of **Sinti, Roma** and other nomadic peoples[328];
6. Crimes against **prisoners of war**[329];
7. The **exploitation of forced labourers** (with some justification called "slave workers") by the state and industry, only recently brought back to public attention around the turn of the millennium.[330]

VI. The Period of Occupation; the Federal Republic of Germany

1. Transformation

After the capitulation of the German Wehrmacht on 8 May 1945, the victorious Allies divided Germany into occupation zones held together—though ever decreasingly so—by the Allied Control Council (Fig. 19). Within the occupation zones, the Allies held governmental power. Today we can hardly grasp the sheer extent of the social and logistical tasks they faced. Germany's cities were destroyed and (in consequence) there was a severe housing shortage; there was a shortage of food and, in addition, millions of new refugees to take care of. The primary concern thus was to ensure the immediate necessities of life. The governing forces achieved this through planning, the occupied Germans through improvising. The focus on this daily struggle for survival may have contributed to the German population's

researcher Wolfgang Benz has commented on the doubts voiced by right-wing extremists over the number (standardised in federal German discourse) of 6 million Jewish victims. After intense research, he concluded that the number lies in between a minimum of 5.29 million and a maximum of just above 6 million; *Wolfgang Benz* (Ed.), Dimension des Völkermords. Die Zahl der jüdischen Opfer des Nationalsozialismus. Munich 1996, p. 15 ff.; on the so-called Wannsee conference of 20 January 1942 that marks the beginning of the systematic "final solution to the Jewish question", cf. the exhibition catalogue of the Wannsee villa, where the conference was held: *Haus der Wannsee-Konferenz* (Ed.), Die Wannsee-Konferenz und der Völkermord an den europäischen Juden. Catalogue of the permanent exhibition. Berlin 2006; on the jurists' role in the debate, cf. *Alex Jettinghoff*, Die Wannsee-Juristen, in: JoJZG 2007, 129 ff.

[328] On this, cf. the contributions in: *Tilman Zülch*, In Auschwitz vergast, bis heute verfolgt. Zur Situation der Roma (Zigeuner) in Deutschland und Europa. Reinbek nr. Hamburg 1979, p. 89 ff.

[329] On this, cf. *Christian Streit*, Keine Kameraden. Die Wehrmacht und die sowjetischen Kriegsgefangenen 1941–1945. Bonn 1991; *Jochen Böhler*, Auftakt zum Vernichtungskrieg. Die Wehrmacht in Polen 1939. Frankfurt am Main 2006, p. 169 ff.

[330] On this, cf. *Klaus Kastner*, Sklaverei oder Arbeitsverhältnisse? Historische und rechtliche Aspekte der Zwangsarbeit des nationalsozialistischen Regimes, in: Commemorative volume for Wolfgang Blomeyer. Berlin 2004, p. 99 ff.—On efforts to gain compensation for forced labourers, cf. among others *Diemut Majer*, Die Frage der Entschädigung für ehemalige NS-Zwangsarbeiter in völkerrechtlicher Sicht, in: Id., Nationalsozialismus im Lichte der Juristischen Zeitgeschichte. Baden-Baden 2002, p. 226 ff.; most recently *Sascha Koller*, Die Entschädigung ehemaliger NS-Zwangsarbeiter nach Inkrafttreten des Gesetzes zur Errichtung der Stiftung "Erinnerung, Verantwortung und Zukunft". Bonn (jur. Diss.) 2006.

KONTROLLRAT

Gesetz Nr. 10

Bestrafung von Personen, die sich Kriegsverbrechen, Verbrechen gegen Frieden oder gegen Menschlichkeit schuldig gemacht haben.

[...]

ARTIKEL II

1. Jeder der folgenden Tatbestände stellt ein Verbrechen dar:

a) Verbrechen gegen den Frieden. Das Unternehmen des Einfalls in andere Länder und des Angriffskrieges als Verletzung des Völkerrechts und internationaler Verträge einschließlich der folgenden den obigen Tatbestand jedoch nicht erschöpfenden Beispiele: Planung, Vorbereitung eines Krieges. Beginn oder Führung eines Angriffskrieges oder eines Krieges unter Verletzung von internationalen Verträgen, Abkommen oder Zusicherungen; Teilnahme an einem gemeinsamen Plan oder einer Verschwörung zum Zwecke der Ausführung einer der vorstehend aufgeführten Verbrechen.

b) Kriegsverbrechen. Gewalttaten oder Vergehen gegen Leib, Leben oder Eigentum, begangen unter Verletzung der Kriegsgesetze oder -gebräuche einschließlich der folgenden den obigen Tatbestand jedoch nicht erschöpfenden Beispiele: Mord, Mißhandlung der Zivilbevölkerung der besetzten Gebiete, ihre Verschleppung zur Zwangsarbeit oder anderen Zwecken, Mord oder Mißhandlung von Kriegsgefangenen, Personen auf hoher See; Tötung von Geiseln; Plünderung von öffentlichem oder privatem Eigentum; vorsätzliche Zerstörung von Stadt oder Land; oder Verwüstungen, die nicht durch militärische Notwendigkeit gerechtfertigt sind.

c) Verbrechen gegen die Menschlichkeit. Gewalttaten und Vergehen, einschließlich der folgenden den obigen Tatbestand jedoch nicht erschöpfenden Beispiele: Mord, Ausrottung, Versklavung, Zwangsverschleppung, Freiheitsberaubung, Folterung, Vergewaltigung oder andere an der Zivilbevölkerung begangene unmenschliche Handlungen; Verfolgung aus politischen, rassischen oder religiösen Gründen, ohne Rücksicht darauf, ob sie das nationale Recht des Landes, in welchem die Handlung begangen worden ist, verletzen.

d) Zugehörigkeit zu gewissen Kategorien von Verbrechervereinigungen oder Organisationen, deren verbrecherischer Charakter vom Internationalen Militärgerichtshof festgestellt worden ist.

2. Ohne Rücksicht auf seine Staatsangehörigkeit oder die Eigenschaft, in der er handelte, wird eines Verbrechens nach Maßgabe von Ziffer 1 dieses Artikels für schuldig erachtet, wer

a) als Täter oder

Fig. 19 (continued)

b) als Beihelfer bei der Begehung eines solchen Verbrechens mitgewirkt oder es befohlen oder angestiftet oder

c) durch seine Zustimmung daran teilgenommen hat oder

d) mit seiner Planung oder Ausführung in Zusammenhang gestanden hat oder

e) einer Organisation oder Vereinigung angehört hat, die mit seiner Ausführung in Zusammenhang stand, oder

f) soweit Ziffer 1 a) in Betracht kommt, wer in Deutschland oder in einem mit Deutschland verbündeten, an seiner Seite kämpfenden oder Deutschland Gefolgschaft leistenden Lande eine gehobene politische, staatliche oder militärische Stellung (einschließlich einer Stellung im Generalstab) oder eine solche im finanziellen, industriellen oder wirtschaftlichen Leben innegehabt hat.

3. Wer eines der vorstehend aufgeführten Verbrechen für schuldig befunden und deswegen verurteilt worden ist, kann mit der Strafe belegt werden, die das Gericht als gerecht bestimmt. Die folgenden Strafen können – allein oder nebeneinander – verhängt werden:

a) Todesstrafe,

b) lebenslängliche oder zeitlich begrenzte Freiheitsstrafe mit oder ohne Zwangsarbeit.

c) Geldstrafe und, im Falle ihrer Uneinbringlichkeit, Freiheitsstrafe mit oder ohne Zwangsarbeit.

d) Vermögenseinziehung.

e) Rückgabe unrechtmäßig erworbenen Vermögens.

f) Völlige oder teilweise Aberkennung der bürgerlichen Ehrenrechte.

Vermögen, dessen Einziehung oder Rückgabe von dem Gerichtshof angeordnet worden ist, wird dem Kontrollrat für Deutschland zwecks weiterer Verfügung ausgehändigt.

4. a) Die Tatsache, daß jemand eine amtliche Stellung eingenommen hat, sei es die eines Staatsoberhauptes oder eines verantwortlichen Regierungsbeamten, befreit ihn nicht von der Verantwortlichkeit für ein Verbrechen und ist kein Strafmilderungsgrund.

b) Die Tatsache, daß jemand unter dem Befehl seiner Regierung oder seines Vorgesetzten gehandelt hat, befreit ihn nicht von der Verantwortlichkeit für ein Verbrechen; sie kann aber als strafmildernd berücksichtigt werden.

5. In einem Strafverfahren oder einer Verhandlung wegen eines der vorbezeichneten Verbrechen kann sich der Angeklagte nicht auf Verjährung berufen, soweit die Zeitspanne vom 30. Januar 1933 bis zum 1. Juli 1945 in Frage kommt. Ebensowenig stehen eine vom Naziregime gewährte Immunität, Begnadigung oder Amnestie der Aburteilung oder Bestrafung im Wege.

[...]

Fig. 19 Excerpt from Control Council Law No. 10

reluctance to deal with National Socialist crimes, as well as the fact that Allied aerial warfare had caused the Germans to see themselves as victims.

This struggle for survival could not be achieved without passing laws, and for this reason alone the Allies were faced with the question of how to deal with laws originating in the period of National Socialist rule. Were all laws passed between 30 January 1933 and 8 May 1945 to be abolished? This solution was never given any serious consideration. Rather, *one part* of these laws was to be repealed, *another part* to remain in force. The understanding behind this was that *National Socialist* law should be abolished, but *non-National Socialist* law should continue to be valid.

The Allied Control Council repealed a number of laws that it regarded as typically National Socialist and/or in violation of the rule of law. Its very first law abolished the Enabling Act that had provided the formal foundation for Hitler's rule, the Law against Forming New Parties which had established the NSDAP's monopoly, and the Law on the Secret State Police, as well as the race laws and other discriminatory laws; further laws abolished discriminatory regulations in marriage law, inheritance law, employment law, agricultural law and film and press law. A multitude of laws regulating the economy and combating the black market (including the respective sanctions) remained in force.[331]

Criminal law in its form at the end of National Socialist rule also needed to be changed in such a way that it could be put into practice by a community under the rule of law.[332] Here, too, the Allied Control Council and military governments tried to abolish those laws considered insupportable by a combination of individual laws and general principles. Among others, laws and regulations aiming to maintain the war machinery, the war and arms industry and National Socialist propaganda and to persecute so-called *Volksschädlinge* and oppress Poles and Jews were rescinded; those laws that remained in force were no longer allowed to be interpreted in line with "National Socialist ideology", and punishment determined by analogy or the "healthy common sense of the people" in particular was prohibited. Death penalties introduced after 1933 could no longer be imposed; the maximum sentences valid before the National Socialists came to power could not be exceeded. The Criminal Code formally abolished the option of analogous application of laws, introduced in 1935, as well as all offences against the state and the criminal law to protect the Wehrmacht.

However, the compatibility of a number of problematic laws with the rule of law was acknowledged. This included the 1943 Decree on the Alignment of Criminal Law's regulation on purely optional mitigation for attempt. Neither the Allies nor later the German courts called this law into question, although influential voices in

[331] On this as a whole: *Matthias Etzel*, Die Aufhebung von nationalsozialistischen Gesetzen durch den Alliierten Kontrollrat (1945–1948). Tübingen 1992; on commercial criminal law: *Hans Achenbach*, Zur Entwicklung des Wirtschaftsstrafrechts in Deutschland seit dem späten 19. Jahrhundert, in: Jura 2007, 342 ff., 344; *Werner*, Wirtschaftsordnung, p. 571 ff.

[332] In detail on the following, cf. *Jürgen Welp*, Die Strafgesetzgebung der Nachkriegszeit (1945–1953) in: Vormbaum/Welp, StGB, supplementary volume I, p. 139 ff.

the literature voiced their doubts about its compatibility with the rule of law.[333] The same goes for the new version of the offence of using threats or force, introduced on the same occasion. One of the Federal Court of Justice's first decisions in criminal matters declared this offence unobjectionable, giving rather strange reasons.[334]

2. *Eradicating the Injustices of National Socialism*

Apart from removing National Socialist components from the law, the aim was also to eradicate National Socialist injustice through restitution,[335] compensation[336] and revision of verdicts.[337] The correction of sentences is our particular interest here.

The task was to review the **criminal verdicts** passed during the period of National Socialist rule, particularly those of the special courts and the People's Court. Allied legislation, with the involvement of the new federal states, passed a combination of laws and decrees that—partly automatically, partly upon application—reduced punishments considered excessive, and in many cases overturned verdicts altogether.[338] The verdicts against members of the resistance to National Socialism in particular were annulled. In general, more value was placed on convicts' anti-Nazi attitudes than on the objective injustice of the sentences passed, e.g. their disproportionality. It was only over 50 years after the end of National Socialist rule, in August 1998, that a federal law was passed decreeing that all verdicts that contradicted the basic principles of justice were

[333] *Otto Schwarz*, StGB, 13th edition. Munich and Berlin 1949, Section 44 note 1a (which states that the regulation is contradictory to post-National Socialist thought); the 16th edition of 1953 deleted this passage; *Eduard Kohlrausch*, StGB mit Nebengesetzen. Textausgabe mit Erläuterung der Änderungen. Berlin 1947, p. 44: "Thus the new German punishment for attempt marks an overemphasis on the idea of the will, going so far as to become a criminal law that focuses on the offender's attitude. The older regulation is closer to the rule of law" (cited here from *Karitzky*, Kohlrausch, p. 409).

[334] For more detail, cf. *Vormbaum*, Festschrift StA Schleswig-Holstein, p. 75 ff.; *Dencker*, Kontinuität, p. 135 ff.; *Id.*, NS-Justiz vor Gericht. Discussion of further aspects of the Special Part in the period immediately following the War: on **political criminal law** see *Schroeder*, Schutz, p. 175 f.; on **testimony offences** see *Vormbaum*, Eid, p. 144 ff.; on **the offence of omitting to effect an easy rescue** see *Gieseler*, p. 86 ff.; on the **failure to report a crime** see *Kisker*, p. 119 ff.; on **duelling** see *Baumgarten*, p. 222 f. (particularly on the question of the legitimacy of the "*Bestimmungsmensur*", arranged duels between student fraternities; on **theft** see *Prinz*, p. 132 ff.; on **false accusation** and **misleading the authorities about the commission of a crime** see *Bernhard*, p. 136 f.; on **bodily harm** see *Gröning*, p. 44 ff.; on **perverting the course of justice** see *Thiel*, p. 130 ff.; on the **frustration of creditors' rights** see *Seemann*, p. 89 ff.; on **defamation of the head of state** see *Andrea Hartmann*, p. 239 ff.; on **prostitution, procuring and pandering** see *Ilya Hartmann*, p. 215 f.; on **incitement to hatred** see *Rohrßen*, p. 125 ff.

[335] On this, cf. *Wogersien*; also *Vogl*, p. 187.

[336] On this, cf. *van Bebber*, Wiedergutgemacht?; also *Vogl*, Wiedergutmachung, p. 187.

[337] *Vogl*, Wiedergutmachung, p. 190 ff.

[338] *Vogl*, op. cit.

annulled.[339] The condition was that the injustice committed was a specifically National Socialist form of injustice. Legislation provided assistance in determining whether this was the case with some additional criteria and a catalogue of a total of 59 laws from the NS period, any application of which was irrebuttably considered to fulfil this condition.[340]

3. Prosecution of Crimes Committed During the National Socialist Period

The topic of the "prosecution of National Socialist crimes" forms part of Germany's coming to terms (*Aufarbeitung*) with its National Socialist past. While conducted only hesitantly at first, from the 1970s onwards it developed into a central theme in the Federal Republic of Germany, supported by broad political consensus.[341]

It was the Allies who first dealt with **National Socialist crimes**, and with the aspects listed under § 5 V. 8. above all. The most important war criminals, i.e. the 22 surviving NS leaders, were tried in the **Nuremberg Trial of the Major War Criminals** before the International Military Tribunal. The term "war criminals" is inaccurate, for war crimes formed only one of several crime complexes being tried. The tribunal also tried crimes against peace and—most significantly for the future development of law—crimes against humanity, as well as *conspiracy* (a complex hard to grasp under the categories of continental European law), which could be used to declare not just individuals, but organisations criminal.[342]

---

339 Law to Annul Unjust Sentences Imposed during the National Socialist Administration of Criminal Justice of 25 August 1998 (BGBl. I, p. 2501).

340 More detail in *Vogl*, Wiedergutmachung, p. 195.

341 Collection of the verdicts passed on NS crimes: *C.F. Ruter/D.W. de Mildt* (Eds.), Justiz und NS-Verbrechen. Die deutschen Strafverfahren wegen nationalsozialistischer Tötungsverbrechen 1945–1999. 22 vols. Munich 1998; also available digitally: www.jur.uva.nl/junsv/.

342 Most recently on the Nuremberg Trials and their significance for the further development of international criminal law: *Herbert R. Reginbogin/Christoph J.M. Safferling* (Eds.), The Nuremberg Trials/Die Nürnberger Prozesse. International Criminal Law Since 1945/ Völkerstrafrecht seit 1945. Munich 2006: earlier publications include: *Bradley F. Smith*, Reaching Judgement at Nuremberg. London 1977; record of proceedings: *International Military Tribunal Nuremberg* (Ed.), Trial of The Major War Criminals Before The International Military Tribunal Nuremberg (14 November 1945 to 1 October 1946). Nuremberg 1947–1949. Available electronically from the Library of Congress under http://www.loc.gov/rr/frd/Military_Law/NT_major-war-criminals.html. Text of the sentences in: *Lothar Gruchmann* (Introduction), Das Urteil von Nürnberg 1946. 3rd edition. Munich (dtv) 1977; a participant's point of view (that of a member of the prosecution and later chief prosecutor of the so-called follow-up trials) is given in *Telford Taylor*, An Anatomy of the Nuremberg Trials. A Personal Memoir. London 1993; from the point of view of contemporary court reporters: *Steffen Radlmaier* (Ed.), Der Nürnberger Lernprozeß. Von Kriegsverbrechern und Starreportern. Frankfurt am Main 2001; Prosecutor Harris's point of view is given in *Whitney R. Harris*, Tyranny on Trial: The Trial of the Major German War Criminals at the End of the World War II at Nuremberg, Germany 1945–1946. Revised edition

The decision to hold the proceedings before a "tribunal of victors" was in part due to the unsatisfactory results of the approach taken after World War I: in the Treaty of Versailles, Germany had been given responsibility for trying German war crimes in the Reich Supreme Court. The lack of a functioning judicial infrastructure in ravaged post-war Germany also played a role.[343]

After the 218 days of the trial, twelve of the accused were sentenced to death, three were given lifelong prison sentences, and four fixed-term prison sentences; three defendants were acquitted. Four organisations (the SS, Sicherheitsdienst [SD], Gestapo and NSDAP Führerkorps) were declared criminal.

There followed the so-called Nuremberg Follow-up Trials (*Nachfolgeprozesse*)[344] against various occupational groups—including jurists, diplomats (the Ministries or so-called Wilhelmstraße Trial), medics, industrialists[345]—and the so-called Einsatzgruppen Trial. These proceedings were no longer conducted jointly by the main victorious nations (France, Great Britain, the Soviet Union and the USA), but only by the American occupying forces.

International liability had been in the offing ever since the nineteenth century and had for decades informed the debate on criminal and international law; it now took on concrete shape in the Nuremberg Trials.[346] The structure of charges, only agreed on right at the end of preparations,[347] contributed to creating a doctrine of international criminal law. Of course, the acceptability of the "Nuremberg Principles" suffered from the fact that one of the victorious nations, the USSR, was itself already responsible for countless crimes against humanity at the time, and in the time that followed, neither France in the Algerian War nor the US in the Vietnam War were prepared to apply these principles to themselves. Only the crimes against humanity committed after the end of the Cold War in former Yugoslavia and Rwanda led to the creation of ad hoc tribunals in the Hague and Arusha and to the creation of the permanent International Criminal Court.

1999. On *conspiracy* cf. *Grässle-Münscher*, Kriminelle Vereinigung, p. 83; *Christoph Safferling*, Die Strafbarkeit wegen "Conspiracy" in Nürnberg und ihre Bedeutung für die Gegenwart, in: KritV 2010, 65 ff.

[343] On the Leipzig war crimes trial, cf. *Heiko Ahlbrecht*, Geschichte der völkerrechtlichen Strafgerichtsbarkeit im 20. Jahrhundert. Baden-Baden 1999, p. 41 ff., including further references.

[344] An overview of all the subsequent trials can be found in *Gerd R. Überschär* (Ed.), Der Nationalsozialismus vor Gericht. Die alliierten Prozesse gegen Kriegsverbrecher und Soldaten 1943–1953, p. 73 ff.

[345] On the Judges' Trial, cf. *Klaus Kastner*, "Der Dolch des Mörders war unter der Robe des Juristen verborgen". Der Nürnberger Juristenprozeß 1947, in: JA 1997, 699 ff.; updated version in: JoJZG 2007, 81 ff.; on the Wilhelmstraße Trial (1948/49), in: Festschrift für Heinz Stöckel (2010), p. 499 ff.

[346] On this, cf. e.g. *Daniel Marc Segesser*, Die historischen Wurzeln des Begriffs "Verbrechen gegen die Menschlichkeit", in: JJZG 8 (2006/2007), 75 ff.

[347] On the history of the Nuremberg Trials, cf. *Ahlbrecht*, Strafgerichtsbarkeit, p. 65 ff.; *Christina Möller*, Völkerstrafrecht und Internationaler Strafgerichtshof. Kriminologische, straftheoretische und rechtspolitische Aspekte. Münster 2003, p. 75 ff.

Once the Cold War had begun, the Western Allies were keen for (West) Germany to rearm and become a member of NATO, and their eagerness to continue the prosecution of NS crimes waned. A wave of pardons at the beginning of the 1950s[348] put an end to this chapter in Germany's dealing with its past. After jurisdiction passed to the German courts, the prosecution of NS crimes was conducted in a markedly more lax manner.

This was one part of the "hushing up" of the past (*Herrmann Lübbe*) that may have helped to create political consensus and thus a comparatively peaceful economic recovery in the early Federal Republic. During the Cold War, references to formerly high-ranking and discredited National Socialists in the early Federal Republic's political and economic elite and in academic chairs – not least chairs of law – provided the East with ammunition that was all the more difficult to refute as it was partly hard fact.[349] If reminders to engage in *Vergangenheitsbewältigung*, coming to terms with the past, called for actual political consequences rather than appearing as mere soap-box oratory, they were often shrugged off as Communist propaganda.[350]

There was a widespread mentality of "drawing a line" under the past. It was encouraged by the fact that most evidence, particularly for the genocide of the European Jews, was located on the other side of the "Iron Curtain". This evidence was partly kept back for political reasons, but also partly rendered either inaccessible or so difficult to access due to the complicated diplomatic situation that this provided a (perhaps not unwelcome) reason to discontinue proceedings. It was only after the so-called **Ulm Einsatzgruppen Trial** of 1958[351] that the prosecution of NS crimes began to move forward. As chance would have it, a trial was conducted in 1958 in Ulm against former members of an "*Einsatzgruppe*" or task force for mass shootings of Jews on the German-Lithuanian border; it emerged that none of the leaders of these task forces had been prosecuted for these atrocities, neither in the Western Occupation Zones nor in the Eastern Zone. The State Ministers of Justice Conference debated the matter, coming to the realisation that all of this material had been left to chance and fell under the jurisdiction of the prosecution at the individual places where the *notitia criminis* had been received, more or less at random. Therefore, a systematic, clarifying investigation was necessary. It was decided to create a central authority for the whole of Germany under the aegis of the Minister of Justice of Baden-Württemberg and which had its seat in Ludwigsburg. It took up its work on 1 December 1958. In April 1959, its jurisdiction was extended

[348] *Werle*, op. cit., p. 144: "A downright pardoning frenzy broke out".

[349] On the "Braunbuch" campaign against West German "NS blood judges", cf. *Michael Greve*, Der justitielle und rechtspolitische Umgang mit den NS-Gewaltverbrechen in den sechziger Jahren. Frankfurt am Main et al. 2001, 2nd chapter; cf. also *Hans-Eckhard Niermann*, Zwischen Unbehagen und Verdrängung. Die Reaktion in Richterschaft und Justizverwaltung des Oberlandesgerichtsbezirks Hamm auf die „Braunbuch-Kampagne" der DDR 1957 bis 1968, in: Requate, Recht und Justiz im gesellschaftlichen Aufbruch (1960–1975), p. 103 ff.

[350] On the political background, cf. *Frei*, Vergangenheitspolitik; *Peter Steinbach*, Nationalsozialistische Gewaltverbrechen. Die Diskussion in der deutschen Öffentlichkeit nach 1945. Berlin 1981; for Austria, cf. *Rabofsy/Oberkofler*, p. 207 ff.

[351] On this, cf. *Rückerl*, p. 140; *Werle*, Bestrafung, p. 146 ff.; *Werle/Wandres*, Auschwitz, p. 23 f.

to investigate all NS crimes, regardless of whether they had been committed on what was now Federal German territory or outside it. Thus it happened that trials for NS crimes were taken up again in the 1960s. After its initial investigations, the Central Office passed its files on to the prosecution departments responsible, and the trials began.

The creation of the Ludwigsburg **Central Office of the State Administrations of Justice** for prosecuting National Socialist crimes led to an intensification and systematisation of prosecution.[352] The results that followed are remarkable.[353] The **Frankfurt Auschwitz Trials** (1963–1965)[354] were the focus of worldwide attention—not least due to their literary accompaniment, *Peter Weiss's* play "The Investigation".[355]

Years of delay had of course made it impossible to prosecute many crimes, for the **statute of limitation** for all cases except the offence of murder lapsed in the early 1960s, unless interrupted in time. A legislative error made when passing the Introductory Act to the Law on Regulatory Offences (EGOWiG) of 1968, where it is unclear to this day whether it was not engineered by a National Socialist sympathiser in the Federal Ministry of Justice,[356] meant that the statute of limitation also applied for the offence of aiding murder. The start-date for the statute of limitation for violent NS crimes had at first been set as 8 May 1945; when the statute of limitation for murder, which was 20 years at the time, threatened to expire in 1965, the start-date of the statute of limitations was shifted, this time to the foundation of the Federal Republic in 1949.[357] In 1969, the statue of limitation for murder was extended to 30 years and was abolished completely 10 years later.

---

[352] *Rückerl*, p. 141 ff.; cf. also *Rüdiger Fleiter*, Die Ludwigsburger Zentrale Stelle und ihr politisches und gesellschaftliches Umfeld, in: Geschichte in Wissenschaft und Unterricht (GWU) 53 (2002), 32 ff.

[353] Numbers in *Werle*, Bestrafung, p. 148; *Vassalli*, Radbruchsche Formel p. 190, including numerous references. The tremendous difficulties that literally got in the way of the Central Office's work in the first years should not be forgotten. The political and administrative establishment of Baden-Württemberg reacted both frantically and threateningly to prosecutor *Barbara Just-Dahlmann's* official statements. Due to her knowledge of the Polish language, Dahlmann had been transferred to the Central Office to translate as many documents as possible before the statute of limitations barred the prosecution of murder in 1960. In the course of her work, she had to contend with the understaffing of the office, working on the translations day and night with her husband in a race to remain ahead of the expiry of the statute of limitations. More detail in *Helmut Kramer*, Laudatio zur Verleihung des Arnold-Freymuth-Preises an Barbara Just-Dahlmann, in: JJZG 2 (2000/2001), 238 ff.

[354] On this, cf. *Werle*, Bestrafung, p. 148 ff.; *Id./Wandres*, Auschwitz.

[355] *Hermann Langbein*, Der Auschwitz-Prozeß. Eine Dokumentation. 2 volumes. Vienna 1965. Reprint Frankfurt am Main 1995; *Werle/Wandres*, Auschwitz vor Gericht.

[356] More detail in *Michael Greve*, Amnestierung von NS-Gehilfen—eine Panne? In: JJZG 4 (2002/2003), 295 ff.

[357] This was not simply a new "calculation" of the statute of limitation (as implied by the legislator), but rather a retrospective extension of the limitation period (as clarified but not criticised by the Federal Constitutional Court; BVfGE 25, 295).

From the outset, the theory and doctrine of criminal law were confronted with the problem of retro-activity in dealing with National Socialist crimes. There were several strategies for dealing with this:

1. One could appeal to a *natural law*, i.e. the timeless criminal nature of those actions that until the seventeenth and eighteenth centuries had been called *delicta in se* and that today's terminology would class as belonging to the "core of criminal law". If this is taken as a starting point, there is no problem of retro-activity. What was unlawful then is still unlawful now. This was the argument presented by the Nuremberg Major War Criminals Tribunal, which claimed that the defendants had infringed principles of justice recognised by all the world's civilised nations which claimed validity at all times. It was also the starting point of the **Allied Control Council Law No. 10**, which formed the basis for the so-called Nuremberg Follow-Up Trials.
2. An understanding of law that might be termed "sociological" takes a completely opposite position. Anyone who has succeeded in making state and society follow their orders also creates "law" in their orders. Thus the defendants' actions were lawful at the time, as they concurred with the will of those in power. Conversely, criminal judges of the Federal Republic of Germany can only apply the law of the Federal Republic. And if what was lawful according to the law of the past becomes unlawful according to today's law, then—if guilt exists—a verdict is determined according to today's law, i.e. the law of the Federal Republic of Germany. Going on from here, one could either argue that the prohibition of retrospective legislation is only valid within the Federal Republic of Germany's legal system; or one could limit the prohibition of retrospective legislation by a change in the constitution.[358]
3. Neither of these positions was adopted in the prosecution of National Socialist crimes. Rather, a mixed line of argument was used that built on an external factor,

[358] Had this happened, then the offence of genocide—which then was Section 220a StGB, transferred to the German International Criminal Code in 2002 (Section 6 VStGB)—could have been used. But as such a constitution-changing exception provision was not made and the offence of genocide was only added to the Criminal Code in 1954, it played no role in the prosecution of NS crimes. It was also not possible to apply Art. 7 (2) of the European Convention on Human Rights, which makes an express exception for the prohibition of retrospective legislation in cases where the offence, "at the time when it was committed, was criminal according the general principles of law recognized by civilized nations", for the Federal Republic had explicitly made a reservation for this regulation prior to ratification. The viewpoint discussed under 1 ("natural law") and the view based on the Radbruch formula shared one problem, albeit to differing degrees: their criteria are more or less manageable in cases of top-level crime. The evaluation becomes more difficult in cases of less serious crime. With the Radbruch formula, the question arises of whether every case of killing counts as "insupportable" (on the "*Mauerschützen*", border guards, see below); this is not an issue for the parameter of natural law, but it is questionable down to which level its criteria can securely be applied. One measure might be furnished by the area of offences against the person within the classic *delicta in se*; but beyond these, the judgement becomes more insecure (does a normal case of using threats or force still count? On cases of perverting the course of justice and electoral fraud in dealing with GDR history see below).

namely that the offences in question—murder, causing bodily harm, perverting the course of justice etc.—had already existed then. Thus—so the argument—retroactivity was not an issue.[359] But this problem persisted: though shoved out of the "front door" of the offence definition, it simply returned through the "back door" of unlawfulness. Could the defendants invoke the fact that their actions (which conformed to the offence) were *justified* at the time? Up to this point, the second, "sociological" approach had been followed (if rather cryptically), but now the "natural law" approach came in once again, in the shape of the so-called **Radbruch formula**. Gustav Radbruch developed this formula in his essay "*Gesetzliches Unrecht und übergesetzliches Recht*", published in 1946. Whether this really marked an abandonment of legal positivism seems doubtful. Reading the formula closely, one can see it begins with the sentence:

> The conflict between legal certainty and justice should be solved in favour of the positive law, law certified by statute and authority, even in cases where its content is unjust and its purpose is inexpedient;

only then does the limitation follow for cases where

> the discrepancy between the positive law and justice reaches a level so insupportable that the law has to make way for justice as 'erroneous law' ('*unrichtiges Recht*')

Furthermore, Radbruch recognises cases where statutes are not only "*unrichtiges Recht*" but also "*Nicht-Recht*", "Non-Law", where "justice is not even striven for" and equality, "which forms the core of justice", is "consciously disowned" in the process of positive legislation.

Case law and legal theory embraced this "Radbruch formula" early on. Given the exorbitant nature of NS crimes, its vagueness was not an issue, as it was easy to show plausibly that the conditions were met.[360]

Despite its lack of clarity, the formula thus suggested a pragmatic way of solving the cases in question in practice. Of course, in terms of methodology, legal policy and history, this approach was problematic. *Methodologically*, it obscured the fact that despite the denial retroactivity was actually being applied; in terms of *legal policy*, it was simply disastrous that neither natural law nor the criminal law of the Federal Republic, but – at least in principle – the law of the National Socialist state was used as a basis for decisions; and *historically* – as justly pointed out by Werle[361] – it was simply inappropriate to use National Socialist law of all things as the basis for trying National Socialist mass murder.

---

[359] This is criticised in *Dencker*, note 63, in: *Institut für juristische Zeitgeschichte Hagen*, Euthanasie vor Gericht, p. 405; *Id.*, Die Strafverfolgung der Euthanasie-Täter nach 1945, in: JJZG 7 (2005/2006), 113 ff., here 119 ff.

[360] In the meantime enough time has passed to name the cost that had to be paid for *Vergangenheitsbewältigung* and the justified efforts made to prosecute NS crimes. In this matter, the different viewpoints of historians and legal historians becomes evident: more detail in *Pauli/Vormbaum*, Vorwort, in: Id., Justiz und Nationalsozialismus, p. VII ff., XII; also *Th. Vormbaum*, Vergangenheitsbewältigung im Rechtsstaat, in: Festschrift for Knut Amelung (2009), p. 783 ff.

[361] *Werle*, Bestrafung, p. 153:

In practice, the procedure was to first try to prove the unlawfulness of the behaviour in question according the NS state's own law.

The way in which the perpetrators of the so-called euthanasia project were dealt with furnishes one example of how this argumentation worked: in 1939, Hitler handed a letter to Bouhler, the head of the Chancellery, which instructed Bouhler and Hitler's attending doctor Dr. Brandt to authorise doctors to kill people with incurable mental illnesses and deficiencies. This letter was written on writing paper of Hitler's personal Chancellery, bearing the crest of the Nazi Party, an eagle holding the swastika symbol in its claws. The crest of the German Reich looked exactly the same at the time, with the sole exception that the eagle looked to the right while the eagle on the Party's crest looked to the left. After 1945, the prosecutors in the trial against the euthanasia doctors argued that Hitler's order provided no justification for the defendants' actions, for the letter carried not the crest of the German Reich, but the crest of the Party, meaning that even according to the law of the time Hitler was acting not as the holder of sovereign rights, but as a private individual or a party member. As their actions corresponded to the offence of murder, the doctors accused were liable to prosecution.

I have severe doubts whether this argument is immanently accurate (i.e. accurate within the NS legal system), for according to the understanding of the time, the Nazi Party was a statutory body under public law and thus carried sovereign rights. Even if this objection is countered by pointing out that the Party was not responsible even then for authorising initiatives such as the euthanasia project, the objection still remains that a separation of the *Führer's* person into a party and a private person would never have been accepted back then.

This procedure shows that behaviour was first attempted to be proven unlawful according the NS state's own law; only if this proved unsuccessful was recourse taken to the Radbruch formula.[362]

Within the framework thus set, the Federal German criminal justice system created its own hurdles, which meant that a significant number of criminals—if they were even put on trial—escaped punishment.

Concerning National Socialist **violent crime**, the question arose whether those accused were to be punished as principal offenders or secondary participants. The thesis developed by Federal German courts was that according to the subjective theory of participation—which was dominant at the time—only a handful of National Socialist leaders, and above all Hitler, could be regarded as principals, as only they possessed criminal intent; if there was any room for doubt, all other lower-ranking participants were regarded as mere secondary participants.[363] Exceptions were made for so-called "*Exzesstäter*", perpetrators of excessive

[362] On this, *Vera Große-Vehne*, Tötung auf Verlangen etc., p. 130 ff.; cf. also *Id.*, Die nationalsozialistischen Pläne für ein "Euthanasie-Gesetz", in: JoJZG 1 (2007), 2 ff.; a critical point of view in *Friedrich Dencker*, note 62 ff., in: *Institut für juristische Zeitgeschichte Hagen*, Euthanasie vor Gericht, p. 401 ff.

[363] *Jörg Friedrich*, Die kalte Amnestie. NS-Täter in der Bundesrepublik. Frankfurt am Main (Fischer-TB) 1984, p. 321 ff.; most recently, *Heinz-Willi Heinckes*, Täterschaft und Teilnahme

violence, particularly those who had committed sadistic acts or acts that went beyond the orders received and the framework within the system. However, because the form of participation determined the range of applicable sentences and this in turn determined the length of the statute of limitation, the long delay in prosecuting National Socialist crimes took effect here, and many proceedings had to be discontinued as the statute of limitation had expired.

In the area of **unlawful acts committed by the judiciary**, the hurdles to sentencing judicial offenders brought about the remarkable result that *not one single* judge—neither of the special courts, nor the People's Court, nor the military courts—was prosecuted by the Federal German justice system for any of the thousands of death sentences pronounced.[364] The most significant hurdles were the following: on the one hand, it was argued that there was a so-called "*Richterprivileg*" (judicial privilege), according to which a judge could only be prosecuted for the content of their verdicts—for example, capital punishment, imprisonment for murder or false imprisonment as principal by proxy—if these also constituted the offence of perverting the course of justice. Arguments in favour of this privilege stated that it protected the judges' independence and their initiative in reaching a decision, and also took account of the judges' duty to reach a verdict.[365] It would seem that this so-called *Richterprivileg* was invented ad hoc after 1945. As far as can be seen, the first time it can be found is in the aforementioned 1946 essay by *Gustav Radbruch*, "Gesetzliches Unrecht und übergesetzliches Recht".[366]

But this was not the only hurdle: perverting the course of justice can only be committed with intent; if the law or the nature of the matter does not demand otherwise, then according to generally accepted opinion intent is present if there is a *dolus eventualis* i.e. conditional intent. However, judicial practice demanded *dolus directus* for perverting the course of justice intentionally.[367] As the particular structure of the offence of perverting the course of justice means that the awareness of unlawfulness factually coincides with the intent to commit the offence, the judges accused were able to plead that they had not thought their past actions were unlawful. All of the adjudicating judges believed this; indeed, the more

bei NS-Tötungsverbrechen. Analyse und Kritik der Rechtsprechung des Bundesgerichtshofes. Bonn (jur. Diss.) 2005.

[364] On the last (unsuccessful) attempt to prosecute a People's Court judge (the Rehse case), cf. instead of many other sources *Freudiger*, Aufarbeitung, p. 386 ff.

[365] During the 1980s, as part of the research for his habilitation, the author searched through all available textbooks, commentaries and court decisions up to 1945, and found not a single passage referring to such a *Richterprivileg*; his doctoral student Carsten Thiel, who has recently investigated the history of the offence of perverting the course of justice since the 19th century, conducted a further, even broader search and reached the same negative conclusion; cf. *Vormbaum*, Schutz des Strafurteils, p. 354 ff.; *Thiel*, Rechtsbeugung, p. 136 ff.

[366] *Radbruch*, Gesetzliches Unrecht, p. 15.

[367] Cf. references in *Ursula Schmidt-Speicher*, Hauptprobleme der Rechtsbeugung. Berlin 1982, p. 82 ff.

insensitive and hardened the accused judge appeared, the more believable his plea seemed to be.[368]

There certainly are good reasons for a judges' privilege; and there are also good reasons for why only a *dolus directus* corresponds to the offence of perverting the course of justice. It is striking, however, that the sum of both elements – in connection with a sensitive application of the principle *in dubio pro reo*, such as one might wish for in many other proceedings – then led to an "acquittal of the Nazi judiciary", as the historian Jörg Friedrich phrased it in the title of a book.[369] Today, dominant opinion requires only *dolus eventualis* for perverting the course of justice. Lowering the intent threshold is the price paid for the prosecution of NS judges – even though it took place at a time when this chapter of NS *Vergangenheitsbewältigung* was for all purposes over. However, it did take effect when dealing with GDR history.

While sentencing NS criminals was the reactive side of the prosecution of NS crime, the legislation of the late twentieth century pro-actively criminalised denying the Holocaust **(Section 130 (2) StGB)**. Whether this criminalisation of a (doubtlessly heinous) understanding of history has really done the matter any service seems rather doubtful, for reasons of expediency alone. Objectively, however, as a public speech offence it fits in with the late twentieth century trend of "combating" and criminalising the early stages of offences.[370]

4. Early Legislation

While "correcting and coming to terms with the NS period's legal excesses"[371] was of concern on the one hand, on the other hand the early Federal Republic's legislative attitude was one of reticence towards liberal reforms of criminal law. However, this did not preclude tentative, cautious steps towards reform: this phase brought about not only a political criminal law shaped by the Cold War, but also the abolition of capital punishment, the legal regulation of suspended sentences in general criminal law, and the resumption of criminal law reform. Changes in juvenile criminal law were ambiguous: some of the enhanced penalties of the NS period were retained,[372] but juvenile criminal law was (carefully) opened up to young adults.

[368] In more detail, *Schmidt-Speicher*, op. cit., p. 105 ff.; *Freudiger*, Aufarbeitung, p. 395.

[369] *Jörg Friedrich*, Freispruch für die Nazi-Justiz. Eine Dokumentation. Reinbek 1983.

[370] On the state of the law in EU states and the theoretical debate on memory enshrined in criminal law, cf. *Emanuela Fronza*, Recht und Gedenken. Ein schwieriger Dialog, in: JJZG 6 (2004/2005), 435 ff.; on the history of Section 130 StGB cf. the Ph.D. thesis of *Benedikt Rohrßen*, Von der Aufreizung zum Klassenkampf zur Volksverhetzung. Berlin, 2009.

[371] *Welp*, Nachkriegszeit, p. 315.

[372] *Kubink*, Strafen, p. 381; *Meyer-Höger*, Jugendarrest, p. 118 ff.

Art. 102 of the Basic Law abolished **capital punishment**—nearly 80 years after the Reichstag had once before determined this in the second reading stage.[373] The following 15 years were characterised by repeated but unsuccessful attempts to reverse this decision.[374]

The first criminal laws of the new West German Republic were triggered, shaped or accompanied by political events—the Cold War first and foremost, which threatened to develop into another World War with the Korean War, and which caused Germany's division to become ever more entrenched. The **Protection of Personal Liberty Act**, with which the majority of the Bundestag risked conflict with the occupying forces, marked the beginning.[375] The Act made the abduction of a person from the Federal Republic (i.e. primarily: to the GDR) an offence, as well as accusing or reporting a person to the police, if this

> thereby exposes him to the danger of being persecuted for political reasons and, in violation of the principles of the rule of law, of suffering harm to life and limb through violence or arbitrary measures, of being deprived of his freedom or of being seriously prejudiced in his professional or financial circumstances.[376]

While this Act could be seen as a weapon of defence in the Cold War, the Cold War soon after brought about a (now democratic) "strong state"[377] which shaped the **offences against the state**[378] that remained in force until 1968. These offences encountered a criminal justice system that was, once again, an "understanding ally" of the legislator.[379]

The convictions of thousands of communists provided East German propaganda with welcome ammunition. Yet, blatant miscarriages of justice—thus the insights of a conference on political justice 1951–1968[380]—have not come to light; and the legislature itself declared it had a bad feeling when passing the law.

The **Third Criminal Law Amendment Act** of 1953 returned criminal law to a formally secure foundation—but for the area of West Germany only, thus accepting the separation of Germany it made manifest. This included adopting many laws from the National Socialist period, including several problematic ones. At the same

---

[373] *Bernhard Duesing*, Die Abschaffung der Todesstrafe in der Bundesrepublik Deutschland. Offenbach am Main 1952, p. 276 ff.; *Evans*, Rituals, p. 797 ff.

[374] For a detailed study of this topic, cf. *Yvonne Hötzel*, Debatten um die Todesstrafe in der Bundesrepublik Deutschland (1949–1989). Berlin 2011.

[375] Habeas Corpus Act ("Gesetz zum Schutz der persönlichen Freiheit") of 15 July 1951, *Vormbaum/Welp*, StGB, No. 60; *Welp*, Nachkriegszeit, p. 153.

[376] Sections 234a ff. and Section 241a StGB as amended by the Protection of Personal Liberty Act; *Vormbaum/Welp*, StGB, No. 60.

[377] *Kubink*, Strafen, p. 319.

[378] In detail on their development, *Schiffers*, Bürgerfreiheit; *F.-C. Schroeder*, Schutz, p. 178 ff.

[379] *Alexander von Brünneck*, Politische Justiz gegen Kommunisten in der Bundesrepublik Deutschland 1949–1968. Frankfurt am Main (edition Suhrkamp) 1978; also the contributions in: *Justizministerium NRW* (Ed.), Politische Strafjustiz 1951–1968; also *Diether Posser*, Anwalt im Kalten Krieg. 3rd edition. Baden-Baden 1999.

[380] *Justizministerium NRW* (Ed.), Strafjustiz, p. 72.

time, the Act also included pioneering innovations, such as suspended sentences and early release on parole (*bedingte Entlassung*).[381]

The **Juvenile Court Act** of 1953 repealed changes made during the NS period, reintroducing suspended sentences and abolishing short custodial sentences of less than 6 months. However, the juvenile detention introduced in 1943 was retained.[382]

5. Continuation and (Preliminary) Completion of Penal Reform

Beyond the above, the legislator was somewhat reluctant to change the Criminal Code. This was probably due to the fact that soon after the foundation of the Federal Republic of Germany, Federal Minister of Justice *Thomas Dehler*, supported by encouragement from the midst of the Bundestag, initiated the resumption of work on the comprehensive reform of criminal law. To that end, the Federal Ministry of Justice first commissioned 18 leading German teachers of criminal law to create a report on basic questions of the reform of criminal law.[383] Besides these reports, comparative legal studies on all important themes of the General and Special Part were produced.[384] Following this preliminary work, a Grand Criminal Law Commission was convened in the spring of 1954, presided over by Dehler's successor, Federal Minister of Justice *Neumayer*.[385]

---

[381] *Welp*, Strafgesetzgebung, p. 169 ff.

[382] On this, cf. *Meyer-Höger*, Jugendarrest, p. 138 ff.

[383] Materialien zur Strafrechtsreform Vol. 1. Bonn 1954: Gutachten der Strafrechtslehrer. The reports were created by *Edmund Mezger*, *Bernhard Schmidt*, *Paul Bockelmann*, *Hans Welzel*, *Ernst Heinitz*, *Richard Lange*, *Thomas Würtenberger*, *Rudolf Sieverts*, *Wilhelm Gallas*, *Werner Niese*, *Karl Schneidewien*, *Reinhart Maurach*, *Hellmuth Mayer*, *Hellmuth von Weber*, *Horst Schröder*, *Eduard Kern* (2x) and *Arthur Wegner*; cf. also (without numerical attribution to the "Materialien zur Strafrechtsreform"): Gutachten und Stellungnahmen zu Fragen der Strafrechtsreform mit ärztlichem Einschlag. Bonn (Bundesministerium der Justiz) 1958. Reports were created by *W. Bitter*, *K. Ernst*, *R. Gaupp*, *Hans Walter Gruhle*, *E. Kretschmer*, *Albrecht Langelüddeke* and *Theodor Ziehen*. Nine medical and psychiatric professional bodies provided commentaries, including the German Society of Psychotherapy and Depth Psychology accompanied by reports from *Alexander Mitscherlich* and *Jutta von Graevenitz*.

[384] Materialien zur Strafrechtsreform. Vol. 2: Rechtsvergleichende Arbeiten (in 2 separate volumes for the General and Special Part), created by the Department for Foreign and International Law in Freiburg. Bonn 1954.

[385] The Commission was made up of: representatives of the German Bundestag: *Hoogen* (CDU/CSU), *Rehs* (SPD), *Schneider* (FDP), *Czermak* (BG/BHE), *Merkatz* (DP); criminal law theorists: *Paul Bockelmann*, *Wilhelm Gallas*, *Hans-Heinrich Jescheck*, *Richard Lange*, *Edmund Mezger*, *Eberhard Schmidt*, *Hans Welzel*; representative of the German Judges Association: *Resch*; representative of the legal profession: *Dahs*; representatives of the Federal Court of Justice and the Federal Prosecutor General at the BGH: *Baldus*, *Wiechmann*; specially appointed individual members: *Koffka*, *Niethammer*, *Richter*, *Schäfer* and *Skott*.

The Commission first convened on 6 April 1954 and decided to have consultations on the Special Part prepared by three independent subcommittees. The Draft of 1927 (Reichstagsvorlage) was to serve as the main basis for consultation in the subcommittees. In addition—as the guidelines for the work of the subcommittees state with remarkable nonchalance—the variations in the Draft of 1936 were to be read against the Reichstagsvorlage, so as to determine whether any individual changes contained in the former should be given preference over the latter. In the time that followed, the subcommittees developed various suggestions, and these were then collected in a preliminary compilation (*vorläufige Zusammenstellung*, VZ); this in turn was to form the basis for the deliberations of the Grand Commission of Criminal Law in the first reading.

After the first reading by the Grand Commission was completed, the Federal Ministry of Justice compiled all of the resolutions and recommendations and presented **Draft 1959 I**. **Draft 1959 II** combined the results of the consultations of the second reading, the comments of the federal governmental departments and the state administrations of justice, as well as requests for changes submitted by the consultants of the Federal Ministry of Justice.[386] This was presented to a States Commission convened by the Minister of Justice of North Rhine-Westphalia for review. In a total of 17 meetings from September 1959 to January 1962, the Commission developed suggestions for changes, most of which referred to the General Part. Some of the States Commission's preliminary results were taken by the Federal Government and incorporated into Draft 1959 II, thus creating the **1960 Draft.**[387] On 7 October 1960, this Draft was introduced in the Federal Council. In order to speed up the process, the Council passed the draft without changes in its meeting on 28 October 1960. Speed was of the essence, as the end of the third legislative period was approaching.

[386] On the deliberations of individual offences and groups of offences in the Special Part within the framework of the reform of criminal law (including the alternative drafts), cf. on **political criminal law** *Schroeder*, Schutz, p. 211 ff.; on **testimony offences** Vormbaum, Eid, p. 150 ff.; on **the offence of omitting to effect an easy rescue** *Gieseler*, p. 96 ff., 118 ff.; on **criminal and terrorist/anarchist organisations** *Felske*, p. 306 ff.; on the **failure to report a crime** *Kisker*, p. 131 ff.; on **duelling** *Baumgarten*, p. 224 ff.; on **theft** *Prinz*, p. 137 ff., 162 ff.; on **false accusation** and **misleading the authorities about the commission of a crime** *Bernhard*, p. 137 ff.; on **arson** *Lindenberg*, p. 124 ff.; on **assault** *Gröning*, p. 47 ff.; on the **perverting the course of justice** *Thiel*, p. 115 ff.; on **mercy killing** *Große-Vehne*, p. 167 ff.; on the **frustration of creditors' rights** *Seemann*, p. 100 ff.; on **defamation of the head of state** *Andrea Hartmann*, p. 256 ff.; on **prostitution, procuring and pandering** *Ilya Hartmann*, p. 216 ff.; on **trespass** *Rampf*, p. 124 ff.; on **embezzlement** and **unlawful appropriation** *Rentrop*, p. 168 ff.; on **forgery of documents** *Prechtel*, p. 185 ff.; on **road traffic law**, *Asholt*, p. 160 ff.; on **incitement to hatred** *Rohrßen*, p. 173 ff.; on **capital punishment** *Hötzel*, p. 175 ff.—**Richard Lange**, already mentioned several times in the course of the present book, was the only teacher of criminal law in the committee who voted for a reintroduction of capital punishment, cf. *Hötzel*, p. 188, footnote 89.

[387] *Vormbaum/Rentrop*, Reform, Vol. 3, p. 109 ff.

After the federal elections in August 1961, the newly formed Federal Government once again took up the 1960 Draft. It was revised and finally submitted to the Federal Council for deliberation in July 1962 as **Draft 1962.**[388] Draft 1962 adopted most offences in the versions used in the 1960 draft.

In its 248th meeting on 2 and 13 July 1962, the Federal Council raised no objections to the government proposal. However, some state governments thought it appropriate to make some fundamental critical observations on the draft—which Federal Minister of Justice *Stammberger* praised as the most significant German legislative enterprise since the Civil Code—before it was referred to the Bundestag. The Prime Minister of Hesse advocated a gradual revision of criminal law, meant to supplement and improve the current state of the law. Baden-Württemberg, North Rhine-Westphalia and Lower Saxony also expressed disappointment that many of their suggestions and proposals developed by the States Commission had not been included. This disapproval of the government proposals also gradually became established in criminal law academia. Although the critics took very different starting points, they all approved of the reform of criminal law in principle, but broadly concurred in rejecting the Draft of 1962 as a suitable basis. The opinion in the literature mainly seemed to be that neither the Grand Commission for the Reform of Criminal Law nor the federal government had any concrete ideas for criminal policy, and that attempts were being made to compensate for this lack by a continued entrenchment of moral prohibitions and rules in criminal law. The state had the right to impose punishment only where its regulations aimed to create a particular effect in terms of criminal policy, but not where it was concerned merely with citizens' moral or ethical behaviour. The reform debate was sometimes fierce; particular controversy was attached to the question of punishment for simple homosexuality and adultery, artificial insemination using donor sperm, and the criminological and social indication criteria of the offence of abortion. The Tübingen professor of criminal law **Jürgen Baumann** (1922–2003) was the main critic of the Draft of 1962.[389]

The Bundestag passed the Draft in the first reading and referred it to the Committee on Legal Affairs; on 3 May 1963, the Committee appointed a subcommittee for "Criminal Law", which on 4 December 1963 was changed to an autonomous special committee independent of the Committee of Legal Affairs, chaired by former Federal Prosecutor General **Max Güde** (1902–1984).[390] By the end of the legislative period in 1965, it had only been able to debate the General Part in any detail. Only a few weeks prior to the inaugural meeting of the Fifth Bundestag, the draft was introduced anew by the ruling parties CDU/CSU and FDP. Thus they

---

[388] *Vormbaum/Rentrop*, Reform, Vol. 3, p. 245 ff.

[389] *Jürgen Baumann*, Kleine Streitschriften zur Strafrechtsreform. 10 Beiträge. Bielefeld 1965; *Id.* (Ed.), Programm für ein neues Strafgesetzbuch. Der Alternativentwurf der Strafrechtslehrer. Frankfurt am Main 1968; *Id.* (Ed.), Mißlingt die Strafrechtsreform? Der Bundestag zwischen Regierungsentwurf von 1962 und Alternativ-Entwurf der Strafrechtslehrer von 1966. Neuwied and Berlin 1969; *Id.*, Weitere Streitschriften zur Strafrechtsreform. 10 Beiträge. Bielefeld 1969.

[390] On Güde, cf. *Volker Tausch*, Max Güde (1902–1984). Generalbundesanwalt und Rechtspolitiker. Baden-Baden 2002.

hoped to avoid the more time-consuming process of a new federal government bill, which would have required first a cabinet resolution and a response from the Bundesrat before the first reading could have taken place. On 13 January 1966, the first reading in the Bundestag took place and the draft was transferred to the "Special Committee for the Reform of Criminal Law", which commenced its work the very next day.

In the Grand Coalition, Gustav Heinemann, a politician of the SPD – a party which had been hesitant [about the reform] up until then – became Minister of Justice at the end of 1966. Despite his express determination to have the whole of the criminal law reformed by the end of the current legislative period using the Draft of 1962 as a basis, i.e. by 1969, the "breakthrough" anticipated failed to take place due to the changed political situation.[391]

In parallel to the "official" reform work, a circle of criminal law academics came together in 1965. They produced an **alternative draft** of a criminal code, the General Part of which was published in October 1966, soon to be followed by various drafts of selected sections of the Special Part.[392] Besides the Draft of 1962, the Special Committee for the Reform of Criminal Law also considered these alternative drafts in the 101 meetings of its consultation process; the alternative drafts had been submitted on the initiative of the FDP faction, who had been in the opposition since the end of 1966. Due to the sheer quantity of material to be perused, the complexity of the subject-matter and the momentousness of the decisions to be taken, it became clear that the entire reform could not be carried out within one parliamentary term. Therefore the Special Committee deferred revising the Special Part of the StGB for the time being, and suggested that first two acts related to particularly significant reforms of criminal policy should be passed.

The **First Criminal Law Reform Act** (1st StrRG of 25 June 1969) completely overhauled the system of sanctions by using measures such as replacing penitentiary and prison by uniform imprisonment, restricting short-term prison sentences, extending suspended sentences, linking measures of reform and incapacitation to the principle of proportionality, and abolishing workhouses and the loss of civil rights. In the Special Part, provisions that no longer seemed appropriate or expedient were repealed—e.g. facilitating escape of prisoners through negligence, grossly negligent false accusation, adultery, duelling laws and bestiality. At the same time, the areas of offences against religion and forgery of technical records were modified, thus limiting the ambit of criminal law in some areas while extending it in others.

The **Second Criminal Law Reform Act** of 4 July 1969 resulted in changes to individual fundamental regulations of the Criminal Code's General Part. We should here mention derivative omission offences, mistake of fact, mistake of law, attempts, principals and secondary participation, and necessity. The continuing

[391] *Uwe Scheffler*, Das Reformzeitalter 1953–1975, in: Vormbaum/Welp, StGB, supplementary volume I, p. 174, 182 ff.

[392] *Vormbaum/Rentrop*, Reform, Vol. 3, p. 401 ff.

reform of the system of sanctions lay at the heart of the Second Criminal Law Reform Act, for example raising the minimum term for imprisonment to 1 month and introducing the day unit fine system, social therapy institutions and supervision orders. In editorial terms, a completely new General Part was incorporated in the Criminal Code. The section on **transgressions** was deleted. The respective offences were either repealed, changed into regulatory offences or upgraded to misdemeanours.

The initial plan was for this newly edited version to enter into force in 1973. This was postponed to 1 January 1975, as it was intended to coincide with numerous material and editorial changes to the Special Part that proved to require much time and discussion.[393]

The **Third Criminal Law Reform Act** of 20 May 1970 consisted of reforming the "criminal law on demonstrations". Apart from other amendments, Section 110 StGB o.V. was repealed, Sections 111, 113 and 125 StGB were revised, Section 114 StGB o.V. was replaced and Section 125a StGB introduced.

The **Fourth Criminal Law Reform Act** of 23 November 1973 (BGBl. I, p. 1725) saw the legislature commence the revision of family law and the law on sexual offences by limiting penal sanctions—this affected, for example, regulations on the insufficient supervision of young persons, the falsification of personal status, marriage fraud, squandering family property, refusing support to pregnant women or the violation of duties of care or education, constitute extensive protection of juveniles in the area of sexual offences, liberalising the law on adult sexual offences, and placing all the respective offences under the heading "protection of sexual self-determination".

The **Fifth Criminal Law Reform Act** of 18 June 1974 (BGBl. I, p. 1297) was essentially concerned with amending the law on abortion. The previous felony of "abortion"—which the 1st StrRG had already changed into a misdemeanour—was now no longer subject to punishment if certain criteria were met.

The central aspect of the amendment was the "time limit solution" in Section 218a StGB, according to which abortion was not deemed an offence if carried out during the first three months of pregnancy by a physician with the consent of the pregnant woman. Furthermore, abortion was not subject to punishment even *after* the first 12 weeks of pregnancy if there were medical or embryopathic indications. According to Section 218(3) StGB, abortions carried out by the pregnant woman herself were subject to imprisonment not exceeding 1 year. By contrast, according to Section 218(1) StGB the physician was liable to imprisonment not exceeding 3 years. This was a possibility particularly in cases where the procedure was carried out without prior social (Section 218c(1) No. 1 StGB) or medical (Section 218c (1) No. 2 StGB) counselling. Abortion remained an offence according to Section 219(1) StGB if carried out after the first 3 months of pregnancy, without certification of the necessary indication by a suitable authority.

---

[393] These also entered into force on 1 January 1975 with the Criminal Code Introduction Act (*Vormbaum/Welp*, StGB, No. 98); the entire Criminal Code was publicly announced at the same time (*Vormbaum/Welp*, StGB, No. 103).

However, this law never entered into force as an injunction by the Federal Constitutional Court temporarily blocked it.[394] Until the law was revised, an indication model was to apply.[395] The Federal Constitutional Court's final verdict declared the time limit solution unconstitutional.[396] The majority of the Court's senate in particular was of the opinion that unborn life was subject to protection according to Art. 2(1) GG, and fundamentally took precedence over the autonomy of the pregnant woman. Furthermore, the Court deduced a corresponding state duty of protection from the objective substance of the fundamental right contained in the Basic Law, according to which the state was required to protect and nurture unborn life throughout the entire pregnancy. Exceptions could only be considered in cases where a continuation of pregnancy was insupportable, particularly in cases of medical, embryopathic, criminological or social indications. A general exception to liability, based purely on the stage of pregnancy and compliance with certain procedures, was deemed incompatible with the constitution.[397]

Thus the legislator was forced to pass a law that went against its visions of criminal policy. It is no surprise, therefore, that it made full use of the room for manoeuvre that remained. This led to an indication model which assumed that abortion was an offence in principle, but entrenched a medical-social indication that also included embryopathic, criminological and social indications. As far as Section 218(3) 2nd sentence StGB was concerned, the amendment could actually be characterised as a "disguised time limit solution", for the pregnant woman was not punished if the procedure was carried out in the first 22 weeks of pregnancy by a physician after a consultation according to Section 218b(1) Nos. 1 and 2 StGB. No indication had to be proven. The physician was still subject to punishment, but this hurdle could be overcome by having the abortion abroad.

Reviewing the "age of reform" (*Scheffler*), its positive results doubtlessly include the liberalisation of the **law on sexual offences**; the liberalisation of **political criminal law** in 1968 (Eighth Criminal Law Amendment Act), brought about by an easing of tension in world politics; reducing the use of **short-term imprisonment** (Sections 38, 47 StGB) and expanding the ambit of **suspended sentences** (Section 56 StGB) and **conditional early release** (Section 57 StGB). The drastic fall in the number of incapacitation orders following the revision of Section 66 StGB should also be mentioned—a trend that has reversed since the 1990s, making incapacitation orders the focus of criminal politicians' and tabloid journalists' desires for exclusion.

However, closer study would be necessary to determine the extent to which the reform of criminal law has led to a limitation of criminal law in terms of offence descriptions on the one hand, and to increasingly lenient punishments in terms of

[394] BVerfGE 37, 324.

[395] BVerfGE 37, 324, 325.

[396] BVerfGE 39, 1, 65, 68.

[397] The *minority* of the senate argued that deducing a *duty* to punish from the rules of the Basic Law actually turned the liberal content of the fundamental rights into their opposite.

sentences on the other. There are notable counter-examples, for example the upgrading of **petty food theft** (*Mundraub*) to a misdemeanour (compensated—in a manner not really reconcilable with the rule of law—by Sections 248a StGB, 153a StPO), replacing qualified offences by **definitional elements** in aggravated theft and relaxing the **provisions on the statute of limitations** (even without considering those made necessary by the prosecution of violent NS crimes). The Special Part in particular would need to be subjected to close scrutiny to determine whether the idea of equating decriminalisation with reform of criminal law (including the alternative drafts[398]) is really justified. Lastly, for the period of reform as for other periods, a consideration of the development of the supplementary penal provisions would be necessary in order to produce a rounded picture. As far as the increased leniency of sanctions is concerned, one should not forget that this is due to a large extent to the increase in offences—escalating once more since the mid-1970s—which the prison system could hardly have coped with if they had all been converted consistently into immediate prison terms.

6. *Criminal Law Theory*

After 1945, a significant portion of the German theory and practice of criminal law began to float in the wake of the **conservative natural law** embraced in the Adenauer era, which led to the revival of a harsh theory of atonement in criminal law. A highly artificial doctrine of criminal law understood itself as a reaction to the "holistic and intuitively value-sensitive methodology" of the NS period.[399]

This renaissance of natural law was justified by the leading proponent of legal relativism and legal positivism before 1933, *Gustav Radbruch,*[400] who in 1946 put forward the theory that the legal positivism taught as part of legal training in the first third of the century had made judges follow the law blindly and strengthened their attitude that "law is law".[401] It is doubtful whether there is any justification for this theory; today it is considered disproven. Quite apart from the fact that the so-called "*Freirechtsschule*" (free law school) formed a strong counter-movement to legal positivism in the legal theory of the 1920s, calling for the judge's position to be strengthened vis-à-vis the legislator and thus (probably unintentionally) pre-empting one of the National Socialists' later demands, it seems doubtful whether Radbruch's statement is factually accurate, for the greater part of

[398] On the suggestions of the "alternative professors" on Road Traffic Law, cf. e.g. *Asholt*, Straßenverkehrsstrafrecht, p. 209 ff.

[399] *Kubink*, Strafen, p. 389.

[400] See most recently *Klaus Adomeit*, Der Rechtspositivismus im Denken von Hans Kelsen und von Gustav Radbruch, in: JuS 2003, 161 ff.; *Christoph M. Scheuren-Brandes*: Der Weg von nationalsozialistischen Rechtslehren zur Radbruchschen Formel. Untersuchungen zur Geschichte der Idee vom "Unrichtigen Recht". Paderborn, Munich, Vienna, Zurich 2006.

[401] Cf. the essay discussed above, *Radbruch*, Gesetzliches Unrecht, p. 10.

scandalous verdicts of the NS period referred to the manipulation of laws from before 1933, and were characterised precisely by the way that National Socialist ideology was employed against the (yet) extant positive wording of the law.[402] This statement may have been accurate in individual cases as far as following the laws passed by the National Socialist legislature was concerned, although it should be pointed out that these laws were often formulated in such a vague way that judges were left considerable room for manoeuvre. Thus the laws demanded that the judges understandingly accommodate the will of the legislator, but not that they follow the law down to the letter in a positivist manner; and in this regard the legislature of the NS period showed itself to be "creative" rather than "positivist".

A large proportion of the very criminal laws passed by the National Socialists provide an example of how problematic the statement (also by *Gustav Radbruch*) is that any positive law – regardless of its content – is better than no law, as it creates legal certainty.[403] This equation of legal positivism and legal certainty is a short circuit, at least as long as the principle of specificity and certain substantive minimum standards are not also taken into account.

For several years around 1960, a fundamental dispute between the so-called ***kausale Handlungslehre*** (**causal theory of action**) and the so-called ***finale Handlungslehre*** (**teleological theory of action**) dominated German criminal law doctrine. While the former corresponded to the traditional definition of action according to the classic turn of the century structure of offences (action as behaviour directed by will, taking effect in the external world),[404] the teleological definition of action, developed by **Hans Welzel** (1904–1977) before 1945,[405] was contingent on many doctrinal factors. According to the teleological theory of action, human action has an ontological (or perhaps better: ontic) structure fundamentally characterised by its *purposefulness* or *teleology* ("*Finalität*"). It goes through the stages of purpose definition, selection of the means necessary to achieve the purpose and realisation of the purpose.[406]

The so-called ***Handlungsunrecht*** (**unlawfulness of the action**) constitutes a fundamental element of the teleological definition of action, and is accompanied by or subordinate to ***Erfolgsunrecht*** (**unlawfulness of the result of an action**), and the resultant ***personaler Unrechtsbegriff*** (**personal concept of unlawfulness**). For

[402] On this, cf. *Wrobel*, p. 215: "If only they had been positivists then!"; also explicitly contradicted in *Reifner*, p. 18 f.; *Eisenhardt*, Rechtsgeschichte, p. 475 f.; *Jettinghoff*, JoJZG 1 (2007), 129 ff., 131. In detail on the debate on the positivism theory, with extensive references, *Vassalli*, Radbruch Formel, p. 26 ff.

[403] *Radbruch*, Gesetzliches Unrecht, op. cit., p. 10.

[404] Cf. in particular *Gustav Radbruch*, Der Handlungsbegriff in seiner Bedeutung für das Strafrechtssystem (1904). Reprinted, edited and with an introduction by Arthur Kaufmann, Darmstadt 1967.

[405] *Hans Welzel*, Kausalität und Handlung, in: ZStW 51 (1932), 703 ff.; *Id.*, Studien zum System des Strafrechts, in: ZStW 58 (1939), 491 ff.; *Id.*, Das neue Bild des Strafrechtssystems. 4th edition. Göttingen 1961 (1st edition 1951).

[406] *Welzel*, Das neue Bild, p. 2 f.

students of legal theory, the consequences were evident mainly in the recognition of a ***subjektiver Unrechtstatbestand*** (*subjective element of unlawfulness*; "*Tatumstandsvorsatz*") for *all* offences committed with intent.[407] The *finale Handlungslehre* has difficulty in conceptualising omission offences and negligence.[408]

In its strictly observed form, the teleological theory has remained a mere "school" of thought; however, some individual—and fundamental—demands have become established; its definition of action has become dominant as part of a so-called **social theory of action**, with altered grounds.[409]

In order to classify the dispute on the definition of action we must once again distinguish between an immanent-doctrinal viewpoint and a viewpoint based on legal history.

In *doctrinal* terms, the development of the personal definition of unlawfulness resulted in a further differentiation and refinement of the system of offences. The demand of the *finale Handlungslehre* to take intent relating to mistakes of fact and the objective infringement of a duty of care out of the concept of guilt and instead attribute them to the *Unrechtstatbestand*, draws the ultimate consequence of the normative concept of guilt; accordingly, the concept of guilt contains only normative elements. The equation of the differentiation between unlawfulness and guilt with that between objective and subjective is thus finally abandoned. What remains is the differentiation between the *general* and *individual* side of an offence, or in other words, between *shall* and *can*—a transformation the roots of which can be traced as far back as the seminal essay by *Reinhard Frank* on the structure of the concept of guilt (cf. § 5 II 2 above).[410]

In terms of *legal history*, the teleological theory of action forms part of the trend towards subjectivising criminal law, dominant since the first decades of the twentieth century, and transforms it into criminal law doctrine; by contrast, the causal theory of action fitted in with the traditional liberal-positivist system of criminal law, which made the exercise of state control over the citizen first dependent on external, objective criteria and only afterwards considered what went on in his or her "inner self".

The new line of thought, which remains dominant today in its more important consequences, comes close to becoming a criminal law which punishes someone's attitude, a "*Gesinnungsstrafrecht*" (if not necessarily, with a certain inevitability nonetheless). This

---

[407] An unsurpassed account of the development of doctrine in the mid-20th century is given in *Hans Joachim Hirsch*, Der Streit um Handlungs- und Unrechtslehre, insbesondere im Spiegel der Zeitschrift für die gesamte Strafrechtswissenschaft, in: ZStW 1981, 831 ff., 1982, 239 ff. It is required reading for anyone wishing to gain an understanding of the history of the doctrine of criminal law of this period.

[408] On the latter, cf. the solution suggested in *Eberhard Struensee*, Der subjektive Tatbestand des Fahrlässigkeitsdelikts, in: Id., Grundlagenprobleme des Strafrechts. Berlin 2005, p. 1 ff.

[409] *Wessels/Beulke*, Strafrecht AT, p. 32 ff.

[410] On this, cf. the introduction by *Hans Joachim Hirsch* on the reprint of Frank's text (Berlin 2008).

does not necessarily mean that it becomes entangled with National Socialist *Täterstrafrecht*. As this account of the development of criminal law has shown, considering the offender's attitude was not an invention of National Socialist criminal law doctrine, but is already to be found with Franz v. Liszt.[411] Of course, this does not change the fact that the phenomenon's most radical incarnation was to be found in NS doctrine. There is always the significant danger that an evaluation of "attitude" becomes detached from its *relation to the offence* and lapses into a general evaluation of the *offender*.[412] A leading exponent of finalism has – albeit recently – repeatedly criticised elements of *Gesinnungsstrafrecht* and interpretations of current criminal law, emphasising that these do not necessarily follow from the personal theory of unlawfulness.[413]

In *factual* terms, this development in doctrine led mostly to an expansion of the criminal law, in line with the courts and the legislature, and shows the influence of the tendency towards a subjectivisation of the criminal law. As this textbook cannot go into any great systematic depth, only three important consequences shall be mentioned here:

1) A subjective theory of attempt (which takes the "implementation of an attitude inimical to the law" as its starting point) with the consequence of purely optional mitigation (already introduced in law in 1943, not repealed after 1945);
2) Recognition of subjective elements of justification, with the consequence that the objective presence of justificatory preconditions is insufficient, although the law does not require such elements for most grounds of justification;
3) Separation of *Tatumstandsvorsatz* (intent relating to elements of the offence) and *Unrechtsvorsatz* (an intent to commit unlawful acts) (expressed in law by the coexistent regulations of Section 16 and 17 StGB, prepared by the verdict BGHSt 2, 200; first regulated to some extent in the Mistake of Law Decree of 1917), resulting in a treatment of mistake of law that is more unfavourable for the citizen.[414]

Subjectivisation did have a limiting effect on liability, at least from the point of view of *legal history*, as far as result-qualified offences were concerned (today Section 18 StGB), as the previous view regarded the occurrence of the result as

[411] *H.J. Hirsch*, Über Irrungen und Wirrungen in der gegenwärtigen Schuldlehre, in: Festschrift für Harro Otto. Cologne et al. 2007, p. 307 ff., 309 f.

[412] *H.J. Hirsch*, op. cit., p. 313 f., 316.

[413] *H.J. Hirsch*, op. cit.; *Id.*, JZ 2007, 494 ff., 499.

[414] Further investigation would be necessary to ascertain whether the current term "*Verbotsirrtum*" goes back to Binding's theory of norms.—On the criticism of the theory of blameworthiness (*Schuldtheorie*), cf. *Jürgen Baumann*, Die Reform des Allgemeinen Teils eines Strafgesetzbuches, in: Leonhard Reinisch (Ed.), Die deutsche Strafrechtsreform. Munich 1967, p. 56 ff., 59: "How easy it is to commit one of the comprehensive offences of the Criminal Code or even the Supplementary Penal Provisions in good faith and with no sense of wrongdoing! [...] Are the majority of those subject to the law prepared to accept that the punishment for intentional perpetration is meted out in spite of a simple mistake of law if the mistake could have been avoided (e.g. through investigation)?"

sufficient in itself to trigger liability.[415] Subjectivisation would also have a limiting effect in the cases of so-called objective conditions of liability still recognised to this day, if the corresponding efforts to include elements of negligence[416] were followed through.

The triumph beyond the borders of Germany of the theory of **objective ascription**, which razed one of the last bastions of the "classical" system of offences, represents more of a shift within doctrine than a reduction of the subjectivisation and expansion of criminal law.[417] For some problems of doctrine such as "social adequacy",[418] permissible risk and risk reduction as well as the doctrine on negligence[419] it is able to provide more elegant doctrinal solutions,[420] whilst elsewhere it produces new contradictions, for example in the case of atypical causal events, where its consideration of the offender's "special knowledge" actually integrates a *subjective* element. Its aim to establish impunity objectively and as early as possible can be interpreted as an attempt to limit punishment (despite the fact that it is motivated rather by economics of labour); however, problem solving models which decades of work in criminal law doctrine successfully allocated to the various problem and system levels are in significant danger of once more being lumped together. In terms of the rule of law, this approach's topical methodology (i.e. according to "case groups") and its "amorphous structure"[421] give cause for concern; the problem of increased risk has also shown that there is the temptation to use the theory of objective ascription to gloss over the principle of *in dubio pro reo*.[422]

Both the somewhat arbitrary as well as (more importantly) authoritarian consequences drawn from natural law during the postwar period brought any kind of natural law—even a rational natural law in the tradition of Kant—into such disrepute that during the 1960s it was considered progressive to proclaim a "**turning away from Kant and Hegel**" (*Klug*). During the 1960s, utilitarian criminal law allied itself with the anti-authoritarian Zeitgeist (which itself combined individual

---

[415] From a *systematic* point of view, Section 18 StGB of course represents an *extension* of liability in law, for without it the principle of Section 15 would apply and insofar intent would be necessary; thus the words "only" and "at least" in Section 18 only make sense in historical terms.

[416] *H.J. Hirsch*, GA 1972, 65, 77 (passim).

[417] On this, cf. *Claus Roxin*, Strafrecht Allg.Teil/1. 4th edition. Munich 2006, 12/138; *Udo Ebert/ Kristian Kühl*, Kausalität und objektive Zurechnung, in: Jura 1979, 561 ff.; *Eberhard Struensee*, Grundlagenprobleme des Strafrechts. Berlin 2005, p. 1 ff., 31 ff., 37 ff.; for Italy most recently *Massimo Donini*, Imputazione oggettiva dell'evento. Turin 2006; on the history of doctrine cf. *Christoph Hübner*, Die Entwicklung der objektiven Zurechnung. Berlin 2004.

[418] *Claus Roxin*, Strafrecht AT, § 10 marginal note 38 (p. 243).

[419] *Claus Roxin*, Bilanz des Finalismus, in: Festschrift für Androulakis. Athens 2004, p. 573 ff., 588.

[420] Of course, as shown by Struensee, most of the accomplishments this theory lays claim to can also be achieved by a suitable interpretation of offence-specific results or the normal doctrine of intent; cf. e.g. *Eberhard Struensee*, "Objektives Risiko" und subjektiver Tatbestand, in: Id., Grundlagenprobleme des Strafrechts. Berlin 2005, p. 31 ff.

[421] *Paeffgen*, in: Nomos-Kommentar zum StGB. 2nd edition. Before Section 32, marginal note 35.

[422] *Wessels/Beulke*, Strafrecht AT, p. 74.

liberalisation and sociation in a contradictory manner) and the corresponding politics, much in the same way it had with the authoritarian Zeitgeist after 1933.

This optimism towards criminal policy of the 1960s and 70s also influenced **Claus Roxin's** book "Kriminalpolitik und Strafrechtssystem", one of the most (internationally) successful programmatic books of criminal law of the last decades,[423] which aims to create a "systemic unity between criminal policy and criminal law" that "also should be realised in the structure of the theory of crime"[424] and attempts to "view, develop and systematise individual categories of offences a priori from the perspective of their function within criminal policy".[425]

This new utilitarian criminal law was able to take credit for the decriminalisation of several offences that had long been overdue. For a brief moment in history, the potential for limiting punishment within utilitarian criminal law and the concept of protected legal interests prevailed.[426] Its influence was largely responsible for the restriction of the law on sexual offences and political criminal law, the instatement of the daily unit fine system and the further limitation of short-term imprisonment, as well as expanding the application of suspended sentences.

The **liberalisation of the law on sexual offences** had already been on the agenda of criminal policy during the Weimar Republic, but this development had been halted by the National Socialists' accession to power. The law on sexual offences had been one of those areas in which the values of the NS period had persisted into the 1950s. The **liberalisation of political criminal law** basically entailed compensating for the excesses of the Cold War criminal law of the early 1950s; it was encouraged as the Cold War temporarily abated and a policy of detente between the two German states set in.[427]

There are several reasons, all linked to one another in a complicated manner, for why a new wave of utilitarian thought on criminal law encompassed the German (and not only German) theory of criminal law during the 60s and 70s, making Franz von Liszt once again the man of the hour—despite the experiences of National Socialist criminal law and its unbridled utilitarianism:

1. As has already been mentioned, after 1945 a significant portion of German theory and practice of criminal law became caught up in the **conservative natural law** of the Adenauer era, thus causing the revival of a harsh theory of atonement in criminal law. Ironically, this theory found itself confronted with a

[423] *Claus Roxin*, Kriminalpolitik und Strafrechtssystem, 2nd edition 1973; cf. also *Id.*, Zur kriminalpolitischen Fundierung des Strafrechtssystems, in: Festschrift for Günther Kaiser. Berlin 1998, p. 885 ff.

[424] *Roxin*, Kriminalpolitik, p. 11.

[425] *Roxin*, Kriminalpolitik, p. 15.

[426] *Kubink*, Strafen, p. 433.

[427] One reason for the liberalisation of political criminal law in 1968, supported by a wide consensus, was also that at the Olympic Games in 1972, according to the political criminal law in force since 1951, the GDR athletes and functionaries were liable to be arrested. The socialist states thus threatened to boycott the Games; in more detail from a contemporary perspective, *Diether Posser*, Anwalt im Kalten Krieg. 3rd edition, Baden-Baden 1999, p. 419 ff.

Criminal Code which contained fundamental elements of Lisztian criminal policy, these having been incorporated during the NS period. Towards the end of this era, anyone who spoke out in favour of a more lenient utilitarian criminal law was thus liberal and "progressive".

2. Criminal statistics and **empiricism** in general formed an inseparable part of Franz von Liszt's theory; his school is often called the "sociological school" (or the "modern" school). Jurists of a traditional bent have always fought against the encroachment of sociology and criminology on law. Anyone *in favour* of this is thus "modern". This did not take into consideration that not only theorists of criminal law, but also (in particular) many exponents of criminology had willingly offered their services to the NS rulers.[428]
3. Franz von Liszt was an exponent of a line of criminal theory that wanted to abolish *inexpedient* criminal law—inexpedient according to the yardstick of individual incapacitation, i.e. the purpose of preventing the convict from committing future crimes. According to this yardstick, there were a number of possibilities for restricting criminal law, particularly in the area of sexual offences, during the early period of the Federal Republic. The tighter laws on sexual offences introduced during the National Socialist period were an ideal starting point. In contrast, the criminalisations and increases in punishment introduced through the 1943 Decree on the Alignment of Criminal Law were hardly touched.

Since the end of the twentieth century, so-called **positive general deterrence** has become the dominant purpose of punishment. It sees the task of criminal law as effecting the protection of legal interests by strengthening the people's sense of what is lawful. It does not target only those inclined to crime (unlike Feuerbach's general deterrence which threatened punishment), but is directed just as much at the law-abiding citizen, to prevent "temptation" from ever arising. As normative "messages" suffice in principle for it to take effect (an effect that is difficult to ascertain, if it can be ascertained at all),[429] it is closely related to **symbolic criminal law**. But it is precisely the tendency towards passing symbolic laws that is one of the causes of the well-nigh unstoppable expansion of criminal law from the last third of the twentieth century onwards.[430]

---

[428] *Wetzell*, Inventing, p. 179 ff.; *Id.*, Der Verbrecher und seine Erforscher, in: JJZG 8 (2006/2007), p. 256 ff.

[429] For a representative elaborated account of this theory, cf. the textbook by *Günther Jakobs*, Strafrecht Allgemeiner Teil. Die Grundlagen und die Zurechnungslehre. (Berlin, New York, 1st edition 1983; 2nd edition 1991). The passages in question are reproduced in: *Vormbaum*, MdtStrD, p. 330 ff. Whether the theories the same author puts forward on the so-called "*Feindstrafrecht*" ("criminal law for enemies"; cf. § 6, footnote 8 ff. below) can be reconciled with his theory of punishment is the subject of surprisingly little discussion; on this, cf. *Vormbaum*, Einführung, in: Vormbaum/Asholt, Feindstrafrecht, p. XXXI ff.

[430] *Winfried Hassemer*, Das Symbolische am symbolischen Strafrecht, in: *Id.*, Strafrecht. Sein Selbstverständnis, seine Welt. Berlin 2008, p. 93 ff.; there p. 95 (footnote 14) for all necessary references on symbolic criminal law.

The end of the NS regime did not at once herald a new way of thinking in **criminology** and prison practice. The Allies' liberation of most individuals who had been in detention for purposes of incapacitation was criticised strongly by German authorities, who stated that the plans for incapacitation detention had already been discussed and agreed in principle before 1933.[431] German prison practitioners' views were still dominated by the image of a homogenous group of "professional and habitual offenders". Offender evaluations from the NS period were adopted without further thought. In prison practice, the "exploration of the offender's personality" remained a central concern. "Hereditary factors" were criteria used with very little inhibition. Of course, the "Kriminalbiologische Dienst" was not reactivated; nonetheless, probands' own statements regarding themselves, their ancestors and other relatives ("suicides, mental illnesses, alcoholism, hereditary diseases") were to be checked and supplemented by questioning priests, teachers, "confidantes", welfare authorities, school boards and health authorities.[432] New editions of criminology textbooks continued to use NS metaphors such as "*Volksganzes*" (the nation as an entity), "the national community as a relationship of blood", individuals' "superiority" or "inferiority", "aliens to the community", "degeneracy", "selection", "elimination", "combating the gipsy infestation" as well as ideas of crime specific to certain races; the threat to the "body of the nation" posed by "germs of crime" was mentioned; in *Ernst Seelig's* textbook of 1951[433] we can still find the statement that the social group of professional offenders has become "mixed due to the constant influx of Jews and gipsies".[434] In the Grand Commission for the Reform of Criminal Law, *Eduard Dreher* spoke of "negative selection" and "particular types of human characterised by unfortunate endogenous influences".[435] The files of judicial and prison practice contained characterisations such as "*großkotzig*" (snooty), "*ein seltener Dreckspatz*" (an exceptionally filthy bugger), "*Schwätzer*" (gossip), "*Stänkerer*" (troublemaker), "*Faulenzer*" (idler), "*übles Früchtchen*" (rotten good-for-nothing). The viewpoints that had already dominated the staggered levels of prison regime of the 1920s maintained their hegemonic position.[436] It was only the shift in mentality of the 1950s and 60s that created "a new awareness and thus the preconditions for a shift in the focus of criminology".[437]

---

[431] From then on, this pattern of argument reappeared again and again—neglecting the question of *why* the regulations in question had *not* been put into practice before 1933.

[432] *I. Baumann*, Verbrechen, p. 140–143.

[433] Cit. according to *Baumann*, Verbrechen, p. 162 ff.

[434] I. Baumann provides references for all cited passages in new editions of textbooks by *Franz Exner*, *Wilhelm Sauer*, *Edmund Mezger* and *Ernst Seelig*; cf. *Baumann*, Verbrechen, p. 145 ff.

[435] *I. Baumann*, Verbrechen, p. 189.

[436] *I. Baumann*, Verbrechen, p. 205 ff. A 1955 advisory report (taken over from the court files) of Bruchsal prison runs: "Incapacitation detention and detention in a concentration camp were unable to prevent his reoffending as early as 1946, in this particular case committing assault and fraud" (op. cit., p. 211).

[437] *Naumann*, Gefängnis, p. 215.

During the 1970s, the so-called **labeling approach** added a new dimension to criminological debate. This approach added the legal definition (and creation) of crime to the crime factors discussed until then.[438] Closely related to this approach to definition, but not identical with it, is **selection theory**, which examines prosecuting bodies' selective perception and the regularities that occur when identifying offenders.[439] Neither approach became dominant, but they did open up criminology to aspects hitherto neglected. At the same time, they were an indicator that criminal sociology (in the broad sense) had gained the upper hand over approaches favouring individual factors.

7. Post-reform Legislation

One achievement of the period of reform (now nearing its end) was the possibility of **suspending life sentences** (in 1981). This resulted from a decision by the Federal Constitutional Court,[440] which declared that while this sanction could in principle be reconciled with the Basic Law, the postulate of human dignity (Art. 1 (1) GG) meant that the prisoner needed to be able to keep the hope of regaining his or her freedom at some point.[441]

In the wake of the criminal law reform, a national **Prison Act** (Strafvollzugsgesetz—StVollzG) was passed in 1976 which encoded rehabilitation as the primary aim of imprisonment (Section 2(1) StVollzG) as well as the principle of approximation of the prison conditions to those of life outside (Section 3 StVollzG). The enactment of this law was also preceded by a decision of the Federal Constitutional Court, which had declared the (uniform) service and prison regulations of the federal states an insufficient legal basis for (further) restrictions of prisoners' rights, and had demanded a basis be created in law.[442]

The liberal climate of the 1960s and early 70s in criminal policy shifted in the mid-70s. Besides processes in the historical development of mentalities and

[438] Cf. instead of many other sources: *Fritz Sack*, Definition von Kriminalität als politisches Handeln: der labeling approach; in: Arbeitskreis Junger Kriminologen (Ed.), Kritische Kriminologie. Positionen, Kontroversen und Perspektiven. Munich 1974, p. 18 ff.

[439] Instead of many other sources, cf. the contributions in: *Hans Steinert* (Ed.), Der Prozeß der Kriminalisierung. Untersuchungen zur Kriminalsoziologie. Munich 1973; also *Hans-Wilhelm Schünemann*, Selektion durch Strafverfahren? Die Bedeutung des labeling approach für unser Strafverfahren, in: Deutsche Richter-Zeitung 1974, 278 ff.

[440] BVfGE 45, 187, 229, 239.

[441] A further consequence of the Federal Constitutional Court decision was the decision in BGHSt 30, 105 (= NJW 1981, 1965), controversial to this day, which issued the so-called *Rechtsfolgenlösung* (sanction-based solution) of Section 211 StGB in order to fulfil the Court's demand that only those cases of murder that exhibit a maximum of unlawfulness and blameworthiness be given the maximum punishment.

[442] BVfGE 33, 1 (= NJW 1972, 811).

historical structures, which are hard to describe,[443] this was caused by the reciprocal escalation resulting from a series of anarchist **terrorist attacks** by the so-called Red Army Faction and conservative politicians' eager reaction, which took the form of toughening and expanding criminal law. The conservatives were regularly able to push a large portion of their demands through by way of compromise with the social democrat criminal politicians.[444]

A further factor was the critical Zeitgeist's discovery of **economic crime**. Under the aegis of criminalising behaviour harmful to society by both "big" and "small fish" equally, *combating* economic crime led to a considerable expansion of criminal law and was also linked to a further major criminal policy topic of the end of the century, combating **organised crime**.

New social movements—feminism, the green movement—also made their mark by demanding new and tougher criminal laws. The result was a militancy in criminal policy that was heightened further by the German reunification and the economic and social structural challenges it brought with it. From the 1970s onwards, there was a downright race to create new offences between any and all political persuasions. State and economic protectionists, women's, children's and animal rights activists apparently only considered their political programme legally accredited once respective threats of punishment and harsh sentences had been issued. Supreme Court judicature joined this trend by issuing extensive readings, particularly frequently in the area of economic criminal law, apparently wanting to prove that it did not just "catch the small fry".

The link between continuously rendering the criminal law more flexible and the corresponding constant desire to ease the strain on the administration of criminal justice led to an increasing leniency of sanctions—rather than to decriminalisation (or, to use a new term, **diversion**). The gradual expansion of the so-called **offender-victim mediation** (Section 46a StGB) was a visible sign of this. No doubt created with good intent, this mediation—along with other similar changes in criminal procedure law (see below)—rendered the liberal, carefully balanced relationship between the state and the accused increasingly precarious.

8. Criminal Procedure[445]

Similarly to the beginning of the century, the development of criminal procedure followed certain rules of its own compared to substantive criminal law. Until the

[443] The end of the "*Wirtschaftswunder*" (economic miracle), the oil crisis of 1973, the breakup of social structures and milieus, a comparatively high level of structural unemployment after 20 years of full employment, crises in environmental and armaments policy.

[444] This interaction is represented in an instructive and gripping manner in the documentary *Die Anti-Terror-Debatten im Parlament. Protokolle 1974–1978*. Reinbek nr. Hamburg 1978.

[445] An overview of its development from the point of view of 2006 is given in *Peter Rieß*, Tendenzen der Strafprozessgesetzgebung in der Bundesrepublik Deutschland, in: Festschrift for

Criminal Procedure Amendment Act of 1964 (Strafprozessänderungsgesetz—StPÄG), the legislature promoted a careful liberalisation and strengthening of the rights of the accused.[446] The aforementioned series of terrorist attacks triggered the reversal of this trend. And as so often before in the history of criminal law (for example when passing the Emminger Decree in 1924), the arguments of legal doctrine and general politics went hand in hand. A heterogeneous alliance formed by legal politicians and stakeholders believed that only the abolition of the defendant's final word (only introduced in 1964) and of the long-standing judicial pre-trial investigation,[447] a judicial guarantee of protection during the pre-trial investigation procedure, would finally be able to establish the accusatorial principle in criminal procedure. However, in doing this and increasing the possibilities for the prosecution to discontinue proceedings, culminating in the discontinuance combined with a fine introduced in 1975 by Section 153a StPO,[448] the prosecutor was turned into a "judge before the judge",[449] as the prosecution was simultaneously granted powers of intervention that served to make interrogations compellable (Sections 161a, 163a StPO).[450]

The main reason given for the abolition of the judicial pre-trial investigation was that the Reich Code of Criminal Procedure's distrust of the (then) new office of the prosecutor could no longer be justified; however, this shows little sophisticated awareness of the notion of procedural separation of powers. Furthermore, the enactment of the RStPO did not only manifest a "distrust" of the new institution of the prosecution, but built on 30 years of concrete experience of it in its Prussian form.[451] Besides, "trust" in criminal prosecution institutions is hardly a constitutional or democratic virtue.[452]

Following its abolition in war legislation, the **principle of mandatory prosecution** was reinstated. But the trend to relax it that had started with the Emminger Decree continued in the Federal Republic of Germany, too. The possibility for discontinuance in Section 153a StPO in particular took it one step further in this direction.

Roland Miklau. Innsbruck, Vienna, Bolzano 2006, p. 433. Overall, Rieß sees the development in a more favourable light than the present publication.

[446] *Schumacher*, Staatsanwaltschaft, p. 209 ff.

[447] By Art. 1 subparagraphs 52 and 57 of the First Criminal Procedure Reform Act of 9 December 1974 (RGBl. I, p. 3393).

[448] Also introduced by the 1st StVRG (Art. 1 No. 36).

[449] *Erhard Kausch*, Der Staatsanwalt. Ein Richter vor dem Richter? Untersuchungen zum § 153a StPO. Berlin 1980; cf. on a specific case (discontinuance of proceedings against Chancellor Helmut Kohl for embezzlement by breaking the rules on donations to political parties) comments by *Wolfgang Naucke*, *Wilhelm Hennis* and *Thomas Vormbaum*, in: JJZG 2 (2000/2001), 722 ff., 725 ff. and 728 ff.

[450] By Art. 1 subparagraphs 43, 46 of the 1st StVRG; in this, cf. the scathing criticism of *Jürgen Welp*, Zwangsbefugnisse für die Staatsanwaltschaft. Tübingen 1976.

[451] *Schumacher*, Staatsanwaltschaft, p. 233.

[452] Cf. also *Welp*, op. cit. p. 9; *I. Müller*, Rechtsstaat und Strafverfahren, p. 206 ff.

A classic example of "abuse of legislation technique"[453] is furnished by **Section 129a StGB** (forming terrorist organisations). Encouraged by media coverage, during the 1970s and 1980s this offence, in which the preliminary stage to full terrorism-related offences was criminalised, became well-nigh synonymous with the terrorist threat—even though originally it had been designated a *misdemeanour* (pointing out this fact always astonished students at the time). The conviction rate has always been low, as usually it is possible to sentence for the "actual" offence (murder, kidnapping, terrorist attacks).[454] The regulation's main purpose was not substantive in nature, but instead it created a point which subsequent procedural regulations—primarily phone tapping and limiting defence rights—could take up in case of a suspicion under Section 129a StGB.[455] In 1986, hectic legislative activity following a new series of attacks—not by anarchist terrorists this time, but by "ecoterrorists" (attacks on pylons and other similar objects)—led to a "substantiation" of this offence, which was upgraded to a felony.

From the 1980s onwards, **victim protection** found its way into criminal procedure. This was encouraged by victimology, which had flourished since the 1970s and whose exponents for a time even wanted to establish it as a discipline of its own *alongside* criminology (implicitly assuming an orientation towards the *offender* in the latter). However, while victim protection was introduced due to justified criticism of shortcomings—such as the sometimes excessive behaviour of defence counsel in rape proceedings, which in most cases could of course have been stopped if proceedings had be managed appropriately, it soon overstepped the mark. Even the principle that preferring public charges (Section 170 (1) StPO) requires only an *alleged* offence and thus regularly (particularly in problematic cases) also only an *alleged* victim, should advise caution. As our journey through the history of criminal law has so often shown, good intentions do not always produce good results.[456]

VII. The German Democratic Republic

1. Overview of the Development of Criminal Law

A glance at the c. 40 years of history of criminal law in the German Democratic Republic, now concluded, reveals both similarities and differences to the

---

[453] *F.-C. Schroeder*, Die Entwicklung der Gesetzgebungstechnik, in: Vormbaum/Welp, StGB, supplementary volume 1, p. 381 ff., 416 ff.

[454] *F.-C. Schroeder*, op. cit., p. 417.

[455] Ibid.

[456] On this, cf. most recently: *Bernd Schünemann*, Der Ausbau der Opferstellung im Strafprozeß—Fluch oder Segen? in: Festschrift R. Hamm. Berlin 2008, p. 687 ff. For criticism of the "martial" terminology "victim", rather than the traditional "injured party" used in criminal procedure until today, cf. *F.-C. Schroeder*, op. cit., p. 381 ff., 390.

development in the Federal Republic. The "anti-fascist, democratic" revolution of the first postwar years prepared for the construction of a real-life socialist system (*real existierender Sozialismus*), whose beginnings were greeted with hope in the name of progress by at least part of the population, and particularly by those opposed to National Socialism. However, it was under the influence of the Stalinist Russian hegemonic power and under the welfare dictatorship of the leading party from the beginning, and soon lost popular support because of internments[457] and deportations[458] carried out by the Soviet occupying forces.

Like in the West, the Soviet Occupation Zone faced the problems of transforming the National Socialist past and prosecuting its crimes. The laws passed by the Allied Control Council were in force there, too; but unlike in the Western zones, the denazification of the justice system was carried out thoroughly not only during the initial period. Two thirds of the people working in the justice system were dismissed due to denazification, which led to significant staff shortages; between 1945 and 1950, an average 25–30 % of judges' and 5–10 % of prosecutors' positions in the Soviet Zone were vacant.[459] While this problem was solved in the Western zones by gradually reappointing people with a Nazi past, until 1948 the Soviet Zone practiced a system of training ***Volksrichter*** or **People's Judges,**[460] which combined finding a solution to this emergency situation with finding new recruits loyal to the system, but also put into practice an idea of a justice system "close to the people" dating back to the Weimar period.[461]

The justice system in the five Eastern states (which existed until 1952) was built up under the supervision of the legal departments of the Soviet Military Administration (SMAD) in the Occupied Zone and in the states and provinces and by the German Central Justice Administration (*Deutsche Zentralverwaltung für Justiz*—DJV) which had been established on the former's command; from around 1948

[457] In the first years after 1945, 160,000–260,000 Germans were interned, some arbitrarily, as "active fascists" or war criminals; *Helmut Müller-Engbers*, Garanten äußerer und innerer Sicherheit, in: Matthias Judt (Ed.), DDR-Geschichte in Dokumenten. Beschlüsse, Berichte, interne Materialien und Alltagszeugnisse. Bonn 1998, p. 431 ff., 432.

[458] Around 40,000 people were deported to the Soviet Union during this time and forced to work in the reconstruction of the industry destroyed by the Germans; *Müller-Engbers*, ibid.

[459] Figures according to *Andreas Gängel*, Die Volksrichterausbildung, in: BMJ (Ed.), Justiz, p. 47 ff.; these shortages were increased by emigration, including of those with no Nazi past, to the Western zones, ibid. p. 48.

[460] On this, cf. *Gängel*, op. cit.; *Wentker*, Justiz, p. 119 ff.; *Andrea Feth*, Die Volksrichter, in: Rottleuthner (Ed.), Steuerung, p. 351 ff.

[461] Eugen Schiffer, member of the (left-wing liberal) German Democratic Party during the Weimar Republic, Reich Minister of Justice from 1919 to 1921 and President of the German Central Justice Administration in the Soviet Zone from 1945 to 1948, had emphatically declared himself in favour of expanding the position of lay judges; cf. *Joachim Ramm*, Eugen Schiffer und die Reform der deutschen Justiz. Neuwied and Darmstadt 1987, p. 176.

onwards, the justice system was increasingly homogenised.[462] The Party and government, via the control tool of the Supreme Court, centrally controlled the courts in all important legal issues.[463]

Overall, the **prosecution of crimes committed during the National Socialist period** commenced early on and was conducted intensely. As early as 1947—at the same time as the Nuremberg follow-up trials against NS doctors—a major "euthanasia" trial was conducted.[464] By 1977, 127 offenders convicted of NS crimes had been sentenced to death and executed.[465] The credibility of this consistent prosecution of NS crimes was of course damaged by the fact that it was combined—at least in some individual cases—with the political persecution of opponents of the regime on the one hand,[466] and was used on the other as propaganda against former NS functionaries who had risen, returned to or remained in senior positions in West Germany.[467]

Despite its officially proclaimed antifascism, the GDR's views on criminal law theory before 1945 were ambivalent. While the problematic elements of the Lisztian school were certainly noted and criticised—although this criticism became markedly less harsh towards the end of the GDR,[468] elements of normality and continuity were apparently accepted.

The treatment accorded the teacher of criminal law **Eduard Kohlrausch** (1874–1948) is symptomatic in this regard. Kohlrausch, a follower of Liszt, had been one of the leading German teachers of criminal law between 1933 and 1945 and among other things had worked in the Criminal Law Reform Commission of the Reich Ministry of Justice. He became Dean of the Faculty of Law at the University of Berlin, renamed "Humboldt University", and played an important role in rebuilding the faculty and its teaching

[462] *Andrej P. Nikitin*, Die sowjetische Militäradministration und die Justiz in Ostdeutschland, in: JJZG 1 (1999/2000), 123 ff.; *Thomas Lorenz*, Die deutsche Zentralverwaltung der Justiz (DJV) und die SMAD in der sowjetischen Besatzungszone 1945 bis 1949, in: Rottleuthner (Ed.), Steuerung, p. 135 ff.; for Brandenburg, cf. *Dieter Pohl*, Justiz in Brandenburg 1945–1955. Gleichschaltung und Anpassung. Munich 2001; for Saxony-Anhalt *Hermann Wentker*, Anfänge der "Volksjustiz in Sachsen-Anhalt1945–1949. Zum Neuaufbau einer Landesjustiz unter sowjetischer Besatzung, in: JJZG 6 (2004/2005), 141 ff.

[463] *Andreas Gängel*, Das Oberste Gericht der DDR—Leitungsorgan der Rechtsprechung—Entwicklungsstationen, in: Rottleuthner (Ed.), Steuerung, p. 253 ff.—On the **military justice system** cf. *Heinz Josef Wagner*, Die Militärjustiz der DDR. Unter besonderer Berücksichtigung der Rechtsprechung der Militärgerichte. 2 volumes. Berlin 2006.

[464] On this, see *Joachim S. Hohmann*, Der "Euthanasie"-Prozess Dresden 1947. Eine zeitgeschichtliche Dokumentation. Frankfurt am Main et al. 1993.

[465] According to an East German documentary; references in *Koch*, JZ 2007, 719 ff., 720.

[466] In the so-called Waldheim trials; on these, cf. *Marxen/Werle*, DDR-Unrecht, Vol. 5/2, p. 791 ff.; *Haase/Pampel*, Waldheimer "Prozesse"; *Dirks*, Verbrechen der anderen, p. 48 ff.; *Falko Werkentin*, Politische Strafjustiz in der Ära Ulbricht. Berlin 1995, p. 174 ff.

[467] On the show trials (in absentia) against Federal Minister **Theodor Oberländer** and the Secretary of State in the Federal Chancellery (and former commentator on the Nuremberg race laws) **Hans Globke** cf. *Christian Dirks*, Verbrechen der anderen, p. 63 ff. On the "Brown Book" campaign, cf. § 5 VI. 3. above, also *Dirks*, Verbrechen der anderen, p. 59 ff.

[468] Cf. references in *Karitzky*, Kohlrausch, p. 24 ff.

programme; in 1947, however, he was dropped and "sent on leave" for reasons unclear to this day.[469]

In actual fact, there is a large proportion of **normality** in the sense of "modernity" to be found in the development of criminal law in the GDR (apart from the broad political area), which places it within the **continuous** development of criminal law in the twentieth century.[470]

The Reich Criminal Code of 1871 at first remained in force after 1945 in the SBZ/GDR also; however, the Allied Control Council's rules on the repealing of criminal laws applied.[471] In 1957, an extensive "Criminal Code Supplementation Act" was passed.[472] This added, among other options, the possibility of conditional sentences of imprisonment not exceeding 2 years (Sections 1, 2) and sanctions of "public reprimand" (Section 3 ff.), the "public announcement of convictions" (Section 7) and a regulation on "exemption from criminal liability" (Section 8). According to this, no offence was constituted

> if an action corresponds to the wording of a legally defined offence, but is not deemed dangerous due to its minor nature and its lack of harmful consequences for the German Democratic Republic, the building of socialism, the interests of the working people and of the individual citizen.[473]

A comprehensive political criminal law was incorporated into the Special Part (Section 13 ff.).[474] Besides traditional offences, it included the offences of "propaganda and agitation endangering the state" and "defamation of the state" (Sections 19, 20), which had their counterparts in the Cold War criminal law of the Federal Republic, but also offences such as "inducing others to leave the GDR", "diversion", "destructive activity ["*Schädlingstätigkeit*"!] and sabotage" (Sections 21–23). A new part on "Crimes against publicly owned property" was also introduced. A further part (Section 32 ff.) created laws for crimes against military discipline.

---

[469] More detail in *Karitzky*, op. cit., p. 179 ff.; cf. also the secondary analysis in *Vormbaum*, Kohlrausch, op. cit.

[470] On this, cf. the contributions in: *Jörg Arnold* (Ed.), Die Normalität des Strafrechts der DDR. 2 volumes. Freiburg im Breisgau 1995, 1996; on one particular continuous aspect—combating "antisocial elements"—cf. "Asoziale" und "Parasiten" im Recht der SBZ/DDR. Randgruppen im Sozialismus zwischen Repression und Ausgrenzung. Cologne, Weimar, Vienna 2005.

[471] Cf. above all KontrollratsG No. 11 of 30 January 1946 (Repeal of Certain Provisions of the German Criminal Law), in: *Vormbaum/Welp*, supplementary volume II, No. 1, as well as Control Council Law No. 55 (Repeal of German Provisions of Criminal Legislation) of 20 June 1947, in: *Vormbaum/Welp*, supplementary volume II, No. 2; for more detail on early legislation in the SBZ/DDR, cf. *Jörg Arnold*, Einige Aspekte der Entwicklung des StGB der DDR, in: Vormbaum/Welp, supplementary volume I, p. 423 ff.

[472] *Vormbaum/Welp*, supplementary volume II, No. 3.

[473] This regulation was supplemented further by Section 9, which made impunity compulsory if the danger to society had disappeared between act and conviction, or the offender's attitude had undergone a "fundamental change".

[474] *Friedrich-Christian Schroeder*, Die Entwicklung des politischen Strafrechts, in: BMJ (Ed.), Justiz III, p. 107 ff.

A new **Criminal Code** came into force on 1 July **1968.**[475] It differentiated between offences and contraventions ("*Verfehlungen*"). Offences were either dangerous (misdemeanours) or harmful to society (felonies); contraventions consisted of (legally defined) "infringements of legal protected interests of the state or its citizens, in which the effects of the offence and the blameworthiness of the offender were of little significance" (Section 4(1)). The law took over the regulations on **petty crime** (Section 3) from the supplementary act of 1957. **Blameworthiness** was defined in positive and largely objective terms using normative elements ("If the offender, despite the option open to him to behave in a manner appropriate in society, fulfils the legal elements of a misdemeanour or a felony through his irresponsible behaviour") (Section 5). Insanity was defined similarly to Section 20 of the Federal German StGB, however the consciousness disorder did not need to be "profound", and the point of reference of responsibility was not "the unlawfulness" of the act, but the "rules of social communal life infringed by the act". Acts committed in a condition of voluntary intoxication were punished according to the law infringed (Section 15). **Intent and negligence** were defined by law (Sections 6–9).[476] **Self-defence and necessity** were both qualified by the *adequacy* of the action taken (Section 17 ff.).

Purely optional mitigation remained in place for **attempt**, as in the Second Criminal Law Reform Act in the Federal Republic (Section 21(4) 3rd sentence).

Section 21(4) 2nd sentence prescribed a consideration of the offender's motives, the results aimed for or considered possible, the extent to which the offence was realised and the reasons why it was not completed. The semi-official criminal law textbook warned against a "one-sided overemphasis on the lack of results as defined in the offence, the objective impossibility or the likelihood of completing the offence, the unsuitability of the 'object' or means".[477]

As far as sentences are concerned, what is most striking is the provision on the "**consultation and verdict by a social institution for the administration of justice**", which is included as part of the substantive law but was actually a procedural provision (Section 28). The sentencing of contraventions was left up to these institutions, and the trial of minor misdemeanours could also be transferred to them, particularly in cases where the "duties of the work collective, house communities, brigades or other collectives guarantee a successful reform of the offender" (Section 28).[478]

---

[475] *Vormbaum/Welp*, supplementary volume II, No. 4.

[476] Both were included in the part on "guilt".

[477] *John Lekschas/Joachim Renneberg* (Eds.), Strafrecht. Allgemeiner Teil. Lehrbuch. Authors Erich Buchholz et al. Berlin (GDR state press) 1976, p. 366.

[478] For a critical view on the popular courts of the GDR, cf. *Felix Herzog*, Rechtspflege—Sache des ganzen Volkes? Bericht über eine Studie zu den Gesellschaftlichen Gerichten der DDR, in: JJZG 2 (2000/2001), 180 ff.

Capital punishment, which had been taken over with the Reich Criminal Code, was also retained in the new Criminal Code.[479] It was threatened for seven crimes against the state, four war crimes and crimes against humanity, and eight military offences, as well as being permissible for certain cases of murder. It was applied and carried out consistently in NS and war crime trials; only a comparatively small percentage of murder convictions resulted in the death penalty[480]; from 1975 onwards, these death penalties were regularly commuted into life sentences by the President of the State Council (*Erich Honecker*). In 1987, the GDR abolished capital punishment – the first state of the Eastern Bloc to do so.[481]

The **range of sentences** for the basic offences was usually less severe than in Federal German criminal law. The standard maximum for imprisonment, 5 years in FRG criminal law, was only 2 years in the GDR Criminal Code; of course, this says nothing of the actual practice followed in sentencing, which needs to be studied further. The most common sentence for qualified offences was imprisonment from 2 to 8 or 10 years.

"Crimes against the national sovereignty of the German Democratic Republic, peace, humanity and human rights" were placed at the beginning of the Special Part, immediately followed, according to German criminal legislative tradition, by offences against the state, in which the term of "*Staatsfeindlichkeit*" ("hostility towards the state") played a major role (Sections 105–107).

Under the socialist order, too, the largest group of offences—about 50 %—consisted of **property offences**. Half of these again were offences against socialist property.[482] The respective provisions on punishment were located—separated according to "socialist property" and "personal or private property"—in Sections 157 ff. and 177 ff.

Offences against state and public order included *illegal border-crossing* (including the liability of those who "leave the territory of the German Democratic Republic without state authorisation or who fail to return to it", Section 213) and "*Rowdytum*" (hooliganism).[483]

Only five amendment acts were passed to change the Criminal Code until the inner-German border was opened.[484] The third of these, the 3rd Amendment Act of 28 June 1979, brought about a significant toughening of the political criminal law. The Popular Courts Act introduced a catalogue of reformatory measures these courts could impose, in Section 34 of the Criminal Code.

---

479 For more detail on capital punishment in the GDR and its abolition, cf. Evans, *Rituals*, p. 855 ff.; *Arndt Koch*, Das Ende der Todesstrafe in Deutschland, in: JZ 2007, 719 ff.

480 *Koch*, op. cit., p. 720.

481 On the background to the abolition, cf. *Koch*, op. cit., p. 722.

482 *Erich Buchholz/Ulrich Dähn/Hans Weber* (Eds.), Strafrecht. Besonderer Teil. Lehrbuch. Authors: Paul Abisch et al. Berlin (State press of the GDR) 1981; on the theft of socialist property, cf. *Wilhelm Rettler*, Der strafrechtliche Schutz sozialistischen Eigentums in der DDR. Berlin 2010.

483 "Whosever participates in a group which, in disregard of public order and the rules of socialist communal life, commits violent acts against, threatens, or grossly annoys other persons or maliciously damages objects or facilities…".

484 All documented in: *Vormbaum/Welp*, StGB, supplementary volume II.

Following the treaty to create a monetary, economic and social union with the Federal Republic, the GDR Criminal Code provisions listed in Appendix III of the treaty were repealed.[485] The 6th Criminal Law Amendment Act of 29 June 1990,[486] passed by the freely elected People's Parliament, aligned large sections of the GDR Criminal Code with that of the Federal Republic, mainly in the area of commercial criminal law. This notwithstanding, the Unification Treaty enacted on 3 October 1990[487] abolished the Criminal Code of the GDR, with only a few exceptions.[488] Although this was appropriate for offences committed from the reunification onwards, it formed a hurdle for the prosecution of older offences and particularly for part of GDR government crime—albeit a hurdle disregarded by the courts and the dominant view in literature.[489]

2. *Prosecution of Crimes Committed During the GDR Period*

Besides the integration of the new federal states, the German reunification also brought with it the task of dealing with the history of the GDR system. Unlike the method used for processing the apartheid system in South Africa, which was taking place at nearly the same time, Germany once again emphasised **criminal prosecution** (alongside rehabilitation, restitution, and other "positive" measures).[490]

There are several differences between the prosecution of NS crimes and of GDR crimes. For one, this time prosecution commenced without delay. On the one hand, this may have been because the justice system did not wish to be accused of failing in its *Vergangenheitsbewältigung* (coming to terms with the past) a second time. On the other, one important factor was that there was no conflict of interest this time. The state crime of the "other side" was being dealt with, not that of "our own

[485] *Vormbaum/Welp*, supplementary volume II, No. 12.

[486] *Vormbaum/Welp*, supplementary volume II, No. 13.

[487] Relevant regulations of the Unification Treaty in *Vormbaum/Welp*, StGB, No. 141.

[488] Apart from some criminal laws relating to the economy and environment, these were mainly the offences of homosexual acts, which were not subject to punishment in the GDR, and abortion, for which the GDR operated a time limit model.

[489] On questions of the validity of criminal law in connection with the division of Germany, cf. *Gerhard Werle/Florian Jeßberger*, in: Leipziger Kommentar zum StGB. 12th edition. Before Section 3, marginal note 433 ff.

[490] Valuable information on background and details on how this was carried out in *Bettina Lang*, Vergangenheitspolitik.—For a comprehensive account, cf. the recent documentation by *Marxen/Werle*; in summary: *Marxen/Werle/Schäfter*, Strafverfolgung; cf. also *Klaus Lüderssen*, Der Staat geht unter—das Unrecht bleibt? Regierungskriminalität in der ehemaligen DDR. Frankfurt (edition suhrkamp) 1992; *Jörg Arnold*, Strafrechtliche Auseinandersetzung mit Systemvergangenheit am Beispiel der DDR. Baden-Baden 2000; *Ernst-Joachim Lampe* (Ed.), Deutsche Wiedervereinigung. Die Rechtseinheit. Arbeitskreis Strafrecht. Vol. II: Die Verfolgung von Regierungskriminalität der DDR nach der Wiedervereinigung. Cologne et al. 1993.

people" as after 1945. Furthermore, the theoretical issues of coming to terms with the past had been thoroughly discussed due to the experiences made after 1945.

The "Radbruch formula" was used once again to deal the question of validity. It is not clear whether this really was what the formula's inventor had in mind, for he had conceived of it under the impression left by National Socialism's crimes against humanity. As Radbruch had insisted upon the validity of laws, including unjust laws, to the last and had only made an exception for extreme cases, it is not even clear whether he would have included the *Mauerschützen* (border guards who shot GDR fugitives attempting to cross the border) as exceptional cases.[491]

There was also a second line of argument, an interpretation "supportive of human rights", that desired to take GDR law and justificatory grounds (e.g. the rules on the use of firearms at the border) at its word, but did not want to consider state practice that contradicted these rules ("*Schießbefehl*"– shooting orders).[492]

A comparison of the pathology of both 20th century German dictatorships is an endeavour that faces the general difficulty of comparing systems and, in particular, dictatorships.[493] In § 5 V. 8. above we drew a distinction between the general and specific pathology of the NS regime. Turning to the GDR with this categorisation in mind, significant general pathological elements are obvious, for beyond the neutral everyday sphere, anti-constitutional, authoritarian and even totalitarian elements of the regime can certainly be identified within the state. Political trials against opponents of the system up to the imposition of the death penalty are classic examples of this category. The fact that leaving the state territory was also a punishable offence can also be counted among the general pathologies of a dictatorial system. Building an elaborate system of surveillance by the State Security Service (*Staatssicherheitsdienst* or "Stasi") also belongs in this category. *Externally*, the regime was incapable of causing a war like the NS regime, as it was too weak and too dependent on the hegemonic power of the Soviet Union; in the 1980s, it also made active efforts to de-escalate the last wave of the Cold War.[494]

It is doubtful whether one can speak of a *specific pathology* of the GDR, at least with the exception of its early years. If the term is used to encompass those processes and specific characteristics that *Herbert Jäger*, looking at the experience of the NS regime, has analysed as "macrocrime", it is possible to speak of state-amplified crime in the GDR, too; however, it is doubtful whether any claim to comparability on *this* level is still using appropriate categories. Best suited for the assumption of comparability are processes such as

---

[491] On this, cf. *Adomeit*, Gustav Radbruch—zum 50. Todestag, in: JJZG 1 (1999/2000), p. 343 ff., 353 f.; in detail on the use of the Radbruch formula in connection with coming to terms with the GDR past, *Giuliano Vassalli*, Formula di Radbruch e diritto penale. Note sulla punizione dei "delitti di Stato" nella Germania postnazista e nella Germania postcomunista. Milan 2001, p. 60 ff.

[492] Cf. *Vassalli*, Radbruchsche Formel, p. 92 ff.

[493] On this cf. most recently e.g. *Detlef Schmiechen-Ackermann*, NS-Regime und SED-Herrschaft—Chancen, Grenzen und Probleme des empirischen Diktaturenvergleichs, in: Geschichte in Wissenschaft und Unterricht 52 (2001), 544 ff., especially 649 ff.; cf. also *Frank Rohrer*, Strafjustiz im Dritten Reich und in der SBZ/DDR. Frankfurt am Main et al. 2007.

[494] Against the wish of its party and state leadership, the GDR remained excluded from the Warsaw Pact troops' invasion of the CSSR in August 1968.

1. Acts of violence at the border between East and West Germany,
2. Abductions (primarily during the early years of the Soviet Zone/GDR),[495]
3. Forced adoptions,
4. The so-called Waldheim Trials, show trials which no longer had anything to do with the rule of law, where actual NS criminals and opponents of the system branded as NS criminals were given severe punishments determined in advance by politicians, many of them the death penalty.[496]

The majority of the cases prosecuted after German reunification of course involved areas that belong to the *general* pathology: harassing opponents of the system, including with legal measures (particularly in the area of employment law), spying by the Stasi, infringing postal privacy, committing fraud in the People's Parliament elections (which were pointless anyway and were called "*Zettelfalten*" or "paper folding" by the populace), corruption and espionage. Most punishments were in the range where suspended sentences could be applied.[497]

Particularly in cases of **electoral fraud** and **perverting the course of justice,**[498] serious legal concerns resulted from the fact that the unification treaty had abolished the GDR Criminal Code and its offences against institutions, thus also abolishing the legal grounds for prosecuting the offences in question "within the system"; however, these concerns were brushed aside.[499]

GDR judges were also granted Radbruch's "judges' privilege", even though there was no guarantee of judicial independence in the GDR. The changed view of perverting the course of justice had practically no effect, for the Federal Constitutional Court found another way of limiting liability for perverting the course of justice—this time through the actus reus. Accordingly, not "every wrongful application of law" constituted perverting the course of justice, but—at least as far as sentencing GDR judges was concerned—only included those cases "in which the wrongfulness of the decision was obvious and, in particular, the rights of others, mainly their human rights, were infringed to such an extent that the decision constitute[d] an arbitrary act".[500]

[495] On this, cf. as an example *Siegfried Mampel*, Entführungsfall Dr. Walter Linse—Menschenraub und Justizmord als Mittel des Staatsterrors (Schriftenreihe des Berliner Landesbeauftragten für die Stasi-Unterlagen. 10). 3rd edition. Berlin 2006.

[496] On this, cf. *Haase/Pampel*, Waldheimer "Prozesse".

[497] Of course, these statistics are more "favourable" percentage-wise because the prosecution was so speedy (unlike the prosecution of NS crimes), so that there were fewer cases where the statute of limitations applied.

[498] On this, cf. *Thomas Vormbaum*, Der Schutz von Institutionen der DDR durch das bundesdeutsche Strafrecht, in: Festschrift Diether Posser. Cologne et al. 1997, p. 153 ff.; *Ute Hohoff*, An den Grenzen des Rechtsbeugungstatbestandes. Eine Studie zu den Strafverfahren gegen DDR-Juristen. Berlin 2001.

[499] BGHSt 40, 35 ff., 39.

[500] BGHSt 40, 41; on this topic as a whole, cf. also *Friedrich Denker*, Strafrechtliche Aufarbeitung des DDR-Unrechts und Rechtskultur, in: Politisches Denken. Jahrbuch 2009, p. 197 ff.

At first, the prosecution of **GDR spies** was also problematic. However, a decision of the Federal Constitutional Court[501] created exceptional conditions for and thus in practice put an end to it.

On the whole, it can be acknowledged that the prosecution of GDR crimes by the Federal German justice system was proportionate, attempting to do justice to both the demands of legal policy and of justice. Even the sentencing of the ***Mauerschützen*** took account of their personal situation to a large extent; the harsher sentence given to Egon Krenz, member of the National Security Council of the GDR and the last President of the State Council, was not criticised by the European Court of Human Rights.[502]

---

[501] BVerfG 92, 277 ff.—Unlike the cases of the domestic activity of the Ministry for State Security; on this, cf. *Roland Schißau*, Strafverfahren wegen MfS-Unrechts. Die Strafprozesse bundesdeutscher Gerichte gegen ehemalige Mitarbeiter des Ministeriums für Staatssicherheit der DDR. Berlin 2006.

[502] On this, cf. *Lensing/Mertens*, JJZG 3, p. 352 ff.; in detail also *Helmut Kreiker*, Art. 7 EMRK und die Gewalttaten an der deutsch-deutschen Grenze. Zu den Urteilen des Europäischen Gerichtshofs für Menschenrechte. Baden-Baden 2002.

§ 6 Current Events in Criminal Law

With the GDR's accession to the Federal Republic, the FRG's legal system was extended to include the new federal states, where it was only possible to build up the criminal law system by using personnel from the Federal Republic. Their secondment created staff shortages, which once again led to a **reduction in the application of criminal law** through reducing the size of judicial panels, limiting appeals, limiting the formal right to make evidential motions, expanding the summary written procedure (*Strafbefehl*) and extending the principle of discretionary prosecution.[1]

Reunification brought about liberalisation in the area of sexual offences in that the decriminalisation of **homosexual activity**, only partially realised in the criminal law reform of the 1960s but carried through to conclusion in the GDR, now came into force throughout the Federal Republic.[2]

Reunification also resulted in a fresh attempt to introduce a time limit solution for **abortion**.

Reunification meant that two different laws on abortion now coexisted in Germany: the indication model based on evaluation by a third party in the old federal states, and a time limit solution without compulsory consultation in the former GDR. As an immediate agreement seemed highly unlikely, Article 31(4) of the unification treaty gave the legislature a deadline of 31 December 1992 for finding a solution for the whole of Germany. The *Schwangeren- und Familienhilfegesetz* (Support for Pregnant Women and Families Act)[3] contained a time limit solution as a justificatory defence for abortion with compulsory consultation (Section 218a StGB). However, this new regulation was also suspended by the

---

[1] *Rechtspflege-Entlastungsgesetz* [Administration of Justice (Reduction of Workload) Act] *1993*; on this, cf. the critical response of the criminal defence lawyers' associations. Cologne 1991.

[2] On its background, cf. *Christian Schäfer*, "Widernatürliche Unzucht". Reformdiskussion und Gesetzgebung seit 1945. Berlin 2006.

[3] BGBl. I p. 1398 of 27 July 1992, *Vormbaum / Welp*, StGB, No. 146.

T. Vormbaum and M. Bohlander, *A Modern History of German Criminal Law*,
DOI 10.1007/978-3-642-37273-5_6, © Springer-Verlag Berlin Heidelberg 2014

Federal Constitutional Court's interim ruling of 4 August 1992.[4] In the decision on the merits issued on 28 May 1993, the majority of the senate declared Section 218a (1) StGB and Section 219 StGB unconstitutional and thus invalid, as they were incompatible with Article 1(1) in combination with Article 2(2) 1st sentence of the Basic Law.[5] This decision was based mainly on reasoning in the first decision on the time limit solution, and rendered another amendment necessary. On the basis of this decision, the Support for Pregnant Women and Families Act of 1 October 1995 was finally passed. It incorporated the "non-justificatory time limit solution with compulsory consultation" demanded by the Federal Constitutional Court.

According to this Act, abortion remains subject to punishment according to Section 218, but Section 218a(1) encodes the possibility of an exception to liability (time limit solution with compulsory consultation). The medical-social and criminological indications are recognised as grounds justifying abortion in Section 218a(2, 3). The *Schwangerschaftskonfliktgesetz* (Pregnancy Conflict Act) supplements the regulation on consultation in Section 219. The Support for Pregnant Women and Families Amendment Act put an erstwhile end to the debate on the punishability of abortion.

Otherwise, the **legislation on substantive criminal law** continues the line of development evident in the change in trend following the reform period. Its most striking characteristic is the verbal "arms race", reminiscent of earlier phases of criminal policy. "*Bekämpfung*", "combating", is the buzz word of contemporary criminal policy. This is evident in the titles of laws passed at the end of the twentieth and the beginning of the twenty-first centuries. After the 1970s and 1980s had produced a First Law to *Combat* Economic Crime (1976), a Law to *Combat* Environmental Crime (1980), a Second Law to *Combat* Economic Crime (1986) and a Law to *Combat* Terrorism (1986), this series was continued following reunification:

1990 Law on the convention [...] for *the suppression of* unlawful acts against the safety of maritime navigation and the protocol ... for *the suppression of* unlawful acts against the safety of fixed platforms;
1991 Law to *Combat* the Illegal Trade in Drugs and Other Forms of Organised Crime;
1991 Second Law to *Combat* Environmental Crime (31st StÄG),
1994 Law to *Combat* Crime;
1997 Law to *Combat* Corruption;
1998 Law to *Combat* Sexual Offences and Other Dangerous Crimes; Law to Improve the *Combating* of Organised Crime;
2001 Law to *Combat* Tax Evasion;
2001 Law to *Combat* Dangerous Dogs (!);
Law to Improve the *Combating* of Money Laundering and *Combating* the Financing of Terrorism;
Law to Facilitate the *Combating* of Illegal and Clandestine Employment;
2003 Law to Implement the Framework Decision [...] on *Combating* Terrorism[...];
Law to Increase the *Combating* of Illegal Employment.

[4] BVerfGE 86, 390, 393.
[5] BVerfGE 88, 203, 208.

Cases where **detention for the purposes of incapacitation**—a legal institution that seemed close to extinction during the 1970s, not least due to past experience, and that was abolished in the GDR precisely because of this experience—was applied increased fivefold in ten years; more and more new "gaps" in its applicability are being discovered.[6]

1998 Law to Combat Sexual Offences and Other Dangerous Crimes (extending the ambit of detention for purposes of incapacitation);

2002 Reserved Detention for Purposes of Incapacitation (Introduction) Act;

2003 Crimes against Sexual Self-determination (Amendment) Act [. . .] (extending the ambit of detention for the purposes of incapacitation);

2004 Retrospective Imposition of Detention for Purposes of Incapacitation (Introduction) Act;

2008 (June) The Bundestag passes the Retrospective Imposition of Detention for Purposes of Incapacitation for Convictions under Juvenile Criminal Law (Introduction) Act.

Responding to a constitutional complaint of a detainee under an incapacitation order, whose detention had been extended retrospectively beyond the term legally possible at the time of his offence and original sentencing, the **European Court of Human Rights** decided in its judgment of 17 December 2009 that the rights of the appellant had been infringed according to Section 7 of the European Convention on Human Rights (**prohibition of retrospective legislation**). The debate surrounding this judgment and its consequences were still ongoing when this edition went to print.[7]

Soon after the wave of anarchist terrorism had subsided, a new worldwide wave of **Islamist terrorism** began, expressed most spectacularly in the attacks on the World Trade Center in New York (2001), in the Madrid train bombings (2004) and the bombing of the London underground (2005). Germany remains unaffected so far. Besides producing a number of pertinent "combating laws", it also gave rise to heightened debate on the so-called ***Feindstrafrecht*** ("criminal law for enemies") on an international level. This term, at first taken up descriptively and critically,[8] gradually became employed increasingly pro-actively; however, this usage still remains in the minority so far.[9]

---

[6] On this, see also: *Klaus Lüderssen*, Die ewige Versuchung des Täterstrafrechts. Das Verhalten im Strafvollzug als Voraussetzung für vorbehaltene oder nachträgliche Sicherungsverwahrung, in: KJ 2006, 361 ff.

[7] The European Court of Human Rights' judgment is available under: http://cmiskp.echr.coe.int/tkp197/view.asp?action=html&documentId=868979&portal= hbkm&source=externalbydocnumber &table=F69A27FD8FB86142BF01C1166DEA398649.

[8] *Günther Jakobs*, Kriminalisierung im Vorfeld einer Rechtsgutsverletzung, in: ZStW 1985, 751 ff.

[9] For a critical view, cf. e.g. *Francisco Muñoz Conde*, Über das "Feindstrafrecht". German ed. Münster 2007; *Tatjana Hörnle*, Deskriptive und normative Dimensionen des Begriffs "Feindstrafrecht", in: GA 2006, p. 81 ff; *Frank Saliger*, Feindstrafrecht: Kritisches oder totalitäres Strafrechtskonzept? In: JZ 2006, 756 ff.; differentiating between law for enemies and a "criminal law intended to combat", *Massimo Donini*, Das Strafrecht und der Feind. German ed., Münster

The **new discourse on torture** is closely linked to the debate on the "law for enemies". In the USA, under the Bush administration (2001–2008) university scholars close to the government (*John C. Yoo*, *Alan Dershowitz* et al.) basically developed a new doctrine of torture, drafted in detail—though of course torture manifests itself in a modern, enlightened form: for example, needles driven under the fingernails must have been sterilised beforehand.[10]

Unlike in the US, in Germany the issue of torture entered public discourse less in the context of the debate on *Feindstrafrecht* and combating terrorism[11] than in connection with a concrete "normal" criminal case. Acting on the order of his deputy chief of police, an examining police officer threatened a suspect with "considerable pain" if he did not reveal the location of the child he had (allegedly) abducted. Influenced by this threat, the suspect led the investigating team to the child (which he had already killed) and made a confession. The district court gave him a life sentence. It did not take the confession resulting from the threat into consideration, but did consider the evidence thus produced and also based its sentence on a confession repeated later. The particularly serious guilt was noted. The examining officer and the deputy chief of police were sentenced for coercion committed in an official capacity and suborning a subordinate to commit coercion in an official capacity respectively, and were given a warning with a deferred sentence (§ 59 StGB). The disciplinary proceedings against them ended without sanction. After the Federal Constitutional Court had decided not to accept a constitutional complaint brought by the kidnapper, he appealed to the European Court of Human Rights as he had been denied legal aid for proceedings on grounds of misconduct in public office against the state of Hesse. The Grand Chamber of the Court determined that while Section 3 of the European Convention on Human Rights (prohibition of torture and inhuman treatment) had been infringed, Section 6 (right to a fair trial) had not.[12]

2007. A collection of texts on the debate surrounding criminal law for enemies: *Thomas Uwer* (Ed.): Bitte bewahren Sie Ruhe. Leben im Feindrechtsstaat. Berlin 2006; *Thomas Vormbaum / Martin Asholt* (Eds.), Kritik des Feindstrafrechts (incl. introduction by Th. Vormbaum). Berlin, Münster 2009 (contributions by German, Italian and Spanish authors).

[10] On this, cf. *Massimo La Torre*, Ohne Erbarmen. Das Recht der Folter, in: JJZG 10 (2008/2009), p. 266 ff., 277 footnote. "A sterilized needle inserted under the fingernails to produce unbearable pain without any threat to health or life" (thus the American lawyer *Alan Deshowitz*).

[11] Although the "ticking bomb" argument was used very early on by a famous German philosopher and legal theorist. In a 1992 lecture, Luhmann evoked this scenario and suggested "allowing torture by internationally supervised courts, television monitoring of the scene in Geneva or Luxembourg, or remote control using telecommunication": *Niklas Luhmann*, Gibt es in unserer Gesellschaft noch unverzichtbare Normen? Heidelberg 1993, p. 1 ff., 27; here quoted from *La Torre*, op. cit., p. 285.

[12] On the Daschner case and the question of whether the prohibition of torture should be relativised in Germany also—for example, if placed under police law and thus made subject to a balancing assessment—cf. *Olaf Miehe*, NJW 2003, 1219 ff.; *Winfried Brugger*, JZ 2003, 165 ff.; *Rainer Hamm*, NJW 2003, 946 ff.; *Hans Christoph Schäfer*, NJW 2003, 947 ff.—Judgment of the Frankfurt Regional Court of 20 December 2004 in the Daschner case: NJW 2005, 692 ff. The European Court of Human Rights' judgment is available under: http://cmiskp.echr.coe.int/tkp197/viewhbkm.asp?skin= hudoc-en&action=html&table=F69A27FD8FB86142BF01C1166DEA398649&key=82 707&highlight=.

After the establishment of the International Criminal Court,[13] which the Federal Republic of Germany had actively supported, a German **Code of International Criminal Law** was passed, thus taking a further step towards the development of an international criminal law.[14]

By putting international criminal law into the form of positive legislation, the problem of retroactivity in future cases dealing with system injustice will be avoided. At the same time, enshrining international criminal law in a criminal code of its own makes it possible to limit tendencies towards relaxing the standards of the rule of law and the application of strict criminal law doctrine vis-à-vis "macro-criminals" in this area.[15] Any account of events in contemporary criminal law would remain incomplete without a glance at **European criminal law**. Unlike the national uniformity achieved in German criminal law in 1870, where decades of work in the criminal law of the individual states and the theory of criminal law had aimed at developing a balance between protecting the accused and the interests of the prosecution, the criminal law of the EU—in keeping with the times—focuses on "protection" and "combating". At the forefront are directives and framework decisions that, far from obliging member states to raise the standards of the rule of law in criminal law in equal measure, in fact consistently require them to create new laws of criminalisation .[16]

A legislative product with the hardly justified claim to the title of "Criminal Law Reform Act" matches the manifestations of contemporary criminal law described here well.

---

[13] For the previous history, cf. *Heiko Ahlbrecht*, Geschichte der völkerrechtlichen Strafgerichtsbarkeit im 20. Jahrhundert. Baden-Baden 1999, particularly p. 335 ff.; *Christina Möller*, Völkerstrafrecht und Internationaler Strafgerichtshof, Münster 2003, particularly p. 573 ff. The International Criminal Court had been preceded by the *ad hoc* tribunals for crimes committed in the former Yugoslavia in Den Haag and crimes committed in the Rwandan conflict in Arusha. By contrast, after the end of the Iraq war the former dictator Saddam Hussein was executed following a comparatively brief trial; on this, cf. *Massimo Donini*, Der Tod des Saddam Hussein, in: JJZG 8 (2006/2007), p. 408 ff.; a critical view is presented in *Kai Ambos / Primurat Said*, Das Todesurteil gegen Saddam Hussein, in: JZ 2007, 822 ff. Given the power relations, no court investigation into the Iraq war under international law took place; on this, cf. the essay collection *Kai Ambos / Jörg Arnold* (Eds.), Der Irak-Krieg und das Völkerrecht. Berlin 2004; also cf. *Stefan Baufeld*, Der 11. September 2001 als Herausforderung für das Völkerrecht. Münster 2005, p. 24 ff.

[14] On its creation, cf. *Bundesministerium der Justiz* (Ed.), Arbeitsentwurf eines Gesetzes zur Einführung des Völkerstrafgesetzbuchs mit Begründung. Erstellt von der vom Bundesministerium der Justiz eingesetzten Arbeitsgruppe Völkerstrafgesetzbuch. Baden-Baden 2001; *Sascha Lüder / Thomas Vormbaum* (Eds.), Materialien zum Völkerstrafgesetzbuch. Dokumentation des Gesetzgebungsverfahrens. Münster 2002.

[15] On elements of "criminal law for enemies" in international criminal law, cf. *Emanuela Fronza*, Feindstrafrecht und Internationale Strafgerichtsbarkeit, in: JoJZG 1 (2007), 121 ff.

[16] On this, cf. *Wolfgang Naucke*, Europäische Gemeinsamkeiten in der neueren Strafrechtsgeschichte und Folgerungen für die aktuelle Debatte, in: JJZG 3 (2001/2002), 439 ff.; *Massimo Donini*, Ein neues strafrechtliches Mittelalter? Altes und Neues in der Expansion des Wirtschaftstrafrechts, in: Id., Strafrechtstheorie, p. 203 ff.

After the reform of criminal law attempted in the 1950s had remained a mere "torso",[17] reform legislation was revisited a quarter of a century later, with the intention of completing the revision of the Special Part of the Criminal Code "as far as possible".[18] In 1996, the Federal Ministry of Justice developed the draft bill of a **Sixth Criminal Law Reform Act** (RefE–6. StrRG). Besides aligning sentences, this draft also intended to make significant changes to the offences of assault, offences against personal freedom, sexual offences, offences against property and assets and arson; in fact, "at a closer glance it [affected] fundamental questions of how definitions of offences were constructed and was of relevance to many questions of the Special Part of the Criminal Code".[19]

This draft bill was submitted for consultation in October 1996. It was officially sent to a working group of 29 teachers of criminal law, the state administrations of justice, the Federal Supreme Court and the criminal defence lawyers' associations for comments with a deadline of 21 February 1997, just under five months, for their reports.[20] The Federal government and coalition factions tabled draft laws as early as 14 March 1997. These were based on the draft bill, but made initial, significant changes. In May 1997, the Bundesrat commented extensively on these draft bills.

The Federal government's response of September 1997 to the comments of the Bundesrat adopted numerous suggestions from the federal states, and also took into consideration a number of comments received in the interim as well as the results of the expert consultations carried out by the German Bundestag.

On 4 June 1997, a public hearing had been conducted in the Committee of Legal Affairs of the Bundestag, during which some experts had commented on the planned changes.[21] The extent to which the draft's intention to make increased use of typified examples (*Regelbeispiele*) instead of qualified offences was acceptable was a matter of particular controversy amongst the experts. The majority of experts were opposed to an expansion of the typified example method: the expansion of sentencing frames had already transferred more responsibility for determining correct sentences into the hands of the judiciary, and it was highly questionable to increase this transfer even further. However, the ensuing legislative process paid no heed to these concerns.

In line with the Committee of Legal Affairs' recommendation, the 6th Criminal Law Reform Act was passed by the German Bundestag with the votes of the CDU, CSU and FDP on 14 November 1997. Even though the Social Democrat members

---

[17] *H.J. Hirsch*, Bilanz der Strafrechtsreform, in: Gedenkschrift Hilde Kaufmann (Berlin 1986), p. 133 f.

[18] BT-Drucksache 13/7164, Begr. p. 18.

[19] *Freund*, ZStW 109 (1997), p. 455 (455): "It is no exaggeration to state: the scope of this enterprise equates to a Grand Reform of the Special Part".

[20] For individual details, cf. *Freund*, ZStW 109 (1997), p. 455, 469.

[21] Prosecutor General *Frenzel*, Chief Prosecutors *Gold-Pfuhl*, *Hubmann* (Prosecution of the District Court Nuremberg-Fürth), *Kempf* (German Bar Association), Federal Supreme Court judge *Nack*, Federal Supreme Court presiding judge *Schäfer*, Prof. *Sack* (Hamburg), *Weber* (President of the District Court Traunstein), *Wick* (Public Prosecution Office Munich) and lawyer Prof. *Widmaier* (Karlsruhe).

of the Committee of Legal Affairs had agreed to most of the suggested changes, the SPD delegates abstained from voting. The Green Party and PDS delegates voted against the Act. The Bundesrat decided not to object. On 1 April of the election year 1998, the Act came into force.

Hardly ever has a law calling itself a reform act been less deserving of the name. Since the 1960s, this title had been used for laws that critically reviewed the inventory of criminal law, and had thus judiciously not been given to any law since 1975. Now it was used as the title of a law the innovations of which—besides a few conciliatory nods towards equality-compliant language—mainly consisted of tougher sentencing provisions and which furthermore evinced a high number of technical defects.[22]

That this law of all, which followed feminist demands for equality-compliant language, abolished the privileged offence of Section 217 StGB (infanticide), one of the few provisions in the StGB which were really favourable to women, is surely one of the most striking paradoxes of contemporary legislation.[23]

The waning first decade of the twenty-first century produced two important innovations in criminal law and criminal procedure:

Section 46b StGB[24] replaced existing special provisions with a general law on **"turning Crown evidence"**. Apart from general concerns with regard to these kinds of laws, objected to repeatedly by criminal law academia, this new law is objectionable as it is limited to only the most serious offences. Paradoxically, these concerns can at best be alleviated by referring to another dubious regulation—discontinuance according to Section 153a StPO. The completely uncoordinated follow-up provision on false accusation in Section 164(3) StGB[25] shows that legislative technique, which had reached its nadir with the Sixth Criminal Law Reform Act, was not set to improve in the new century. Of course, we should not ignore that both Section 46b StGB and Section 153a StPO will probably be embraced by both prosecution and defendants. With certain reservations, this also applies to the new Section 257c StPO, which gave **plea agreements in criminal proceedings**, already recognised and outlined within a strict framework in previous judicial practice, a statutory form. This trend towards "relieving the pressure" on the administration of justice, the decisive breakthrough of which was achieved with the Lex Emminger of 4 January 1924 as described above, was given a further boost by these new laws.

---

[22] On this, cf. the contributions in: *Friedrich Dencker / Eberhard Struensee / Ursula Nelles / Ulrich Stein*, Einführung in das 6. Strafrechtsreformgesetz 1998. Munich 1998.

[23] On this, see *Andrea Czelk*, "Privilegierung" und Vorurteil. Positionen der Bürgerlichen Frauenbewegung zum Unehelichenrecht und zur Kindstötung im Kaiserreich. Cologne, Weimar, Vienna 2005, p. 234 ff.

[24] Introduced by the 43rd Criminal Law Amendment Act of 29 July 2009 (BGBl. I, p. 2288); more detail in *Streng*, NK. 3rd ed. 2009.

[25] More detail in *Vormbaum*, NK. 3rd ed. 2009, § 164 marginal note 79 ff.

§ 7 Review and Outlook

I. Review

Now that we have reached the end of our journey through the history of criminal law of our legal-historical period, it is worth casting our minds back to our initial statements on broadening the perspective of the history of law and the history of criminal law. Contemporary legal history should examine the development of law in our legal-historical period critically, and its questions should be based on legal theory. In order to conduct such an examination, we considered the state of the criminal law at the beginning of the legal-historical period, and encountered Enlightenment philosophy's postulate of a secular, rational and humane criminal law. Of course, we also saw the danger posed to the humanitarian aspect by Enlightenment thought's utilitarian rationalism, which was opposed by Immanuel Kant's philosophy of law. Furthermore, we observed that this philosophy was characterised by strict respect for legality and the citizen's autonomy, but that criminal law on the whole maintained a high degree of punitiveness throughout the nineteenth century, moving from a protection of rights to the less strict protection of legal interests, and with interventionist, opportunist political and police criminal legislation as its constant companion.

Towards the end of the nineteenth century, this liberal but strict retributive criminal law dissolved—not because of its strictness (which could have been countered by a more lenient retributive criminal law), but because of its actual or supposed inability to combat crime effectively. This fresh wave of utilitarian thought produced an expansion of criminal law (this time only thinly disguised as humanitarian), the full extent of which only becomes clear if the flood of supplementary penal provisions that followed political demand are considered. This created a stealthy dilution of strict legality in criminal law. However, at least it also again showed ways of retracting inexpedient criminal law and/or forms of imprisonment. The reform of criminal law that set in shortly after the beginning of the twentieth century was led by Lisztian demands: on the one hand, avoiding **short-term imprisonment**, on the other, expanding judicial discretion at the cost of legal certainty and

T. Vormbaum and M. Bohlander, *A Modern History of German Criminal Law*, DOI 10.1007/978-3-642-37273-5_7, © Springer-Verlag Berlin Heidelberg 2014

the introduction of **security measures** in addition to a criminal punishment commensurate with the blameworthiness of the crime in question. It was precisely the least problematic aspect of the modern school of criminal law, the demand for a reduction of inexpedient criminal law, that earned the criminal reform the enmity first of conservative, and later of National Socialist legal theorists and criminologists.

The dissolution of legality in criminal law can be seen on all levels of criminal law (theory of offences, criminal legislation, case law), which became increasingly **material**, **ethicised**, **subjective** and **flexible**. This is expressed in the *Tätertypenlehre* (subjectivisation), the supplanting of the doctrine of the infringement of protected legal interests by the **doctrine of the infringement of duty** (materialisation), in the dilution of the distinction between legality and morality recognised at least since Kant (ethicisation), and in the increased importance of the role of the judge and the admission of **analogy** *in malam partem* (flexibilisation). Brutal wartime criminal legislation (already evident, if less strongly so, during the First World War) clearly shows the utilitarian criminal law's potential to violate human rights, regardless of its disguise as "atonement".

A historical moment of shock after 1945 led to a **renaissance of natural law**. Admittedly, it took on an authoritarian guise that was reflected primarily in the judiciary (most judicial staff had received their training during the NS period), and that furthermore relied on the numerous legal sanctions created under the NS regime which remained in force after 1945. This was countered by a **fresh emphasis on the concept of finality**, which in its misapprehension of historical context thought itself able to propagate a "turning away from Kant and Hegel" as a means of achieving a liberal criminal law. It benefited not only from the 1960s *Zeitgeist* that demanded reform in state and society, but also from the fact that the toughening and expansion of criminal law during the NS period had created considerable—if initially ignored—potential for decriminalisation. The toughened sexual offences, which were not retracted after 1945, were the focus of most of the public attention and debate of all the areas of reform. And thus a revival of the *concept of protected legal interests* was used to legitimise decriminalisations of an area the criminalisation of which in the nineteenth century had been a reason for "inventing" the concept of protected legal interests in the first place. While functionalised, politicised utilitarian criminal law had been radicalised under the NS regime, a variety that was more lenient on the whole succeeded in gaining the upper hand for a short period between 1965 and 1975. From the mid-1970s onwards, the climate in criminal policy became harsher once more. Especially since German reunification, which here forms the boundary of our "contemporary legal events", **criminal law is becoming tougher once again**, even though there is no rise in crime that might justify this movement. The parallels to the previous century are unmistakeable. Politics is reacting to stories in the tabloid press with frenzied activity in criminal policy (and criminalisation). Anyone demanding decriminalisation—a catchphrase of criminal policy around 1970—is nowadays accused of being naive and unworldly. Between 1995 and 2006, the number of prisoners in Germany rose by over a third.[1]

[1] Cf. the report in: *Frankfurter Allgemeine Zeitung* of 12 December 2006, p. 11.

Of course, there are many indications that the expansion (and the recent toughening) of criminal law is not restricted to Germany alone, at least to some extent. Silva Sanchez's 2003 analysis, which has now become practically an international classic in the field of criminal law, notes phenomena and their causes that apply to all industrial nations—especially in the age of globalisation.

For these reasons, a survey of the development of criminal law in the past 200 years is unable to confirm modern criminal law's frequently cited trend towards leniency and humanisation. While criminal law may have become more modern, it has become more liberal, humane and lenient at best in a few strictly demarcated areas and during brief phases, and the present is certainly not one of these phases.[2] The fact that this expanded criminal law, the offence definitions of which are increasingly vague, is generally applied with restraint by the Federal German justice system is no cause for reassurance, for under the rule of law the liberal practice of criminal law should not be guaranteed by the insight of criminal judges, but by the legislator.

II. Continuities

As has already been mentioned several times, the question of **continuity** forms a particular problem of legal history and is particularly pertinent to the history of criminal law in the twentieth century. This problem can be pinpointed in the question of whether the period of National Socialism follows the general development of criminal law or constitutes a break. The aspect of normality and modernity has already been mentioned in regard to the National Socialist period (cf. § 5 V. 1. above). Furthermore, our complete overview should already have rendered the continuity perspective plausible, so that the examples of criminal offences issued during the NS period that remain in force today, used elsewhere by the author to illustrate the concept of continuity,[3] need not be repeated here. We can see in all of these examples that the problematic offences were already discussed earlier in the context of the reformatory work on criminal law during the Weimar period, and in

[2] This observation can be generalised, arriving at a criticism of the unreflectingly optimistic faith in progress that can be seen, for example, in a condescending criticism of medieval criminal law (already voiced by Enlightenment thinkers). On this, cf. *Evans*, Rituals, p. 2: "But the unhistorical, complacent and self-congratulatory aspects of this view have long been obvious." As our survey has shown repeatedly, secularisation is no guarantee for humanisation. On this, cf. *Evans*, op. cit., p. 3: "Where ideology has been used to justify state violence in the twentieth century, it has often little in common with religion."

[3] *Vormbaum*, Festschrift OLG Schleswig-Holstein, p. 71 ff., 74 ff.: purely optional liability for attempt; measures for reform and incapacitation; the offence of using threats or force (Section 240 StGB); the offence of abuse of trust (Section 266 StGB); omission to effect an easy rescue (Section 323c StGB); false testimony (Section 153 StGB).

some cases even earlier. They are embedded in the aforementioned elements of *materialisation*, *ethicisation*, *subjectivisation* and *flexibilisation*,[4,5]

> In criminal legislation, all of the characteristics mentioned converge in two aspects: a rise in the *number* of offences, thus in **criminalisation**, and in the rise of **indeterminate** criminal laws. Even after 1945, this trait of criminal legislation has continued to flourish. The line of "combating" laws listed in the section on "Current events in criminal law" shows clearly the connection between the four cited elements, and particularly the functionalisation of criminal law.[6] This style of legislation begins in the 1930s (precursors aside). Since then, legislation has been discovering a need for "protection" and "combating" at ever shorter intervals. This development corresponds to the development of the intensity of legislative activity: of more than 200 changes to the Criminal Code between 1871 and the present, 32 occurred between 1871 and 1933, 59 between 1871 and 1949, and well over 150 occurred in the roughly 55 years of the Federal Republic alone. This does not even take into consideration that a significant part of the new criminal laws – namely the larger part – is no longer contained in the Criminal Code, but in supplementary penal provisions, and that the rise in their number (as well as the rise in the number of regulatory offences) keeps pace with this development. Despite the reform of criminal law in the 1960s, changes leading to the abolition of offences remain negligible.[7]

Asking the question about the continuity of the criminal law in the twentieth century—and perhaps even longer—and thus not regarding the National Socialist period as a break,[8] seems provocative. The associations conjured up by key words

---

[4] *Gerhard Pauli*, Rechtsprechung, uses a comparison of the criminal jurisprudence of the Reich Supreme Court from 1933 to 1945 and that of the Federal Supreme Court, arriving at the similar shared traits of *materialisation*, *subjectivisation* and a *tendency towards social law* (he understands "a tendency towards social law" as a tendency oriented towards what is "socially necessary", which is closely related to materialisation).

[5] The development of the so-called *factual point of view* also forms part of materialisation and flexibilisation. One important characteristic of liberal criminal law is its **subsidiarity** to the legal order as a whole; it should not penalise behaviour that civil or public law does not regard as unlawful or at least does not consider worthy of punishment. While the factual point of view is not unproblematic as far as these areas are concerned, it can—for example in social and employment law—serve to create a fair balance of interests that legal regulations have not made sufficient provision for; however, in criminal law it only serves to expand the ambit of what is punishable and thus comes into conflict with the principle of *nullum crimen sine lege*. The "progenitor" of this line of argument is **Hans-Jürgen Bruns** (1908–1994). In his habilitation "Die Befreiung des Strafrechts vom zivilistischen Denken", published in 1938, he additionally based it on the "healthy common sense of the people". Despite this shady provenance, it is still highly popular with the criminal courts; on the character of the factual manager in connection with Section 14(2) StGB, cf. *Marc Büning*, Die Strafbarkeit des faktischen Gesellschafters einer GmbH. Münster 2004.

[6] This has also been pointed out by *Michael Hettinger*, NJW 1996, 2263, (2264): "It is possible to combat vermin and disease, and maybe even an enemy who has invaded the country. However, criminal law under the rule of law has other aims". I doubt whether we are dealing with a (mere) "*linguistic* subversion of a legal field" [sc.: criminal law] (as stated by *Hettinger* op. cit., p. 2263).

[7] Elsewhere I have attempted to sum up the dubious elements in a ten-point list: *Vormbaum*, "Politisches" Strafrecht, in: ZStW 1995, 734 ff., 738.

[8] An understanding of continuity that was naive and immanent within the system, so to speak, existed early on in the 1950s. In his *Einführung in die Geschichte der deutschen Strafrechtspflege*, first published in 1947, **Eberhard Schmidt** stated that "the continuity of genuine theory of criminal law did not break off [during the National Socialist period]" (*Eb. Schmidt*, Einführung, § 360, p. 451; cf. § 5 footnote 204 above); naturally, this constitutes more or less the opposite of the

such as "concentration camp", "Holocaust" and "*Vernichtungskrieg*" shape our understanding of that period so strongly (and justifiably so) that it is easy to assume that these elements must have influenced all other spheres of life. However, this assumption makes it hard for us to access certain problems and ultimately hinders us in critically questioning today's criminal law. This will be discussed further below. First, however, some further points on the theory of continuity.

1) During the early years of the Federal Republic, there was a palpable element of continuity in terms of a **continuity of personnel**: a number of the academics still teaching criminal law during the 1960s had already done so during the National Socialist period.[9] The aforementioned Edmund Mezger is a classic example of this.[10] However, the attention paid to this aspect of continuity has now subsided due to biological reasons; it can itself also be problematic, for a focus on personal elements potentially threatens to distract from structural continuity, a threat one might term the "trap of personalisation".[11]
2) The concept of a **structural continuity** in the theory of criminal law in the twentieth century has by now become the dominant one among legal historians. The "caesura model" ("perversion" 1933—"convalescence" 1945) scarcely has any more adherents. General history, too, needed a long time before it could face analysing those areas where the National Socialist period represents not a break, but a continuation of earlier lines of development—and more and more of these areas are being discovered (cf. § 5 V. 1. above).[12]
3) Apparently the development of criminal law criticised here experienced a particularly strong surge during the time of the National Socialist regime. Legal-historical discourse attempts to take account of this by speaking of the

understanding of continuity referred to here.—In the preface to this first edition, Eb. Schmidt states that he wrote this book "during the darkest days of German history". As he immediately adds that the plan for the book already existed "before the political collapse", these darkest days of Germany history can only refer to the days *after* this collapse. The survivors of the Holocaust and opponents of the regime will more likely have been of the opinion that the "collapse" marked the end of the darkest years of German history. Whether the author really tackled "aberrations in the field of criminal law in the spoken and written word", as he attests in *ibid.*, and "dealt with the different manifestations of degenerate [!] utilitarian jurisprudence" is a subject for future research; there are some arguments against it. Even with the recent substantial monograph by *Simone Gräfin von Hardenberg*, Eberhard Schmidt. (1891–1977), Ein Beitrag zur Geschichte unseres Rechtsstaats, 2009, a critical biography of Eberhard Schmidt is still lacking. Closer consideration should be paid to the statement of *Georg Dahm* in his letter to *Eberhard Schmidt* of 4 February 1948 (reproduced in the annual JZG 7 (2005/2006), 199 ff.), which the above-mentioned author interprets rather generously in *Schmidt's* favour on page 366 ff.

[9] To point this out was regarded as improper, probably due to a silent, more or less reflective assumption of continuity (soon to prove double-edged), besides the need for loyalty between colleagues, which could also be termed cronyism.

[10] As already discussed in § 5, footnote 240; on this, cf. *Francisco Muñoz Conde*, Edmund Mezger. Beiträge zu einem Juristenleben. Berlin 2007.

[11] *Pauli/Vormbaum*, Preface, in: Id., Justiz und Nationalsozialismus, p. VII.

[12] Ibid.

radicalisation or **acceleration** of this development. This has the advantage that an awareness for lines of continuity remains, but at the same time the special features of this period are taken into consideration. For, of course, there is no reason why the differences in quality between the Weimar and post-war democracy on the one hand and the NS regime on the other should be neglected. While many of the dubious laws enacted by the National Socialists had been debated in the time before the NS regime, they had—crucially—*not* been enacted then. It was precisely the NS regime, with its less scrupulous maxims of legal policy, its greater hermeticism and its continuous rule unbroken by an electoral vote, that was easily able to put these legislative plans into practice.

Of course, the theory of radicalisation cannot change the fact that the ground for the manifest unlawfulness of the National Socialist regime and its exorbitant crimes was also laid by tradition, and that a large part of the "abnormal" features of National Socialism can be understood not as a break in tradition, but as the ultimate consequence of important elements of tradition that still continue to have an effect today.

4) In any case, identifying a provision's origin in the National Socialist period is thus of heuristic value for the current debate in criminal policy, i.e. as a starting point for questioning. In the National Socialist past and its criminal law, German criminal law doctrine—if you will—*also* possesses a chance that other nations do not: the fact that a criminal law or figure of thought in criminal law was compatible with National Socialism gives us cause to question it critically.

For decades, Germany has used the catch-phrase of "coming to terms with the past". However, "coming to terms with the past" can only mean: coming to terms with the present, or—even better—the future.[13]

III. Outlook

As mentioned several times earlier, the characteristics of the line of development criticised here are:

Flexibilisation: Dominance of the idea of finality rather than the idea of law. Any half-plausible purpose, usually formulated as serving the purpose of protection or—in its stricter variety—combating, stands good chances of gaining support from criminal law.

Moralisation: The strict demarcation—recognised since Kant—of legality on the one hand and morality on the other, of law on the one hand and of ethics on the other, of moral condemnation on the one hand and adjudication for disturbance of

[13] *Arthur Kaufmann*, Rechtsphilosophie und Nationalsozialismus, in: Recht, Rechtsphilosophie und Nationalsozialismus. (ARSP supplement No. 18). Wiesbaden 1983, p. 1: "It seems to me we must come to terms with the future, if we have to come to terms with anything".

communal life on the other, is driven back. Often this is disguised by emotionally charged formulations giving out the purpose of protection.

Materialisation: The dismantling of protective forms of the rule of law, and the establishment of evaluations based on content. A popular means of achieving this end is employing the argument of "liability loopholes".[14]

Subjectivisation: An increased tendency to evaluate an offence according to standards internal to an offender; in terms of *legislative technique*: an increase in subjective characteristics of offences as opposed to objective characteristics; in terms of *theory of criminal law*: an increase in elements taken from *Gesinnungsstrafrecht* rather than *Tatstrafrecht*. Personalisation ("terrorist", "dealer", "child molester", "speeder") plays a significant role in the borderline area between the doctrine of criminal law and criminal policy.

If this development is considered ominous—and it merits being thought of thus—then the question of the practical implications for the present day arises. However, this is no longer a topic for a textbook on the history of criminal law. Therefore, only two general and thus necessarily somewhat abstract points will be mentioned here: the **punishment limitation theory** and the **idea of law**.

The first aspect affects our understanding of the theory of criminal law. Following *Wolfgang Naucke*, it is possible to distinguish between two prior understandings that can be employed in the theory of criminal law:

1) Theory of criminal law as an attempt "to equip [the state] with a clear description of the behaviour that requires combating as criminal, i.e. to sharpen criminal law as a tool following a specific purpose". In this case, the doctrine of criminal law is a *doctrine of prosecution*, a technical tool to render prosecution more effective.
2) Theory of criminal law as liberal doctrine or doctrine of decriminalisation. *Punishing* is always authoritarian. What other word can be used for it if the state imposes fines on its citizens, forbids them to use their motor vehicle for a certain period of time, takes away their freedom or even (in some countries, including democratic countries) takes their lives? If this is considered the nature of criminal law, then any criminal *law* must indeed be authoritarian. However, if one rather believes that these are only characteristics of *punishment*, but that the most important task of criminal law—precisely because it is law—lies in setting boundaries to state activity and society's desire for punishment, then the fundamental nature of criminal law is actually anti-authoritarian; and whether it is liberal or not depends only on the *extent* to which it limits state punishment.

Both of these terms are ideal-typical ones; in reality, they cannot always be neatly distinguished. Ideal-typical terms have the advantage that they give us guidelines for practical action we can attempt to approximate in our everyday practice. In this sense, the concept of a theory limiting punishment is promoted here. However, if the functionalisation and expansion of criminal law (or rather: of

[14] On this, see *Thomas Vormbaum*, Glosse: Strafbarkeitslücken, in: JZ 1999, 613.

punishment) is to be countered by autonomous ideas of law, and the idea of pure finality to be set against the idea of law, then *all* elements of the idea of law—*justice*, *legal certainty* and finally (also) practicality—need to achieve recognition.[15] Every criminal law and every interpretation of the law must stand up to each of these three criteria. We cannot go into detail here on what shape this might take.[16] Measured against this threefold yardstick, there are several features of our criminal law that should look very different from the way they do at present.

[15] Cf. *Gustav Radbruch*, Rechtsphilosophie. 7th ed., ed. Erik Wolf. Stuttgart 1970, p. 124 ff., 146 ff., 168 ff.

[16] Cf. the approach taken in *Thomas Vormbaum*, Aktuelles zur Lage des Strafrechts, in: Festschrift for Dimitris Th. Tsatsos. Baden-Baden 2003, p. 703 ff.

Important Primary and Secondary Sources

Only works that are cited more than once, particularly in more than one paragraph (and abbreviated), or that are of seminal importance are listed here. In citations, authors of more than one work are referenced by including a meaningful word from the work's title, insofar as a differentiation between works is not obvious from the context.

ACHENBACH, Hans: Historische und dogmatische Grundlagen der strafrechtssystematischen Schuldlehre. Berlin 1974.

ALBER, Peter-Paul: Die Geschichte der Öffentlichkeit im deutschen Strafverfahren. Berlin 1974.

AMELUNG, Knut: Rechtsgüterschutz und Schutz der Gesellschaft. Untersuchungen zum Inhalt und zum Anwendungsbereich eines Strafrechtsprinzips auf dogmengeschichtlicher Grundlage. Zugleich ein Beitrag zur Lehre von der "Sozialschädlichkeit" des Verbrechens. Frankfurt am Main 1972.

ANGERMUND, Ralph: Deutsche Richterschaft 1919–1945. Krisenerfahrung, Illusion, politische Rechtsprechung. Frankfurt am Main 1990.

ARMBRÜSTER, Klaus: Die Entwicklung der Verteidigung in Strafsachen. Ein rechtsgeschichtlicher Beitrag von den Anfängen einer Verteidigertätigkeit in Deutschland bis zum Ende der Weimarer Zeit. Berlin 1980.

ARNOLD, Jörg (Ed.): Die Normalität des Strafrechts der DDR. Band 1. Gesammelte Beiträge und Dokumente. In collaboration with Birte E. Keppler et al. Freiburg im Breisgau 1995.

ASHOLT, Martin: Straßenverkehrstatbestände—Reformdiskussion und Gesetzgebung seit dem Ausgang des 19. Jahrhunderts. Berlin 2007.

BANDEMER, Dagmar: Heinrich Albert Zachariae. Rechtsdenken zwischen Restauration und Reformation. Frankfurt am Main 1985.

BARRENECHE, Ninette: Materialien zu einer Strafrechtsgeschichte der Münchener Räterepublik. Berlin 2004.

BAUMGARTEN, Immanuel: Dem Verbrechen auf der Spur. Eine Geschichte der Kriminologie und Kriminalpolitik in Deutschland 1880–1980. Göttingen 2006.

T. Vormbaum and M. Bohlander, *A Modern History of German Criminal Law*,
DOI 10.1007/978-3-642-37273-5,

BAUMGARTEN, Ralf: Zweikampf—§§ 201–210 StGB a.F. Reformdiskussion und Gesetzgebung von 1870 bis zur Aufhebung der Zweikampfbestimmungen. Berlin 2002.

BEBBER, Katharina van: Wiedergutgemacht? Die Entschädigung für Opfer der nationalsozialistischen Verfolgung nach dem Bundesergänzungsgesetz durch die Entschädigungsgerichte im OLG-Bezirk Hamm, in: Pauli / Vormbaum, p. 251 ff.

BECCARIA, Cesare: Cesare Beccaria, On Crimes and Punishments (1764). Mit einer Einführung von Wolfgang Naucke. Berlin 2004.

BECKER, Peter: Verderbnis und Entartung. Eine Geschichte der Kriminologie des 19. Jahrhunderts als Diskurs und Praxis. Göttingen 2002.

BERNER, Albert Friedrich: Die Strafgesetzgebung in Deutschland vom Jahre 1751 bis zur Gegenwart. Leipzig 1867 (Reprint Aalen 1978).

BERNHARD, Lars: Falsche Verdächtigung—§§ 164, 165 StGB—und Vortäuschung einer Straftat—§ 145 d StGB. Reformdiskussion und Gesetzgebung seit 1870. Berlin 2003.

BLASIUS, Dirk: Bürgerliche Gesellschaft und Kriminalität. Zur Sozialgeschichte Preußens im Vormärz. Göttingen 1976.

[BMJ] BUNDESMINISTERIUM DER JUSTIZ (Ed.): Im Namen des Volkes? Über die Justiz im Staat der SED. Exhibition of the Federal Ministry of Justice. I: catalogue vol., II: documentarz vol., III: academic companion vol. Leipzig 1994.

BOHNERT, Cornelia: Zu Straftheorie und Strafverständnis im Schulenstreit der Jahrhundertwende. Pfaffenweiler 1992.

BOLDER, Paul Otto: Der Versuch einer Reform des Strafverfahrens und der Strafgerichtsverfassung in den Jahren 1885, 1894 und 1895. Freiburg (jur. Diss.) 1934.

BRUNS, Hans-Jürgen: Die Befreiung des Strafrechts vom zivilistischen Denken. Berlin 1938.

BUMKE, Erwin: Verordnung über Gerichtsverfassung und Strafrechtspflege vom 4. Januar 1924. Berlin 1924.

BUSCH, Jost-Dietrich: Die Strafbarkeit der erfolglosen Teilnahme und die Geschichte des § 49a StGB. Marburg (jur. Diss.) 1964.

BUSCH, Tim: Die deutsche Strafrechtsreform—Ein Rückblick auf die sechs Reformen des deutschen Strafrechts (1969–1998). Baden-Baden 2005.

BUSCHMANN, Arno: Nationalsozialistische Weltanschauung und Gesetzgebung 1933–1945. Vol. 2 (all published so far): Dokumentation einer Entwicklung. Wien 2002.

BUSCHMANN, Arno: Das Strafgesetzbuch in der Zeit von 1933 bis 1945—Die Novellierungen des Strafgesetzbuchs in der Epoche des Nationalsozialismus, in: Vormbaum / Welp (Eds.), Das Strafgesetzbuch. Supplementary vol. I, p. 53–138.

BYRD, B. Sharon, and Joachim Hruschka: Kant zu Strafrecht und Strafe im Rechtsstaat, in: Juristenzeitung 2007, 957–964.

CARSTEN, Ernst: Die Geschichte der Staatsanwaltschaft in Deutschland bis zur Gegenwart (Wroclaw 1932). Reprint Frankfurt am Main / Tokyo 1970.

CATTANEO, Mario A.: Aufklärung und Strafrecht. Beiträge zur deutschen Strafrechtsphilosophie des 18. Jahrhunderts. Baden-Baden 1998.

CIPOLLA, Tamara: Friedrich Karl von Strombeck. Leben und Werk. Berlin 2010.

COLLIN, Peter: "Wächter der Gesetze" oder "Organ der Staatsregierung"? Konzipierung, Einrichtung und Anleitung der Staatsanwaltschaft durch das preußische Justizministerium. Von den Anfängen bis 1860. Frankfurt am Main 2000.

CORNELIUS, Kai: Vom spurlosen Verschwindenlassen zur Benachrichtigungspflicht bei Festnahmen. Berlin 2006.

CZEGUN, Ignazio: Die Mitwirkung von Bundesrat und Reichstag bei der Kolonialgesetzgebung, in: JJZG 8 (2006/2007), 174–202.

CZELK, Andrea: "Privilegierung" und Vorurteil. Positionen der Bürgerlichen Frauenbewegung zum Unehelichenrecht und zur Kindstötung im Kaiserreich. Cologne, Weimar, Vienna 2005.

DANNECKER, Gerhard: Die Entwicklung des strafrechtlichen Rückwirkungsverbots und des Milderungsgebots in Deutschland, in: JJZG 3 (2001/2002), 125–202.

DENCKER, Friedrich: Die strafrechtliche Beurteilung von NS-Rechtsprechungsakten, in: Peter Salje (Ed.), Recht und Unrecht im Nationalsozialismus. Münster 1985, p. 294 ff.

DENCKER, Friedrich: Kontinuität und Diskontinuität im materiellen Strafrecht am Beispiel des Nötigungstatbestandes, in: Pauli / Vormbaum, p. 129 ff.

DENCKER, Friedrich: NS-Justiz vor Gericht, in: Jörg Requate (Ed.), Recht und Justiz im gesellschaftlichen Aufbruch (1960–1975). Bundesrepublik Deutschland, Italien und Frankreich im Vergleich. Baden-Baden 2003, p. 93 ff.

DERSCH, Gisela: Begünstigung, Hehlerei und unterlassene Verbrechensanzeige in der gemeinrechtlichen Strafrechtsdoktrin bis zum Erlass des Reichsstrafgesetzbuchs. Göttingen 1980.

DETTMAR, Juliane: Legalität und Opportunität im Strafprozess. Reformdiskussion und Gesetzgebung von 1877 bis 1933. Berlin 2008.

DEZZA, Ettore: Beiträge zur Geschichte des modernen italienischen Strafrechts. Berlin 2004.

DEZZA, Ettore: Beiträge zur Geschichte des italienischen Strafprozesses im Kodifikationszeitalter. Münster 2007.

DEZZA, Ettore: Der Feind der Wahrheit. Das Verteidigungsverbot und der Richter als "Faktotum" in der habsburgischen Strafrechtskodifikation (1768–1873), in: JJZG 9 (2007/2008).

DEZZA, Ettore, und Loredana Garlati: Beiträge zur Geschichte der habsburgischen Strafgesetzgebung in Italien. With an appendix: Cesare Beccarias Gutachten zum Allgemeinen Gesetzbuch über Verbrechen und Strafen aus dem Jahre 1791. Münster, Berlin 2010.

DIRKS, Christian: "Die Verbrechen der anderen". Auschwitz und der Auschwitz-Prozeß der DDR. Das Verfahren gegen den KZ-Arzt Dr. Horst Fischer. Paderborn 2004.

DONINI, Massimo: Strafrechtstheorie und Strafrechtsreform. Beiträge zum Strafrecht und zur Strafrechtspolitik in Italien und Europa. Berlin 2006.

DURYNEK Jürgen: Korruptionsdelikte (§§ 331 ff. StGB). Reformdiskussion und Gesetzgebung seit dem 19. Jahrhundert. Berlin 2008.

DÜWELL, Franz Josef, and Thomas Vormbaum (Eds.): Themen juristischer Zeitgeschichte (1). Schwerpunktthema: Recht und Nationalsozialismus. Baden-Baden 1998.

ECKERT, Jörn: Die Kieler rechtswissenschaftliche Fakultät—"Stoßtruppfakultät", in: Heribert Ostendorf / Uwe Danker (Ed.), Die NS-Strafjustiz und ihre Nachwirkungen. Baden-Baden 2003, p. 21 ff.

EISENHARDT, Ulrich: Deutsche Rechtsgeschichte. 4th edition. Munich 2004.

ELLING, K.: Die Einführung der Staatsanwaltschaft in Deutschland. Ein Beitrag zur Geschichte des Strafprozesses. (Wroclaw 1911). Reprint Frankfurt am Main 1977.

ELOBIED, Tarig: Die Entwicklung des Strafbefehlsverfahrens von 1846 bis in die Gegenwart. Berlin 2010.

EVANS, Richard J.: Rituals of Retribution. Capital Punishment in Germany 1600–1987. Oxford 1996.

FELSKE, Karsten: Kriminelle und terroristische Vereinigungen (§§ 129, 129a StGB). Reformdiskussion und Gesetzgebung seit dem 19. Jahrhundert. Baden-Baden 2001.

FEUERBACH, Paul Johann Anselm: Revision der Grundsätze und Grundbegriffe des positiven peinlichen Rechts. 2 Vols. Jena 1799, Chemnitz 1800.

FEUERBACH, Paul Johann Anselm: Lehrbuch des gemeinen in Deutschland gültigen Peinlichen Rechts (first published 1801), last edition Gießen 1847.

FEUERBACH, Paul Johann Anselm: Betrachtungen über das Geschwornengericht. Landshut 1813.

FEUERBACH, Paul Johann Anselm: Betrachtungen über die Öffentlichkeit und Mündlichkeit der Gerechtigkeitspflege (1821). Reprint Aalen 1969.

FÖGEN, Marie Theres: Der Kampf um Gerichtsöffentlichkeit. Berlin 1974.

FRANZ, Oliver: Ausgehverbot für Jugendliche ("Juvenile Curfew") in den USA. Reformdiskussion und Gesetzgebung seit dem 19. Jahrhundert. Mit einem Exkurs: Ausgehverbot für Jugendliche in Deutschland während des Zweiten Weltkrieges. Baden-Baden 1999.

FREI, Norbert: Vergangenheitspolitik. Die Anfänge der Bundesrepublik Deutschland und die NS-Vergangenheit. 2nd edition Munich 1997.

FREUDIGER, Kerstin: Die juristische Aufarbeitung von NS-Verbrechen. Tübingen 2002.

FRIEDRICH, Jörg: Die kalte Amnestie. NS-Täter in der Bundesrepublik. Frankfurt am Main 1984.

FRIEDRICH, Jörg: Freispruch für die Nazi-Justiz. Die Urteile gegen NS-Richter seit 1948. Eine Dokumentation. Reinbek nr. Hamburg 1983.

FROMMEL, Monika: Strafjustiz und Polizei. Muß man die Strafrechtsgeschichte vom Kopf auf die Füße stellen?, in: Akten des 26. Deutschen Rechtshistorikertages 1986. Frankfurt am Main 1987, p. 169 ff.

Frommel, Monika: Präventionsmodelle in der deutschen Strafzweck-diskussion. Beziehungen zwischen Rechtsphilosophie, Dogmatik, Rechtspolitik und Erfahrungswissenschaften. Berlin 1987.

Frommel, Monika: Die Implementation der liberalen Forderung nach einer Reform des Strafverfahrens in der jüngeren Strafrechtsgeschichte, in: Heinz Monhaupt (Ed.), Rechtsgeschichte in den beiden deutschen Staaten (1988–1990). Beispiele, Parallelen, Positionen. Frankfurt am Main 1991, p. 548 ff.

Gadebusch bondio, Mariacarla: Die Rezeption der kriminalanthropologischen Theorien von Cesare Lombroso in Deutschland von 1880–1914. (Abhandlungen zur Geschichte der Medizin und der Naturwissenschaften. No. 70). Husum 1995.

Gadebusch bondio, Mariacarla: From the "Atavistic" to the "Inferior" Criminal Type. The Impact of the Lombrosian Theory of the Born Criminal on German Psychiatry, in: Peter Becker / Richard F. Wetzell (Eds.), Criminals and Their Scientists. The History of Criminology in International Perspective. New York (Cambridge University Press) 2006, p. 183 ff.; German: Vom "atavistischen" zum "minderwertigen" Verbrechertypus. Der Einfluss der Lehre Lombrosos vom geborenen Verbrecher auf die deutsche Psychiatrie, in: JJZG 8 (2006/2007), 280 ff.

Garlati, Loredana: cf. Dezza, Ettore.

Geppert, Klaus: Der Grundsatz der Unmittelbarkeit im deutschen Strafverfahren. Berlin 1979.

Gieseler, Kirsten: Unterlassene Hilfeleistung—§ 323 c StGB. Reformdiskussion und Gesetzgebung seit 1870. Berlin 1998.

Glaser, Julius: Handbuch des Strafprozesses. Vol. 1. Leipzig 1883.

Gneist, Rudolf: Freie Advocatur. Die erste Forderung aller Justizreform in Preußen. Berlin 1867 (reprinted without changes 1911).

Goltsche, Friederike: Der Entwurf eines Allgemeinen Deutschen Strafgesetzbuches von 1922 (Entwurf Radbruch). Berlin 2010.

Grässle-Münscher, Josef: Kriminelle Vereinigung. Von den Burschenschaften bis zur RAF. Hamburg 1991.

Greco, Luis: Lebendiges und Totes in Feuerbachs Straftheorie. Ein Beitrag zur gegenwärtigen strafrechtlichen Grundlagendiskussion. Berlin 2009.

Gribbohm, Günter: "Geführte Strafjustiz"—Reichsgericht und Kriegsstrafrecht im Zweiten Weltkrieg. Berlin, Münster 2009.

Grolman, Karl: Grundsätze der Kriminalrechtswissenschaft nebst einer systematischen Darstellung des Geistes der deutschen Criminalgesetze (1805). Reprint Glashütten 1970.

Gröning, Christian: Körperverletzung—§§ 223 ff, 340 StGB. Reformdiskussion und Gesetzgebung seit 1933. Berlin 2003.

Gröschner, Rolf, and Gerhard Haney: Die Bedeutung P.J.A. Feuerbachs (1775–1833) für die Gegenwart, Tagung der Internationalen Vereinigung für Rechtsphilosophie (IVR) in Jena, 15. und 16. März 2002. Wiesbaden 2003.

Grosse-vehne, Vera: Tötung auf Verlangen (§ 216 StGB), "Euthanasie" und Sterbehilfe. Reformdiskussion und Gesetzgebung seit 1870. Berlin 2005.

GRUCHMANN, Lothar: Justiz im Dritten Reich 1933–1940. Anpassung und Unterwerfung in der Ära Gürtner. Munich 1988.

GUMBEL, Emil Julius: Vier Jahre politischer Mord (reprint of the 1924 edition). Heidelberg 1980.

GÜNTHER, Hans: Staatsanwaltschaft. Kind der Revolution. Berlin 1973.

GUSY, Christoph: Weimar—die wehrlose Republik? Verfassungsschutzrecht und Verfassungsschutz in der Weimarer Republik. Tübingen 1991.

HAASE, Norbert, and Bert Pampel (Eds.): Die Waldheimer "Prozesse"—50 Jahre danach. Baden-Baden 2001.

HABER, Günter: Strafgerichtliche Öffentlichkeit und öffentlicher Ankläger in der französischen Aufklärung. Mit einem Ausblick auf die Gesetzgebung der Konstituante. Berlin 1979.

HAEBERLIN, C.F.W.J.: Sammlung der neuen deutschen Strafprocessordnungen. Mit Einschluß der französischen und belgischen sowie der Gesetze über die Einführung des mündlichen und öffentlichen Strafverfahrens mit Schwurgerichten. Greifswald 1852.

HÄLSCHNER, Hugo: Das preußische Strafrecht. In 3 parts. Part 1: Geschichte des brandenburg-preußischen Strafrechts. Ein Beitrag zur Geschichte des deutschen Strafrechts. Bonn 1855. Reprint Aalen 1975.

HANNOVER, Heinrich, and Elisabeth Hannover-Drück: Politische Justiz 1918–1933 (first edition Frankfurt 1966). Hamburg 1977.

HARTMANN, Andrea: Majestätsbeleidigung und Verunglimpfung des Staatsoberhauptes (§§ 94 ff. RStGB, 90 StGB). Reformdiskussion und Gesetzgebung seit dem 19. Jahrhundert. Berlin 2006.

HARTMANN, Andrea: "Chronik der Majestätsbeleidigungsprozesse" im "Vorwärts": Massenphänomen Majestätsbeleidigung, in: JoJZG 1 (2007), 49 ff.

HARTMANN, Ilya: Prostitution, Kuppelei, Zuhälterei. Reformdiskussion und Gesetzgebung seit 1870. Berlin 2006.

HERRMANN, Joachim: Die Reform der deutschen Hauptverhandlung nach dem Vorbild des anglo-amerikanischen Strafverfahrens. Bonn 1971.

HERTZ, Adolf: Die Geschichte des Legalitätsprinzips. Diss. Freiburg im Breisgau 1935.

HETTINGER Michael: Das Fragerecht der Verteidigung im reformierten Inquisitionsprozeß, dargestellt am badischen Strafverfahrensrecht von 1845/51 im Vergleich mit anderen Partikulargesetzen. Berlin 1985.

HILGENDORF, Eric, and Jürgen Weitzel (Eds.): Der Strafgedanke in seiner historischen Entwicklung. Ringvorlesung zur Strafrechtsgeschichte und Strafrechtsphilosophie. (Schriften zum Strafrecht 189). Berlin 2007.

HIPPEL, Robert von: Beiträge zur Geschichte der Freiheitsstrafe, in: ZStW 18 (1898), 419–494, 608–666.

HIPPEL, Robert von: Deutsches Strafrecht. In two volumes. Reprint of the Berlin 1925 edition. Aalen 1971.

HIRSCH, Hans Joachim: Die subjektive Versuchstheorie, ein Wegbereiter der NS-Strafrechtsdoktrin, in: Seminara / Hirsch, p. 61 ff.

Hirsch, Hans Joachim: Der Streit um Handlungs- und Unrechtslehre, insbesondere im Spiegel der Zeitschrift für die gesamte Strafrechtswissenschaft, in: ZStW 1981, 831–863, 1982, 239–278.

Hirsch, Martin, Diemut Majer und Jürgen Meinck (Eds.), Recht, Verwaltung und Justiz im Nationalsozialismus. Cologne 1984.

Holtzendorff, Franz von (Ed.): Handbuch des deutschen Strafrechts. Vol. I: Die geschichtlichen und philosophischen Grundlagen des Strafrechts. Berlin 1871.

Holzhauer, Heinz: Willensfreiheit und Strafe. Das Problem der Willensfreiheit in der Strafrechtslehre des 19. Jahrhunderts und seine Bedeutung für den Schulenstreit. Berlin 1970.

Hötzel, Yvonne: Debatten um die Todesstrafe in der Bundesrepublik Deutschland (1949–1989). Berlin 2010.

Institut für juristische zeitgeschichte hagen: "Euthanasie vor Gericht". Die Anklageschrift des Generalstaatsanwalts beim OLG Frankfurt/M. gegen Dr. Werner Heyde u.a. vom 22. Mai 1962. Ed. Thomas Vormbaum. Berlin 2005.

Justizministerium nrw (Ed.): Politische Strafjustiz 1951–1968 (Schriftenreihe Juristische Zeitgeschichte NRW. Vol. 7). (With contributions by Dirk Blasius, Diether Posser, Alexander von Brünneck, Reinhard Schiffers, Gerhard Pauli and Gerhard Wolf and discussion reports by Markus Rheinländer and Thomas Vormbaum). Düsseldorf 1998.

Karitzky, Holger: Eduard Kohlrausch—Kriminalpolitik in vier Systemen. Eine strafrechtshistorische Biographie. Berlin 2002.

Kern, Eduard: Geschichte des Gerichtsverfassungsrechts. Munich and Berlin 1954.

Kesper-biermann, Sylvia: Einheit und Recht. Strafgesetzgebung und Kriminalrechtsexperten in Deutschland vom Beginn des 19. Jahrhunderts bis zum Reichsstrafgesetzbuch 1871. Frankfurt am Main 2009.

Kissener, Michael: Zwischen Diktatur und Demokratie. Badische Richter 1919–1952. Konstanz 2003.

Klesczewski, Diethelm: Die Rolle der Strafe in Hegels Theorie der bürgerlichen Gesellschaft. Eine systematische Analyse des Verbrechens- und des Strafbegriffs in Hegels Grundlinien der Philosophie des Rechts. Berlin 1991.

Klingebiel, Hans: Die Gerichtsverfassung des Strafprozesses in ihrer Entwicklung seit 1879. Göttingen (jur. Diss.) 1936.

Knapp, Wolfgang: Der Verteidiger—ein Organ der Rechtspflege? Cologne, Berlin, Bonn, Munich 1974.

Knollmann, Johann Wilhelm: Die Einführung der Staatsanwaltschaft im Königreich Hannover. Studien zur Einführung des reformierten Strafprozesses. Berlin 1994.

Koch, Arnd: Das Ende der Todesstrafe in Deutschland, in: JZ 2007, 720 ff.

Köhler, Michael: Einführung, in: v. Liszt, Zweckgedanke, p. V ff.

Korn, Frank: Körperverletzung—§§ 223–233, 340 StGB. Reformdiskussion und Gesetzgebung von 1870 bis 1933. Berlin 2003.

Korzelius, Sven: "Asoziale" und "Parasiten" im Recht der SBZ/DDR. Randgruppen im Sozialismus zwischen Repression und Ausgrenzung. Cologne, Weimar, Vienna 2005.

Krause, Thomas: Geschichte des Strafvollzugs. Von den Kerkern des Altertums bis zur Gegenwart. Darmstadt 1999.

Krauss, Detlef: Das Prinzip der materiellen Wahrheit im Strafprozeß, in: Herbert Jäger (Ed.), Kriminologie im Strafprozeß. Zur Bedeutung psychologischer, soziologischer und kriminologischer Erkenntnisse für die Strafrechtspraxis. Frankfurt am Main 1980, p. 65 ff.

Kroeschell, Karl: Rechtsgeschichte Deutschlands im 20. Jahrhundert. Göttingen 1992.

Kubink, Michael: Strafen und ihre Alternativen im zeitlichen Wandel (Kölner Kriminalwissenschaftliche Schriften 37). Berlin 2002.

Küper, Wilfried: Die Richteridee der Strafprozeßordnung und ihre geschichtlichen Grundlagen. Berlin 1967.

Küper, Wilfried (Ed.): Carl Joseph Anton Mittermaier. Symposium 1987 in Heidelberg. Vorträge und Materialien. Heidelberg 1988.

Landsberg, Götz: Karl Joseph Anton Mittermaier (1787–1867). Ein Professorenleben in Heidelberg; in: Heidelberger Jahrbücher XII (1968), p. 29 ff.

Lang, Bettina: Strafrechtsbezogene Vergangenheitspolitik. Politischer Wille und Strafrechtsrealität im Spannungsverhältnis am Beispiel von Deutschland und Südafrika. Freiburg im Breisgau 2005.

Laubenthal, Klaus: Strafvollzug. Berlin, Heidelberg, New York, Tokyo 1995.

Lensing, Hans, und Thomas Mertens: Der Europäische Gerichtshof für Menschenrechte und die "Mauerschützen". Die Radbruchsche Formel oder: Innerer Widerspruch, in: JJZG 3 (2001/2002), 352 ff.

Lindenberg, Stefan: Brandstiftung—§§ 306 ff. StGB. Reformdiskussion und Gesetzgebung seit 1870. Berlin 2004.

Liszt, Franz von: Strafrechtliche Aufsätze und Vorträge (AuV). 2 Vols. Berlin 1905.

Liszt, Franz von: Der Zweckgedanke im Strafrecht (first published in ZStW 3 [1883], 1 ff.). With and introduction by Michael Köhler. Baden-Baden 2002 (text excerpt in *Vormbaum*, Strafrechtsdenker, p. 468 ff.).

Liszt, Franz von: Die deterministischen Gegner der Zweckstrafe, in: ZStW 1893, 325 ff. (text excerpt in *Vormbaum*, Strafrechtsdenker, p. 484 ff.).

Liszt, Franz von: Das Verbrechen als sozial-pathologische Erscheinung, in: Id., Strafrechtliche Aufsätze und Vorträge Vol. 2, p. 230 ff.

Loening, Richard: Über geschichtliche und ungeschichtliche Behandlung des deutschen Strafrechts, in: ZStW 3 (1883), p. 219 ff.

Löhr, Holle Eva: Der Grundsatz der Unmittelbarkeit im deutschen Strafprozeßrecht. Berlin 1972.

Löw, Christine: Die Erkundungspflicht beim Verbotsirrtum nach § 17 StGB. Frankfurt am Main, Berlin, Bern 2003.

Löw, Christine: Die Entwicklung des Verbotsirrtums und der Erkundigungspflicht seit dem 19. Jahrhundert, in: JJZG 4 (2002/2003), 312 ff.

Luge, Jens: Die Rechtsstaatlichkeit der Strafrechtspflege im Oldenburger Land 1932–1945. Hannover 1993.

LUGE, Jens: Konflikte in der regionalen Strafrechtspflege 1932–1945, in: Festschrift 175 Jahre OLG Oldenburg. Cologne 1989, p. 217 ff.

MAJER, Diemut: "Fremdvölkische" im Dritten Reich. Ein Beitrag zur nationalsozialistischen Rechtssetzung und Rechtspraxis in Verwaltung und Justiz unter besonderer Berücksichtigung der eingegliederten Ostgebiete und des Generalgouvernements. Boppard am Rhein 1981.

MAJER, Diemut: Nationalsozialismus im Lichte der Juristischen Zeitgeschichte. Ideologie—Staat—Besatzungsregime in Europa 1939–1945. Baden-Baden 2002.

MALSACK, Birgit: Die Stellung der Verteidigung im reformierten Strafprozeß. Eine rechtshistorische Studie anhand der Schriften von C.J.A. Mittermaier. Frankfurt am Main 1992.

MARXEN, Klaus: Der Kampf gegen das liberale Strafrecht. Eine Studie zum Antiliberalismus in der Strafrechtswissenschaft der zwanziger und dreißiger Jahre. Berlin 1975.

MARXEN, Klaus: Das Volk und sein Gerichtshof. Eine Studie zum nationalsozialistischen Volksgerichtshof. Frankfurt am Main 1994.

MARXEN, Klaus: Das Problem der Kontinuität in der neueren deutschen Strafrechtsgeschichte, in: KritV 1990, 287 ff.

MARXEN, Klaus, Koichi Miyazawa and Gerhard Werle (Eds.): Der Umgang mit Kriegs- und Besatzungsunrecht in Japan und Deutschland. Berlin 2001.

MARXEN, Klaus, and Holger Schlüter: Terror und "Normalität". Urteile des nationalsozialistischen Volksgerichtshofs 1934–1945. Eine Dokumentation. (Juristische Zeitgeschichte NRW 13). Düsseldorf 2004.

MARXEN, Klaus, and Gerhard Werle (Eds.): Strafjustiz und DDR-Unrecht. Dokumentation. *Vol. 1*: Wahlfälschung. Berlin 2000; *Vol. 2*: Gewalttaten an der deutsch-deutschen Grenze. 2 vols. Berlin 2002; *Vol. 3*: Amtsmissbrauch und Korruption. Berlin 2002; *Vol. 4*: Spionage. 2 vols. Berlin 2004; *Vol. 5*: Rechtsbeugung. 2 vols. Berlin 2007; *Vol. 6*: MfS-Straftaten. Berlin 2006. (Series to be continued.)

MARXEN, Klaus, Gerhard Werle und Petra Schäfter: Die Strafverfolgung von DDR-Unrecht. Fakten und Zahlen. Berlin 2007.

MARXEN, Klaus: Strafrecht nach der Überwindung zweier Unrechtsregime in Deutschland. Ein Plädoyer für eine zeithistorische Rechtsschule im Strafrecht, in: Festschrift 200 Jahre Juristische Fakultät der Humboldt-Universität zu Berlin. Berlin 2010.

MELBER, Henning: Kontinuitäten totaler Herrschaft: Völkermord und Apartheid in "Deutsch-Südwestafrika". Zur kolonialen Herrschaftspraxis im Deutschen Kaiserreich, in: Jahrbuch für Antisemitismusforschung 1 (1992), 91 ff.

MEYER-HÖGER, Maria: Der Jugendarrest. Entstehung und Weiterentwicklung einer Sanktion. Baden-Baden 1998.

MEYER-REIL, Arndt: Strafaussetzung zur Bewährung. Reformdiskussion und Gesetzgebung seit 1870. Münster 2006.

MITTERMAIER, Carl Joseph Anton: Anleitung zur Vertheidigungskunst im deutschen Criminalprocesse und in dem auf Öffentlichkeit und Geschwornengerichte gebauten Strafverfahren mit Beispielen. 2nd edition. Landshut 1820.

MITTERMAIER, Carl Joseph Anton: Das deutsche Strafverfahren in der Fortbildung durch Gerichts-Gebrauch und Partikular-Gesetzbücher und in genauer Vergleichung mit dem englischen und französischen Straf-Prozesse. Erste Abtheilung. Heidelberg 1927.

MITTERMAIER, Carl Joseph Anton: Die Lehre vom Beweise im deutschen Strafprozesse nach der Fortbildung durch Gerichtsgebrauch und deutsche Gesetzbücher in Vergleichung mit den Ansichten des englischen und französischen Strafverfahrens. Darmstadt 1834.

MITTERMAIER, Carl Joseph Anton: Die Strafgesetzgebung in ihrer Fortbildung geprüft nach den Forderungen der Wissenschaft und nach den Erfahrungen über den Werth neuer Gesetzgebungen, und über die Schwierigkeiten der Codifikation, mit vorzüglicher Rücksicht auf den Gang der Berathungen von Entwürfen der Strafgesetzgebung in constitutionellen Staaten. 2 vols. Heidelberg 1841, 1843.

MITTERMAIER, Carl Joseph Anton: Die gesetzliche Beweistheorie in ihrem Verhältniß zu Geschworenengerichten, mit besonderer Rücksicht auf den neuesten Entwurf eines Gesetzbuchs über das Verfahren in Strafsachen von 1831 für das Königreich Baiern; in: NArchCrR 13 (1833), 120–140.

MITTERMAIER, Carl Joseph Anton: Der deutsche Strafprozeß, verglichen mit dem auf Oeffentlichkeit, Mündlichkeit und Anklageprinzip gebauten Verfahren, mit Prüfung der neuesten Ergebnisse der Strafprozeßgesetzgebung, mit besonderer Beziehung auf den neuesten köngl. sächsischen Entwurf des Criminalverfahrens, in: ArchCrR 1842, 424–458.

MITTERMAIER, Carl Joseph Anton: Die Mündlichkeit, das Anklageprinzip, die Oeffentlichkeit und das Geschwornengericht in ihrer Durchführung in den verschiedenen Gesetzgebungen dargestellt und nach den Forderungen des Rechts und der Zweckmäßigkeit mit Rücksicht auf die Erfahrungen der verschiedenen Länder geprüft. Stuttgart und Tübingen 1845.

MITTERMAIER, Carl Joseph Anton: Das englische, schottische und nordamerikanische Strafverfahren im Zusammenhange mit den politischen, sittlichen und socialen Zuständen und in den Einzelheiten der Rechtsausübung dargestellt. Erlangen 1851.

MÜLLER, Christian: Das Gewohnheitsverbrechergesetz vom 24. November 1933. Kriminalpolitik als Rassenpolitik. Baden-Baden 1997.

MÜLLER, Christian: Verbrechensbekämpfung im Anstaltsstaat. Psychiatrie, Kriminologie und Strafrechtsreform in Deutschland 1871–1933. Göttingen 2004.

MÜLLER, Helga: Der Begriff der Generalprävention im 19. Jahrhundert. Von P.J.A. Feuerbach bis Franz v. Liszt. Frankfurt am Main, Bern, New York 1984.

MÜLLER, Ingo: Rechtsstaat und Strafverfahren. Frankfurt am Main 1980.

MÜLLER, Ingo: Der Wert der "materiellen Wahrheit", in: Leviathan 5 (1977), 522 ff.

MÜLLER, Ingo: Furchtbare Juristen. Die unbewältigte Vergangenheit unserer Justiz. München 1987.

MÜLLER, Ingo: Kontinuität und Diskontinuität im Strafprozessrecht, in: Pauli / Vormbaum, p. 161 ff.

MÜLLER-DIETZ, Heinz: Justiz und Nationalsozialismus. Gesammelte Beiträge. Baden-Baden 2000.

MÜLLER-STEINHAUER, Sandra G.: Autonomie und Besserung im Strafvollzug. Resozialisierung auf Grundlage der Rechtsphilosophie Immanuel Kants. Münster 2001.

MUMME, Helmut: Ernst Ferdinand Kleins Auffassung von der Strafe und den sichernden Maßnahmen. Hamburg 1936.

MUÑOZ CONDE, Francisco: Edmund Mezger. Beiträge zu einem Juristenleben. Berlin 2007.

MUÑOZ CONDE, Francisco: Die Besuche Edmund Mezgers im KZ Dachau im Jahre 1944, in: JJZG 4 (2002/2003), 369 ff.; Reprinted in: Id., Mezger, p. 95 ff.

MUÑOZ CONDE, Francisco: Das Erbe Franz von Liszts, in: Festschrift für Winfried Hassemer. Heidelberg 2010, p. 535–558.

NAUCKE, Wolfgang: Über die Zerbrechlichkeit des rechtsstaatlichen Strafrechts. Materialien zur neueren Strafrechtsgeschichte (Juristische Zeitgeschichte. Section 1, Vol 4). Baden-Baden 2000.

NAUCKE, Wolfgang: Die Kriminalpolitik des Marburger Programms 1882, in: Id., Zerbrechlichkeit, p. 223 ff. (First published in: ZStW 1982, 525 ff.).

NAUCKE, Wolfgang: Über den Einfluss Kants auf Theorie und Praxis des Strafrechts im 19. Jahrhundert; in: Id., Zerbrechlichkeit, p. 131 ff.

NAUCKE, Wolfgang: Zur Entwicklung des Strafrechts in der Französischen Revolution, in: Id., Zerbrechlichkeit, p. 29 ff.

NAUCKE, Wolfgang: Der materielle Verbrechensbegriff im 19. Jahrhundert, in: Diethelm Klippel (Ed.), Naturrecht im 19. Jahrhundert. Kontinuität, Inhalt, Funktion, Wirkung. Goldbach 1997, p. 269 ff.

NAUCKE, Wolfgang: Deutsches Kolonialstrafrecht 1886–1918, in: Id., Zerbrechlichkeit, p. 265 ff.

NAUCKE, Wolfgang: Über das Strafrecht des Ersten Weltkriegs, in: Id., Zerbrechlichkeit, p. 287 ff.

NAUCKE, Wolfgang: Die Aufhebung des strafrechtlichen Analogieverbots 1935, in: Id. Zerbrechlichkeit, p. 301 ff.

NAUCKE, Wolfgang: Die Mißachtung des strafrechtlichen Rückwirkungsverbots 1933–1945, in: Id., Zerbrechlichkeit, p. 337 ff.

NAUCKE, Wolfgang: NS-Strafrecht: Perversion oder Anwendungsfall moderner Kriminalpolitik?, in: Id., Zerbrechlichkeit p. 361 ff.

NAUCKE, Wolfgang, and Regina Harzer: Rechtsphilosophische Grundbegriffe. 5th edition. Munich 2005.

NAUMANN, Kai: Gefängnis und Gesellschaft. Freiheitsentzug in Deutschland in Wissenschaft und Praxis 1920–1960. Münster 2006.

Neh, Siegfried W.: Die posthumen Auflagen von Feuerbachs Lehrbuch. Zu der Konzeption C.J.A. Mittermaiers und seinem Wissenschaftsverständnis. Berlin 1991.

Niermann, Hans-Eckhard: Die Durchsetzung politischer und politisierter Strafjustiz im Dritten Reich. Ihre Entwicklung aufgezeigt am Beispiel des OLG-Bezirks Hamm (Juristische Zeitgeschichte NRW 3). Düsseldorf 1995.

Nobili, Massimo: Die freie richterliche Überzeugungsbildung. Reformdiskussion und Gesetzgebung in Italien, Frankreich und Deutschland seit dem Ausgang des 18. Jahrhunderts. Baden-Baden 2001.

Nobis, Frank: Die Strafprozeßgesetzgebung der späten Weimarer Republik (1930–1932). Berlin 2000.

Oehler, Dietrich: Wurzel, Wandel und Wert der strafrechtlichen Legalordnung. Berlin 1950.

Ogorek, Regina: Richterkönig oder Subsumtionsautomat? Zur Justiztheorie im 19. Jahrhundert. Frankfurt am Main 1986.

Ogorek, Regina: Richterkönig oder Subsumtionsautomat? Zur Justiztheorie im 19. Jahrhundert. 2nd edition. Frankfurt am Main 2004.

Ollinger, Thomas: Die Entwicklung des Richtervorbehalts im Verhaftungsrecht. Von den Anfängen bis zur Paulskirchenverfassung. Berlin 1997.

Pack, Wolfgang: Das parlamentarische Ringen um das Sozialistengesetz Bismarcks 1878–1890. Düsseldorf 1961.

Pauli, Gerhard, and Thomas Vormbaum (Eds.): Justiz und Nationalsozialismus—Kontinuität und Diskontinuität. Berlin 2003.

Peters, Edward: Folter. Geschichte der Peinlichen Befragung. Translated from the American by Jobst Christian Rojahn. With an updated preface to the German paperback edition by Kurt Groenewold. Hamburg 2003.

Peters, Karoline: J.D.H. Temme (1798–1881) und das preußischen Strafverfahren in der Mitte des 19. Jahrhunderts. Berlin 2010.

Plate, Hartwig: Ernst Beling als Strafrechtsdogmatiker. Seine Lehren zur Begriffs- und Systembildung. Berlin 1966.

Prechtel, Dietmar: Urkundendelikte (§§ 267 ff. StGB). Reformdiskussion und Gesetzgebung seit 1870. Berlin 2005.

Prinz, Felix: Diebstahl—§§ 242 ff. StGB. Reformdiskussion und Gesetzgebung seit 1870. Berlin 2003.

Putzke, Sabine: Die Strafbarkeit der Abtreibung in der Kaiserzeit und in der Weimarer Republik. Eine Analyse der Reformdiskussion und der Straftatbestände in den Reformentwürfen (1908–1931). Berlin 2003.

Rabofsky, Eduard, and Gerhard Oberkofler: Verborgene Wurzeln der NS-Justiz. Strafrechtliche Rüstung für zwei Weltkriege. Vienna, Munich, Zurich 1985.

Radbruch, Gustav: Paul Johann Anselm Feuerbach. Ein Juristenleben. 3rd edition. Ed. by Erik Wolf. Göttingen 1969.

Radbruch, Gustav: Gesetzliches Unrecht und übergesetzliches Recht (first published in: Süddeutsche Juristenzeitung 1 [1946], 105 ff.). With a preface by Winfried Hassemer. (Juristische Zeitgeschichte. Kleine Reihe 4). Berlin 2002.

RADBRUCH, Gustav: Drei Strafrechtslehrbücher des 19. Jahrhunderts, in: Festschrift für Ernst Heinrich Rosenfeld. Berlin 1949, p. 7 ff.

RAMPF, Christina: Hausfriedensbruch (§ 123 StGB). Reformdiskussion und Gesetzgebung seit 1851. Berlin 2006.

RASEHORN, Theo: Justizkritik in der Weimarer Republik. Das Beispiel der Zeitschrift "Die Justiz". Frankfurt am Main, New York 1985.

REIFNER, Uwe: Juristen im Nationalsozialismus. Kritische Anmerkungen zum Stand der Vergangenheitsbewältigung, in: ZRP 1983, 13–19.

RENTROP, Kathrin: Untreue und Unterschlagung (§§ 246, 266 StGB)—Reformdiskussion und Gesetzgebung seit 1870. Berlin 2007.

RENTZEL-ROTHE, Wolfgang: Der "Goldschmidt-Entwurf". Inhalt, reformgeschichtlicher Hintergrund und Schicksal des Entwurfs eines Gesetzes über den Rechtsgang in Strafsachen 1919/1920. Pfaffenweiler 1995.

REQUATE, Jörg (Ed.): Recht und Justiz im gesellschaftlichen Aufbruch (1960–1975). Bundesrepublik Deutschland, Italien und Frankreich im Vergleich. Baden-Baden 2003.

RICHSTEIN, Christine: Das "belagerte" Strafrecht—Kriegsstrafrecht im Deutschen Reiche während des Ersten Weltkrieges. Münster, Hamburg, London 2000.

RIESS, Peter: Zur Entwicklung der Verteidigung im deutschen Strafprozess, in: Strafverteidigung im Rechtsstaat. 25 Jahre Arbeitsgemeinschaft Strafrecht des Deutschen Anwaltvereins. Baden-Baden 2009, p. 773 ff.

RIESS, Peter: Zur Entwicklung der gesetzlichen Aufgabenverteilung im Ermittlungsverfahren im deutschen Strafprozess, in: Festschrift für Klaus Volk. Munich 2009, p. 559 ff.

RIESS, Peter: Zur Entwicklung der Vorschriften über die Unmittelbarkeit in der Strafprozessordnung, in: Festschrift für Manfred Maiwald. Berlin 2010, p. 661 ff.

ROSENBERG, Hans: Theologischer Rationalismus und vormärzlicher Vulgärliberalismus, in: Id., Politische Denkströmungen im deutschen Vormärz. Göttingen 1972, p. 18 ff.

ROTTLEUTHNER, Hubert (Ed.): Steuerung der Justiz in der DDR. Einflussnahme der Politik auf Richter, Staatsanwälte und Rechtsanwälte. Cologne 1994.

RÜCKERL, Adalbert: NS-Verbrechen vor Gericht. Versuch einer Vergangenheitsbewältigung. Heidelberg 1982.

RÜPING, Hinrich, and Günter Jerouschek: Grundriß der Strafrechtsgeschichte. 5th edition. Munich 2007.

RÜPING, Hinrich: Staatsanwaltschaft und Provinzialjustizverwaltung im Dritten Reich. Aus den Akten der Staatsanwaltschaft bei dem Oberlandesgericht Celle als höherer Reichsjustizbehörde. Baden-Baden 1990.

RUSCHE, Georg, and Otto Kirchheimer: Sozialstruktur und Strafvollzug. Frankfurt am Main, Cologne 1974.

SCHÄFER, Christian: Die Strafbarkeit "widernatürlicher" Unzucht §§ 175, 175a, 175b, 182 a.F. StGB)—Reformdiskussion und Gesetzgebung seit 1945 (2006).

SCHAUZ, Désirée: Strafen als moralische Besserung. Eine Geschichte der Straffälligenfürsorge 1777–1933. Munich 2008.

SCHIFFERS, Reinhard: Zwischen Bürgerfreiheit und Staatsschutz. Wiederherstellung und Neufassung des politischen Strafrechts in der Bundesrepublik Deutschland 1949–1951. Düsseldorf 1989.

SCHMIDT, Eberhard: Einführung in die Geschichte der deutschen Strafrechtspflege. 3rd edition. Göttingen 1965.

SCHMIDT, Eberhard: Die geistesgeschichtliche Bedeutung der Aufklärung für die Entwicklung der Strafjustiz aus der Sicht des 20. Jahrhunderts, in: Schweizerische Zeitschrift für Strafrecht (SchwZStrR) 73 (1958), 341 ff.

SCHMIDT, Eberhard: Zuchthäuser und Gefängnisse. Zwei Vorträge. Göttingen n.d.

SCHMIDT-RECIA, Adrian, and Holger Steinberg: Eine publizistische Debatte als Geburtsstunde des "Marburger Programms", in: ZStW 119 (2007), 195 ff.

SCHMITZBERGER, Johanna Gertrude: Das nationalsozialistische Nebenstrafrecht 1933 bis 1945. (Rechtshistorische Reihe. 376). Frankfurt am Main 2008.

SCHROEDER, Friedrich-Christian: Der Schutz von Staat und Verfassung im Strafrecht. Eine systematische Darstellung, entwickelt aus Rechtsgeschichte und Rechtsvergleichung. (1st edition Munich 1970) 2nd edition. Goldbach 1995.

SCHROEDER, Friedrich-Christian: Der Schutz von Staat und Verfassung im Strafrecht. Eine systematische Darstellung, entwickelt aus Rechtsgeschichte und Rechtsvergleichung. Munich 1970.

SCHROEDER, Friedrich-Christian: Die Entwicklung der Gesetzgebungstechnik, in: *Vormbaum / Welp*, Das StGB. Supplementary vol. 1, p. 381 ff.

SCHUBERT, Werner, und Jürgen Regge (Eds.): Quellen zur preußischen Gesetzgebung des 19. Jahrhunderts. *Gesetzrevision* (1825–1848). I. Section. Straf- und Strafprozeßrecht. 6 Vols. Vaduz 1981–1996.

SCHUBERT, Werner, Jürgen Regge, Pater Rieß and Werner Schmid (Eds.): Quellen zur Reform des Straf- und Strafprozessrechts. 3 Sections (1918–1932; 1933–1939—Strafrecht; 1933–1939—Strafprozessrecht). Berlin, New York 1988 ff.

SCHUBERT, Werner, and Jürgen Regge (Eds.): Entstehung und Quellen der Strafprozeßordnung von 1877. Frankfurt am Main 1989.

SCHUBERT, Werner, and Thomas Vormbaum (Eds.): Entstehung des Strafgesetzbuchs. Vol. 1 (1869). Baden-Baden 2002; Vol. 2 (1870). Berlin 2004.

SCHULZE, Reiner, Thomas Vormbaum, Christine D. Schmidt and Nicola Willenberg (Eds.): Strafzweck und Strafform zwischen religiöser und weltlicher Wertevermittlung. Münster 2008.

SCHUMACHER, Ulrich: Staatsanwaltschaft und Gericht im Dritten Reich. Zur Veränderung der Kompetenzverteilung im Strafverfahren unter Berücksichtigung der Entwicklung in der Weimarer Republik und in der Bundesrepublik. Cologne 1985.

SCHÜNEMANN, Bernd: Einführung in das strafrechtliche Systemdenken, in: Id., Grundfragen, p. 1 ff.

SCHÜNEMANN, Bernd (Ed.): Grundfragen des modernen Strafrechtssystems. Berlin, New York 1984.

SCHÜTZ, Sigrid Susanne: Die Entwicklung des Betrugsbegriffs in der Strafgesetzgebung vom Codex Juris Bavarici Criminalis (1751) bis zum Preußischen Strafgesetzbuch (1851). Munich 1987.

SEEMANN, Ralf: Strafbare Vereitelung von Gläubigerrechten (§§ 283 ff., 288 StGB). Reformdiskussion und Gesetzgebung seit 1870. Berlin 2006.

SELLERT, Wolfgang, and Hinrich Rüping: Studien- und Quellenbuch zur Geschichte der deutschen Strafrechtspflege. Vol. 1: Von den Anfängen bis zur Aufklärung *(Sellert)*; Vol. 2: Von der Aufklärung bis zur doppelten Staatsgründung *(Rüping)*. Aalen 1989 and 1994.

SEMINARA, Sergio, and Hans Joachim Hirsch: Zur strafrechtlichen Versuchslehre im 19. und 20. Jahrhundert. Münster 2008.

SEMINARA, Sergio: Die Versuchsproblematik in der deutschen Strafrechtswissenschaft der ersten Hälfte des 19. Jahrhunderts, in: Seminara / Hirsch, p. 1 ff.

SENN, Marcel: Rechtsgeschichte—ein kulturhistorischer Grundriß. 4th edition. Zurich 2007.

SENN, Marcel, and Lukas Gschwend: Rechtsgeschichte II—Juristische Zeitgeschichte. 2nd edition. Zurich 2004.

SENN, Marcel, and Andreas Thier: Rechtsgeschichte III—Textinterpretationen. Zurich 2005.

SILVA SANCHEZ, Jesús María: Die Expansion des Strafrechts. Frankfurt am Main 2003.

STAPENHORST, Hermann: Die Entwicklung des Verhältnisses von Geldstrafe zu Freiheitsstrafe seit 1882. Eine rechtshistorische Untersuchung anhand von Kriminalstatistiken. Berlin 1993.

STENGLEIN, Melchior: Sammlung der deutschen Strafgesetzbücher. 3 vols. Munich 1858.

STINTZING, Roderich, and Ernst Landsberg: Geschichte der deutschen Rechtswissenschaft. 3 sections in 4 vols. 2nd reprint of the Munich 1880–1884 edition. Aalen 1978.

STÖLZEL, Adolf: Brandenburg-Preußens Rechtsverwaltung und Rechtsverfassung. Dargestellt im Wirken seiner Landesfürsten und obersten Justizbeamten. Vol. II. Berlin 1888.

SÜNDELIN, P.: Sammlung der neueren deutschen Gesetze über Gerichtsverfassung und Strafverfahren. Berlin 1861.

THÄLE, Brigitte: Die Verdachtsstrafe in der kriminalwissenschaftlichen Literatur des 18. und 19. Jahrhunderts. Frankfurt am Main 1993.

THIEL, Carsten: Rechtsbeugung—§ 339 StGB. Reformdiskussion und Gesetzgebung seit 1870. Berlin 2005.

THOMAS, Sven: Die Geschichte des Mordparagraphen—eine normgenetische Untersuchung bis in die Gegenwart. Bochum 1985.

VASSALLI, Giuliano: Formula di Radbruch e diritto penale. Note sulla punizione dei "delitti di Stato" nella Germania postnazistae nella Germania postcomunista. Milan (Giuffrè) 2001.

VASSALLI, Giuliano: Radbruchsche Formel und Strafrecht. Zur Bestrafung der "Staatsverbrechen" im postnazistischen und postkommunistischen Deutschland. Berlin 2010.

VERRI, Pietro: Betrachtungen über die Folter, in: Thomas Vormbaum (Ed.), Folter und Schandsäule. Der Mailänder Prozeß wegen "Pestschmierereien" in Rechtskritik und Literatur. Berlin 2008, p. 3 ff.

VIEREGGE, Bianca: Die Gerichtsbarkeit einer "Elite". Nationalsozialistische Rechtsprechung am Beispiel der SS- und Polizei-Gerichtsbarkeit. Baden-Baden 2002.

VOGEL, Joachim: Einflüsse des Nationalsozialismus auf das Strafrecht. Berlin 2004.

VOGL, Ralf: Die Wiedergutmachung von nationalsozialistischem Unrecht durch die Bundesrepublik Deutschland und die DDR, in: Marxen / Miyazawa / Werle, p. 177 ff.

VORMBAUM, Thomas: Die Lex Emminger vom 4. Januar 1924. Entstehung, Inhalt und Auswirkungen. Berlin 1988.

VORMBAUM, Thomas: Aktuelle Bezüge nationalsozialistischer Strafgesetzgebung, in: Strafverfolgung und Strafverzicht. Festschrift zum 125jährigen Bestehen der Staatsanwaltschaft Schleswig-Holstein. Cologne, Berlin, Bonn, Munich 1992, p. 71 ff.

VORMBAUM, Thomas: Strafjustiz im Nationalsozialismus. Ein kritischer Literaturbericht, in: GA 1998, 1 ff.

VORMBAUM, Thomas: Eid, Meineid und Falschaussage. Reformdiskussion und Gesetzgebung seit 1870. Berlin 1990.

VORMBAUM, Thomas: Der Schutz von Institutionen der DDR durch das bundesdeutsche Strafrecht, in: Festschrift für Diether Posser zum 75. Geburtstag. Cologne 1975, p. 153 ff.

VORMBAUM, Thomas (Ed.): Strafrechtsdenker der Neuzeit. Baden-Baden 1998.

VORMBAUM, Thomas: Der Judeneid im 19. Jahrhundert. Ein Beitrag zur juristischen Zeitgeschichte. Berlin 2006.

VORMBAUM, Thomas: 130 Jahre Strafgesetzgebung—Versuch einer Bilanz, in: Vormbaum / Welp, Das StGB, supplementary vol. I, p. 456 ff.

VORMBAUM, Thomas: "Die Einheit im Denken und Sinnen". Zensur und totalitäre Gefahr im "Wintermährchen" (Kommentar II), in: Heinrich Heine, Deutschland ein Wintermährchen (1844). Berlin 2006, p. 115 ff.

VORMBAUM, Thomas: Beccaria und die strafrechtliche Aufklärung in der gegenwärtigen strafrechtswissenschaftlichen Diskussion, in: Helmut Jacobs (Ed.), Gegen Folter und Todesstrafe—Aufklärerischer Diskurs und europäische Literatur vom 18. Jahrhundert bis zur Gegenwart. Frankfurt am Main 2007, p. 305–319.

VORMBAUM, Thomas, and Kathrin Rentrop: Reform des Strafgesetzbuchs. Sammlung der Reformentwürfe. 3 vols. Berlin 2008.

VORMBAUM, Thomas, and Jürgen Welp (Eds.), Das Strafgesetzbuch. Sammlung der Änderungen und Neubekanntmachungen. Baden-Baden (from 2002 onwards Berlin) *4 text vols:* (I) 1870–1953 (1999); (II) 1954–1974 (1999); (III) 1975–1992 (2000); (IV) 1993–2000 (2002); *3 supplementary vols.:* (I)

130 Jahre Strafgesetzgebung. Eine Bilanz. With contributions by Andreas Roth, Theo Rasehorn, Arno Buschmann, Jürgen Welp, Uwe Scheffler, Eric Hilgendorf, Friedrich Christian Schroeder, Jörg Arnold and Thomas Vormbaum (2004); (II) Das Strafgesetzbuch der DDR (2006); (III) supplementary and index volume (2006).

VORMBAUM, Thomas, and Martin Asholt: Kritik des Feindstrafrechts. Berlin, Münster 2009.

VORMBAUM, Thomas (Ed.): Moderne deutsche Strafrechtsdenker. Berlin, Heidelberg 2010.

VORMBAUM, Thomas: Opportunismus oder Kontinuität? Eduard Kohlrausch (1874–1948), in: Festschrift 200 Jahre Humboldt-Universität. Juristische Fakultät. Berlin 2010.

VOSSIECK, Eckhard: Verbotene Veröffentlichung strafprozessualer Schriftstücke—§ 353 d StGB. Gesetzgebung und Rechtsanwendung seit 1851 (2003).

WÄCHTERSHÄUSER, Wilhelm: Das Verbrechen des Kindesmordes im Zeitalter der Aufklärung. Berlin 1973.

WACHSMANN, Nikolaus: Gefangen unter Hitler. Justizterror und Strafvollzug im NS-Staat. Munich 2004.

WAGNER, Joachim: Terrorismus und Strafrecht im deutschen Kaiserreich von 1871. Heidelberg 1981.

WEBER, Judith: Die sächsische Strafgesetzgebung im 19. Jahrhundert bis zum Inkrafttreten des Reichsstrafgesetzbuches. Berlin 2008.

WEBER, Robert: Die Entwicklung des Nebenstrafrechts 1871–1914. Baden-Baden 1999.

WEHLER, Hans-Ulrich: Deutsche Gesellschaftsgeschichte. 4 vols. Munich. Vol. 1: 1700–1815 (2nd edition 1989), Vol. 2: 1815–1845/48 (2nd edition 1989), Vol. 3: 1849–1914 (1989), Vol. 4: 1914–1949 (2003).

WEISSLER, Adolf: Geschichte der Rechtsanwaltschaft. Leipzig 1905.

WELP, Jürgen: Die Strafgesetzgebung der Nachkriegszeit (1945–1953), in: Vormbaum / Welp, supplementary vol. 1, p. 139 ff.

WENTKER, Hermann: Justiz in der SBZ/DDR 1945–1953. Transformation und Rolle ihrer zentralen Institutionen. (Quellen und Forschungen zur Zeitgeschichte 51). Munich 2001.

WERLE, Gerhard: Justiz-Strafrecht und polizeiliche Verbrechensbekämpfung im Dritten Reich. Berlin, New York 1989.

WERLE, Gerhard: Die Bestrafung von NS-Unrecht in Westdeutschland, in: Marxen / Miyazawa / Werle, p. 137 ff.

WERLE, Gerhard, and Thomas Wandres: Auschwitz vor Gericht. Völkermord und bundesdeutsche Strafjustiz. Munich 1995.

WERNER, Stefan: Wirtschaftsordnung und Wirtschaftsstrafrecht im Nationalsozialismus. Frankfurt am Main, Bern, New York, Paris 1991.

WESSELS, Johannes / Werner Beulke (cont.): Strafrecht. Allgemeiner Teil. Die Straftat und ihr Aufbau. 36th edition. Heidelberg 2006.

WESTPHALEN, Daniela: Karl Binding (1841–1920). Materialien zur Biographie eines Strafrechtsgelehrten. Frankfurt am Main, Bern, New York, Paris 1989.

WETZELL, Richard F., Inventing the Criminal. A History Of German Criminology 1880–1945. Chapel Hill, London (University of North Carolina Press) 2000.

WETZELL, Richard F.: Der Verbrecher und seine Erforscher. Die deutsche Kriminologie in der Weimarer Republik und im Nationalsozialismus, in: Jahrbuch der juristischen Zeitgeschichte 8 (2006/2007), p. 256 ff.

WINKLER, Heinrich August: Der lange Weg nach Westen. Deutsche Geschichte. Vol. 1: Vom Ende des Alten Reiches bis zum Untergang der Weimarer Republik. Munich 2000.

WOGERSIEN, Maik: Restitution, in: Pauli / Vormbaum, p. 271 ff.

WOLF, Erik: Große Rechtsdenker der deutschen Geistesgeschichte. 4th edition. Tübingen 1963.

WROBEL, Hans: Verurteilt zur Demokratie. Justiz und Justizpolitik in Deutschland 1945–1989. Berlin 2008.

ZACHARIÄ, Heinrich Albert: Die Gebrechen und die Reform des deutschen Strafverfahrens, dargestellt auf der Basis einer konsequenten Entwicklung des inquisitorischen und des accusatorischen Prinzips. Göttingen 1846.

ZACHARIAS, Hans: Die amtlichen Reformversuche zur Strafgerichtsverfassung seit Entstehung der Strafprozeßordnung. Göttingen (jur. Diss.) 1921.

ZIEMANN, Sascha: Neukantianisches Strafrechtsdenken. Die Philosophie des Südwestdeutschen Neukantianismus und ihre Rezeption in der Strafrechtswissenschaft des frühen 20. Jahrhunderts. Baden-Baden 2009.

ZIMMERLING, Jürgen: Die Entwicklung der Strafrechtspflege für Afrikaner in Deutsch-Südwestafrika 1884–1914. Eine juristisch/historische Untersuchung. Bochum 1995.

List of Translated Texts

BECCARIA, Cesare: Beccaria. 'On Crimes and Punishments' and other Writings. Ed. Richard Bellamy, transl. Richard Davies. Cambridge: Cambridge University Press, 1995.

FICHTE, Johann Gottlieb: Foundations of Natural Right. Ed. Frederick Neuhauser, transl. Michael Bauer. Cambridge: Cambridge University Press, 2000.

GROTIUS, Hugo: The Rights of War and Peace, ed. Richard Tuck. From the edition of Jean Beyberac, transl. John Morrice. Indianapolis: Liberty Fund, 2005.

HEGEL, Georg Wilhelm Friedrich: Elements of the Philosophy of Right. Ed. Allen W. Wood, transl. H. B. Nisbet. Cambridge: Cambridge University Press, 1991.

HUMBOLDT, Wilhelm v.: The Limits of State Action. Ed. J. W. Burrow, transl. Joseph Coulthard. Cambridge: Cambridge University Press, 1969.

KANT, Immanuel: Perpetual Peace and Other Essays. Transl. Ted Humphrey. Indianapolis: Hackett, 1983.

KANT, Immanuel: Metaphysical Elements of Justice, transl. John Ladd. Indianapolis: Hackett, 1999.

KANT, Immanuel: Grounding for the Metaphysics of Morals, transl. James W. Ellington. Indianapolis: Hackett, 1985.

MONTESQUIEU, Charles-Louis de Secondat, baron de La Brède et de: The Spirit of the Laws. Ed. and transl. Anne M. Cohler, Basia Carolyn Miller, and Harold Samuel Stone Cambridge: Cambridge University Press, 1989.

NIETZSCHE, Friedrich: On the Genealogy of Morality. Ed. Keith Ansell-Pearson, transl. Carol Diethe. Cambridge: Cambridge University Press, 2007.

SCHOPENHAUER, Arthur: Prize Essay on the Freedom of the Will. Ed. Günther Zoller, transl. Eric F. J. Payne. Cambridge: Cambridge University Press, 1999.

The Emperor's new code of criminal laws: published at Vienna, the 15th of January, 1787 [Josephina]. Dublin: John Rea, 1787.

T. Vormbaum and M. Bohlander, *A Modern History of German Criminal Law*, DOI 10.1007/978-3-642-37273-5,

Index of Persons

T. Vormbaum and M. Bohlander, *A Modern History of German Criminal Law*, DOI 10.1007/978-3-642-37273-5, © Springer-Verlag Berlin Heidelberg 2014

L

Subject Index

DOI 10.1007/978-3-642-37273-5, © Springer-Verlag Berlin Heidelberg 2014

MIX
Papier aus verantwortungsvollen Quellen
Paper from responsible sources
FSC® C105338

If you have any concerns about our products,
you can contact us on
ProductSafety@springernature.com

In case Publisher is established outside the EU,
the EU authorized representative is:
Springer Nature Customer Service Center GmbH
Europaplatz 3, 69115 Heidelberg, Germany

Printed by Libri Plureos GmbH
in Hamburg, Germany